THE

GENESIS OF THE CIVIL WAR

THE STORY OF SUMTER

1860-61

BVT CAPT TRUMAN SEYMOUR
1st Artillery

1ST LIEUT. G.W. SNYDER
Corps of Engineers.

1ST LIEUT. JEFF. C. DAVIS
Co. E. 1st Artillery.

2ND LIEUT. R.K. MEADE
Corps of Engineers.

CAPT ABNER DOUBLEDAY.
Co. E. 1st Artillery.

MAJ. ROBT ANDERSON.
1st Artillery Comdg. Officer.

ASST SURG. SAM W. CRAWFORD.
Medical Staff.

CAPT J.G. FOSTER.
Corps of Engineers.

THE

GENESIS OF THE CIVIL WAR

THE STORY OF SUMTER

1860-1861

BY

SAMUEL WYLIE CRAWFORD

BREVET MAJOR-GENERAL, U. S. A., A.M., M. D., LL. D.

NEW YORK
CHARLES L. WEBSTER & COMPANY
1887

PREFACE.

A TRAGIC story is easily told. Battle pictures are not hard to paint with words or brush. It is more difficult to trace with accuracy the beginning of revolutionary movements, for these are from their very nature secret, and hidden from the common view, and often the more carefully concealed in proportion to their importance. It has been my pleasure and my purpose to seek into these hidden things. In these pages I have undertaken to touch the spring of a fresh impulse, and to unfold the story of those events which led to the great national struggle between the North and the South in the war for the union of the States. I had a singular introduction to the scenes which ushered in the mighty conflict. It was this:

"ADJUTANT-GENERAL'S OFFICE,
"WASHINGTON, September 7, 1860.
"To ASSISTANT-SURGEON S. W. CRAWFORD, U. S. A.,
"NEWPORT, R. I.
"The Secretary of War directs that you proceed forthwith to Fort Moultrie, South Carolina, and report for duty to the commanding officer of that station. Answer.
"Respectfully, your obedient servant,
"W. A. NICOLS,
"*Adjutant-General.*"

The manner of transmitting this command was unusual. In those early days the telegraph was not always used for the ordinary business of the War Department. The imperative terms of the one I had just received added to my appreciation of its importance. At the moment of its reception I was at breakfast with some friends at Newport, R. I., where I was enjoying a short respite from frontier service. Leaving the table at once, I was soon on my way to Charleston. As I journeyed,

there was time for earnest reflection as to the cause which had so
suddenly interrupted my visit and sent me to the far South in a
sickly season.   The heat was intense, and seemed to grow more
and more oppressive after we passed the Potomac.   Our train had
reached South Carolina, and was crossing the Santee River. I
had fallen into a reverie, when I was aroused by a conversation
directly behind me.   The words spoken gave me my first intimation of the emergency that had called me so suddenly from my
vacation.   The stranger said:

"There is no use denying it, and the papers cannot suppress
the facts.   The yellow fever is in Charleston, for the doctor at
that fort in the harbor has just died of it."

The speaker was a typical Southerner, and he spoke with a
good deal of emphasis.   So I was on my way to take the place
of an officer of my corps who had died at his post, in attendance,
possibly, on an epidemic of yellow fever. My position at the
moment was that of an officer of the medical staff of the army,
with the rank of captain of cavalry, and I was now called upon
to face new responsibilities.   I approached them with grave
apprehensions.

It was after dark when the train reached the city near which
I was to be stationed.   The streets were almost deserted, and I
found my way to the chief hotel with some difficulty, to find few
signs of life there.   A rather dogmatic clerk and a sleepy negro
were the only persons on duty.   The clerk suggested, as I registered my name:

"You are an officer of the army to be stationed in this harbor
-No?"

I replied in the affirmative.

"Where have you come from?"

"From Newport, R. I.," I replied.

"Don't you think you had better go down to-night?" he said
to me, in rather a marked way.

"It is five miles or more; what means of conveyance is
there?" I asked.   "I have never been here before in my life."

"None, that I know of," he replied; "the steamers stop running after 3 o'clock, but you might get a negro to row you
over in a skiff.   It is dangerous to stay here."

"No," I replied, "that is out of the question. I shall remain
over night here."

"If you do," replied the clerk, "you will be one of the few people in this house."

I remained all night. In the morning I proceeded to Fort Moultrie, on Sullivan's Island. I had only just entered the fort, when a message from the commanding officer summoned me to the bedside of the servant of his household. He had attended upon the deceased medical officer and was now stricken, as was believed, with the same disease. The general thought was that the officer himself had died of yellow fever. Recollection of the scourge of 1856, which so seriously affected Charleston, was still fresh in the minds of everyone. Fortunately there was no yellow fever. The epidemic changed to one of "broken bone fever," or "dengue." It affected the entire community, but without fatal results in any case.

I was one of the few medical men in the vicinity. This brought me into friendly and rather close relations with the community. Thus my being hurried away from Newport was turned to great account. This accident and sudden transfer to Fort Moultrie gave me a favorable opportunity of noting, studying and commenting upon the social and political phases of the secession movement, just as it began to take shape immediately after Mr. Lincoln's election.

At this distance from the mighty events of those days, the value of the associations I was fortunate enough to have with those who were planning the first strokes of disunion can readily be appreciated. The records are uniformly silent upon most of these grave events. The files of the War Department, in the letters and reports of Major Anderson, and in the admirable and almost daily communications and journal of Captain J. G. Foster, the senior engineer, contain a wellnigh complete record of the events in their special military relations to Forts Moultrie and Sumter. But any connected record of the great political complications, decisions and actions that influenced the Government is wholly wanting. There are few documents in the State Depart ment, or in any of the others, which give authentic information as to the minor details of the early features of the struggle with secession. Cabinet councils keep no minutes. The only record of its action that can be reached is when some Cabinet officer defends before another generation matters which cannot be spoken of at the time of their occurrence. Much was done

orally, and to such an extent was this carried that the important
instructions of the Secretary of War to Major Anderson on the
7th of December, 1860, instructions involving to a greater extent
than any other the question of peace or war to the country, were
carried to him by Major Don Carlos Buell verbally. Not only
executive officers, but whenever it could be done, statesmen and
soldiers, seemed to avoid any record. Therefore it is that personal observation and inquiry at the time becomes of such vital
value in writing the history of the early hours of the controversy,
which finally provoked civil war.

Besides constant associations with leading Southern people in
the city of Charleston during those days, I was in almost daily
attendance upon the convention which passed the Ordinance of
Secession, until its doors were closed to all but the members. I
kept a general record of the events as they transpired, as far as
it was possible for me to do so. I did it for the purpose of
embodying at some future time, in such a narrative as this, the
events which constituted so important an era in the history of the
country. The story has never been told, save in fragments.
Volumes have been written about the battles which followed the
intellectual combat which provoked the war. Statesmen, philo-
sophers and laymen have given utterance to much that occurred
after the clash of arms began. But the connected story of the
beginning, and a picture of what the combat was about, have never
yet been presented in consecutive form. As the medical officer
of Fort Moultrie and Fort Sumter, I was brought into close
relations with Major Anderson, and was a part of the beginning
and end of our first combat with secession at Sumter. The
Major often spoke to me of his anxieties, and of the difficulties
which surrounded him. With him I saw the first and the last
shot sent against that fort that aroused the country to war.
Besides personal association with and a study of the secession
movement at its very initiative, I have, through years of inquiry,
at both the North and the South, reached documents and conclusions of great importance. I have studied and here presented
them with much care. We are far enough away from the prejudices of that period to deal dispassionately with them. I have
called my work "The Genesis of the Civil War," and advisedly.
It is not intended to embrace a recital of the long train of those
predisposing causes, which sprang into life at the formation of

the Government and developed into a fatal antagonism with the growth of the nation, but rather those of an immediate and exciting nature, which, precipitated by the secession of South Carolina and proceeding unchecked in their course, finally from logical and irresistible conclusion plunged the country into war.

In a spirit of what I have meant to be judicial fairness, I have written ideas, stated facts and compiled documents in these pages, to which, with every consciousness of the imperfection of my work, I invite the best judgment of my countrymen.

S. W. CRAWFORD,
Brevet Major-General, U. S. A.

UNIVERSITY OF PENNSYLVANIA,
PHILADELPHIA, April 12, 1887.

CONTENTS

—————

CONTENTS.

CHAPTER IV.

CHAPTER V.

CHAPTER VI.

CHAPTER XIV.

CHAPTER XV.

CHAPTER XVI.

CHAPTER XVII.

CHAPTER XXI.

CHAPTER XXVII.

CHAPTER XXVIII.

CONTENTS.

CHAPTER XXIX.

CHAPTER XXX

CHAPTER XXXI.

ILLUSTRATIONS

THE

GENESIS OF THE CIVIL WAR

THE STORY OF SUMTER

1860-61

CHAPTER I.

United States Property in the Harbor of Charleston–Description of the Forts
and their Armament–Their Defenseless Condition–Social Relations between the Officers and the People of Charleston.

THE summer of 1860 found the United States in possession
of certain public property within the territorial limits of South
Carolina. It had been acquired and the jurisdiction yielded by
the Legislature of the State in the usual way. There was no
special contract between the Federal Government and this Commonwealth, nor any feature which distinguished the legal relations
between them from those maintained with the other States of the
Union. She had accepted the Constitution of 1787 as her sister
States had done, and, notwithstanding the political agitations of
which she had been the peculiar theatre at various crises, the
Constitution of the United States and the laws passed in pursuance thereof had been, up to the time when this narrative begins,
the supreme laws of the land there, as they had been elsewhere.
The military property of the United States in and about the
harbor of Charleston, the scene of the events with which we are
principally concerned, consisted of the forts in the harbor and a
large arsenal within the city limits. The latter was surrounded
by four acres of neatly kept grounds, and was in charge of a
military storekeeper of ordnance, with fourteen enlisted men. Its
stores consisted of over 22,000 stand of arms, besides heavy
ordnance, with a variety of munitions and supplies, and were very
valuable. Had they subsequently been within reach of the

I

beleaguered garrison of Sumter, the story now to be written might have assumed a different aspect.

Three forts with historic names guarded the entrance of the harbor of Charleston from the sea. They had been designed solely to meet invasion from abroad, and were constructed, in every particular, in suggestive indifference to the possibility of domestic insurrection or civil war.

Castle Pinckney, a small round structure of brick, stood at the extremity of a sandy spit at the mouth of the Cooper River, three-quarters of a mile from the city of Charleston. It was occupied only by an ordnance sergeant and his family. Practically, it had long been abandoned. Grass grew on its walks, its casemates had cracked here and there, and signs of neglect and decay were apparent on every side; but twenty-two heavy guns still stood upon its parapet,* and the old sergeant busied himself in keeping bright the lacquer upon the guns and round shot, and in trimming the harbor light that gleamed from its walls by night.

Nearly four miles farther down, and tight in the jaws of the channel, in its narrowest part, stood Fort Sumter, a large brick pentagonal fort, fifty feet in height, with its faces making an angle at the salient on the channel front, and its flanks running perpendicularly to a gorge that formed its rear. It was unfinished, and without armament of any kind. A few heavy guns of old pattern lay in rows on the parade, amid dressed masonry and large stones and material for the completion of the work. One hundred and twenty workmen, under the charge of a lieutenant of engineers, were busy in the completion of the fort, under an appropriation of the Act of Congress of June, 1859.

From its very origin Fort Sumter seemed destined to notoriety. As early as 1805 the State of South Carolina had formally ceded "to the United States of America all the right, title and claim" of the State to Castle Pinckney, Forts Moultrie and Johnson, as well as other "sites for the erection of forts" at the exposed parts of the State.† But it was not until 1827 that, impressed with the exposed condition of the harbor of Charleston, additional defenses were determined upon. The sea had

---

* Four 42-pounders, fourteen 24-pounders, four 8-inch seacoast howitzers, Chief of Ordnance, December 21, 1860.

† Statutes at Large of South Carolina, Vol. V., p. 501.

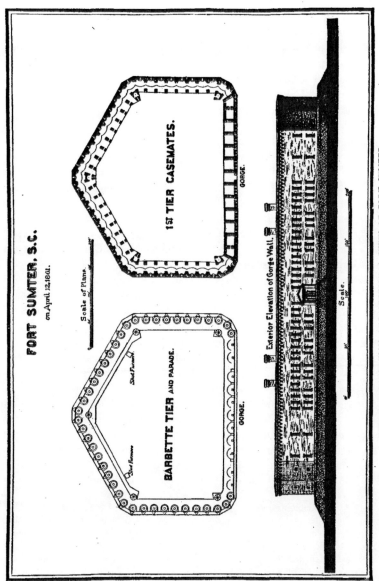

EXTERIOR ELEVATION AND SECTIONAL VIEW OF FORT SUMTER.

encroached upon the site of Fort Moultrie, on Sullivan's Island, and it became necessary to look for other positions for defensive works. The shoal opposite Fort Moultrie was selected. Without consulting the State, experimental operations were begun upon the shoal on which the fort now stands, and a report, with a plan for a "casemated battery" for this shoal, was submitted by a board of United States engineers, and was approved by the Secretary of War (P. B. Porter) in 1828. This action, without their advice or consent, at once aroused the Legislature of the State, and upon the 17th of December, 1834, the committee on Federal relations of the House was instructed to inquire and report as to the work going on, and whether the navigation of the harbor, as well as "the interests of the good people of the State, might not be affected thereby." But the committee were "not able to ascertain by what authority the Federal Government assumed to erect the works" referred to, when the Legislature formally requested the Governor "to apply to the Executive Department of the United States Government to ascertain by what authority such works are erected," and to report the correspondence to the Legislature.* Satisfactory explanations being made, the formal cession to the United States of all right, title and claim of South Carolina to the site of Sumter and the requisite quantity of adjacent territory was made on the 17th day of December, 1836. It was in 1829 that work was begun upon the fort; when finished, its armament was to consist of 146 guns of all calibres, and a war garrison of 650 men.

Directly across the channel eastward, on the sandy beach of Sullivan's Island and near the sea, stood Fort Moultrie, a low water battery built of brick, sixteen feet high, with one tier of guns *en barbette,* some bearing directly upon the channel, that ran within short range of its walls. It enclosed an area of one and one-half acres. On its cramped parade were piles of balls and shells, and an old furnace for heating shot. In its rear, or

---

* Reminiscences of South Carolina: Gen. W. G. De Saussure.

NOTE. —When it was known that the General Government was working upon this shoal, with the prospect of occupying it, one William Laval a resident of Charleston, obtained a grant of it from the Legislature. The shoal was covered at high tide, and thus became a part of the waterway of the harbor, and was not disposable to any one, nor could the State itself occupy it. It was soon discovered, therefore, that the grant to Laval was an error, and proceedings had been instituted in the courts to revoke what was done, when the formal cession took place.

gorge, two stories high, were its sally-port, its guard-house and its offices. On the left, of double stories, were the quarters for officers, and opposite were the barracks for the men. Its name and its association were dear to every Carolinian. It stood near the site of the old palmetto fort, where the troops of the State line repulsed the British fleet under Admiral Sir Peter Parker, on the 28th of June, 1776. Bearing the name of one of her most distinguished sons, every child in South Carolina had spelled the story and had grown up in the belief that that fort and its history were peculiarly his own inheritance. Two companies of the

SAND-BAG PARAPET AT FORT MOULTRIE, AS COMPLETED BY THE CONFEDERATES.

First Regiment of Artillery, under the command of the Lieutenant-colonel of the regiment, John L. Gardiner, with the regimental band, garrisoned the fort, which had been continuously occupied for many years. Its armament consisted of fifty-five guns of all calibres, including ten 8-inch Columbiads, eleven howitzers, thirty 24 and 32 pound guns, with four brass field-pieces. Its fire commanded all approaches except the rear, and a number of its guns concentrated upon a single point in the channel, by which every vessel was compelled to pass to enter the inner harbor. Unprepared for an attack, it had, in long years of disuse, fallen into a condition similar to Castle Pinckney. The winds had piled up the sands on the sea front to a level with and against the parapet, and communication was easy from all sides. Without a ditch, without defensive arrangements of any kind, it was an easy prey to any force that should choose to attack it. Some of its officers and men lived habitually outside of the work, and its hospital had long been established a short distance beyond the walls.

The sea winds had piled up long rows and hillocks of sand on all sides of it, and to the northward especially, and commanding the approach from the main part of the island. At a distance of 180 or 200 yards from the fort, a range of sand-hills had been formed, covered with a sparse, stunted vegetation, which completely commanded the parapet upon that side of the work, and which, if occupied by riflemen, would greatly embarrass, if not effectually prevent, any service of its guns on that side. To its defenseless condition the attention of the Government had been earnestly called. As long before as the 18th of June, 1860, the acting Assistant Quartermaster of the post had called the attention of the general commanding the department to the condition of the work, and had made a request that the sum of $500 might be sent to him for the purpose of removing the sand from the walls of the fort. He urged that, if it was the intention "that the walls should fulfill at all the conditions for which they were built," it was necessary to remove the sand. "A child," said he, "ten years old can easily come into the fort over the sand-banks, and the wall offers little or no obstacle." He declares that the ease with which the walls could be gotten over, rendered the place more of a trap in which the garrison might be shot down from the parapet than a means of defense. "It looked strange," said he, "not to say ridiculous, that the only garrisoned fort in the harbor should be so much banked in with sand that the walls were in some places not a foot above the banks." Unfit for attack, incapable of resistance, Fort Moultrie presented an appearance anything but formidable, in the summer of 1860. The harbor of Charleston had not been overlooked in the general appropriation made by Congress for the national defenses in 1860, and the sum of $8,500 had been specially designated for the repairs of Fort Moultrie, by the act approved on the zest of June. Brevet-Captain J. G. Foster, of the Corps of Engineers, had relieved Capt. G. W. Cullum, the officer in charge of the engineering operations in the harbor, and to him the condition of Fort Moultrie, as set forth in the letter of the post quartermaster, was referred by the War Department for a report.

A prompt and exhaustive reply was received from that officer on July 2, when he was ordered to proceed without delay to Charleston and commence work at once upon the fortifications in that harbor. By the 14th of September, the work was begun at Moultrie, and "a full force of masons" renewed the work at Fort Sumter on the following day. It was thus, in the ordinary routine of army administration, and in pursuance of an Act of Congress making appropriations for the specific purpose, that work upon the fortifications in Charleston Harbor was begun and prosecuted in the summer of 1860.

But however regularly and in accordance with routine that work might have been undertaken, it soon became manifest that the renewed activity in regard to the forts had attracted the attention of the authorities and people of the city and of the State. It had come to be accepted as a fact that the coming elections in November would result in the defeat of the party in power, and in view of this the deliberate purpose of the State had been formed.

Between the officers of the garrison and the summer inhabitants of the island, as well as the people of Charleston, the relations had ever been of the most agreeable character. The military band furnished an attractive feature, and the parapet at Fort Moultrie was the daily promenade of the fashionable throng. To the officers of the little garrison, upon whom the events of a few weeks suddenly devolved, perhaps, the gravest responsibilities connected with the beginning of the Civil War, the severance of these social ties-some of them close and prized, and some of them strengthened by birth and connection—was one of the earliest as well as the saddest consequences of their peculiar position. But it was an inevitable consequence, and they so accepted it.

The officers of the garrison were no exception to the general rule which influenced other officers of the army. Reserving to themselves the right to hold their individual political sentiments, it was without reference to any part in the struggles so often renewed in the country; their allegiance holding to the Government, whose servants they were, without regard to the political complexion of any special administration. Embracing every shade of politics, they were nevertheless a unit in their convictions of duty under the peculiar circumstances that surrounded them. Long habits of discipline and obedience, acquired in years of service, had wrought their full effect, and kept them unwavering in the discharge of simple duty until the last. They early appreciated the earnestness of the leaders and people of South Carolina, but they left the solution of the difficulties to the same tribunal to which they were accustomed to refer their own—the Government at Washington. But as the days went by, and the determination of South Carolina became more manifest to them, and they realized that they and their trust were the offending features, they became animated by a single purpose—*resistance.*

CHAPTER II.

SOUTH CAROLINA was at this period the only State in the Union where the Presidential electors were appointed by the Legislature. In accordance with an Act of Congress of 1846, the electors for President and Vice-President of the United States were to be appointed on the Tuesday next after the first Monday of November, of the year in which they were to serve. The Governor of the State availed himself of the law to call the Legislature of 1860 together in special session on the 5th of November, not only that they might carry into effect the Act of Congress, but that they might take action, "if deemed advisable for the safety and protection of the State." It was the new Legislature that was thus called upon to act. Elected in the previous month of October, and composed of the younger men, it had been chosen with reference to the anticipated difficulties. Promptly upon the day specified the Legislature met in special session at Columbia, when the presiding officer of the Senate (Porter) announced that they were "all agreed as to their wrongs;" and he urged unanimity of sentiment and action, "as the destiny and very existence of the State" depended in great part upon the action they should take. The special object of this call of the Legislature could soon have been attained, but the Governor, in transmitting his message, embraced the opportunity to call their attention to the existing political condition—that "a sectional candidate" would be elected to the Presidency was deemed strongly probable, and that the party electing him were committed to measures which, if carried out, would "reduce the Southern States to mere provinces of a consolidated despotism,"

9

He suggested, therefore, that the Legislature remain in session, and take such action as would prepare the State for any emergency that might arise, and he earnestly recommended that, in the event of Abraham Lincoln's election to the Presidency, "a convention of the people of this State be immediately called to consider and determine for themselves the mode and measure of redress." . . . "The only alternative left, in my judgment," said he, "is the secession of South Carolina from the Union." He thought that it would be followed by the entire South, and that the co-operation of other States was near at hand. He recommended that the militia be reorganized; the whole military force of the State placed in a position to be used at the shortest notice; that every man in the State between the ages of eighteen and forty-five should be well armed with the most efficient weapons of modern warfare; and that the services of 10,000 volunteers should be immediately accepted."

In a retrospect of events after the nomination of Mr. Lincoln, we find no act so full of meaning, so much the result of long conceived and cherished purpose, as this. It seemed that the moment had come when the hopes of those who for so long had influenced Southern sentiment were to be realized; and as the Legislature gathered in extra session in Columbia on the 5th of November, it was with a determination, long before reached, to put into operation that machinery which should separate the State from the federal union and render her free and independent. In this conclusion they were largely supported by the representatives of popular sentiment throughout the State. Prominent men, who had long been known as the representatives of the "co-operative sentiment," had now changed their minds, and, in speeches made to the people during the summer, were openly and boldly for separate State action. Conspicuous among them was W. W. Boyce, a Member of Congress from South Carolina, who had long been a recognized advocate of co-operation. In a speech delivered by him at Winsboro, on the 9th day of August, 1860, he said: "If Lincoln be elected, I think that the Southern States should withdraw from the Union. All, but if not all, as many as will, and if no other, South Carolina alone, in the promptest manner and by the most direct means." He consid-

---

* Governor's Message, Extra Session, 1860.

ered the success of the Republican party in the Presidential election as involving the necessity of revolution. Upon the 7th of November, ere the result of the election was definitely known, in an address to the people of Columbia, he said: "The way to create revolution is to start it. I think the only policy for us, the only thing left for us to do, as soon as we receive authentic intelligence of the election of Lincoln and Hamlin, is for South Carolina, in the quickest manner and by the most direct means, to withdraw from the Union. To submit to Lincoln's election is to consent 'to death.'" Such sentiments, and from such a source, produced an effect marked and immediate. They were received with enthusiasm. They were the first public assertions of a sentiment growing daily in the minds of a large portion of the people, and when the Legislature, and subsequently the Convention, met and acted, their decision was deemed the simple interpretation of the popular will.

A short time before this extra session of the Legislature, a caucus had been called to meet in Columbia. At this caucus, letters from leading public men (Pugh, Bullock, Yancey and others) of other Southern States were read, in reply to categorical questions put to them as to what action they desired South Carolina to take. These letters unanimously counselled that, as South Carolina was the foremost State in secession sentiment, more unanimous in her people, and with less division than any other State, she should take the lead, and they pledged the cotton States in her support. These letters not only silenced the claim that the other States were jealous of South Carolina, but at once negatived the pretexts of the co-operationists and largely influenced the action of the Legislature. But while the determination to call a convention was general, if not unanimous, the time at which it should be called was made the subject of short but earnest discussion, both within and without the Legislature. It was thought, by some, that there should be co-operation with the other Southern States; that it was the better and more expedient course. Others, again, believed that the State should await the commission of some, *overt act* of hostility to South Carolina upon the part of the General Government. But the counsels of those who, at this early period, had begun to assume the control of the movement prevailed. "If we wait for co-operation," said they, "slavery and States rights must be abandoned and the cause of the South lost forever."* It was not difficult to see that postponement or delay would be hazardous, if not fatal, to the movement. The failure of co-operation in 1850-51 was recalled to the minds of the prominent men, and they instanced the action of Virginia in now declining to join the proposed conference of the Southern States upon the invitation of South Carolina, as discrediting the cause and repudiating the action of the State. Openly and earnestly they urged that the State should act alone. Public meetings were everywhere held, and in Columbia the arguments for immediate action were loudly applauded, and endorsed by the people. The result of the election had now become known and was received with deep feeling and with a conviction that the crisis so long anticipated, and for so long inevitable, had at last come; that it would unite the South, and that the course to be pursued by the State was now clear, while any apprehension of the establishment of a free-soil party in their midst, which the success of Mr. Douglas would have created, was now set at rest.

In Charleston the feeling had assumed a distinct and definite shape. On the 7th of November the Grand Jury of the United States District Court refused to perform the duties of their office. The ordinary business had been disposed of, when, in response to an inquiry from the presiding judge, as to whether they had any presentments to make, the foreman, Mr. Robert N. Gourdin, a prominent citizen of Charleston, replied:

"May it please your Honor, It is understood to be one of the functions of the Grand Jury to make presentments of nuisances, and to suggest to the court and to the country such reforms in law or in its administration as may to them seem proper. These presentments are predicated upon the stability of the Government, and are designed to promote its gradual and steady progress to the highest civilization.

"Hence it was the purpose of this jury to lay before the court some matters suggested by the indictments submitted to them, but the events of yesterday seem to render this unnecessary now.

"The verdict of the Northern section of the Confederacy, solemnly announced to the country through the ballot-box on yesterday, has swept away the last hope for the permanence, for the stability, of the Federal Government of these sovereign States, and the public mind is constrained to lift itself above the consideration of details in the administration of law and justice

---

* Mullins in reply to McGowan; Journal of the House, 1860.

up to the vast and solemn issues which have been forced upon us. These issues involve the existence of the Government of which this court is the organ and minister. In these extraordinary circumstances, the Grand Jury respectfully decline to proceed with their presentments. They deem this explanation due to the court and to themselves."

A profound silence followed this announcement, when the Judge of the court, the Hon. A. G. Magrath, rose in his place and formally resigned his office. He said:

"The business of the term has been disposed of, and under ordinary circumstances it would be my duty to dismiss you to your several avocations, with my thanks for your presence and aid. But now I have something more to do, the omission of which would not be consistent with propriety.

"In the political history of the United States an event has happened of ominous import to fifteen slaveholding States. The State of which we are citizens has been always understood to have deliberately fixed its purpose whenever that event should happen.

"Feeling an assurance of what will be the action of the State, I consider it my duty, without delay, to prepare to obey its wishes. That preparation is made by the resignation of the office which I have held.

"For the last time I have, as a Judge of the United States, administered the laws of the United States within the limits of the State of South Carolina.

"While thus acting in obedience to a sense of duty, I cannot be indifferent to the emotions it must produce. That department of government which I believe has best maintained its integrity and preserved its purity has been suspended.

"So far as I am concerned the Temple of Justice, raised under the Constitution of the United States, is now closed.

"If it shall never again be opened, I thank God that its doors have been closed before its altar has been desecrated with sacrifices to tyranny.

"May I not say to you, that, in the future which we are about to penetrate, next to the reliance we should place in the goodness of that God who will guide us in the right way, should be our confidence in our State and our obedience to its laws? We are about to sever our relations with others, because they have broken their covenant with us. Let us not break the covenant we have made with each other. Let us not forget that what the laws of our State require become our duties, and that he who acts against the wish or without command of his State, usurps that sovereign authority which we must maintain inviolate."

The address was received with profound silence, and during its delivery many of the spectators were in tears.

The resignation of the United States District-Attorney followed at once upon the same day; the judge, who had left the bench and divested himself of his robes, resuming his seat to formally accept it. That of the Collector of the Port followed soon after, and as the news was received at Columbia, it produced the greatest impression, and added strength to the arguments of those who urged immediate action. A meeting of the prominent politicians of South Carolina, including the whole Congressional delegation except one, had been held at the residence of United States Senator Hammond, near Augusta, on the 25th of October, 1860. Governor Gist, the Governor of the State, ex-Governor Adams and ex-Speaker Orr were present, and it was unanimously resolved by them that South Carolina should secede from the Union in the event of Mr. Lincoln's election. But of all the circumstances that indirectly exercised an influence on the Legislature in their action, the proceedings in the United States Court, then sitting in the city of Charleston, and which have just been described, were by far the most important in their effect. The views of the presiding judge were not known. During the fierce conflict as to the necessity of separate State action, in 1850, when the "denial of equal rights in the Territories" reopened the whole controversy, and when the demand for separate action rang through the State, and divided its people as did the tariff question of 1829, he was fixedly opposed to the separate action of the State, and was a zealous advocate of the co-operation of all the Southern States in whatever conduct should be adopted. It was not, then, the question of the right of a State to secede from the Union; this was not doubted anywhere in the State; the question was simply one of the expediency of its exercise under the then existing circumstances. Invisible forces, acting upon the popular heart, had induced a great political change during the time that had passed; radical differences, born with. the Constitution itself as to the nature of the Federal Union and the limits of the Federal Government, had meantime greatly developed themselves; and the people of South Carolina, with a new generation just entering upon the theatre of political action, found themselves year by year anticipating then time when they would become a party to a controversy with the General Government. The maintenance of that theory of government adopted by South Carolina, was deemed not only essential to its welfare, but as the one recognized in the foundation of the Union. No encroachment upon it should be over-looked, and when a proper opportunity was presented it must be met, and that opportunity, it was thought, was presented when it was ascertained that the popular voice had been expressed in favor of one for the Presidency who was believed to be in sympathy with the political enemies of the slave-holding States, and whose elevation to that high office, threatened, as was supposed, the existence of their industrial pursuits and the overthrow of their political institutions.

Nor was this view confined to the men in prominent political place only: it was the conviction of all. The result of the election for President was accepted by every class as decisive of the action of the State, and that action must be the separation from the Federal Union. Its form of political faith had been affirmed and proclaimed by its Governors, its General Assemblies and its judges in the most positive and solemn manner, and had been recognized and accepted by the people.

They recognized no more allegiance to the General Government, as sovereign, than to any entirely foreign State, excepting as determined by the conditions of the Union and the Constitution. And they held that, whenever these conditions were violated by the Federal Government, the sovereign people and Commonwealth of South Carolina had the right, if they deemed it expedient, to dissolve such allegiance.

When, therefore, the election of Mr. Lincoln was announced to them, they saw in it the sure precursor of danger and ruin. They had no leader, they needed none, but rushed on without further thought to the adoption of what they considered a proper exercise of their right and their most certain protection. Like others who had been the advocates of co-operation in 1850, the United States Judge had accepted the conclusion that not only was there now sufficient cause for separate State action, but that the dissolution of its relation with the Union was necessary to the welfare of the State.

In accordance with this conviction his sudden announcement and action in the United States District Court at Charleston produced an effect so marked and immediate as to give an increased impetus to the movement. Its result was felt not only in Charleston and in the State; it reached to Washington. The President saw the whole Federal machinery, upon which he relied in the exercise of his constitutional powers to enforce the laws, swept away at once, and himself without any power to restore it. Meantime a large and enthusiastic meeting was held in Charleston, at which a committee, consisting of the three prominent citizens who had lately resigned from Federal office, was appointed to go to Columbia and urge immediate action upon the Legislature. The members of the Charleston delegation had been divided in opinion as to the time at which the Convention should be called. It was urged that more efficient action could be relied upon if the call for a Convention was postponed until near the close of Mr. Buchanan's administration. Upon the arrival of the committee from Charleston, however, the delegation was called together to confer with them, when, after the interview, they became a unit for immediate action.

It was under such influences that the Legislature had met in extra session, when, without discussion, without the display of emotion or feeling inseparable from debate, without any demand for hasty action, a resolution was offered in the Senate on the second day of the session, making so much of the Governor's message as refers to a call of the people of this State, the reorganization of the militia, and preparations for the defense of the State the special order for the following day. The committee on Federal relations was ordered to report a bill, which was done on the 8th of November. It provided for calling a convention for the purpose of secession. It was soon disposed of. Upon its second reading, on the 9th, it received but one dissenting voice, that of Mr. McAlilley, Senator from Chester, and upon its final passage, on the 10th, the vote was 42 in the affirmative, and in the negative, none. In the House a similar course had been pursued. The Senate Bill, with the report of the committee on Federal relations of the House, was recommitted to the committee of the whole House, which discussed it, and on the 12th it was passed

NOTE.–In a conversation with Judge Black on the 10th of January, 1883, I mentioned to him that I was about to visit Charleston, S. C.; that some of those who had been conspicuous in the early days of the war were still living; and that I hoped to see them, and especially to converse at length with Judge Magrath. "Is Judge Magrath still living?" inquired Judge Black; "the act of that man caused more anxiety to Mr. Buchanan than any other event that occurred, except Anderson's movement from Moultrie to Sumter." He thought that the only thing to be done was to refill the Federal offices thus vacated, and that he believed to be difficult, if not impossible.–[AUTHOR.]

by a vote of 114 in the affirmative, and in the negative none. The election for delegates was to be held on the 6th of December, and the Convention to meet on the 17th. Other resolutions were adopted, authorizing the committees on military affairs of the Senate and House to meet during the recess, and to prepare a plan for arming the State, to organize a permanent military bureau, and to reorganize the militia. On the 13th the Governor communicated to the Legislature the resignation of United States Senator Hammond. Resolutions were at once passed in both Houses, recognizing the act of Senator Hammond as one of loyalty and devotion to the sovereignty of South Carolina, "at once worthy of his high character and filial devotion." The Legislature then adjourned, having fully accomplished the object of their extra session.

On the 26th of November, the Legislature of the State again met in regular session. So confidently was the secession of the State anticipated that measures looking to its prospective political relation were freely discussed and commented upon. The Governor, upon the reassembling of the Legislature, transmitted a message rehearsing the arguments for secession and counselling prompt and independent action. "In looking forward," said he "to the separate nationality of South Carolina, many changes will have to be made in existing laws;" and among others he recommends that the law prohibiting masters from permitting negroes to hire their own time and make contracts, should be so amended as to attach a penalty of fine and imprisonment to the parties violating it; that no slave mechanic should be permitted to hire white men to work under his direction; and that it must be distinctly understood that the white is the governing race without an exception, and without regard to a disparity of intellect, merit or acquirements; and he recommends the enactment of a law "punishing summarily and severely, if not with death, any person that circulates incendiary documents, avows himself an abolitionist, or in any way attempts to create insubordination or insurrection among the slaves;" that the effort to call a convention of the Southern States had failed, and that there was but one course left for South Carolina to pursue, and that was, "to go straight forward to the consummation of her purpose;" that she would not stand alone; she had the right to secede peaceably, and the Government could not rightfully prevent a State from seceding, but that "men having arms in their hands may use them;" and he earnestly urged upon the Legislature the necessity of arming the State at the earliest practicable period, and thus be prepared for the worst. "It is gratifying to know," he said, "that if we must resort to arms in defense of our rights, and a blow should be struck at South Carolina before the other States move up in line, we have the tender of volunteers from all the Southern and some of the North ern States, to repair promptly to our standard and share our fortunes." At the close of his official term, the Governor trans- mitted a second and final message, reiterating the fact that the State had at last determined to "part company with those that treat her as aliens and enemies," and that, "having forever closed the door from which we have passed out of the Union, we may with safety seek co-operation and unite with other States."*

The delay of the Convention for a single week to pass the ordinance of secession would have a blighting and chilling influ- ence upon the other Southern States, and he trusted that by the 25th of December no flag but the Palmetto would float over any part of the State of South Carolina. At the same time he presented to the Legislature "one of the pikes intended by John Brown to be used by the negroes of Virginia upon the unoffending and peace- able inhabitants of that State;" and he repeated the request of Mr. Ruffin, of Virginia, who had brought it, that it might be placed in some conspicuous position in the State House at Columbia, there to remain and be preserved as an abiding and impressive evidence of the fanatical hatred borne by the dominant Northern party to the institutions and people of the Southern States, and he recommended that the thanks of the State be returned to Mr. Ruffin for this memento of Southern wrongs too long and too patiently borne. It was thus that public sentiment was formed and supported by personal and official influences, and with a special reference to its effect upon the Convention so soon to assemble at Columbia.

But even at this early period the current of events was lead- ing to the open assertion of what was considered in South Carolina as the rights of their State; and a conviction was rapidly growing in the minds of the people that such assertion, if maintained,

---

* It would appear that co-operation before individual State action was regarded as unwise, and in the nature of a conspiracy.

would inevitably result in a conflict with the General Government. Military organizations had begun to act, and as early as the 20th of October the Washington Light Infantry, an elite corps of Charleston, at a special meeting held by them had taken into consideration "the threatening aspect of affairs and the necessity of preparing to meet the emergency." Their commanding officer, Captain Simonton, suggested that preparations be made "to take the field at a moment's warning," and a resolution was offered by one of their number, Sergeant W. A. Courtenay,* and unanimously adopted, that the services of the organization should be offered to the Governor as an independent Battalion of Light Troops "of not less than two hundred men," and in case of service they should be so recognized.

To this prompt tender of their services the Governor replied, accepting it conditionally, and expressing an opinion that, from the signs of the times, "South Carolina will require the support of all her sons," when he would place the organization in "the front rank of its country's defenders."

As soon as the result of the election was known, the Governor called for the services of the Washington Light Infantry, and, as will be subsequently seen, stationed them as a guard over the United States Arsenal in the city of Charleston, on the 12th of November.

---

* The present efficient mayor of Charleston, S. C.

CHAPTER III.

MEANTIME, the Government at Washington was not indifferent to the movements in South Carolina. The President and Cabinet had recognized the certainty of a great political change; and the prospect of the advent to power of a party wholly committed to a national policy diametrically opposed to their own was fully anticipated. Men of prominence in the South had gone northward, and had satisfied themselves of the impending change, and, in passing through Washington on their return, had freely expressed their convictions. In spite of the angry discussions in and out of Congress, the full meaning of which but few realized, the country and the Cabinet simply drifted through the long summer into a condition of things the only solution of which was war. The great national issues which had divided the Whig and Democratic parties had ceased to interest or control popular opinion. The fierce discussions of the slavery question, which had for some years past excited and embittered the popular temper, had resulted in the complete extinction of the Whig party; and in the coming contest the Democratic party found itself opposed by a new organization, which, from the very character of its principles and measures, made the political issue one between the North and the South. It was obvious that if this party succeeded, and the South, believing itself placed on the defensive, should carry out the policy of resistance which it had declared in advance, the close of Mr. Buchanan's administration would be a troubled one, and his Cabinet would be divided into hostile factions. In the condition of things just developing, there could be no unity of administration in a Cabinet which represented such conflicting interests and opinions. Mr. Buchanan's Cabinet consisted of three Northern men, General Cass, of Michigan, Secretary of State; Mr. Toucey, of Connecticut, Secretary of the Navy, and Judge J. S. Black, of Pennsylvania, Attorney-General; and of four Southern men, Mr. Howell Cobb, of Georgia, Secretary of the Treasury; Gov. J. B. Floyd, of Virginia, Secretary of War; Mr. Jacob Thompson, of Mississippi, Secretary of the Interior; and Mr. J. Holt, of Kentucky, Postmaster-General.

Mr. W. H. Trescot, the Assistant Secretary of State, who had been Acting Secretary under the President's warrant during the absence of General Cass, from June to October, 1860, was a native of South Carolina. His relations to the Secretary of State and the President were known to be close, while he was naturally in friendly connection with the Southern members of the, Cabinet, and intimately so with the leaders of the movement in his own State; and he was soon sought as the exponent and the vehicle of their views and intentions in the antagonism that seemed to be daily developing between the Government at Washington and South Carolina. After severing his connection with the Cabinet, he became the agent of his State, and immediately upon his return to South Carolina, in February, 1861, he made a record of his impressions of the ('events which have been the subject of so much controversy, and the truth about which is of essential importance to the future history of the country." A record thus made may well be considered a valuable contribution to the materials of that future history. It is from this manuscript the writer has drawn largely; and oftentimes the clear and vigorous narrative has been inserted in the terse and graphic words of the author himself. He says:

"Placed thus, at the head of the State Department, my relations with the President, the Cabinet and the foreign ministers were naturally and necessarily freer and more intimate than they would have been under ordinary circumstances. I was thus familiar with the hopes and fears, the opinions and expectations, which. agitated the rulers of the country during that exciting period which preceded the secession of South Carolina, while my correspondence from home kept me fully informed how public opinion there was preparing for the inevitable issue. During the summer all the political signs confirmed the belief that the defeat of the Democratic party was certain. The Southern Senators and members who had at the close of the session gone North to judge for themselves, all in passing through Washington bore the same invariable testimony as to what they had seen and heard. Evidence of all sorts flowed in upon the Executive Committee of the party which sat at the Capitol, and to the same effect. One sort of testimony struck me particularly. The State Department had the selection of papers in which to publish the Laws, so many papers for each State, and as the patronage was not very considerable, it was distributed, of course, with a view to party influence. The applications for these appointments brought me in contact with political editors from all parts of the country, and, with every disposition and every temptation to be sanguine, their statements only confirmed the certainty of a great political defeat;

"The President and the Cabinet had full time to consider their positions.

"The President and Governor Toucey, the Secretary of the Navy, seemed to agree most perfectly. They thought that the Republican victory was only illusory–that the party could not survive success–that, after four years of power, checked and crossed by a powerful opposition, a great and universal reaction, already commenced, would complete its destruction–and restore the old Democracy, purified and strengthened, to its ancient rule. They did not believe that the South was in earnest, and thought secession only probable in the case of South Carolina, a result which, being manageable, might after all have a very wholesome effect.

"Mr. Cobb, the Secretary of the Treasury, held and expressed but one opinion, that it was the duty of the South, in defense both of honor and, interest, to dissolve the Union. He thought that every State should secede by itself, and that secession should be practically accomplished on the 4th of March, upon the close of Mr. Buchanan's administration. This he thought most likely to unite the South, and only due to Mr. Buchanan's consistent support of Southern rights. Of the earnestness of these opinions he gave convincing proof by writing to his friends in Georgia that, if upon the election of Mr. Lincoln there was a probability that the State would acquiesce, he wished his name withdrawn as a candidate for the United States Senate, as, with his views, he could no longer continue in public life with hope or honor.

"Governor Floyd, Secretary of War, thought secession unwise and a dissolution of the Union unnecessary. Like Mr. Buchanan and Mr. Toucey, he believed the Black Republican triumph only temporary, and that its success would be its destruction. As a matter of policy, therefore, he wished to fight in the Union, but he recognized the right of a State to secede, fully sympathizing with the South in the opinion that, as far as the North was concerned, enough had been done to justify any action the South might take, and was resolute that no force should be employed by the Government to restrain the action of an independent State.

"Mr. Thompson, Secretary of the Interior, seemed to me, while holding the general opinions entertained by Southern men, to be governed in his personal conduct by a strong attachment to Mr. Buchanan, an unwillingness to believe in the necessity of the extreme measure of secession, and a readiness to acquiesce in any course which his State—Mississippi—should adopt.

"General Cass, Secretary of State, like Mr. Cobb, held clear and well-defined opinions. From the beginning he believed Lincoln's election certain, and the' dissolution of the Union, or at least the secession of the South, inevitable. Not recognizing any right in a State to secede except as a revolutionary measure, he would have. resisted the attempt at the commencement, and, as the sworn officer of the United States, he would have done his utmost to preserve its integrity. 'I speak to Cobb,' he would say, 'and he tells me he is a Georgian; to Floyd, and he tells me he is a Virginian; to you, and you tell me you are a Carolinian. I am not a Michigander; I am a citizen of the United States. The laws of the United States bind you, as they bind me, individually; if you, the citizens of Georgia or Virginia or Carolina, refuse obedience to them, it is—my sworn duty to enfore them.' That he believed to be his duty, and he would have done it, 'although he believed he would not succeed in the attempt, for he also believed that great wrong and injustice had been done the South; that the Black Republican party was organized for its destruction; and, as he always predicted, that a long and bloody civil war was the sure and necessary result of the existing condition of things. Judge Black, the Attorney-General, to a great extent agreed with

General Cass, but he treated the question exclusively as one of constitutional law. At least, it always seemed to me that he was unwilling to look at the political consequences of secession, and the question which he proposed to himself for solution was, What is the legal wrong involved in secession, and what is the legal remedy? a question to be solved judicially, not politically. His views were always supposed to be specially enforced in the full and forcible argument afterwards embodied in the President's message.

"Of the opinions and feelings of Mr. Holt, the Postmaster-General, I never knew more than was to be inferred from his position in the Cabinet and his action when appointed Secretary of War."

Of the members of the Cabinet thus enumerated, those who, in view of the threatening aspect of affairs, occupied the most prominent positions, were the Attorney-General, Judge Black, and the Secretary of War, Mr. Floyd. The trained and vigorous mind of Judge Black did not long hold him to any technical solution of the difficulties, and, as the time passed, and brought with every day events and momentous issues that pressed upon the country, the views of Judge Black expanded, and he grew daily in appreciation and harmonious sympathy with the demands of the situation. Stern partisan as he was, he yielded to the demands of the country, until the same brain that created and the same hand that penned the Attorney-General's opinion of November, 1860, came equally to trace the able comments of the statesman upon the President's letter to the South Carolina Commissioners, as well as the utterances of the patriot in the letter of January 17, 1861, to Lieutenant-General Scott.

His prejudices were as deep-seated as his convictions were strong, and when he took occasion to express his opinions, it was often done with little reference to their harmony or discord with those of other men. Wholly in accord with his party, "he found himself at all times opposed to the same enemy," and his opinions were often formed amid the stress and passion of action." His relations to the President had ever been close through a long career. He was his counsellor, and, as will be seen, his influence was potential. His personal attachment was deep and real, and although the public acts of the President were often the subject of close, logical criticism, the utterance of any conclusion of con-

demnation was ever avoided, while his respect for his good qualities never failed to find in him a vigorous expression while he
lived."

Mr. Holt, the Postmaster-General, was a native of Kentucky.
His State was divided probably more than any other upon the
questions of public policy now agitating the country, but his
own views were well known, and afterward found assertion in his
able. speeches to his people, denouncing the proposed neutrality
of the State.

A distinguished lawyer, he had been called by Mr. Buchanan
in 1857 to his first public office, that of Commissioner of Patents.
Subsequently, upon the death of Aaron V. Brown, the position of
Postmaster-General was tendered to him by the President, which
he accepted. Upon the retirement of Governor Floyd from the
Cabinet he became the Secretary of War, and through the trying
scenes at the close of Mr. Buchanan's administration, to the
inauguration of Mr. Lincoln and beyond it, he guided the affairs
of the War Department with patriotic firmness and ability.   What
in the exercise of his office he was called upon to do will be seen
as this narrative progresses; but it may not now be amiss if the
writer recalls with gratitude his defense of Anderson and his
command, in their position in Charleston harbor, his able argument in defining the position of the Government in its course as to
Sumter, and his support of the little garrison, as his words came
to them encouraging them in their duty.

The question which from first to last agitated all minds, which,
both before and after the secession of the State loomed up as
almost the only subject of immediate danger to the success of the
movements, and which at once engaged the attention of the Government at Washington, of the authorities of the State, and the
Convention, was the status of the public property in the city and

---

*On the 22d of March, 1882, I had a long and earnest conversation with
Judge Black upon the subject of the interview between the President and the
Congressional delegation of South Carolina, as to the understanding or arrangement agreed upon at that interview. The details of his interview with the President, when the commissioners of South Carolina were in Washington, were stated,
when at the end I said, "Well, then, Judge Black, there appears to be but one
inference to be drawn, but one conclusion to be reached; the President did
make that agreement." The Judge rose, and, looking steadily at me for a
moment, said, "Remember, that is *your* conclusion."—[AUTHOR.]

harbor of Charleston. The necessity and the policy of reinforcing the forts in Charleston harbor in advance of the anticipated secession of the State were subjects of constant discussion in the Cabinet. General Cass, the Secretary of State, and Judge Black, the Attorney-General, were urgent that the forts in the South, and especially those in Charleston harbor, should be reinforced at once.

The Secretary of War, Mr. Floyd, remained firm in his determination that no reinforcement should be sent. "He said," says the Assistant Secretary of State in his narrative, that with his opinions he never could and never would consent to the coercion of a sovereign State; that while he did not think the anticipated action of South Carolina wise, he sympathized deeply with her spirit; that, considering the reinforcement of the garrisons in Charleston harbor as looking very like coercion, and at any rate only calculated to excite and irritate the popular feeling, he would not consent to it. But that, on the other hand, he would not submit to any attempt on the part of the people to take the forts; that he was bound to resist, and would resist. What would be the consequence of the secession of the State was a grave question, but one which had not yet arisen. That at present he was only resolved upon two things: not to reinforce the forts, and not to allow them to be taken by an unlawful force. In these positions I agreed with him; and we agreed further in believing that there was no danger of an attack on the forts by an unlawful mob, and that the State would take the action she might deem necessary, regularly, and with due notice to the Government at Washington. The position of Governor Floyd I explained fully, and at his own request, by letters to those at home who could, in my opinion, best use the knowledge for the purpose of quieting the alarm and apprehensions of the citizens of Charleston. The apprehensions of the people of Charleston, however, were not easily quieted, and General Cass and Judge Black were urgent that the forts should be reinforced. The subject was one of constant discussion. Governor Floyd was earnest in his determination and resolved not to reinforce, but he thought that if such were his opinions, he ought to be trusted by the State; that if in the ordinary routine of the business of the War Department he sent a few men to Fort Sumter, or a few boxes of ammunition to Fort Moultrie, to supply the vacancies caused by death or desertion and to furnish the usual amount of powder kept in the garrison, these acts ought not to be objects of suspicion; that in fact this jealousy and clamor against his ordinary action was weakening his power to act when an extraordinary emergency did arise. Besides, as he argued on one occasion with great force, 'You tell me that if any attempt is made to do what under ordinary circumstances is done every day, you will be unable to restrain your people. Suppose you are not able to restrain them *now,* am *I* bound to leave these garrisons unprotected, to the mercy of a mob; am I not bound to enable them to resist an unlawful violation which you cannot control?' While I felt the strength of this reasoning, I knew also that in the then condition of feeling in Charleston anything that could be even misunderstood or misrepresented as reinforcement would lead to an explosion that would injure the whole Southern cause. I therefore saw Mr. Cobb and explained to him what I understood to be Governor Floyd's position. I told him that while I admitted its strength, things were in that condition that he could not act from it; that I had the most perfect confidence in him, and had pledged myself at home that our people could trust him implicitly, but that any nice difference between what was reinforcement for the purpose of reinforcement, and what was ordinary routine business, would not be understood at such a time; and that unless the Secretary of War could make up his mind to allow no change in the forts, important or not, I could not answer for the consequences, and, after what I had written home, would feel bound to resign and tell the authorities there to judge for themselves. I believed that such a step would lead to the occupation of Fort Sumter in forty-eight hours, and I told him that I was on my way to Governor Floyd to announce to him my conclusion. He proposed that I should postpone my visit until after a conference that he was to have that morning with the Governor and Mr. Thompson. I did so. That night Governor Floyd called at my house, and in a long and very free conversation expressed his former convictions, his feeling that the State ought to accept his action without suspicion, as his opinions were well known, fixed, and had been acted on constantly long before this crisis had come. But that if I thought collision between the people of the State and the Government forces would be precipitated, he would not consent that a man or a gun should be sent to any of the forts in the harbor of Charleston; and

if his sense of duty induced any change in his determination, I
should be informed by him in advance of any action and in ample
time to pursue such a course as I deemed proper. Things continued upon this footing during the preparation of the President's
annual message, the contemplation of which it seemed certain
must produce a dissolution of the Cabinet, for the nearer the
time came for opinion to take the form of action, the more utterly
impossible was it to reconcile the differences. Those members
of the Cabinet who desired that reinforcements should be sent to
Charleston pressed their policy, and a few evenings after the
conversation with Governor Floyd, just related, he called upon me
evidently much excited. He said that just after dinner the
President had sent for him (at the room in the State Department,
which he occupied while preparing his message); that when he
reached him he found General Cass and Judge Black, who retired
immediately upon his entrance. The President then informed
him that he had determined to reinforce the garrisons in Charleston harbor, upon which a very animated discussion arose. The
President finally consented to suspend his decision until General
Scott could reach Washington, and he had been telegraphed to
come on immediately. Governor Floyd felt confident that he
could satisfy General Scott of the impolicy of such a step, that it
could not be supported, and that the distribution of United States
troops was such as to render anything looking like the use of force
not only idle but disastrous, as it must provoke attack, which the
Government was in no condition to resist successfully." When,
therefore the pressure of General Cass and Judge Black upon the
President for the immediate reinforcement of the forts became
urgent, it seemed to the Southern members of the Cabinet to be
important to devise some means by which such a necessity should be
obviated. The practical question that presented itself was, by what
means the President could be induced to change his purpose; they
were anxious both that any action taken by the Southern States
be regularly made—in their opinion, constitutionally made—and
that Mr. Buchanan should be spared the embarrassment and
difficulty which would result from any premature and violent
demonstration in them. They desired that time should be
allowed for the development of a complete unity of purpose in all
the Southern States, and that the issue which now seemed inevitable should be met by the new Administration, whose advent to
power was considered by them the provocation.

"Governor Floyd declared," says the Assistant Secretary in his narrative, "that his mind was made up, that he would cut off his right hand before he would sign an order to send reinforcements to the Carolina forts, and that if the President insisted, he would resign. Mr. Thompson, Secretary of the Interior, agreed with him perfectly, and said he would sustain his course and follow him."

After considerable discussion, various propositions were suggested, among them one from the Assistant Secretary of State, who proposed that he should go to the President, "state to him that the Secretary of War had communicated to me his intention, and then endeavor to disabuse his mind of any unfounded apprehensions as to the action of the State, and submit to him the reasons, based upon information in my possession, against such a policy as he thought of adopting, should I make no impression. I would then say that under the circumstances it was my duty, however painful, to submit my resignation then and there, and leave for Columbia the next morning, to lay the facts before the executive of South Carolina. I would be in Columbia in thirty-six hours, and upon such information there could be no earthly doubt that the forts would be occupied in the following twenty-four. Such a resolution, respectfully but firmly stated, would I thought make the President hesitate. Indeed, he could not have acted, for he would have been forced to remove Governor Floyd, and the time occupied in the changes and the execution of the orders would have been more than enough to give the State the necessary opportunity. Such a proceeding was of course only to be adopted as a last resort, because it involved necessarily such a breach between the President and Governor Floyd as would compel his resignation, if not anticipated by his dismissal, and because while it gave the State warning it only precipitated the issue. For, once taken, the die was cast, the forts would be seized, and the Government could not have submitted either to its defeat or to the manner in which it was effected."

Another proposition was one to the effect that the Member of Congress from Charleston should be at once summoned to Washington, in the hope that his representation of the public feeling, which had been possibly exaggerated, would relieve the President's mind of any fear of an outbreak. The proposition which was finally adopted, says the Assistant Secretary of State, was that

"I should write to the Governor of the State—Governor Gist—tell him that the President was under very strong apprehensions that the people of Charleston would seize the forts; that in consequence he felt bound to send reinforcements. That the Southern members of the Cabinet would resist this policy, to resignation, but that they thought that if he felt authorized to write a letter assuring the President that if no reinforcements were sent, there would be no attempt upon the forts before the meeting of the Convention, and that then commissioners would be sent to negotiate all the points of difference; that their hands would be strengthened, the responsibility of provoking collision would be taken from the State, and the President would probably be relieved from the necessity of pursuing this policy." They added: "If such a letter was written, and failed, he should have information in ample time to take such steps as the interest of the State required."

"I therefore addressed Governor Gist the following letter:

[STRICTLY   CONFIDENTIAL.]
WASHINGTON, November 26, 1860.

"Dear Sir: I am aware (and I do not deem it necessary to specify my source of information) that apprehensions exist in the mind of the President that before the State acts in convention some attempt will be made to take the forts in Charleston harbor. Feeling that his personal honor would be involved in such an attempt, he may make his apprehensions the pretext or ground on which to order an increased force to those posts. This order will be resisted to the very last, and at any cost, by the Southern members of the Cabinet, but they would be incalculably strengthened in their position if you were at liberty to say directly to the President that you could answer, on your responsibility, that so long as no change was made in these garrisons, so long as no additional force was sent there and the State remained in the Union, no such attempt would be made, and that any increase of force made in the face of this notice would lead to instant collision, and that for every drop of blood shed under such circumstances he, and he alone, would be responsible.

"I wish you distinctly to understand that there is no possibility of such an order being issued without the dissolution of the Cabinet and your receiving ample notice. While I answer, for this, I write with the confidence that such an assurance will prevent any hasty and indiscreet movement on the part of the State. Believing that you agree fully with me that, for the sake of the State and of the South, our move toward secession ought to be regular and orderly, and that all collision should be avoided, and feeling that the Southern members of the Cabinet are entitled to the support of the State, I write to you to indicate how you can support them. To that point alone, this letter is addressed. If it becomes necessary for the State to look to itself, you shall know promptly and certainly.

"If, therefore, you can write such a letter as I indicate, the Southern members of the Cabinet can rest upon it triumphantly no such order will be issued in the face of it, and if it is, you will be free to act, will have ample information as to the necessity of action, and the whole responsibility of what comes will be, not on the head of South Carolina, but of the President of the United States.

"If so, your letter must be here by return mail, directed under cover to me. Telegraph me also when this is received, and if you intend to answer yes or no to my proposition. Details I cannot give you, but trust that my signature will command your confidence.   I am, yours respectfully,
"WM. HENRY TRESCOT."
"To GOVERNOR GIST."

To this letter I received the following answer:

"EXECUTIVE OFFICE,
"COLUMBIA, S. C., November 29, 1860.
"MR. WM. HENRY TRESCOT.

"Dear Sir: Although South Carolina is determined to secede from the Federal Union very soon after her Convention meets, yet the desire of her constituted authorities is, not to do anything that will bring on a collision before the ordinance of secession has been passed and notice has been given to the President of the fact; and not then, unless compelled to do so by the refusal of the President to recognize our right to secede, by attempting to interfere with our exports or imports, or by refusal to surrender the forts and arsenals in our limits. I have found great difficulty in restraining the people of Charleston from seizing the forts, and have only been able to restrain them by the assurance that no additional troops would be sent to the forts, or any munitions of war. Everything is now quiet, and will remain so until the ordinance is passed, if no more soldiers or munitions of war are sent on. That is to say, I will use my utmost efforts to effect that object, and believe I will succeed; but the Legislature and myself would be powerless to prevent a collision if a single soldier or another gun or ammunition is sent on to be placed in the forts, If President Buchanan takes a course different from the one indicated and sends on a reinforcement, the responsibility will rest on him of lighting the torch of discord, which will only be quenched in blood. I am under a pledge to sanction resistance, and to use all the military power of the State to prevent any increase of troops in these garrisons, and had to make the pledge

to restrain the people, who are restive, and hope no necessity will arise to compel me to redeem the pledge. I write to you knowing that, while you will be faithful to the Government of the United States as long as you hold office under it, yet you are also a South Carolinian, and would desire, by all means, to avoid the needless shedding of blood. If you think there is no impropriety in showing this letter to the President you are at liberty to do so, for I do not wish him to be mistaken and act in such a way as to bring upon the country a bloody war, without the most imperious necessity.   Very truly yours,

"WM. H. GIST."

At the same time I received the following letter from Governor Gist, which had crossed mine to him on the road:

"[CONFIDENTIAL.]

"EXECUTIVE DEPARTMENT,

"COLUMBIA, S. C., November 29, 1860.

"MR. W. H. TRESCOT.

"*Dear Sir:* I take the liberty, from your general character and without the pleasure of a personal acquaintance, to ask if you have any objections, in the event of your connection with the Federal Government ceasing, to remain in Washington and act as confidential agent for this Department. It is important to have some one at Washington to give me the earliest information of what transpires affecting the interest of this State, and I know no one so acceptable as yourself. It is probable that the Convention will want some one on the spot through whom the information of its final action can be authoritatively communicated to the President at the earliest moment and an answer received. If you remain I will inform the Convention that you are in Washington, and suggest that you be selected to perform this delicate and important duty. If there is any inquiry as to the course South Carolina will pursue, you may safely say that she will not permit any increase of troops or munitions of war in the forts or arsenal, and, considering it an evidence of intention to coerce and an act of war, she will use force to prevent it, and a collision must inevitably ensue. I have had great trouble, as it is, to prevent an attack upon the forts, and will not be able (if willing) to prevent an attack upon them if another soldier is sent there. Of course, I do not expect you to act in the premises until your duty to the Federal Government ceases, but I cannot but anticipate such a result soon. An early answer is requested.

"Very respectfully and truly yours,

"WM. H. GIST."

In view of this letter, and from the fact that the action of the State was now considered certain, the Assistant Secretary determined to offer his resignation to the President, remaining, however, for a few days in office, in order that the President might have an opportunity to select his successor. The President replied to him that "however much he regretted the necessity, he had anticipated it for some time," and then, in language which it is unnecessary to repeat, expressed his pleasure at the relations which had always existed between them. He said that it was due to him to make his appointment of a successor as soon as possible, and that it certainly should be done before the Convention of South Carolina had taken any action:* "I cannot but express my grateful recollection of Mr. Buchanan's uniform kindness and confidence in his conduct to me. The absence of General Cass for the summer, and his health when in Washington, brought me into very constant personal association with the President. Having been Minister both to Russia and England, and also Secretary of State, he took special interest in that department, and watched its proceedings with minute and well-informed interest. His diplomatic experience was large, and his general views very cautious and very clear, and his knowledge always accurate. My official intercourse with him was invariably pleasant. With the ordinary mass of the business of the Department he never interfered, and, on all matters large and important enough for his decision, gave careful and most considerate attention to views and opinions with which he did not agree; while he never failed to manifest, when he felt it, his cordial approval of the manner in which his own instructions were carried out."

The President had now concluded his annual message, and, in view of the sentiments expressed by the Governor of South Carolina, he determined to send to him a copy, in advance of its publication, by the hands of the Assistant Secretary of State, who, in view of the confidential relations he had held with the President, was thoroughly informed upon the subject of the President's views. He could explain in Columbia what might be misunderstood there, and, from the relations he held with the authorities in South Carolina, could bring back to the President a clear and reliable account of the state of feeling and opinions in the State, and thus prepare the way, if possible, to a peaceful solution of the difficulties.

That the State would pass the ordinance of secession he was now convinced, and, in the uncertainty of the result of any issue made with the General Government, his chief anxiety. was in reference to the collection of the revenue and the safety of the forts.

* Trescot's Narrative.

He was assured "that the people of South Carolina not only held the right of secession, but that they would take special pride in carrying out that right, regularly, peaceably, as a *right,* not as a revolutionary measure; that I really believed it would mortify them to be compelled to resort to force; that they would pass the ordinance of secession, and then send regularly accredited agents to negotiate with the Government." 'But,' said he, 'you know I cannot recognize them. All I can do is to refer them to Congress.' I told him that I believed such a reference, courteously made and in good faith, would be accepted, and that the State would wait a reasonable time for the decision of Congress. This he seemed to think would be sufficient, if the secession was inevitable; but still he was very cautious, and his great hope seemed to be, by temporizing, to avoid an issue before the 4th of March.

"On Sunday night, when I saw him, he went over the old ground; said that he thought his message ought to be acceptable to the South; that he had spoken the truth, boldly and clearly; and that all he had declared was that, with regard to the laws and property of the United States, he would discharge the obligations of his official oath, as far as his constitutional powers enabled him.

"I told him that I would take the message with pleasure, because it was a courtesy to the Executive of the State, and because I thought that, waiving the opinions expressed as to the right of secession, it was as conciliatory as it was possible for him to make it from his position; and, indeed, more so than I had expected. But that I must say, in candor, that it would have no effect upon the action of the Convention; that my recent letters satisfied me that the State would not only secede, but that it would secede immediately; that delay until the 4th of March was impossible; but that, having said that much, I was perfectly willing to take the message as he desired, and I felt confident that he might rely upon my assurances that there would be no violence used towards the forts by any unlawful assemblage or mob; that I had with me a letter from the Governor of the State, which I would read to him if he desired, and the tenor of which I then communicated to him. He then asked me if I had seen General Cass. I said not that day; but that I had talked over the whole subject with him again and again, and we always ended where we began. He said, however, that I must see him when I left the White

House—he wished it, particularly—and repeat our conversation. I saw the General, of course, but our conversation was very brief. He said he was very sorry; he saw what was coming, but that nothing could prevent it. I left for Columbia on Monday morning, where I arrived early on Wednesday."

Governor Gist received the message of the President kindly, recognizing the courtesy of the communication, but at once declared that "the State was determined upon immediate secession; that no scheme of policy, however plausible, could induce delay until the 4th of March, either in deference to Mr. Buchanan's position or with a view to the co-operation of other States," and the opinion of the South Carolina Legislature, then in session, was strong in support of this declaration. It was at the same time evident that an issue of force was not desired by the leaders in South Carolina, that the State would go on resolutely to the attainment of its end, and that, to avoid such an issue of force, it was believed in South Carolina that the Federal Government, however it temporized, would have to concede the principle upon which the State stood. Satisfying himself that there was a strong feeling against any popular demonstration of force, either in violation of the law or in the seizure of the public property, the Assistant Secretary returned to Washington and communicated at once to the President, in person, the result of his mission. During his absence the representatives of South Carolina had reached Washington, to take their seats in Congress.

They were apprised of the precise condition of things, and of the views of the President, and upon the day after the return of the Assistant Secretary from South Carolina, he found them in the act of having their important interview. The Assistant Secretary had no authority to. make any proposition or suggestion on behalf of the President to the Governor of the State. He was simply to deliver a copy of the message. He found, upon his arrival in Charleston, that he had been anticipated. He had hardly left Washington before M. L. Bonham, then a Member of Congress from South Carolina, and afterwards its Governor, telegraphed from Washington to Columbia of the mission of the Assistant Secretary. At the same time a letter from the same source was sent to the Governor of South Carolina, announcing the purpose and object of the visit of Mr. Trescot, who, upon his arrival, was at once made aware that no postponement of the call for a Convention to the 4th of March was now possible.

CHAPTER IV.

President recognizes condition of things–His message of 3d December, 1860
Its reception by his Cabinet–Resignation of Secretary of the Treasury,
Mr. Cobb, who is succeeded by Mr. Thomas, of Maryland–Effort to pre-
serve the military status in Charleston Harbor–South Carolina delegation
wait upon the President–Their interview–Written statement left with the
President–Understanding of the delegation, of what was accomplished–
Their impression–Explanation of Messrs. Miles and Keitt to the South
Carolina Convention, of the understanding after Anderson's movement to
Fort Sumter–Governor of South Carolina claims that the Government at
Washington was pledged–Major Anderson not informed of it–Return of Assistant Secretary of State from Charleston–His interview with
the President–General Cass, Secretary of State, urges reinforcement of
the forts–President declines–Resignation of the Secretary, who seeks to
withdraw it–Declined by the President, who tenders to Judge Black, the
Attorney-General, the position of Secretary of State.

THE President had now definitely determined upon a policy,
which he maintained until the last. He knew that the country
was waiting anxiously upon the words of his coming message.
He had finally recognized the actual condition of things around
him, but he equally felt that whatever view he might take, or
whatever measure he might recommend to Congress, the State of
South Carolina would in a few days, by a convention of her people,
pass an ordinance of secession from the Federal Union. It was
the last opportunity he could hope for, as the President, to use
the power and prestige of his high office, and to exert any influence
of a personal character that might remain to reconcile interests
daily becoming more and more threatening to the existence of
the Union. But while he believed that the cotton States would
probably sever their connection with the Union, he thought that
the border States might be secured.

It was thus, after much "serious reflection," that he arrived
at his conclusions, which he announced in his message to Congress of the 3d of December, 1860.

In submitting this message to his Cabinet, it had met the
warm approval of every member, except that part of it that denied

the right of secession and claimed it to be a national duty to defend the public property and to collect the revenue.

It was this announcement that hastened the resignation of the Secretary of the Treasury, Mr. Cobb, who had, however, previously intimated his intention. He stated that, with his well-known views, the message of the President gave the opportunity for his resignation without harshness, and that he could be more useful at home, notwithstanding that he owed his position in Mr. Buchanan's Cabinet to the fact that during his canvass for the Governorship of Georgia he had. made a powerful argument against the right and doctrine of secession.

In his letter to the President resigning his position, he said, "A sense of duty to the State of Georgia requires me to take a step which makes it proper that I should no longer continue to be a member of your Cabinet." His remaining in the Cabinet would expose him to unjust suspicions and put Mr. Buchanan in a false position. His association with the President had been pleasant. "The evil has now passed," he said, "beyond control, and must be met by each and all of us, under our responsibility to God and our country;" and he believed that history would have to record the administration of Mr. Buchanan as the last one of our present Union, and would place it "side by side with the purest and ablest of those that preceded it."

The place of Mr. Cobb was filled by Mr. Philip F. Thomas, of Maryland, who had formerly been its Governor. He differed, however, so widely from the President upon the questions immediately involved, that he remained in office but one month, giving way to the appointment to the Treasury Department of General John A. Dix, of New York.

While positive action seemed to be suspended, both upon the part of the General Government and that of the State, a conviction had grown up in the minds of the people of South Carolina that the public property in their midst would certainly be theirs, either by negotiation or force, when the State should have formally passed the ordinance of secession from the Federal Union. That the State would pass such an ordinance, was generally believed, and, in the uncertainty of the result of any issue made with the General Government, it was deemed wise, if not essential, that until the Convention should meet and act, the "military status" that then existed in the harbor of Charleston should remain unchanged, and that some positive understanding or agreement should be had with the General Government, that would maintain the relative condition of things precisely as they were.   To this end, on the 8th of December, the majority of the South Carolina delegation in Washington, with the exception of Mr. Ashmore, waited upon the President, who left a Cabinet meeting to confer with them. Rumors were rife that the forts in the harbor of Charleston were to be supplied and garrisoned, and it was known that the subject had engaged the attention of the Cabinet, and that some of the members were urgent that action should be taken. It was believed, too, by many, that the garrison of Fort Moultrie, on Sullivan's Island, was threatened by a mob and its safety imperilled, and the President himself was not without anxiety in regard to that command, as he stated to the delegation. He seemed much disturbed, and expressed a sense of the deep responsibility resting upon him to protect the lives of Major Anderson and his command. The delegation replied to him that the news that reinforcements were on their way to Charleston would be the surest way to provoke what he seemed so anxious to avoid; that the general sentiment of the State was against any such proceeding, and that they felt satisfied that there would be no attempt to molest the forts in any way prior to the action of the Convention, then shortly to meet; that while they could not undertake to say what that body would see fit to do, they "hoped and believed" that nothing would be done until Commissioners should negotiate for the delivery to the State of the public property; and they stated that it was their "solemn belief" that any change in the existing status would in the excited state of feeling precipitate a collision. The President asked that a written memorandum of what was said should be given to him, and the following paper was handed to him on the 10th of December:*

"To His Excellency James Buchanan,
                    "President of the United States.
     "In compliance with our statement to you yesterday, we now express to you our strong convictions that neither the constituted authority nor any body of the people of the State of South Carolina will either attack or molest the United States forts in the harbor of Charleston previous to the act of the Convention, and,

---

*Appendix to Journal of the Convention, 1860-61. *Charleston, 1861.* Statement of Messrs. Miles and Keitt

we hope and believe, not until an offer has been made through
an accredited representative to negotiate for an amicable arrangement of all matters between the State and the. Federal Government; provided that no reinforcement shall be sent into those
forts, and their relative military status shall remain as at present.
"(Signed.)

"JOHN MCQUEEN.
"WILLIAM PORCHER MILES.
"M. L. BONHAM.
"W. W. BOYCE.
"LAWRENCE M. KEITT.

"WASHINGTON, 9th December, 1860."

The President objected to the word "provided," because it
looked as if *he* was to be bound, while there was no authority to
bind or pledge the Convention. The delegation did not so understand it, and they endeavored to convince the President that the
maintenance of the condition of things was wholly and absolutely
in his power; that if he maintained the existing condition of
things, they believed that any collision would be avoided until an
attempt at peaceable negotiation had failed. If he did not maintain such condition, then a collision would inevitably, and at
once, be precipitated. The whole effort of the delegates was
directed to the avoidance of a collision until peaceable negotiation had failed. The words ((military status" were commented
upon, and the delegation expressly stated that the transfer of the
garrison of Fort Moultrie to Fort Sumter would be equivalent to
a reinforcement, and would as certainly lead to a collision as the
sending of fresh troops. As the delegates rose to go, the President said, substantially, "After all, this is a matter of honor
among gentlemen; I do not know that any paper or writing is
necessary; we understand each other." But not yet satisfied that
they were thoroughly understood, one of the delegation observed:
"Mr. President, you have determined to let things remain as they
are, and not to send reinforcements; but suppose you should hereafter change your policy for any reason, what then? That would
put us, who are willing to use our personal influence to prevent
any attack upon the forts before commissioners are sent on to
Washington, in rather an embarrassing position." The President at
once remarked, "Then I would first return you this paper." The
impression made upon the delegation, as the result of this interview, was that the President was wavering, and had not wholly

decided as to what course he would pursue. The importance of this interview cannot be over-estimated. By it a conviction was established in the minds of the people, not only of South, Carolina, but of the entire South, that the status then existing would be maintained under the most solemn assurances. When, therefore, his officer in Charleston Harbor made his sudden movement to Fort Sumter, and the President failed to restore the status, it gave rise to serious accusations of breach of faith, and of his failure to keep his pledged word. It is fortunate that the views held by either party to the interview, and of its obligation, are matters of record. On the 4th of January, 1861, in the secret session of the Convention of South Carolina, a resolution was passed, calling upon Messrs. Miles and Keitt, two of the late Representatives in Congress, for a statement "setting forth exactly the understanding which existed between them and the President of the United States, and the circumstances which attended that understanding." The statement was duly furnished to the Convention,* in which "a full and exact account of what passed between the President and the delegation" was recited, as well as their conception of what they believed had been secured at that interview. They held that the understanding, or "agreement," was a "pledge;" that the President, in putting the matter upon the high footing "as a matter of honor among gentlemen, in which no paper or writing is necessary," was acting in a double capacity, "not only as a gentleman whose share in carrying out the agreement was potential, but as the head of the army, and therefore having the absolute control of the whole matter of reinforcing or transferring the garrison at Charleston." The delegation left the President, considering him after their interview as bound in honor, if not by treaty stipulation, not to make any change in the status then existing in Charleston Harbor, while all of the delegation, and especially those who had been elected to the Convention, felt equally bound to do everything on their part to prevent any premature collision, The authorities of the State of South Carolina had taken a similar view. On the 2d of January, in a communication to Brigadier-General Simons, commanding the Fourth Brigade of the South Carolina Militia, the Governor stated that there was, when he came to the city, a "distinct pledge of faith between the Gov-

---

* Statement of Messrs. Miles and Keitt to South Carolina Convention.

ernment at Washington and those who had a right to speak for South Carolina, that everything in the harbor and all the forts should remain precisely *as they then were,* and that there should be no increase of force or any reinforcements sent from abroad until our Commissioners presented themselves at Washington and made regular negotiations for the forts. I acted with confidence upon this pledge.* Suddenly we were surprised at the step taken by Major Anderson, now acknowledged and proclaimed by the late Secretary of War to be in open violation of the faith of the Government.†" On the 3d of January, in his message to the Legislature, the Governor formally stated that "it was distinctly understood" that those who had a right to pledge the parties on both sides had agreed that the status in the harbor should in no way be disturbed until the Commissioners to be sent by the State should present themselves at Washington. There was no positive stipulation entered into. The delegation was not empowered to bind the Convention or the State in any way, and were in no way accredited for any like purpose. They assumed, "as gentlemen" and in view of their prominent position, to indicate the course and policy of the State, and they claimed that this "very fact" should have made the President more ready to strengthen their hands to bring about and carry out that course and policy which he pro-fessed to have as much at heart as they had.‡ How the Presi-dent himself came to look upon this "understanding," or "agree-ment," when late in December the secession ordinance had been passed by the Convention of South Carolina and Major Ander-son had transferred his command from Fort Moultrie to Fort Sumter, will be seen in his answer to the South Carolina Commis-sioners in a subsequent part of this narrative. But, however the President or his advisers may have regarded it, it was not deemed essential that Major Anderson should be informed of it. It was not anticipated that he or his command would change the existing status, but that anything requiring such action would be referred to Washington. Hardly had the interview between the President and the South Carolina delegation terminated, when the Assistant

---

*Journals of both Houses, p. 148. Journal of the Senate, January 4, 1861. Governor's Message.

† Pickens in reply to General Simons's report, Record of Sumter, 1862, p. 17.

‡ Statement of Messrs. Miles and Keitt to the South Carolina Convention.

Secretary of State was announced, and a long conference with the President took place. The President referred to his interview with the delegation, and expressed his great satisfaction at the character of the paper presented to him by them.

"He then showed me a paper," says the Assistant Secretary, "signed by all of them but Colonel Ashmore, the paper which he afterwards quoted in his letter to the Commissioners. He appeared to be much gratified and relieved by it, and said that he had asked them to see me and he would then have a talk with me. I told him, I had not seen them, but that the paper did not go any further, if as far, as the Governor's letter which I had communicated to him."

"What letter?" said he. "I do not recollect it; and when did you show it to me?'

"The evening," I replied, "on which you gave me your message to carry to Columbia." He said he did not remember it.

"Have you got it?"

I said it was at my house, and I could get it in a few minutes; and that, as the Secretary of the Interior had just come in, I would leave them to their business while I went for it. I brought it back with me, and read it to the President in Mr. Thompson's presence. We then discussed it and the whole subject, and I told the President that my visit confirmed exactly what I had said to him before I went.

"Well," said he, "that is all very well up to the point where the negotiation stops, for Congress may refuse to entertain it."

"Then, sir," said I, "I will speak with the most perfect candor: the State will take the forts. What else can she do, if she is in earnest? But I hope the negotiation will not fail." And I added:

"Mr. President, why keep troops in the forts at all? If I understand your message rightly, you consider them simply as property, just as you do the Post Office, the Custom House and the Sub-Treasury buildings. You don't propose to guard *them*, do you?"

He said "No."

"Then," said I, "why not treat the forts precisely in the same manner?—keep an orderly-sergeant and one or two men there only."

He said he had great faith in the honor of the State; and that

the Governor's letter and the memorandum of the Carolina delegation were a guarantee, he believed, that nothing violent would
be done; that he would receive the Commissioners kindly and
refer the whole matter to Congress, and so on, traveling round in
the same circle; and I took my leave.   Soon after my return I
placed my resignation, dated the 10th of December, in the hands
of General Cass.   When I went into his room to give it to him,
he begged me to keep it for a day or two, for events might render
it unnecessary—at least he perhaps could not act on it.   He said
he could not speak more plainly, but the next day he would explain
all, although I probably understood him.   This, of course, I knew
meant only one thing. From the beginning of the controversy he
had held but one opinion and one language, and he had now submitted to the President the alternative of reinforcing the forts or
accepting his resignation; and the next day, the President having
refused to consent to this course, he resigned. Under the circumstances, I felt bound to say to the President that I would continue
in office until he had appointed a new Secretary, provided the appointment was made before the ordinance of secession was passed
by the Convention. For the refusal to adopt the advice of General
Cass was in the interest of the State, and it would have embarrassed
the President very much to have had the Department without
either a Secretary or Assistant Secretary. Judge Black the Attorney-General, who was appointed General Cass's successor, was
very busy in the Supreme Court, and it was not, I think, before
the 17th that I fairly ceased official action at the Department,
and the 20th before Judge Black acknowledged the resignation
left with General Cass."

Meantime, a despatch had arrived from Major Anderson stating
that he felt secure in his position, and this, in connection with the
influence exercised by the Southern members of the Cabinet, induced the President to change his purpose, and reinforcements
were not sent to the forts in Charleston Harbor.   In consequence,
the Secretary of State now submitted to the President, in the
presence of the Cabinet, a paper recommending the immediate
reinforcement of the forts in the harbor of Charleston. The
President received it without comment, and a few days later General Cass tendered his resignation.

In a previous interview with the Attorney-General, General
Cass had intimated to him his intention to resign his office. He

was asked by Judge Black if he had communicated his intention to the President, when he replied that he had not yet. Subsequently, the resignation of General Cass was carried by Judge Black to the President. Two days afterward, the Secretary called upon Judge Black, and said to him that he had been hasty in tendering his resignation; that he had yielded to a pressure brought upon him by those about him, who had, in a measure, compelled him to it; that, upon reflection, he thought that the matter involved was a question that belonged to the War Department rather than to his own, and that he desired to withdraw his resignation, and requested Judge Black to mention his wish to the President. In an interview which took place soon after, the wish of General Cass was mentioned by Judge Black to the President, who declined to return his resignation to General Cass, and who at once tendered to Judge Black the position of Secretary of State, which was accepted, with the understanding that Edwin M. Stanton should receive the appointment of Attorney-General. The resignation of General Cass took effect on the 14th of December, when he left the Cabinet.

CHAPTER V.

PROMPTLY on the morning of the 17th of December, the Convention met at Columbia, without a single absentee, and proceeded to organize by calling to the chair Mr. D. F. Jamison, of Barnwell. Upon taking his place Mr. Jamison announced that it was their fixed determination to throw off a Government to which they had been accustomed, and to provide for their future safety; that if anything had been decided by the elections for a Convention, it was that South Carolina must dissolve her connection with the Confederacy as speedily as possible. Overtures from without were to be feared, and he trusted "that the door is forever closed to all further connection with our Northern confederates;" and he closed his speech by advising the South, as did Danton at the commencement of the French Revolution, "To dare! and again to dare! and without end to dare."

Having been elected as permanent President of the Convention, Mr. Jamison said, in a short speech, that there was no honor he should esteem more highly than to sign the ordinance of secession as a member of the Convention, but to sign it as its President would be the greatest honor of his life.

In view of the subsequent action of this body, and that by it secession was inaugurated in the South, it is instructive as well as

45

interesting to glance at its composition, its character and capacity, and to follow in part its career.

When the call for a Convention was presented to the people of South Carolina it found them not unprepared. They well knew the object of its creation. Twice before, in her history, South Carolina had called conventions of her people to consider what steps should be taken to resist what she considered the infringement of her sovereignty by the General Government. It is true that her Nullification Ordinance and her legislative acts dependent upon it in 1832, were rendered nugatory by the passage of Mr. Clay's Compromise Tariff of the 12th of February, 1833; it is true that the general acquiescence of the Southern States in the compromise measures of the same great statesman in 1850 (but which she regarded as a surrender of the whole matter at issue) had induced her to forego secession; still, the spirit that had animated these conventions survived.

Men that had sat in them, as well as those who by pamphlet or speech had been conspicuous in their advocacy of the right of secession, were taken up by the people and returned by large majorities. For a whole generation the people of South Carolina had discussed the question of separation from the Federal Union, and when asked again to vote for a Convention for the purpose of taking into consideration the dangers incident to the position of the State in the Federal Union, to take measures for providing against the same, and to take care that the Commonwealth suffered no detriment, they knew well what was expected of them, and they cordially and eagerly responded to the summons, by the election of a body of men as unanimous in sentiment, as calm and deliberate in feeling, but as earnest and able, as ever assembled in any State of the Union. This Convention of 1860, unlike the Legislature that called it into being, was a body of elderly men. Half of its members were upwards of fifty years old; three-fourths were over thirty-five. A large proportion had occupied prominent public positions; four—R. Barnwell Rhett, Robert W. Barnwell, William F. De Saussure and James Chesnut, Jr.—had represented South Carolina in the Senate of the United States; two of these, Messrs. Barnwell and Rhett, had previously served in the lower House; and one, James L. Orr, had also once been Speaker of the House of Representatives. Five—J. P. Richardson, J. H. Means, John L. Manning, J. H. Adams, and W. H. Gist—had been Governors of the State. The Honorable I. W. Hayne had been for ten years Attorney-General.

The Judiciary was largely represented. Elected by the Legislature, and for life, with ample support to maintain the dignity of the position, their office was scarcely deemed second, in point of honorable distinction, to the United States senatorship itself. In this Convention were ex-United States Judge A. G. Magrath; Chancellor Benjamin Dunkin, afterwards the Chief Justice, a native of Massachusetts; Chancellors Wardlaw, Carroll, and Inglis, a native of Maryland; Judges Withers, Glover, Whitner, and D. L. Wardlaw. There were leading lawyers from different portions of the State. Eminent clergymen of the Baptist and Methodist churches, railroad presidents, large manufacturers and influential planters and merchants. Eight of the delegates had been members of the State Convention of 1833, which nullified the Protective Tariff Acts of 1828 and 1832. Twenty-eight had been members of the State Convention of 1852, when the question of the *status* of the territory acquired by the Mexican war was under discussion; a Convention that affirmed the right of the State to secede from the Federal Union, and that declared that "the frequent violations of the Constitution of the United States by the General Government and its encroachments upon the reserved rights of the sovereign States of the Union, especially in relation to slavery, amply justify this State, so far as any duty or obligation to her confederates was involved, in dissolving at once all political connection with her co-States, and that she forbears the exercise of this manifest right of self-government, from considerations of expediency only," viz., the want of co-operation.

Original and thorough-going secessionists were in a minority in the Convention. Those who were formerly of the co-operation party largely predominated. There was an element of over-caution in the Convention, that showed itself abundantly in the shrinking, temporizing policy in regard to Fort Sumter, and in the elaborate and repeated efforts at peaceful diplomacy, which drifted the State with the issue unsettled to the time when the incoming administration, seated firmly in power, were ready to use the whole power of the Government upon the first hostile movement made upon the public property or upon the flag.

Hardly had the Convention assembled at Columbia when a

resolution was introduced by Chancellor J. A. Inglis to the effect that "it is the opinion of the Convention that the State should forthwith secede from the Federal Union known as the United States of America, and that a committee be appointed to draft an ordinance to be adopted by the Convention in order to accomplish this purpose of secession." *(Vide* Journal of Convention, 1860, p. 13.) It passed without a dissenting voice.

Meantime, a contagious disease having broken out in the city, the Convention resolved to change its session to Charleston, and it reassembled in that city on the 18th. Already the impatience of the people began to be manifested, and open dissatisfaction was expressed that the Secession Ordinance had not been passed before adjournment to Charleston; and Mr. W. P. Miles, a delegate from Charleston, earnestly opposed the resolution to adjourn to that city, "or anywhere else," until the Secession Ordinance should be passed. There appeared to be but one unanimous sentiment, and that was for immediate separation from the Union. If any attachment remained for the old Union, it was not manifested. Argument had exhausted itself after a discussion of thirty years, and the sole question now was as to the manner of accomplishing the object in view. There was no place for mild counsels, and as one by one the links that connected them with the Government were. broken the enthusiasm of the people grew more and more intense, until, firm as one mind in what they believed to be the right, and sustained by the confident hope of a united South, the people of South Carolina did not hesitate to go steadily on in the course marked out for them, until it brought them face to face with the General Government, and at a point from which neither felt that they could retire.

No concession, no compromise, no constitutional guarantee was now possible to an amicable arrangement that had not for its basis the separation and independence of the State; the people scorned the idea of compromise, and it was under these auspices and in view of a future clearly determined upon, that the Convention of South Carolina reassembled in Charleston on the 18th of December.

In the large room of Institute Hall, the Convention reassembled at 4 o'clock on the afternoon of the 18th of December. Crowds of excited people thronged the streets and open squares

INSTITUTE OR SECESSION HALL.

of the city, and filled the passage and stairways of the hall. Congratulations were exchanged on every side, while earnest dissatisfaction was freely expressed that the passage of the Secession Ordinance had been delayed.

Blue cockades* and cockades of palmetto appeared in almost every hat; flags of all descriptions, except the National colors, were everywhere displayed. Upon the gavel that lay upon the Speaker's table, the word "Secession" had been cut in deep black characters.† The enthusiasm spread to the more practical walks of trade, and the business streets were gay with bunting and flags, as the tradespeople, many of whom were Northern men, commended themselves to the popular clamor by a display of coarse representations on canvas‡ of the public men, and of the incidents daily presenting themselves, and of the brilliant future in store for them.

The session of the Convention lasted but one hour; there was great unanimity. After a resolution for a committee to prepare an address to the people of the Southern States, at the head of which was Mr. R. B. Rhett, Judge Magrath moved, "That so much of the message of the President of the United States as relates to what he designates the property of the United States in South Carolina,' be referred to a committee of thirteen to report of what such property consists, how acquired, and whether the purpose for which it was so acquired can be enjoyed by the United States, after the State of South Carolina shall have seceded, consistently with the dignity and safety of the State; and that the said committee further report the value of the property of the United States not in South Carolina, and the value of the share thereof to which South Carolina would be entitled upon an equitable division thereof among the United States." And it was made the order of the day for one o'clock the next day, when it was unanimously adopted.

To enable the speakers to be better heard, the Convention

---

* Cockades had been worn during the Nullification excitement.

† Personal observation.

‡ One canvas represented Judge Magrath in the act of firing a piece of artillery in his library; another represented Mr. Lincoln endeavoring to split a palmetto log; while a third showed the anticipated prosperity of Charleston, the wharves crowded with cotton bales and negroes, and the harbor filled with shipping.

adjourned their session to a building known as St. Andrews Hall, and here the question of the Government property in the harbor was first discussed.

From the very initiation of the movement the State, however unwillingly, found herself involved with the General Government. At this period peaceable separation was the undoubted wish of all. Those who desired a conflict with the Government were few indeed; and while the most sagacious of the leaders knew that to preserve the Union there would be war, it was essential that this should not appear. It was vital, at least in the initiation of the movement, that there should be no conflict until a united South could speak and act; and the whole course of those who now led the movement was undoubtedly in favor of a peaceful solution of the difficulties daily presenting themselves. Not that either the people or the leaders shrank from any issue necessary to successful separation, but, in order to induce and to secure the hearty co-operation of the people, and thus involve them in a common risk and a common cause, it was necessary to induce the belief that the separation of the State would be peaceful.

On the 19th the Convention reassembled at St. Andrews Hall, when the President of the Convention submitted a communication from J. A. Elmore, the Commissioner from Alabama, enclosing a telegram received on the night of the 17th from Governor A. B. Moore, of Alabama.

"Tell the Convention," said he, "to listen to no propositions of compromise or delay;" and Mr. Elmore assures the President of the Convention that the Governor "offers it" in no spirit of dictation, but as the friendly counsel and united voice of the true men of Alabama.

After some discussion, it was determined that no reports of the speeches should be made or permitted. Propositions were made to sit with closed doors, in order that the Convention might keep in their own hands all reports of their proceedings. Doors were closed to all but the members. Several of the delegates who were absent when the vote was taken upon the resolution, that it was the sense of the Convention that the State should forthwith withdraw from the Union, now appeared and asked to have their votes recorded in the affirmative.

The special order of the day being the resolution in reference to that part of the message of the President of the United States which refers to the property of the United States. in South Carolina, it was considered, and a committee of thirteen was appointed, at the head of which was A. G. Magrath, to report to the Convention upon the resolution.*

It was resolved, also, to send three commissioners, bearing an authenticated copy of the Secession Ordinance to Washington to be laid before the President and Congress. And, also, that these commissioners should be empowered to treat for the delivery of the forts, magazines, and other "real estate;" and they were authorized to treat of the public debt, and for a division of all the property held by the United States as the agents of the States, and until a new Confederacy should be formed. This latter resolution was referred to the "Committee on Foreign Relations."†

As on the previous day, the feeling exhibited was intense; each man, through the day, as he met his neighbor, anxiously asked if the Ordinance had yet passed. The public offices were all thronged by earnest men awaiting the final action of their State. Deep-settled purpose was apparent upon the countenances of all, and a determination everywhere manifested to stand by the State in her action to the last. The Convention was composed of men in whom the people had the utmost confidence, and with anxious hearts they awaited the result of their deliberations. Not to be behind in any effort to advance the movement, and at the same time to afford security to the State, the Board of Pilot Commissioners compelled the pilots to promise that they would not bring any United States vessels into the harbor.

Early on the morning of the 20th knots of men were seen gathered here and there through the main streets and squares of Charleston. The Convention was not to meet until 12 o'clock, but it was understood that the Committee were ready to report the Ordinance of Secession, and that it would certainly pass the Convention that day. The report soon spread. Although this action had been fully anticipated, there was a feverish anxiety to

---

*As the proceedings of the Convention have been published, reference is here made only to those resolutions referring to the public property and to Fort Sumter.

† Other resolutions were introduced to define the status of the State, in view of 'her new relations to the General Government, and among them one to determine the amount of legislation of Congress that had been abrogated by secession, and how much remained in force, notwithstanding that act.

know that the secession of the State was really accomplished, and as the hour of noon approached, crowds of people streamed along the avenues towards St. Andrew's Hall and filled the approaches. A stranger passing from the excited throng outside into the hall of the Convention would be struck with the contrast. Ordinary business was quietly disposed of; the Mayor and Governor and the officials of the Legislature were invited to seats upon the floor; committees authorized by previous resolutions were announced by the President, the more noticeable being that of the late United States Judge Magrath, to head the Committee on so much of the President's message as related to the property in the harbor, and W. P. Miles on Foreign Relations looking to the ordeal in Washington. Quietly the Convention had met and had been opened with prayer to God. There was no excitement. There was no visible sign that the Commonwealth of South Carolina was about to take a step more momentous for weal or woe than had yet been known in her history.

Then followed the introduction of a resolution by Mr. R. B. Rhett, that a committee of thirteen be appointed to report an ordinance providing for a convention to form a Southern Confederacy, as important a step as the secession of the State itself, It was referred to the appropriate committee, when Chancellor Inglis of Chesterfield, the Chairman of the Committee to report an ordinance proper of secession, arose and called the attention of the President.

An immediate silence pervaded the whole assemblage as every eye turned upon the speaker. Addressing the chair, he said that the Committee appointed to prepare a draft of an ordinance proper, to be adopted by the Convention in order to effect the secession of South Carolina from the Federal Union, respectfully report that they have had the matter under consideration, and believe that they would best meet the exigencies of the occasion by expressing in the fewest and simplest words all that was necessary to effect the end proposed, and so to exclude everything which was not a necessary part of the "solemn act of secession." They therefore submitted the following:

ORDINANCE

to dissolve the Union from the State of South Carolina and other States united with her under the compact entitled "The Constitution of the United States of America."

We, the people of the State of South Carolina, in convention assembled, do declare and ordain, and it is hereby declared and ordained, that the Ordinance adopted by us in convention, on the 23d day of May, in the year of our Lord, seventeen hundred and eighty-eight, whereby the Constitution of the United States was ratified, and also all the acts and part of acts of the General Assembly of this State ratifying amendments of the said Constitution, are hereby repealed, and that the union now subsisting between South Carolina and other States under the name of "United States of America" is hereby dissolved.

A proposition that business be suspended for fifteen minutes was not agreed to, and the question was at once put, with the result of a unanimous vote, at 1:30 P. M., of 169 yeas, nays none. An immediate struggle for the floor ensued. Mr. W. Porcher Miles moved that an immediate telegram be sent to the Members of Congress, at Washington, announcing the result of the vote and the Ordinance of Secession. It was then resolved to invite the Governor and both branches of the Legislature to Institute Hall, at seven o'clock in the evening, and that the Convention should move in procession to that hall, and there, in the presence of the constituted authorities of the State and the people, sign the Ordinance of Secession. That a clergyman* of the city should be invited to attend, and upon the completion of the signing of the Ordinance, he should "return thanks to Almighty God in behalf of the people of this State and to invoke His blessings upon our proceedings." The Ordinance was then turned over to the Attorney-General and solicitors to be engrossed.

The invitations to the Senate and House of Representatives having been accepted, the Convention moved in procession at the hour indicated to Institute Hall, amid the crowds of citizens that thronged the streets, cheering loudly as it passed. The galleries of the hall were crowded with ladies, who waved their handkerchiefs to the Convention as it entered, with marked demonstration. On either side of the President's chair were two large palmetto trees. The Hall was densely crowded. The Ordinance, having been returned engrossed and with the great seal of the State, attached by the Attorney-General, was presented and was signed by every member of the Convention, special favorites being received with loud applause.† Two hours were thus occupied.

* Dr. Bachman was the one invited.

† Delegates from St. Pauls and St Michaels; also Mr. Rhett, Governor Gist and others.

The President then announced that "the Ordinance of Secession has been signed and ratified, and I proclaim the State of South Carolina," said he, "an independent Commonwealth."

At once the whole audience broke out into a storm of cheers; the ladies again joined in the demonstration; a rush was made for the palmetto trees, which were torn to pieces in the effort to secure mementos of the occasion. As soon as the passage of the Secession Ordinance at St. Andrews Hall was accomplished, a messenger left the house and rode with the greatest speed to the camp of the First Regiment of Rifles, South Carolina Militia, Colonel Pettigrew, one mile distant, where in front of the paraded regiment the Ordinance was read amid the loud acclamations of the men.

The adjournment of the Convention was characterized by the same dignity that had marked its sessions. Outside, the whole city was wild with excitement as the news spread like wild-fire through its streets. Business was suspended everywhere; the peals of the church bells mingling with salvos of artillery from the citadel. Old men ran shouting down the street. Every one entitled to it, appeared at once in uniform. In less then fifteen minutes after its passage, the principal newspaper of Charleston had placed in the hands of the eager multitude a copy of the Ordinance of Secession. Private residences were illuminated, while military organizations marched in every direction, the music of their bands lost amid the shouts of the people. The whole heart of the people had spoken. Men in elegant life, who had never known labor for a day, stood side by side with the "poor white" from the towns and, the country. From the quiet plantation, from the factory and the workshop, from the sand-hills in the interior and the cities on her coast, the manhood of South Carolina hastened without condition to offer themselves and their services to their State.

CHAPTER VI

Colonel Gardiner at Moultrie–Makes requisition for Ordnance Stores–Issue
made–Excitement in consequence–Telegrams to Washington–Relieved
by Major Anderson–Sketch of a letter of Anderson to War Department,
24th of November–Importance of this letter–Force under Anderson
Work going on–Attempt to enroll workmen–Correspondence with War
Department on the subject.

THE old and worthy soldier who commanded the post of Fort
Moultrie was slow to awaken to the reality of his position. As
early as the month of October the engineer officer had suggested
to his chief in Washington that a few small-arms should be
placed in the hands of his workmen at Fort Sumter for the protection of the Government property in that work. The Chief
of Ordnance* approved of the suggestion, and recommended to
the Secretary of War that, with the concurrence of the commanding officer of the troops in the harbor, he might be authorized to
issue forty muskets to the engineer officer. This proposition was
approved by the Secretary and submitted to the commanding
officer at Fort Moultrie for his approval and action, who replied
that he saw no objection to the "propriety" of the issue. The
workmen were bound by the principles of common law, as well
as by the articles of war, to defend the public property in their
charge. As to the "expediency," it was another question; that
most of the 109 laborers in Fort Sumter were of foreign nationality, of whom it is prudent to be somewhat suspicious, were
indifferent as to which side they took, and could at any moment
discharge themselves of their obligations, and take any side they
saw fit. That while some might be safely trusted with arms,
others might not be, and unless some precaution was taken to
keep the arms from the latter class, they might deliver up the
post "on a bribe or demand." He thought that the only proper
precaution was to, fill up his companies with drilled recruits,
fifty men, and to occupy Fort Sumter and Castle Pinckney.†

---

* Colonel Craig, Chief of Ordnance, to Secretary of War. W. of R., I
ser., I vol., p. 60.
† Colonel Gardiner to Chief of Ordnance, November 5, 1860.

The issue being contingent upon the approval of Colonel Gardiner, was, in view of his communication, not made, and the requisition remained unacted upon in the hands of the military storekeeper of the arsenal. But the military stores at Fort Moultrie were diminishing daily, and no effort was made to replace them until, urged by the repeated solicitation of his officers, the commanding officer finally made an attempt to replenish them from the arsenal at Charleston, and that effort cost him his position. On the 7th of November he directed that a list of what was immediately necessary should be made out and sent to the military storekeeper at the arsenal.* The list was confined to fixed ammunition for small-arms, consisting principally of musket cartridges, percussion caps, primers, etc, and also of hand-grenades, and paint and lacquer and priming-tubes. There was a deficiency in the first, and there were none of the last on hand that were serviceable. The military storekeeper had informed the proper officer that he had these stores on hand for issue, and this was the usual and official mode of obtaining supplies—a matter of ordnance routine. But the existence of a hostile and excited feeling in Charleston in regard to the forts was well known to the commandant of Fort Moultrie. The arsenal was already watched by the troops of the State by night; and in view of this, and in order to avoid observation, it was thought advisable to put the soldiers detailed for the duty in citizens' dress and send them in a schooner to a private wharf near the arsenal. The object of the disguise was to avoid drawing attention to the men employed, and from the apprehension of a collision. Before the schooner started, the appearance of the men in citizens' dress attracted the attention of the people on the island, and developed the fact that the movements of the men were watched. Information was sent at once to Charleston. The men embarked upon the schooner and proceeded to the arsenal wharf, which ran some distance back into the town. Proceeding to the arsenal under Brevet-Captain Seymour, who had accompanied them, arrangements were made with the military storekeeper to transfer the required ammunition on board the schooner. Some carts had been sent for to the city, but failing from some reason to arrive, the single cart at the arsenal was employed to transport the boxes. While this

* Porter's Report, November 11, 1860.

was in progress (some of the boxes having been already put on board) a citizen made his appearance and informed the corporal in charge of the men that the proceeding must stop, and that no more ammunition must be transferred. The corporal went at once to the arsenal and informed the officer in charge, who proceeded to the wharf to inquire the cause of the interference. He was informed by a citizen that the wharf was a private one, that it was his property, and that he would not permit anything of that character to leave it, unless by permission of the authorities; that he had sent word to them, and that they would soon be down. Captain Seymour expostulated, but the citizen was firm, and said that he could and would prevent it; that he only needed to raise his hand, and he could get one hundred men from a factory near by. It was thought better to avoid a collision, as a crowd had collected; and the boxes were removed from the vessel, which had grounded in the stream, where she was soon after visited by, the authorities. On the next morning Captain Seymour was sent to the Mayor, who gave the requisite permission, which Colonel Gardiner, the commanding officer of Fort Moultrie, then declined to avail himself of, as the city authorities had no right in any way to control his supplies. Meantime, and without delay, a telegram had been sent to the Assistant Secretary of State at Washington, reciting the facts, and saying that if the removal of the ammunition was by order of the War Department it ought to be revoked, otherwise collision was inevitable.

What took place in Washington is thus described in the words of the Assistant Secretary of State himself:

"After the call of the Convention, but before the election of members of that body, just as I was sitting down to dinner one day, I received a telegram from Charleston, saying that intense excitement prevailed in the city, on account of the removal by Colonel Gardiner, then in command at Fort Moultrie, of some arms and ammunition from the United States arsenal in the city to the fort, and that if the removal was by orders from the Department of War it ought to be revoked, otherwise collision was inevitable. Knowing that the Cabinet were then in session, I went over immediately to the White House, and met the members coming from the President's room. I took Governor Floyd aside, and he was joined, I think, by Messrs. Cobb and Toucey, and showed them the telegram.

Governor Floyd replied, 'Telegraph back at once; say you have seen me, that no such orders have been issued, and none such will be issued under any circumstances.'

"This I did immediately. When, a day or two after, I received letters giving me a more detailed account of the whole transaction, I again saw Governor Floyd, who communicated to me in a very full conversation, the official information he had received, his impressions of the folly of Colonel Gardiner's conduct, and his final determination to remove him and supply his place with Major Robert Anderson, in whose discretion, coolness and judgment he put great confidence. He also determined to send Colonel Ben. Huger to take charge of the arsenal, believing that his high reputation, his close association with many of the most influential people in Charleston, and the fact of his being a Carolinian, would satisfy the State of the intentions of the Government."

The action of Colonel Gardiner in his legitimate attempt to replenish his stores from the arsenal at Charleston, brought the whole subject at issue so plainly before the Cabinet at Washington as to define with great precision the position of some of the members. It was upon this occasion that the Secretary of War announced without hesitancy the position he held. He maintained "that with his opinions he never could and never would consent to the coercion of a sovereign State." His entire view of the question and his conclusions were in advance of the secession of a State. The consequence of such a condition "was a grave question, and had not yet arisen; that at present he was only resolved upon two things: not to reinforce the forts, and not to allow them to be taken by an unlawful force." This position of the Secretary of War was fully explained at his own request by letters from the Assistant Secretary of State to prominent and influential men in South Carolina, for the purpose of quieting the alarm and apprehensions of the people of Charleston. Meantime, in order to acquaint himself more thoroughly with the actual condition of things in Charleston Harbor, he had despatched Major Fitz John Porter,* an able officer of the Adjutant-General's Department, on the 7th of November, to inspect the fortifications and troops in Charleston Harbor. Major Porter proceeded to

---

* Official Report of Major F. J. Porter, W. D. November 11, 1860. W. of R. Vol, I, p. 70.

Charleston on the 7th of November, and after a thorough inspection submitted his report to the Secretary of War. He reported that there was an absence of strict discipline in the command; that no sentinel was posted over the buildings and storehouses outside the fort; and that an incendiary could in a few moments destroy all the supplies and workshops; that sufficient personal attention was not given to the Quartermaster and Subsistence departments; that the troops were grossly ignorant of their drill as infantry; and that their commanding officers manifested a want of familiarity with the tactics; and that all military exercises had been suspended for a long time; that the commanding officer neglected to appear at inspection or drill, and that "such neglect was due to indifference to the performance of military duty;" that no precautions had been taken to guard against an attempt at surprise or the destruction of the buildings, which, in the highly inflamed condition of the mass of the community, was not improbable. "The unguarded state of the fort invites attack, if such design exists, and much discretion and prudence are required on the part of the commander to restore the proper security without exciting a community prompt to misconstrue actions of authority. I think this can be effected by a proper commander, without checking in the slightest the progress of the engineer in completing the works of defense. All could have been easily arranged several weeks since, when the danger was foreseen by the present commander." In concluding his report Major Porter, contrary to the opinion and recommendation of Major Anderson, thought it unadvisable to occupy Fort Sumter, "so long as the mass of engineer workmen" were engaged in it, but that the "completion of those parts essential for the accommodation of a company might be hastened." In regard to Castle Pinckney, he thought that "under present circumstances" he would not recommend its occupation. In view of this report, and of the action of Colonel Gardiner in attempting to replenish his stores from the arsenal at Charleston, it was determined to believe him from his command. Accordingly, on the 15th of November, a special order was issued by command of Lieutenant-General Scott, directing Major Robert Anderson, First Artillery, to "proceed to Fort Moultrie, and immediately relieve Brevet-Colonel John L. Gardiner, Lieutenant-Colonel First Artillery, in command thereof."

Major Anderson had been promoted to his present grade in 1857.

He was the senior major of the regiment, two companies of which with the headquarters constituted the garrison of Fort Moultrie. A graduate of the Military Academy of the class of 1825, he had been in continuous service and in various capacities, both civil and military. He had been instructor of Artillery at West Point, and had largely cultivated the literature of his profession. During the war with Mexico he had served upon the staff of General Scott, who had maintained a high opinion of his character and abilities, which opinion was shared by the Secretary of War. He had been brevetted captain "for gallantry and successful conduct" in the Florida war, and major for gallant and meritorious conduct in the battle of Molino del Rey in Mexico, where he was severely wounded. While Southern by birth and connection, as well as in his sympathies, he was yet controlled by a high sense of honor, which influenced him in his duty to his Government to the last. Independently of his regimental position, he appeared to be especially fitted for the command in Charleston Harbor, in view of the complicated and threatening relations almost daily presenting themselves; and in sending him to Fort Moultrie the authorities in Washington believed that while he was likely to be acceptable to the authorities and people of South Carolina, they could wholly rely upon him to protect and defend the interests of this Government.

He was at this time wholly in accord with the views of Lieutenant-General Scott, and he clearly saw and announced the result of any other policy. Later, as the responsibility pressed upon him, and his position in Fort Sumter seemed to give him control, he became largely impressed and influenced by the political complication; and as State after State severed its connection with the Union, he became more and more despairing of any good result. Of pure morals and of strong religious nature, he sought Divine guidance to sustain him in all his acts. He never at any time believed that the coercion of the South was possible. He became devoted to a peaceful solution of the troubles, and in his effort to attain it he at times wellnigh compromised his position as a soldier. His true views, as well as the convictions which influenced him, appear more clearly in his private correspondence, as will be seen subsequently.

Major Anderson proceeded at once to his post, and, without delay, in company with the engineer officer in charge, instituted a close inspection of the forts in the harbor. On the 23d of November he reported to the Government that the outer defenses of Fort Moultrie would be finished and the guns mounted in two weeks, should nothing unforeseen occur to prevent; that his position was rendered insecure by the existence of several sand hillocks within a few hundred yards of the eastern wall, which offered admirable cover for sharpshooters, and that two of these hillocks commanded the work; these he should feel compelled to level; that his garrison was so weak as to invite attack, and that "this was openly and publicly threatened;" that the guns in the lower tier of casemates of Fort Sumter would be mounted in seventeen days, and that the fort itself was then ready "for the temporary reception of its proper garrison;" that the magazines contained 40,000 pounds of powder and a full supply of ammunition for one tier of guns.

"This work, Sumter," said he, "is the key of the entrance to the harbor; its guns command this work, Moultrie, and could soon drive out its occupants. It should be garrisoned at once."

He recommended the immediate occupancy of Castle Pinckney by a garrison of two officers and thirty men, as by such occupancy he thought his own garrison would be safer and more secure from attack. He thought it was "essentially important" that it should be immediately occupied. "The Charlestonians," he says, "would not venture to attack this place, when they knew that their city was at the mercy of the commander of Castle Pinckney;" and so important did he regard this, that he asks for authority to occupy it by an officer and twenty-six laborers to make repairs, and that they might be instructed in the use of the guns to defend it. This request was refused by the Secretary of War.* He earnestly asked that reinforcements might be sent to him, and that Fort Sumter and Castle Pinckney should be garrisoned; and he assumed the responsibility of making the above suggestion because he firmly believed that as soon as the people of South Carolina learned that he had demanded reinforcements, they would occupy Castle Pinckney and attack him at Fort Moultrie. The importance of this communication of Major Anderson to his Government cannot be over-estimated. It was the result of his earliest impressions. He had just taken com-

---

* Adjutant-General's office, December 1, 1860. S. Cooper, Adjutant-General.

mand, and after an inspection of his position and surroundings his military instincts at once suggested the only proper course to be pursued; and he did not cease to, urge upon the Government the necessity for immediate reinforcement until he came to feel how powerless he was. This communication was submitted to

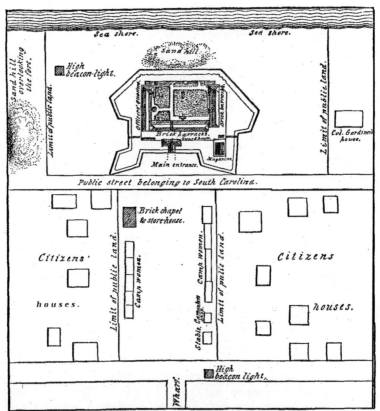

SECTIONAL VIEW OF FORT MOULTRIE.

the Secretary of War, and on the 28th of November Major Anderson was informed by the Adjutant-General that authority had been given by the Engineer Bureau to Captain Foster to send to Castle Pinckney the engineer workmen, as he had suggested, and he was directed to forward any information he might have directly to the Department or to the Secretary himself, thus avoiding General Scott.

But while opposed to the sending of any enlisted men to Fort Moultrie, the Secretary of War was willing to employ civilians, and upon the 24th of November, through the Adjutant-General of the Army, he had asked for information upon the present state of the command and the condition and "capabilities of defense," and, "whether in view of maintaining the troops ready for efficient action and defense, it might not be advisable to employ reliable persons not connected with the military service for purposes of fatigue and police." Part of this letter had been anticipated. In reply, Major Anderson stated that the excitement was too great, and he doubted whether such persons could be obtained there. Again, on November 28, he repeats his recommendation that Castle Pinckney should be garrisoned, as more could be done for his security by that means than by anything that could be done by strengthening the defenses of Fort Moultrie. And he reports that, had he been in command at an earlier period and before the work was begun, he would have advised the removal of the garrison to Fort Sumter, "which so perfectly commands the harbor and this fort."*

The whole force under the command of Major Anderson consisted of seven officers, two non-commissioned staff, seventeen non-commissioned officers and seventy-five enlisted men, of whom eight were musicians. There was no restriction at this period upon any intercourse with Charleston, many of whose citizens were temporary residents of Sullivan's Island. The activity about the fort drew to it a large number of visitors daily, and the position of the garrison and the probable action of the State in regard to the forts were constant subjects of discussion. There was as yet no unfriendly feeling manifested, and the social intercourse between the garrison and their friends in Charleston was uninterrupted. But as the days went on the feeling assumed a more definite shape, and found expression in many ways. The officers of the garrison were informed by prominent citizens of Charleston that the people were greatly excited, that not another man or any kind of stores would be allowed to land at or for these forts, and that the action of the General Government in putting the forts in

---

*Anderson, November 28, 1860, to Adjutant-General.

a more defensive state would be regarded as an act of "aggression," which would cause an attack to be made upon them. It was openly announced, both to the commanding officer and to his officers, that as soon as the State seceded a demand for the delivery of the forts would be made, and if resisted, they would be taken. Major Anderson was greatly impressed by these statements, and on December 1 again renewed his request for troops or "vessels of war," and he informed the Government that the question to be decided—and the sooner it was done the better—was, whether, when South Carolina secedes, these forts are to be surrendered or not. Meantime, all of the able-bodied men in Charleston were enrolled, military companies were formed everywhere, and drilling went on by night and day, and with the impression among them that they were to attack Fort Moultrie. Speeches of the most inflammatory character were made, in view of the assembling of the Convention to meet on the 17th of December, and the determination to take possession of the fort, at all hazards, increased in strength from day to day.

Meantime, the work on the forts went on steadily under the engineer officers in charge. On the 12th of September, the same day that the work upon Fort Moultrie was begun, the engineer officer in charge reported to his chief that "a full force of masons will commence work on two casemate arches of Fort Sumter to-morrow morning," and on the 14th of September he requested that the several appropriations made by Congress for the repairs and construction of Forts Sumter and Moultrie be placed to his credit. This was at once done, and on the 18th of September he was informed by the acting chief engineer that the remittances had been applied for, and that he would be charged as follows:

    For Fort Sumter . . . . $ 20,000
    For Fort Moultrie   8,500
    For Preservation of the site of Fort Moultrie . . .   5,000

It was under these specific appropriations of Congress, in the ordinary routine of departmental business, and directed by the proper officials, that work upon the forts in the harbor of Charleston was begun and continued in the summer and fall of 1860. It soon became manifest that assistance to the engineer in charge of the works was necessary, and accordingly, on the 21st of September, First Lieutenant G. W. Snyder, corps of engineers, reported for duty under special orders of the War Department, as an assist-

ant to the engineer in charge of the works, and was shortly afterwards assigned especially to the work on Fort Sumter. An able,
active and sagacious officer, much of the valuable work done was
the result of his personal suggestion and superintendence. Owing
to the difficulty of obtaining efficient white labor in Charleston,
fifty laborers were brought from Baltimore by the engineer in
charge of the works.   During September, October and November
the work on the forts progressed steadily and rapidly. The large
mass of sand in front of the scarp wall of Fort Moultrie was
removed, and a permanent glacis formed, flanking arrangements
built, the guard-house pierced with loop-holes for musketry and
made defensible, the construction of temporary platforms and the
placing of four field-pieces in position for flank defense, as well
as the digging of a wet ditch around part of the work. One hundred and twenty men were employed, and the work had so far and
so satisfactorily progressed that on the 2d of December Major
Anderson reported to his Government that the work on Fort
Moultrie would soon be finished, and that even his small command would be enabled to make such a resistance that the South
Carolina authorities would hardly venture to attack him." On the
13th of December the engineer in charge reported to his chief
that, "with a sufficient war garrison, he would consider Fort
Moultrie as secure against any attack of the State."†
   Meantime, the work upon Fort Sumter was steadily progressing. The casemate arches of the second tier were constructed
and the flagging laid, the officers' quarters completed, and the
whole of the upper tier made ready for the armament, and on
the 24th of November Fort Sumter, in the opinion of Major Anderson, was ready for and ought to receive one company.
   The activity at the forts had not failed to draw the attention
of the authorities of the State and people of Charleston to them,
and it was the conviction of every officer that an attack was
imminent. The greatest irritation existed that the Government
was engaged in strengthening them. It was claimed that their
guns were trained upon the city, and in speeches made to the
crowds that assembled in different sections, the people were called
upon to go and "turn those guns backward." Effective use was
made of this in the pressure brought to bear upon the Conven-

* Anderson, December 2, 1860, to Adjutant-General.
† Anderson, page 26. Engineer Officer.

tion, but wiser counsels prevailed, and it was finally determined, by those controlling the movement, to refrain from any immediate hostile demonstration against the forts, provided that the Government at Washington would agree that no change in the military status should be made until at least the Convention should meet and act, and entrust the subject to commissioners for its final adjustment at Washington. It was at this time that an application was made by an adjutant of a South Carolina regiment to the engineer officer at Moultrie for his rolls, as it was desired to enroll the men upon them for military duty. The engineer officer refused, as the men were in the employment and pay of the United States. Major Anderson, to whom the subject had been referred, without delay asked the special instructions of his Government. "What shall I do," said he, "if the State authorities demand from Captain Foster men whom they may have enrolled into the State's service?" Upon the 14th of December the War Department replied to him, that if the State authorities demand any of Captain Foster's workmen, on the ground of their being enrolled into the service of the State, and the subject is referred to you, you will, after fully satisfying yourself that the men are subject to enrollment, and have been properly enrolled, cause them to be delivered up or suffer them to depart." This reply was not satisfactory to Major Anderson, who, upon the 18th of December, informed the Department that, as he "understood it, the South Carolina authorities sought to enroll as a part of their army intended to work against the forces of the United States men who are employed by and in the pay of that Government, and could not, as I (he) conceived, be enrolled by South Carolina under the laws of the United States and of the State of South Carolina."* To this no answer was returned, and the rolls were not furnished.

---

* Anderson to Adjutant-General, November 28, 1860.

CHAPTER VII.

Letter of War Department declining to reinforce–Feeling in Charleston that
    forts would be taken–Anderson's views–Letter to R. N. Gourdin and
    to his rector at Trenton, N. J.–Sand-hills around the Fort–Refusal of the
    Government to allow him to reduce them–Importance of Sumter–Instruc-
    tions of War Department to Anderson by Major Buell–Substance of his
    interview with Anderson–Buell's order given to Anderson–Criticism on
    it from Buell himself–Further instructions from President not to make a
    desperate defense–Force of engineer workmen sent to Pinckney–Muskets
    sent to Pinckney and Sumter on Foster's requisition–Excitement in con-
    sequence–Action in Charleston and Washington–Muskets returned.

As the time passed, Major Anderson found his position at
Fort Moultrie growing more and more irksome. The threatening
attitude of the State added to his embarrassment, and he reported
to his Government that there were "intelligent and efficient men
in this community who, by intimate intercourse with our army
affairs, had become perfectly acquainted with this fort, its weak
points, and the best means of attack."* There was no concealment of the purposes of the State, as in private conversation and
in public speeches their determination to take the forts was openly
asserted, and the officers of the garrison were frankly and repeatedly told of the feeling of the people in opposition, as already
stated, to any supplies to the forts, or any effort to place them in
a special state of defense. Drilling went on nightly, and the
streets were daily enlivened by the march of armed bodies of
men, whose purpose of attack upon Fort Moultrie was at times
loudly proclaimed.†

The Government had declined to reinforce the forts, and, in
response to the urgent applications made by Major Anderson,
had definitely informed him of its purpose. "It is believed,"
said the Adjutant-General upon December 1, "from information
thought to be reliable, that an attack will not be made on your
command, and the Secretary has only to refer to his conversation

---

* Anderson, December 28, 1860.
† Personal observation.

68

with you, and to caution you that, should his convictions unhappily prove untrue, your actions must be such as to be free from the charge of initiating a collision. If attacked, you are of course expected to defend the trust committed to you to the best of your ability.

"The increase of the force under your command, however much to be desired, would, the Secretary thinks, judging from the recent excitement produced on account of an anticipated increase, as mentioned in your letter, but add to that excitement and might lead to serious results."*

On the 1st of December, Major Anderson reported to his Government that the people were "making ready for the fight which they say must take place, and insist upon our not doing anything." And he recommended, on the 6th of December, that in view of the approaching action of the State, it would be well to discontinue all engineering work on Fort Moultrie, except what was necessary to increase its strength, and "apply our science" to making every means available to resist an assault; and added that if Fort Sumter was not to be garrisoned, "the guns certainly ought not to be mounted, as they might be turned upon him in Moultrie." "Our time is short enough for what we have to do," said he, and should the stores or reinforcements not arrive, he feared that we should not "distinguish ourselves by holding out many days." But little hope was entertained by him that any settlement of the difficulties could be had without bloodshed, and he so reported to his Government. His sentiments found expression in his private letters. On the 11th of December, he wrote to a friend in Charleston:†

"You need no assurance from me that, although I am exerting myself to make this little work as strong as possible and to put my handful of men in the highest state of discipline, no one will do more than I am willing to do to keep the South in the right and to avoid the shedding of blood. You may be somewhat surprised at the sentiment I express, being a soldier, that I think an appeal to arms and to brute force is unbecoming the age in which we live. Would to God that the time had come when there should be no war, and that religion and peace should reign throughout the world.
"I am, dear Sir,
"Yours very respectfully,
"ROBERT ANDERSON."

---

* Adjutant-General's office, December 1, 1860,
† Mr. Robert N. Gourdin,

To the rector of the church he attended in Trenton, N. J., he writes more fully of his position, and of the difficulties that surrounded him; and in view of his subsequent action, his statements become important. His letter was as follows:

FORT MOULTRIE, S. C.,
"December 19, 1860.

MY DEAR FRIEND,

"A word or two about my position, and so on. As soon as I had time to inspect my position and ascertain the feeling and temper of the people here, I found that to enable me to comply with my orders to defend this fort, it was absolutely necessary that more troops and ordnance stores must be sent. And I recommended that they should be sent at once. The Government has, as you see it stated, declined for prudential reasons to send them, and I must now do the best I can. This fort is a very weak one in its capacity of being defended; it is surrounded by houses that I cannot burn or destroy until I am certain that I am to be attacked, and I shall not be certain of it until the South Carolinians are in possession; but I have so little ammunition that I cannot waste it in destroying houses. And again, within 160 yards from the walls are piles of sand-hills, some of them higher than our fort, which will give the best and safest shelter for sharpshooters, who may pick off in a short time our band of sixty men –all we have."

Meantime, his position at Fort Moultrie became more and more critical. He had applied to the War Department for authority to remove the low range of sand-hills so near to and which commanded his work on the north side-the approach from the land. These hills, if occupied by sharpshooters, would have rendered the service of the guns on that side impossible. His application was denied. "If deemed essential," said the Secretary of War, through the Adjutant-General, on the 14th of December, "to the more perfect defense of the work, the leveling of the sand-hills, which command the fort, could not under ordinary circumstances be considered as initiating a collision." But the delicate question of its bearing on the popular mind in its present excited state demands the coolest and wisest judgment. The fact of the sand-hills being private property and having houses upon them, decided the question in the negative; the houses could be destroyed at any moment, but, being leveled in anticipation of an attack, "might betray distrust and prematurely bring on a collision." Major Anderson at once replied—on the 18th of December—that there were no houses built upon the sand-hills, they were between him and them, but that he would not remove them until convinced that an attack would be made upon him; and he at the same time informed the Department that these sand-hills and the houses surrounding the fort would afford safe shelter for sharp-shooters, who might pick off the greater part of his command, if they stood to their guns, in a few hours. His conference with Colonel Huger and with the mayor of the city and promi-nent citizens, convinced him that, so far as their influence or power extended, no unauthorized attack would be made upon him, but all were equally decided that the forts must be theirs after the State had passed the Ordinance of Secession and its Commissioners had gone to Washington.

Meantime, the attention of the State authorities and the people had been turned more especially to Fort Sumter. They were not slow to realize that, well provisioned and manned, its possession would give the control of the harbor to the force occupying it. So much was Major Anderson impressed with this belief that he communicated the fact to his Government, and recommended that it might be advisable and prudent to cause all of the ammunition, except what was needed for the immediate defense of the forts, to be destroyed or rendered unserviceable. "Fort Sumter," said he, "is a tempting prize, the value of which is well known to the Charlestonians, and once in their possession, with its ammunition and armament and walls uninjured, and gar-risoned properly, it would set our navy at defiance, compel me to abandon this work, and give them perfect command of this harbor." And thus, in almost daily communication, Major Anderson reported to the Government not only the details of his position in their military relations, but his anxieties and well-founded appre-hensions, and he was persistent in his applications for instructions that should fully guide him in the extraordinary circumstances in which he was placed.

It was impossible to leave him longer without such instruc-tions, and accordingly Major Don Carlos Buell, a discreet and able officer of the Adjutant-General's Department, was selected by the War Department to proceed to Charleston Harbor and convey to Major Anderson instructions, which were given to Major Buell verbally by the Secretary of War at his residence in Washington.

The subject had been discussed in the Cabinet, but without deciding upon the character of the instructions, it was left to the Secretary of War to transmit such as the deemed necessary. Sending for Major Buell on the 7th of December, the Secretary informed him that he desired him to go to Charleston to inspect Major Anderson's situation and communicate instructions to him. These instructions were "explanatory of the policy to be observed, rather than absolute or explicit with reference to the things to be done."* Nor did they assume the form of orders. "The duty of maintaining defensively the authority of the Government was distinctly affirmed." The critical condition of affairs at Charleston, the question of reinforcing Major Anderson, and the importance of allaying the public excitement and avoiding a collision," were alluded to in the conversation, and the impression produced upon the mind of Major Buell was that, whether from prudential reasons or because of the difficulty of providing for every contingency in the defensive attitude required of Major Anderson, any committal to writing "was purposely avoided by the Secretary." The Secretary spoke of his own authority only, and made no allusions to the President, and no memorandum was made by Major Buell of the conversation until the morning of the 11th of December, at Major Anderson's headquarters at Fort Moultrie, when he had completed the object of his visit, including an inspection of Fort Sumter, and was about to start upon his return. Major Buell had passed the night not only in the same quarters with Major Anderson, but in the same room with him. In the morning the verbal instructions he had given, were reduced to writing at the voluntary offer of Major Buell himself. That memorandum was entirely in his own language. It was not, nor did it profess to be, a literal record of the Secretary's communication to him, but was his interpretation of the Secretary's intentions, adapted to the condition of things as the messenger found them, and of which the Secretary himself could have had no exact knowledge, From the manner in which the instructions had been communicated to Major Buell, it might have been inferred that they were not to be conveyed by him in any other

---

* Major Buell's letter to author.

way; but, impressed with the importance of the occasion, he said to Major Anderson, after discussing with him suggestively the application of them to particular questions, "You ought to have written evidence of these instructions;" and without waiting for any reply he immediately "committed them for the first time to paper." They were as follows:

"Memorandum of verbal instructions to Major Anderson, First Artillery, commanding Fort Moultrie, South Carolina.

"You are aware of the great anxiety of the Secretary of War, that a collision of the troops with the people of this State shall be avoided, and of his studied determination to pursue a course with reference to the military force and forts in this harbor which shall guard against such collision. He has, therefore, carefully abstained from increasing the force at this point, or taking any measures which might add to the present excited state of the public mind, or which would throw any doubt on the confidence he feels that South Carolina will not attempt by violence to obtain possession of the public works or interfere with their occupancy. But as the counsel and acts of rash and impulsive persons may possibly disappoint these expectations of the Government, he deems it proper that you should be prepared with instructions to meet so unhappy a contingency. He has, therefore, directed me verbally to give you such instructions.

"You are carefully to avoid every act which would needlessly tend to provoke aggression; and for that reason you are not, without evident and imminent necessity, to take up any position which could be construed into the assumption of a hostile attitude. But you are to hold possession of the forts in this harbor, and if attacked you are to defend yourself to the last extremity. The smallness of your force, will not permit you, perhaps, to occupy more than one of the three forts, but an attack on or an attempt to take possession of any one of them will be regarded as an act of hostility, and you may then put your command into either of them which you may deem most proper, to increase its power of resistance. You are also authorized to take similar steps whenever you have tangible. evidence of a design to proceed to a hostile act.

(Signed.)   "D. C. BUELL,

"Assistant   Adjutant-General.

"Fort Moultrie, South Carolina, December 11, 1863."

This is an exact copy of the original instructions now on file in the War Department, in the handwriting of Major Buell, and there is no other record of the instructions in the archives of the Government. In furnishing a copy of them to the President

on the 21st of December, the Secretary of War appended the
following:

"This is in conformity to my instructions to Major Buell."
              (Signed.)   "JOHN B. FLOYD,
                        "Secretary of War."

It could not have been important, and may have been entirely
accidental, but it is nevertheless to be observed that the word
defensive, not in the original, appears in the last sentence of the
copy furnished to the President.

In handing the paper to Major Anderson, Major Buell said,
"This is all I am authorized to say to you, but my personal
advice is, that you do not allow the opportunity to escape you."

Anderson understood his remark only as "a friendly encour-
agement," while there was still much in the nature of his orders
and the attitude of the Government to embarrass him.

Major Buell had remained over Sunday in Charleston, and
became impressed with the feeling manifested. There was no
noisy demonstration, but "there was everywhere evidence," he
thought, "of a settled purpose." The determination to obtain
possession of the forts was with them as fixed as the act of secession itself.

All the indications and all the information he could obtain
convinced him "that Fort Sumter would be seized, with or without the State authorities, unless the Government should occupy
it," and these considerations largely influenced him in his interpretation of the instructions of the Secretary of War, and which
were expressed in the memorandum order.

He thought, too, that "it was evident Fort Moultrie would any
day be liable to assault and reduction unless Sumter was occupied
by a Government garrison," and he thought that Anderson "fully
realized the fact."

After some suggestions to Anderson, "all looking to the contemplated transfer of his command," Major Buell returned at
once to Washington with a copy of the memorandum he had
given to him. His report to the Secretary was verbal, but he
left with the chief clerk, Mr. W. R. Drinkard, who enjoyed confidential relations with the Secretary, a copy of the memorandum
for the files of the War Department. Whether the Secretary ever
read it until it was called for by the President is questionable.

Anderson reported the visit of Major Buell and his instructions to him, but they were not made known to the President until the 21st of the same month. The President was dissatisfied with that part of the instructions which directed Anderson to defend himself to "the last extremity," and a special messenger was sent with a communication to Major Anderson, in which he was informed that it was not the President's intention that he should make a useless sacrifice of his own life or that of his men, upon a mere point of honor.   He was to exercise a sound military discretion, and if he was attacked by a greatly superior force it would be his duty to yield to necessity and make the best terms in his power." The sending of Major Buell and the object of his mission were known in Washington, and on the 13th of December the principal newspaper of Charleston published, from its correspondent in Washington, the following despatch:

"Major Buell and several other officers of the army have been sent to Fort Moultrie to look after the forts.   Keep a sharp lookout upon them.   They were sent for no good to us.   See that they make no change in the distribution of soldiers, so as to put them all in Fort Sumter; that would be dangerous to us."

The instructions delivered by Major Buell were of the first importance, both as a warrant to Major Anderson in the course he subsequently pursued, as well as in enabling the President to support him in that course.

Meantime, the difficulties of Anderson's position at Fort Moultrie increased daily.   His pressing request of the 23d of November, to occupy Castle Pinckney with laborers in case the Government declined to send troops for that purpose, had been acceded to by the War Department on the 28th of that month, and an additional officer, Second Lieutenant R. K. Meade, of the Corps of Engineers, detailed as an assistant to take charge. But since his letter of the 23d of November, Major Anderson had modified his views, and on December 1, had reported to the War Department that it was probable that, in the highly excited state of the people, the sending of the detachment of engineer laborers to Castle Pinckney "may bring on that collision which we are so anxious to avoid." He would consult the engineer officer in charge, and if convinced that it would lead to that result.

---

*Floyd to Anderson, December 21, 1860.

he would assume the responsibility, and suspend the execution of the plan. Satisfying himself that no opposition would be made, the measure was allowed to proceed; and considering that this detachment was in reality an advance guard for his command, he assigned First Lieutenant Jefferson C. Davis to occupy the work until the engineer officer should arrive, and work was begun on Castle Pinckney on the 3d of December. It was hoped and believed by Major Anderson and his engineer that this force, consisting of four mechanics and thirty laborers, could be made available for the active defense of the work in default of troops. It had so been presumed in the letter of Major Anderson of the. 28th of November, and in accordance with this view a request was made by the engineer in charge, on the 2d of December, to the War Department, through the chief of this corps, that four boxes of muskets, with cartridge-boxes and belts, be issued to him, as he required fifty muskets for Fort Sumter and fifty for Castle Pinckney. Colonel Huger, who was then in Charleston, and had command of the arsenal, declined to recommend their issue, even temporarily, without orders from the War Department, but upon consultation with Captain Foster and Major Anderson it was agreed that it was best to write for the requisite authority at once. The application was made, and laid before the Secretary of War on the 6th of December. It was returned by the Adjutant-General on the 7th, with the endorsement that action "was deferred for the present," and reference made to a recent letter of Captain Foster of the 4th of December. In this letter Captain Foster had stated that in consequence of "recent developments" of the state of feeling among his men, he did not "judge it proper to give them any military instruction or to place arms in their hands." This applied more especially to Fort Sumter, where his overseer had ascertained that his men were disinclined to resist the citizen soldiers of the State, although willing to resist a mob; and he reported that the feeling in regard to secession was so strong that almost all were entirely influenced by it.

On the 6th of December Major Anderson reported that he feared the same might be anticipated from the force in Castle Pinckney. But as his confidence in his laboring force increased, and his conviction that without arms he was at the mercy of a mob became real, Captain Foster proceeded to the arsenal on the 17th. of December, "for the purpose of procuring two gins which were required at Fort Sumter," and to the transmission of which there was no objection. While there, he arranged with the military storekeeper that the old order of the Ordnance Department of November 1, allowing him forty muskets, should be complied with. This order had been suspended at the time, on account of the objection of Colonel Gardiner, the commanding officer of Fort Moultrie, as its execution would appear like arming the employees. It was suspended only, and they were now sent to Captain Foster, and placed in the magazines of Fort Sumter and Castle Pinckney on the 17th of December. The act occasioned an excitement that ought to have been foreseen. Early on the following morning the military storekeeper addressed a note to Captain Foster, stating that the shipment of the forty muskets had caused "intense excitement." A military official of the State had called upon him and assured him that some "violent demonstration" was certain, unless the excitement could be allayed, and he also informed him that Colonel Huger had assured the Governor of the State that no arms should be removed. He had pledged his word that the muskets should be returned at once, and he asks that this request be complied with. Captain Foster declined to return the arms, stating that he knew nothing of the pledge of Colonel Huger to the Governor, but was willing to refer the matter to Washington.

Meantime, a telegram had been sent from Charleston to the Assistant Secretary of State, on the 19th of December, informing him of the removal of the forty muskets from the arsenal in Charleston to Fort Moultrie, and that great excitement prevailed. And he was requested to ask the Secretary of War to have the arms instantly returned, or a collision might occur at any moment; that this act, not instantly countermanded by telegraph, would be decisive, and that not a moment should be lost. An immediate reply also should be sent.

"In the meantime," says the Assistant Secretary of State, "the difficulties were increasing. On the 19th of December I received the following telegram:

W. H. TRESCOT, late Ass't Sec'y of State, Charleston.
"Captain Foster yesterday removed forty muskets from the arsenal in Charleston to Fort Moultrie; great excitement prevails; telegraph to have the arms instantly returned, or a collision may occur at any moment. Three days will determine, in convention, peace or war, and this act, not instantly countermanded by

telegraph, will be decisive. Not a moment's time should be lost. Telegraph immediately to me."

The telegram reached the Assistant Secretary at a late hour of the night of the 19th. He at once sought the Secretary of War at his residence. He was ill, but he gave immediate orders to the chief clerk of his department to telegraph, in his name, to Captain Foster, that if he had removed any arms, to return them instantly, and to answer by telegraph. Major Anderson, who had upon the 18th advised Captain Foster to return the arms, was at the same time informed by the Secretary, by telegram of like date, of his order to Captain Foster, and the telegraph office was kept open all night for the reply. The arms were returned at once upon the receipt of the Secretary's order, and the following telegram was received by the Assistant Secretary of State:

"The Governor says he is glad of your despatch, for otherwise there would have been imminent danger. Earnestly urge that there be no transfer of troops from Fort Moultrie to Fort Sumter, and inform the Secretary of War.

(Signed.)   "J. JOHNSTON PETTIGREW,

"Aide-de-Camp."

CHAPTER VIII.

UPON the 11th of December, in accordance with the provisions of her constitution, the Legislature of South Carolina proceeded to the election of a Governor in place of W. H. Gist, whose term of office was about to expire. Upon the seventh ballot on the 14th of December, Francis W. Pickens, a distinguished citizen of the State, was declared to be the choice of the Legislature. While engaged in the peaceful pursuit of agriculture and away from the strife of public political life, he had been called by the President to represent the country at the Court of St. Petersburg, and had returned at a moment when a crisis in political affairs seemed to be imminent. A student of classical literature, of varied and extensive information, he had served his State in various capacities, and he was now, as he had ever been, in devoted sympathy with her in all that she had done, and in all that she proposed to do. He was identified with no clique nor trammelled by partisan obligation. His social foundations were deeply laid, and this was, to his fellows, a commendation sure and strong. For three generations his family name had held conspicuous place, and in the struggle of the Revolution and afterward in high civil and military position, his immediate ancestors had illustrated it by heroic deeds that still live in history. An earnest disciple of the school of Calhoun, he had become the mouth-piece of its creed and the willing apostle of its doctrines. While a Member of Congress, he had, like his great exemplar, opposed the reception of petitions for the abolition of slavery, and in a powerful speech against the constitutional power of the Government to abolish slavery in the District of Columbia, had given utterance to sentiments that proved to be strangely prophetic.

79

He advocated the independence of Texas in opposition to Mc-Duffie, and greatly impressed the people by a powerful speech upon the relation of the Government to banks and banking. He had been a member of the State Senate, and also of the Nashville Convention of 1850, and, as a member of the State Convention of 1852, he had drawn up the ordinance asserting the right of secession

Presidents Tyler and Polk had each tendered to him a Foreign Mission, the former to France, and the latter to England, which he had declined. When, however, that to St. Petersburg was offered to him by President Buchanan, he accepted it, and had now returned from Russia to share the fortunes of his State.

Hospitable, generous, kind by nature, he had yet not at all the genius of government, and when called to a position which made him the conspicuous figure at the outbreak of the great revolution, and which required the exercise of great qualities, he failed to respond to the emergency. Desirous at all times of the credit to follow from conspicuous acts in the service of his State, he nevertheless shrank from the responsibility so inseparable to its attainment.

His enthusiasm often led him into error, and he allowed his better judgment to be overcome "by the glow of the fight." He had a certain ability, not unmixed with shrewdness, that enabled him at times to maintain himself in default of stronger qualities. His zeal was better and stronger than his discretion.

Of a character so contradictory in its nature and so inconsistent in its purpose it is difficult to form an estimate. Influenced as he was by a strong will, and without clear perceptions, it was hardly possible to trace the relations between his declared purposes and the course he pursued under the peculiar circumstances of his position; not upon a review of his career do we find in him the characteristics to be looked for in a chosen political leader in such a crisis.

His long absence and his separation from the politics of his State had induced a conservative feeling which was not in harmony with that of the leaders. He had been influenced too by the views of the President, whom he had consulted after his return. He was in favor of a postponement of any call for a convention until the administration of Mr. Buchanan should have closed. He was believed to be moderate in his views, and it was from this, in connection with his services and prominent position,

that he was suggested by some as a candidate for the Governorship of the State. But many, and especially those holding
extreme views, were opposed to him, and among them some of his
immediate family connection. Repeated interviews were held
with him, when he finally became convinced that unless he put
himself at once in line with the advanced sentiments and in favor
of immediate action and the secession of his State, he could not
be nominated. A public meeting, to be held in Columbia, was
arranged, where he was to announce his views upon immediate
State action. At this meeting, he took such advanced ground as
to leave no illusion as to his sentiments and wishes. He placed
himself in line with the ultra men of his State and maintained
himself in advance of the sentiment until the end.

Almost from the moment that he became the chief executive
of South Carolina, he found himself at the head of a commonwealth that, so far as its own act could accomplish it, was free and
independent.

No provision had been made, either by the Convention or by
the Legislature, for the new and extraordinary condition of
things after the passage of the Ordinance of Secession. Every
detail required the personal decision of the executive, and the
whole was greatly complicated by the constant presence of military questions demanding immediate decision and action, and
upon the solution of which depended the greatest consequences,
of good or evil, to the State.

On the 17th of December, the day after he was inaugurated,
he despatched a confidential agent to the President demanding
possession of Fort Sumter. The agent was Major D. H.
Hamilton, First Regiment, S. C. V. This official had been the
United States Marshal, and had just resigned his office. The
letter entrusted to him was marked "strictly confidential." Its
tone was firm and courteous. It was as follows:

[STRICTLY CONFIDENTIAL.]*

"COLUMBIA, December 17, 1860.
"My DEAR SIR: With a sincere desire to prevent a collision
of force, I have thought proper to address you directly and truthfully on points of deep and immediate interest.

"I am authentically informed that the forts in Charleston

---

*Correspondence No. 1. Governor Pickens to President Buchanan.
The Record of Fort Sumter. Columbia, S. C., 1862.

harbor are now being thoroughly prepared to turn, with effect, their guns upon the interior and the city.

"Jurisdiction was ceded by this State expressly for the purpose of external defense from foreign invasion, and not with any view they should be turned upon the State.

"In an ordinary case of mob rebellion, perhaps it might be proper to prepare them for sudden outbreak. But when the people of the State, in sovereign convention assembled, determine to resume their original powers of separate and independent sovereignty, the whole question is changed, and it is no longer an act of rebellion.

"I, therefore, most respectfully urge that all work on the forts be put a stop to for the present, and that no more force may be ordered there.

"The regular Convention of the people of the State of South Carolina, legally and properly called, under our constitution, is now in session, deliberating upon the gravest and most momentous questions, and the excitement of the great masses of the people is great, under a sense of deep wrongs and a profound necessity of doing something to preserve the peace and safety of the State.

"To spare the effusion of blood, which no human power may be able to prevent, I earnestly beg your immediate consideration of all the points I call your attention to. It is not improbable that, under orders from the commandant, or, perhaps, from the commander-in-chief of the army, the alteration and defenses of those posts are progressing without the knowledge of yourself or the Secretary of War.

"The arsenal in the city of Charleston,, with the public arms, I am informed, was turned over, very properly, to the keeping and defense of the State force at the urgent request of the Governor of South Carolina. I would most respectfully, and from a sincere devotion to the public peace, request that you would allow me to send a small force, not exceeding twenty-five men and an officer, to take possession of Fort Sumter immediately, in order to give a feeling of safety to the community. There are no United States troops in that fort whatever, or perhaps only four or five at present, besides some additional workmen or laborers, lately employed to put the guns in order.

"If Fort Sumter could be given to me as Governor, under a permission similar to that by which the Governor was permitted to keep the arsenal, with the United States arms, in the city of Charleston, then I think the public mind would be quieted under a feeling of safety, and as the Convention is now in full authority, it strikes me that it could be done with perfect propriety. I need not go into particulars, for urgent reasons will force themselves readily upon your consideration. If something of the kind be not done, I cannot answer for the consequences.

"I send this by a private and confidential gentleman, who is authorized to confer with Mr. Trescot fully, and to receive through him any answer you may think proper to give to this.
"I have the honor to be, most respectfully,
(Signed.) "Yours truly,
"F. W. PICKENS.
"To the PRESIDENT OF THE UNITED STATES."

By the same messenger Governor Pickens addressed a letter to the Assistant Secretary of State, whose resignation had not yet been accepted, requesting him to attend to his messenger, to go with him to the President, and see that he was "certainly able" to deliver the letter entrusted to him. One day was allowed by the Governor for the stay of his messenger, and, if he thought it necessary, the Assistant Secretary might bring the answer himself. It was no doubt supposed by the Governor that the resignation of the Assistant Secretary, which he knew had been tendered, had been accepted, and that he was acting then, as he subsequently did act, as the agent of the State.

Major Hamilton proceeded with the utmost haste to Washington, and upon the 20th of December procured an interview with the President through the Assistant Secretary of State, who thus relates what took place. He says:

"The communication brought by Colonel Hamilton for the President was sealed, but I had received notice of this extraordinary missive in a confidential letter by the previous mail, not, however, from the Governor. I saw the President, and returned to him with Colonel Hamilton at the hour he appointed. The President received us in the library, read the letter, and asked Colonel Hamilton when he expected to return. He replied, the next morning. The President said it was impossible to give him the answer by that time—could he not wait longer? Hamilton said, (Yes, until the next evening.' The President said the answer would then be ready. Hamilton then said, Mr. President, I am aware of the contents of that letter, and think that if you would accept them, it would greatly facilitate the negotiations between my Government and the United States.' The President replied that he would consider it, and give Mr. Hamilton his answer next day. He then, as we were leaving the room, called me back, gave me the letter and asked me to read it, and return to him when I had done so."

"The letter proposed that, in order to quiet the apprehensions of the people of the State as to the forts, Governor Pickens should be authorized by the President to occupy Fort Sumter with a small body of State troops, the answer to the request, or demand, to be given in twenty-four hours.*   If Governor Pickens had simply asked the President for an assurance that Fort Sumter should not be occupied, and that Anderson should be so instructed, I think it could have been obtained; as it was, this demand, if persisted in, released the President from his pledge to the delegation, placed them in a very awkward attitude, and, in my opinion, would have led to exactly what it wanted to avoid, an issue before the arrival of the Commissioners. Besides which the Convention was in session; the very day on which Colonel Hamilton had his interview with the President the Ordinance of Secession was passed, and that body properly was in charge of the conduct and policy of the State.   I consulted Senators Davis and Slidell, and they were both of opinion that to press this demand could do nothing but mischief. Generals Bonham and McQueen, two of the Carolina delegation, the only two, I believe, then in Washington, happened to dine with me that day, and as Hamilton had told them the object of his mission, I communicated to them the contents of the letter, and proposed that we should send a joint telegram to the Governor suggesting its withdrawal. We did so, and late that night I received the following telegram:

"CHARLESTON, December 20, 1860.

Hon. W. H. TRESCOT.

"You are authorized and requested to withdraw my letter by Dr. Hamilton immediately I have seen General Cushing. Despatch back immediately. Have you seen Huger?

"F. W. Pickens."

"The next morning I withdrew the letter. The President expressed his gratification, repeated to me over and again his desire to avoid collision, his readiness to receive Commissioners, to refer them to Congress in good faith, and his determination not to disturb the status of the forts, but to wait the result of their negotiation.   He was pledged, he said, not to disturb the status in favor of the United States, and the Governor ought not and could not justly ask him to disturb it in favor of the State. He was trusting to the honor of Carolina, and they ought not to suspect him; he was acting under the obligations of his honor; and I—and the State might rely upon it—would redeem it to the uttermost. He

---

* See letter in Journal of House of Representatives, South Carolina, December 11, 1861.

said he had taken no copy of the letter, but would be glad, if I had no objections, to have a copy of the telegram under which I withdrew it, which I gave him. I accordingly returned the letter to Hamilton, with another to the Governor, explaining my reasons for asking authority to withdraw it." This letter of the Assistant Secretary, in view of its clear and important statements, is here given entire.

"WASHINGTON, December 21, 1860.

"To His EXCELLENCY F. W. PICKENS,
        "Governor of South Carolina:
    "*Sir:* Your confidential letter to the President was duly delivered to him yesterday by D. H. Hamilton, Esq., according to your instructions. It was withdrawn (no copy having been taken) this morning by me, under the authority of your telegraphic despatch. Its withdrawal was most opportune. It reached here under circumstances which you could not have anticipated, and it produced the following effect upon the President:

    "He had removed Colonel Gardiner from command at Fort Moultrie, for carrying ammunition from the arsenal at Charleston; he had refused to send reinforcements to the garrison, there; he had accepted the resignation of the oldest, most eminent, and highest member of his Cabinet, rather than consent to send additional force; and the night before your letter arrived, upon a telegraphic communication that arms had been removed from the arsenal to Fort Moultrie, the Department of War had issued prompt orders, by telegraph, to the officer removing them, to restore them immediately. He had done this upon his determination to avoid all risk of collision, and upon the written assurance of the majority of the Congressional Delegation from the State that they did not believe there was any danger of an attack upon the forts before the passage of the Ordinance, and an expression of their trust and hope that there would be none after, until the State had sent Commissioners here. His course had been violently denounced by the Northern press, and an effort was being made to institute a Congressional investigation. At that moment he could not have gone to the extent of action you desired, and I felt confident that, if forced to answer your letter then, he would have taken such ground as would have prevented his even approaching it hereafter—a possibility not at all improbable, and which ought to be kept open. I considered, also, that the chance of public investigation rendered the utmost caution necessary as to any communications from the State; and having presented the letter, and ascertained what the nature of the reply would be, you had all the advantage of knowing the truth, without the disadvantage of having it put on record. Besides this, the President seemed to think that your request was based upon the impossibility of your restraining the spirit of our people-an interpretation which did you injustice, and the possibility of which I deemed it due to you to avoid. He also appeared to labor under the impression that the representations of the Members of Congress and your own differed essentially, and this, I thought, on account of both, should not be stated in any reply to you. I was also perfectly satisfied that the status of the garrisons would not be disturbed.

"Under these circumstances, if I had been acting under formal credentials from you, and the letter had been unsealed, I would have delayed its presentation for some hours until I could have telegraphed you; but that was impossible. As Major Hamilton, therefore, had brought with him General McQueen and General Bonham, when he called upon me and delivered the letter, and had even gone so far as to express the wish that they should be present when he delivered it to the President—a proposition which they declined, however—I deemed it not indiscreet, nor in violation of the discretionary confidence which your letter implied, to take their counsel. We agreed perfectly, and the result was the telegraphic despatch of last night. The withdrawal of the letter was a great relief to the President, who is most earnestly anxious to avoid an issue with the State or its authorities, and, I think, has encouraged his disposition to go as far as he can in this matter, and to treat those who may represent the State with perfect frankness.

"I have had, this morning, an interview with Governor Floyd, the Secretary of War. No order has been issued that will at all disturb the present condition of the garrisons; and while I cannot even here venture into details, which are too confidential to be risked in any way, I am prepared to say, with a full sense of the responsibility, that nothing will be done which will either do you injury or properly create alarm. Of course, when your Commissioners have succeeded, or failed to effect their negotiations, the whole issue is fairly before you, to be met as courage, honor and wisdom may direct.

"My delay in answering, your telegram concerning Colonel Huger was caused by his absence from this place. He came, in reply to my telegram, last night, and this morning I telegraphed you his decision, which I presume he has explained by a letter of this same date. As Major Hamilton leaves this evening, I have only time to write this hurried letter, and am, sir,

"Very respectfully,
"WM. HENRY TRESCOT.

"I enclose your confidential letter in this."

Two days before the interview with Major Hamilton, the

President, having appointed the Hon. Caleb Cushing a special agent in his behalf for the Purpose of changing or modifying the action of the State, sent him with the following letter to the Governor of South Carolina:*

"WASHINGTON, December 18, 1860.

"MY DEAR SIR:

"From common notoriety, I assume the fact that the State of South Carolina is now deliberating on the question of seceding from the Union. While any hope remains that this may be prevented, or even retarded so long as to allow the people of her sister States an opportunity to manifest their opinion upon the causes which have led to this proceeding, it is my duty to exert all the means in my power to avert so dread a catastrophe.

"I have therefore deemed it advisable to send to you the Hon. Caleb Cushing, in whose integrity, ability and prudence I have full confidence, to hold communication with you on my behalf, for the purpose of changing or modifying the contemplated action of the State in the manner I have already suggested.

"Commending Mr. Cushing to your kind attention, for his own sake as well as that of the cause, I remain,

"Very respectfully,
"Your friend,

(Signed.)   "JAMES BUCHANAN.

"HIS EXCELLENCY FRANCIS W. PICKENS."

While the object of Mr. Cushing's mission was a secret one, its purpose was understood to be a proposition from Mr. Buchanan that the call for a convention in South Carolina should be postponed until his administration had ended, and that the existing status should remain undisturbed.

The interview with Governor Pickens was short. He told Mr. Cushing, frankly, that he would return no reply to the President's letter, except to say "very candidly, that there was no hope for the Union, and that, as far as he was concerned, he intended to maintain the separate independence of South Carolina, and from this purpose neither temptation nor danger should for a moment deter him.

In regard to the status in the harbor, Mr. Cushing informed him that while he could not say what changes circumstances might produce, when he left Washington there was then no intention whatever to change the status of the forts in the harbor in

---

* "The Record of Fort Sumter." Columbia, S. C., 1862.

any way." Official courtesy was not overlooked in the reception of Mr. Cushing.

On the 20th of December a joint committee of both Houses of the Legislature was appointed to invite him to attend in Institute Hall in the evening, when, in presence of both branches of the general assembly, the Ordinance of Secession passed that day was to be signed by the President and members of the Convention. This, as well as the tender of the privileges of the House of Representatives, was declined by Mr. Cushing, who, finding it impossible to attain the object of his mission, returned at once to Washington.

Meantime, Governor Pickens, not satisfied to await a response to his letter to the President, went to Charleston on the 18th, the day after his messenger left, and at once proceeded to take into his own hands the enforcement of the existing status in the harbor. Sending at midnight of the 18th for Captain Charles H. Simonton, who with his command, the Washington Light Infantry, had been guarding the arsenal to prevent the removal of ammunition or stores to the forts, he informed him that he had heard of an intention upon the part of the commandant of Fort Moultrie to evacuate that work and take possession of Fort Sumter; that this must be prevented at all hazards; but that, if possible, an actual conflict with the United States troops must be avoided; that he had determined to send Captain Simonton, with such men from his company as he could rely upon, to cruise between the two forts. His orders were specific and in writing. He was to hail every boat passing between the forts; if he found that any were boats with United States troops on board, he was ordered to state to the officer in charge his orders and to prevent the passage at all hazards. If the officer persisted he was to resist it by force, to sink his boats and then immediately to take Fort Sumter. He was to use his own discretion in accomplishing the object in view.†

Obeying his instructions, Captain Simonton moved a detachment of his command from the arsenal at once, and placing them on a small steamer, proceeded down the harbor to cruise between

*See Message No. 1 to Legislature of South Carolina at extra session of November, 1861.

† Governor Pickens's Message at called session of Legislature, convened November 5, 1861.

Fort Moultrie and Fort Sumter. This was repeated night after night until the 23d instant, when he was relieved from duty by the Charleston Rifles under Captain J. Johnson, Jr.

The day after his inauguration the Governor sent Lieutenant-Colonel John Green to Fort Monroe with instructions to furnish him with information of all military operations; and he employed a Mr. Charles Norris, who was at the head of the minute men of Norfolk, to keep him informed. He also hired a workman to work in the yard and to keep him posted; and the Governor says that he owes much to Mr. Norris for this.

It was believed by many that, while there was no hope of preserving the Union, a peaceable solution of the difficulties might yet be arrived at by negotiation, provided that the public property in the harbor should be secured in the possession of the State now; while the administration at Washington, although not friendly, was at least committed to such a course as to bar any active interference. Within a few months that administration was to pass away, and there was nothing to induce any other belief than that the incoming administration, securely seated in power and in possession of the immense resources of the Government, would prove hostile to any proposition for the transfer of the public property. Under such circumstances there was no hope for peace, for it was the conviction of all minds that the forts in the harbor of Charleston should and would be taken by the State.

A strong pressure had been brought to bear upon the Governor soon after his inauguration, in reference to the public property in the harbor, and especially in regard to Fort Sumter. The subject had engaged the attention of the prominent men; and the leaders, in accordance with the wishes of the people, felt the necessity of vigorous action. So earnest was the feeling on the subject of the immediate seizure of the forts that parties were formed both for and against the measure. Among the suggestions made and urged upon the Governor was one by Colonel R. B. Rhett, Jr., that a large steamer of the Boston line should be chartered, 500 riflemen put on board, and the ship anchored abreast of the fort and commanding the entrance of the inner harbor.

Early in November, when the election of Mr. Lincoln was known, but had not yet been promulgated, a party representing various military organizations in Charleston presented themselves to two of the leading military men of the city, and offered to go, under their command, and take possession of Fort Sumter. These gentlemen dissuaded the applicants from any immediate action, but promised co-operation in case that any movement should be made.

Upon the arrival of Colonel Huger to take command of the arsenal in Charleston, he sought an interview with one of these gentlemen, and informed him that it was known that such a proposition had been made. Shortly after the inauguration and arrival of Governor Pickens in Charleston, he was waited upon by four members of the Legislature, consisting of Colonel Rhett, Mr. W. S. Mullins, and two others and earnestly urged to take measures to prevent any movement to Fort Sumter.

Governor Pickens replied that he had made all necessary arrangements in reference to preventing Major Anderson from occupying Fort Sumter, and he endeavored to satisfy these gentlemen that any such movement would be prevented. The desire to avoid any collision with the General Government, and the growing belief that the status, as it then existed, would not be disturbed until the Convention should act, mainly influenced Governor Pickens to content himself with an effort to enforce it. Nor had the Governor himself been indifferent to the importance of Fort Sumter, as conferring upon the force that held it the control of the harbor.

Soon after his arrival in Charleston in December, he directed Major Walter Gwynn, an accomplished engineer, to make an inspection and report of the condition of Fort Sumter. This officer at once made a thorough inspection and report of the work. The result of this inspection was soon known, and added to the deep-seated feeling already existing in regard to the immediate possession of the fort.

The press throughout the State teemed with the most earnest arguments in favor of an immediate seizure of the forts, and the principal journal of Charleston, the leader of secession sentiment, was incessant in its demands for the seizure of Fort Sumter. Resolutions- were introduced into the Legislature, and public speeches were made by prominent men, all urging immediate action. "The forts," said a distinguished speaker to an assemblage at Charleston, "will be ours as soon as we secede, and we will secede as surely as the sun will rise on to-morrow."

Almost immediately after the meeting of the Convention in Charleston, and upon the second or third day of its session, a party consisting of Ex-Governor J. A. Winston, of Alabama, Benjamin McCullough, George Saunders, and Mr. Sherrod, of Alabama, proceeded to Fort Sumter, and thoroughly inspected it as to its offensive and defensive qualifications, and as to its power of resisting an attack from the land.

On the morning of the 26th of December, Colonel R. B. Rhett, Jr., accompanied by Mr. Williams Middleton, of Charleston, waited again upon the Governor. A letter had been received by Colonel Rhett, from a friend in Washington who was likely to be well informed, to the effect that Anderson was about to seize Fort Sumter, and Governor Pickens was urged again to secure it. Mr. Middleton was not present at the interview, having been called away, but the name and the opportunities for information of his informant were given by Colonel Rhett to the Governor. On that night, Anderson transferred his command from Fort Moultrie to Fort Sumter. Two signal guns were fired, as has been before described, which announced to Lieutenant Hall—who, in command of two lighters with the women and children, and stores of the garrison, had awaited the signal to make sail for Fort Sumter-that the command had arrived there.

As the report of these guns echoed through the city of Charleston, the distinguished gentleman who had accompanied Colonel Rhett in the morning, and who knew the purport of the letter received from Washington, announced to his guests at his residence that the Governor had taken Fort Sumter,

CHAPTER IX.

WORK was now pushed on at the forts with the greatest activity, and Major Anderson considered that an attack upon him was more and more imminent. He manifested the greatest anxiety in regard to the progress and character of the defensive works going on, while at the same time he was conscious that over their nature or construction he could exercise no absolute control, and this added greatly to his embarrassment. He had differed from the engineer in charge in regard to the building of a caponiere, or bastionette, at one of the angles of the work for flanking defense. One at an opposite angle had already been constructed, and the foundation of the other had been laid. But Major Anderson considered that it was now too late to commence its construction, and on the 6th of December he had communicated his views to the War Department, and suggested the substitution of some other arrangement of more speedy construction.

On the 20th, the day upon which the Ordinance of Secession was passed by the Convention of South Carolina, he called the attention of the War Department to the fact that no reply had been made to his suggestion; that the engineer officer did not feel authorized to make any change, and would commence the work on the next day. This he regretted very much, "for," said he, "if an attack is made while that work is going on, our fort can be very easily carried." On the 22nd inst., in submitting to the Government a statement of the engineer officer, that he would have the work defensible in five and have it finished in nine working days, he replied, "God knows whether the South Carolinians will defer their attempt to take this work as long as that;" and he urges upon the Government that when an officer was placed in as delicate a position as he then was, "he should have the entire control over all persons connected in any way with the work entrusted to him." Major Anderson felt the restrictions upon him keenly. In the same communication he reports the presence of the steamer—guard-boat—between him and Fort Sumter; that the authorities of the State were determined to prevent, if possible, any troops from being placed in that fort; and that they would seize it as soon as they thought it questionable as to its being turned over to the State. He again urged upon the Government that if they would give him orders he could throw his garrison into Fort Sumter, although he must sacrifice the greater part of his stores, as it was now too late to remove them. But once in Fort Sumter, he could keep the entrance to the harbor open until works should be constructed outside of him. He thought that no one could tell what would be done; that action might be deferred until the Commissioners return from Washington; or, if they saw that their demands were not likely to be complied with, the State would act without waiting for their return. He did not think that he could rely upon any assurances, and he "wishes to God that he only had men enough to fully man his guns."

In view of the importance of this communication from Major Anderson, it is here given in full:

No. 10.]   "FORT MOULTRIE, S. C., December 22, 1860.
                    "(Received A. G. O., December 26.)
"Col. S. COOPER, *Adjutant-General* :

"COLONEL: Captain Foster is apprehensive that the remarks in my letter of the 20th instant may be considered as reflecting upon him, and I told him that I would cheerfully state distinctly that I do not intend to pass any criticism upon his proceedings.

"I stated in my last letter fully all the reasons I intended to give against commencing the second caponiere. The Captain has put a very large force of masons on it, and they are running up the walls very rapidly. He says, as he has all the material on hand, the men, having just completed the first one, will be enabled to construct the second caponiere as soon as they could finish any temporary work in its stead. He says that he will have the 'work defensible in five more working days, and have it finished in nine more working days.' God knows whether the South Carolinians will defer their attempt to take this work so long as that. I must confess that I think where an officer is placed in as delicate a position as the one I occupy, that he should have the entire control over all persons connected in any way with the work intrusted to him. Responsibility and power to control ought to go together.

"I have heard from several sources that last night and the night before a steamer was stationed between this island and Fort Sumter. That the authorities of South Carolina are determined to prevent, if possible, any troops from being placed in that fort, and that they will seize upon that most important work as soon as they think there is reasonable ground for a doubt whether it will be turned over to the State, I do not doubt. I think that I could, however, were I to receive instructions so to do, throw my garrison into that work, but I should have to sacrifice the greater part of my stores, as it is now too late to attempt their removal. Once in that work with my garrison I could keep the entrance of their harbor open until they construct works outside of me, which might, I presume, prevent vessels from coming into the outer harbor.

"We have used nearly all the empty barrels which Captain Foster had wisely saved, for embrasures, traverses, &c., and Captain Foster is now making use of our gun pent-houses for the same purpose, filling them with sand.

"No one can tell what will be done. They may defer action until their Commissioners return from Washington; or, if apprised by the nature of the debates in Congress that then demands will not probably be acceded to, they may act without waiting for them.

"I do not think that we can rely upon any assurances, and wish to God I only had men enough here to man fully my guns. Our men are perfectly conscious of the dangerous position they are placed in, but are in as fine spirits as if they were certain of victory.

"I am, Colonel, very respectfully, your obedient servant,
"ROBERT ANDERSON,
" *Major First Artillery, Commanding.*

"P. S.—I have just heard that several of the men at work in Fort Sumter wear the blue cockade. If they are bold enough to do that the sooner that force is disbanded the better. The public property would be safer there under Lieutenant Snyder and a few men than it now is.

"R. A."

Through the activity and ability of the Engineer Department Fort Moultrie was now in a condition of defense, so far as the peculiar circumstances of its position permitted. On the 13th of December, the engineer officer reported to his chief that the auxiliary defenses would be completed in four days, and that with a sufficient war garrison he would consider the fort secure against any attack that the State could bring against it, but that the garrison was a mere handful of sixty men, and he could hardly spare men for the flanking defenses he had built. Its armament was complete. Its heavy battery numbered forty-five guns, including sixteen 24-pounders, nineteen 32 pounders and ten 8-inch Columbiads. In addition to these, there were one 10-inch seacoast mortar, four brass field-guns and three howitzers of 12 and 24 pounds for flanking defense. There was a large supply of ammunition both for artillery and infantry, and with some exception, a complete service for the guns.

On the 20th of December, the day upon which the State passed the Ordinance of Secession, 137 men were at work upon the defenses of Fort Moultrie. The wet ditch that partly surrounded the work, half quicksand, was completed. The east front of the work was raised, and the guns facing the sand-hills were provided with siege-battery embrasures faced with hides, with heavy merlons between them, and strong traverses to prevent an enfilading fire. A bridge connecting the barracks and guard-house—which had been loop-holed for musketry and arranged for sharpshooters—was finished. Positions were established for sharpshooters, and a picket fence was built bordering the ditch and running half around the fort. The embanking of the glacis was completed, and it was proposed by the engineer officer to connect a powerful Daniells Battery with the magazine of Fort Sumter, as well as with mines around Fort Moultrie and under the sand-hills, and to explode these mines if the position should be taken by an armed force. A strict watch was kept night and day, and entrance to the fort forbidden to all but the garrison. Hitherto the freest access had been permitted, but as the position of the garrison became more critical, and interested persons—among them military officials—came down to observe and make notes and sketches of the work going on, it became necessary to close the gates to all but the garrison—a proceeding that occasioned complaint and increased the already excited feeling of the people. Newspaper correspondents and crowds of visitors came daily, and among them persons of position and distinction, who conversed freely with the officers with regard to their position. The venerable James Pettigrew, accompanied by Judge George S. Bryan, of Charleston, came to visit the garrison and to convey their sympathy with its position, while frankly expressing their opinion that if the fort was not given up it would be taken. They thought that a continuance of the work under the circumstances would be unwise. Their engineers came down as the defenses progressed, studying the points of attack and defense. It became questionable for the officers to visit the city of Charleston. There was no social or public gathering in which the great question of the forts in the harbor was not discussed. Just previous to the secession of the State a distinguished gentleman of Charleston, in addressing a large meeting at Columbia, said "that the forts in the harbor had their guns pointed upon the city," and he called upon the people to go down and turn these guns backward." The occupants of the fort were called hirelings and mercenaries, and every effort was made to stimulate the people and excite them against the garrison. In the Legislature a motion was made by Mr. R. B. Rhett that the forts be taken at once. This was seconded, but the motion was postponed by the influence of the more conservative men.

At Castle Pinckney all of the guns and carriages were placed. in good working order, but the general work was delayed, as the Charleston merchants refused to sell to the engineer officer, as an agent of the United States, the necessary lumber.

The embrasure shutters of the main gate were repaired and secured, the cisterns rebuilt, and work upon the wooden banquettes in the half-bastion commenced. The working party at Castle Pinckney were picked men, and the engineer officer believed them to be wholly reliable for service against any mob that should assault the fort.

Work had rapidly advanced also at Fort Sumter, upon which 150 men were actually at work. The casemate arches for the second tier of guns were now completed, the flagging laid and the traverse rails mounted, but the construction of the embrasures had been delayed, as the material necessary had not yet arrived. The barracks for the men on the eastern side of the fort had been finished. The traverse stones of the first tier were reset; the flagging of the second tier was laid, and the construction of the embrasures of that tier begun. But few of the guns had been mounted at Fort Sumter, as Major Anderson had recommended

---

*This statement induced the Hon. John Tyler, of Virginia, to ask the President if it were true.

a suspension of the armament until the future of the fort was more definitely determined. Nor did the engineer officer think it safe to proceed with the work, although everything was in readiness to mount all of the guns when it was deemed necessary and safe so to do. In communicating to his chief on the sad of December the progress and completion of the work upon Fort Moultrie, Captain Foster had reported the presence of the guard-boats near the forts, whose movements had been of such a character that on the night of the 20th the night-watch at Fort Sumter had reported to Lieutenant Snyder, the officer in charge of the work, the near presence of the guard-boat. Upon visiting the ramparts, Lieutenant Snyder found the vessel close under the west flank of the fort, apparently sounding. At Castle Pinckney another steamer remained close to the work, and when hailed by the night-watch as to her purpose, an answer was returned, "You will know in another week." In a report made to his chief, the engineer stated that he had taken no steps to ascertain the object of this espionage, as the recent orders of the War Department had assured him that every cause that might irritate the people must be avoided. This communication from Captain Foster was deemed so important that the officer in charge of the Engineer Bureau at Washington* took the letter in person to the Secretary of War on the 26th of December, and read it to him. After listening to the reading of the letter, the Secretary merely remarked that "it was very satisfactory," and expressed a wish that the troubles would pass without bloodshed. While commending the course of his subordinate, the officer in charge of the Engineer Bureau informs him that, although his several letters had been laid before the Secretary of War and instructions for him earnestly requested, "thus far no such instructions had been received."

This important communication, with its official indorsements, is here given entire:

"SULLIVAN'S ISLAND, S. C., December 22, 1860.
"Col. R E. DeRUSSY,
    "*Commanding Corps of Engineers, U. S. Army, Washington. D.C.:*
    "COLONEL: I feel it my duty to inform you that on the last two nights steamers from town have remained in the close vicinity

*Captain H. G. Wright, Corps of Engineers.

of Fort Sumter, apparently with the object of maintaining guard over the fort. On the first night, that of the 20th, only one came. She approached from the direction of town, as though running for the wharf, and her movements attracting the attention of the watchman, he awoke Lieutenant Snyder, who, when he went upon the ramparts, found her close under the west flank, apparently sounding. She afterwards moved off to a second position about six hundred yards from the fort, and remained during the night. She showed no lights. On the same night this or another steamer reconnoitred and remained around Castle Pinckney for some time, and when hailed by the night-watch on the Castle as to what she wanted, some one replied, 'You will know in a week.' Last night two steamers kept watch around Fort Sumter.

"These steamers are the small harbor or coast steamers, and one of them was named the Nina. Judging it best not to incur any risk of an unpleasant occurrence, I have not taken any steps to ascertain the object of this surveillance, nor of those in command of the steamers. The recent orders emanating from the War Department have given me the assurance that every cause that might irritate these people must be avoided. However mortifying it may be to know that there are no means for defense in Fort Sumter, and that the military men of the city have their eyes fixed upon it as the prize to obtain, I feel bound to carry out this idea in my every act.

"I do not even feel authorized to vary my present plan of operations, either by a reduction or an increase of force, although my expenses are very heavy, and my present liabilities barely covered by my requisitions just made. Whenever the Department desires that I may make a change of operations, I beg that it may soon be communicated to me.

"At Fort Moultrie I am still exerting myself to the utmost to make it so defensible as to discourage any attempts to take it. The wet ditch is now completed. The whole of the east front is now raised by solid merlons, two barrels high, and in three positions to a greater height, to serve for cavaliers. The guns are provided with good siege-battery embrasures, faced with green hides, and two of them 8-inch howitzers, one in addition furnished with musket-proof shutters working on an axis, elevated over the throat of the embrasure by supports on each side, and manœuvred by double bars extending back over the gun.

"A field howitzer has been put in position on the parapet at the northeast salient by means of a palmetto stockade, so as to sweep the vicinity of that angle better than it was before. Traverses to intercept shot from the sand-hills have been placed on the parapet and upon the terrepleins.

"The bridge connecting the barracks and guard-house is completed, the doors arranged with fastenings, doors cut through the partition walls of the barracks, trap-doors cut in the floors, and ladders made. The howitzers in the finished caponiere are put in good working order. The second caponiere was commenced yesterday morning, with a full force of masons, and by to-night was over six feet in height, with both embrasures completed. Major Anderson wanted me to adopt some more temporary construction, but I showed him that this would be far more valuable in the defense, and having the materials and masons ready, I could construct it just as quickly and cheaply. On Monday I shall erect a lookout tower, or sharpshooter stand, on top of the guard-house, at Major Anderson's request. I have stopped for the present the work upon the glacis in front of the sea front, and put all my force upon the above works. The glacis has, however, assumed fine proportions, and is in fact nearly completed. One-half of the interior slope is well sodded, and half of the glacis slope covered with muck six inches thick.

"It will take very little work to complete the whole of it, as soon as the present pressing work is finished.

"Very truly yours,   J. G. FOSTER,
"Captain Engineers."

[Endorsement No. I.]
ENGINEER DEPARTMENT, December 24, 1860.

"Respectfully submitted to the honorable Secretary of War for his information, and with the earnest request that the instructions solicited by Captain Foster may be promptly given.

"H. G. WRIGHT,
"Captain. of Engineers, in charge."

[Endorsement No. 2.]
"ENGINEER DEPARTMENT, December 26, 1860.

"Respectfully referred to the honorable Secretary of War, and his attention urgently called to the within report as one of great importance.   "H. G. WRIGHT,

"Captain of Engineers, in charge."

[Endorsement No. 31
"ENGINEER OFFICE, December 26, 1860.

"Have just seen the Secretary of War, and read to him the within letter. His only remarks in regard to it were that it was very satisfactory, and that he hoped, or thought, I don't distinctly remember which, that we should get over these troubles without bloodshed. He further said he did not wish to retain the letter —this in answer to my question.   " H. G. W."

Whatever agreement or understanding may have been entered into between the Government at Washington and those who acted for the State of South Carolina, in regard to the existing status in the harbor of Charleston, it is evident that Major Anderson had not been informed of it. After the transmission of the orders of the War Department by Major Buell he was left without further instructions, although reporting his position almost daily. The true nature of these orders seemed to have been regarded by the Government on the one hand and Major Anderson on the other in very different lights.   By the former they were almost ignored, the President himself having apparently forgotten their existence, although the character of the order to be sent was discussed at a Cabinet meeting before their transmission to Major Anderson; by the latter they were regarded, in their letter and spirit, as conferring upon him authority to act in case of "tangible evidence" that a hostile act was imminent, and of this he was to be the judge. Major Anderson believed that he had such tangible evidence.   What he heard were the almost daily threats that his position would be attacked; and these threats became more numerous and more positive after the State had passed the Ordinance of Secession. He knew that he could not long defend himself. What he saw was the nightly watch upon him lest he should transfer his command to the stronger and safer position of Fort Sumter. It was this latter action on the part of the State authorities—wholly in violation of any agreement that might have been made-that impressed him beyond all others and mainly influenced his actions. Upon the 14th of December he wrote to a personal friend as follows:*

"When I inform you that my garrison consists of only sixty effective men, that we are in a very indefensible work, the walls of which are only about fourteen feet high, and that we have within 100 yards of our walls, sand-hills which command our work, and which afford admirable sites for their batteries and the finest covers for sharpshooters, and that besides this there are numerous houses, some of them within pistol-shot—you will at once see that if attacked in force, headed by any one not a simpleton, there is scarcely a probability of our being able to hold out long enough to enable our friends to come to our succor.

"Trusting that, etc.,

(Signed.)   "ROBERT   ANDERSON."

He had never ceased to urge upon the Government the necessity of action in regard to Fort Sumter.   His opinions in regard to the importance of that work, the impossibility of any occupancy of the harbor by the Government troops should the State seize and garrison it, and his desire to occupy it, were no secrets to his officers.

---

* From the Richmond *Whig,* December 24 1860.

On Monday, the 24th of December, the Commissioners appointed by the Convention on the 21st, the day following the passage of the Ordinance of Secession, proceeded to Washington to treat with the Government for the delivery of the forts and public property within the limits of the State, and to negotiate generally in regard to the existing relations of the parties.

The object of their mission was generally known, and Major Anderson had become convinced, as he had reported to his Government, that upon the success or failure of their mission an immediate attack upon him depended. It was the intention of the State authorities, and tacitly approved by the general sentiment of the people, that, the present status being preserved, there should be no authorized attack upon the public property until the Commissioners formally sent by the Convention to Washington should have failed in their effort at negotiation. The apprehension entertained in some quarters of mob action, and even alleged by the President himself, had no place in the calculations of those who were now guiding the course of the State. Mob law or its measures were unknown in South Carolina, and the tone and temper of those in control were too well known to encourage its existence now. The earnestness of the authorities and people of the State seemed to have impressed itself more forcibly upon Major Anderson since the visit of Major Buell and the departure of the Commissioners to Washington, and he felt that upon him mainly the responsibility of a conflict seemed to rest. A change in his manner was evident to the officers about him, who inferred the reception of unwelcome news. His whole desire was to avoid bloodshed, and he believed that if he and his command, as the offending feature, were removed to a position of greater safety and more enlarged control, the issue would be at least postponed. When, then, the Commissioners had been formally sent to Washington by the Convention, Anderson anticipated their reception and the rejection of their proposals by the Government; and believing that the critical moment as to his position had come, he resolved to take advantage of the "tangible evidence" he believed he had, and to act under the plain instructions given to him through Major Buell. His determination to transfer his command to Fort Sumter was accordingly taken, and he proceeded to execute it.

CHAPTER X.

THE morning of the 26th of December brought with it no apparent change in the relative status in the harbor of Charleston. The garrison of Fort Moultrie, following its ordinary routine of duty, were early at work in carrying out the preliminary instructions of Major Anderson before his movement.

The large number of women and children of the garrison and the necessary supplies were to be transferred apparently to Fort Johnson, an old barrack on the western shore of the harbor. The hospital, which had been established outside of Fort Moultrie, was moved into the fort. Rumors were rife that a selection of the troops to make the attack upon Fort Moultrie had been determined upon in the city. To meet this, an order assigning to each officer his duty was read upon parade.

Christmas of 1860, with its attendant festivities, had come. Taking advantage of the day, as likely to divert from him temporarily the close scrutiny under which he had labored for so long, Major Anderson pushed forward the preparations for the movement he had determined upon, under the disguise of preparation for action; his intention being to accomplish his movement on Christmas Day, which was only prevented by rain. Orders were given for the immediate packing up of all articles considered essential in the transfer to Fort Johnson, and to all outward appearances the garrison of Fort Moultrie seemed to be on the very eve of action.

A feeling prevailed that this movement was only preliminary to a conflict, and the co-operation of the men was actively manifested.

Work upon the defenses went on with its accustomed vigor, and that upon Fort Moultrie was fast approaching completion. In Fort Sumter 150 men were actively at work under the engineer officer in charge, and at Castle Pinckney the necessary repairs were being rapidly pushed forward. To ensure secrecy in the movement, Major Anderson had not communicated his intention to any of his officers until their co-operation and assistance were indispensable. As the principal means of transportation for the troops were the boats in use by the Engineer Department at Fort Sumter and Castle Pinckney, and the assistance of the officers of that department was important, Lieutenants Snyder and Meade, the officers in charge of those works, were early informed of his purpose and intention. By noon the women and children had embarked upon the two lighters in readiness at the wharf at Sullivan's Island. The provisions for four months had been put on board, and Lieutenant Hall, the adjutant of the post, who had, been put in charge by Major Anderson, received, for the first time, his orders to proceed towards Fort Johnson. He was not to land, but to await the firing of two signal guns from Fort Moultrie, when he was to make all sail for Fort Sumter, as the report of those guns would inform him that the command had safely arrived there. The unusual number of lighters (three) at the wharf had attracted attention.

Two citizens presented themselves to watch the operations. They followed the movements of Lieutenant Hall everywhere except into the fort itself, and finally demanded of him the reason for the transfer of so large an amount of provisions. An evasive answer was given, when the men left at once for the steamer for Charleston, which postponed its departure until the lighters had left. Through an oversight, one box marked "A thousand ball cartridges" had been put on board. A boat of the Chief Engineer came to the lighter, which had grounded, and removed the box, and this action seemed to satisfy another citizen, who had watched the whole operation and who soon afterwards left. Preparations for the defense of the work went steadily on through the day. Intending to visit the city, the writer found that the boats had been sent on other duty, when he crossed to Fort Sumter. 'While there he was led to believe, from a conversation with the officer in charge, that something unusual might be expected to occur, and he was earnestly advised to return to Fort Moultrie and remain there." Upon reaching the fort he joined Major

---

*"Crawford," said he, "go back to Fort Moultrie, and don't take your eyes off Anderson."

Anderson upon the parapet of the work looking seaward. A large steamer of the Savannah line was passing southward in the offing. She had arrested her course for a moment, as if to enter the harbor. The attention of Major Anderson was called to it by the writer. Anderson watched the steamer with great earnestness, when, turning to the writer he said: "I hope she will not attempt to come in. It would greatly embarrass me. I intend to move to Fort Sumter to night." Enjoining the utmost secrecy as to his statement, he replied, in answer to a question as to the disposition to be made of the hospital department, that he had determined to leave it in the fort as it was, until the next morning; that it was less likely to be disturbed in case of any interference by the troops of the State than other interests which it was important to transfer at once. The defensive preparations went on steadily until "retreat roll-call"—when the order was given to evacuate the fort. Shortly after dusk the movement began. The sea was still, the moon shining brightly. Three six-oared barges and two four-oared boats were in readiness on the beach below the fort. Half an hour before starting, Major Anderson sent for Captain Doubleday, whose company formed part of the garrison, and informed him of his intention to transfer his command to Fort Sumter; that he wished him to have twenty men under arms, with knapsacks, to go in the first boat.

Sending his family with those of the other officers at once to safe quarters upon the island, Captain Doubleday formed his men without delay and marched them to the boats, leaving the remainder, under the charge of First Lieutenant J. C. Davis, to await transportation. Major Anderson was awaiting the appearance of the men at the gateway of the fort, when he led the way in person to the boats. The men entered the three boats awaiting them, silently and in order. Their arms were so disposed as to avoid attracting attention in the bright moonlight, and when all was in readiness, Lieutenant Snyder, the engineer officer in charge at Fort Sumter in the leading boat, accompanied by Major Anderson with the flag of the garrison, they pushed off from shore. They were followed by Lieutenant Meade, the engineer officer in charge at Castle Pinckney, in his boat, while Captain Doubleday with the rest of the men followed in the remaining boat. When half-way across the channel, one of the boats which for several nights had been used as a guard-boat to cruise between the forts, made its appearance directly in the path of the rearmost boat. To avoid her the boats under Major Anderson and Lieutenant Meade diverted their course along Sullivan's Island. Captain Doubleday's boat pushed directly across and was the first to arrive. For the moment it was thought best to turn back, but the men took off their hats and coats, concealing their arms and belts, so as to give themselves the appearance of workmen, and the boat pushed on. The steamer passed close by—within a distance of 100 yards—but instead of being upon her ordinary mission she was in the act of towing a vessel to the harbor bar. This was the only night since the establishment of the guard that the service had been interrupted. A second boat, the *Emma,* lay at her wharf in Charleston with the armed force on board, ready to move down the harbor on her usual tour of duty. She was awaiting the orders which were regularly transmitted by an aide-de-camp from the Governor's headquarters, but which, from some unexplained reason, failed to come at the usual hour, and the boat was still at her dock when the signal guns were fired from Moultrie. The officers on board thought that they had been forgotten, when, after the shots were fired, Colonel Pettigrew, an aide-de-camp of the Governor, came hastily to the boat and asked for an explanation of the firing, and at once ordered her upon her mission. But it was then too late; the command had crossed without interruption, which, had the guard-boat been present at her usual hour and carried out her orders, it would have been impossible to accomplish. Upon reaching Fort Sumter the command disembarked amid the surprise and protests of the workmen, who gathered about the boat and demanded the reason for the presence of the soldiers. Many of them wore the secession cockade. Captain Doubleday landed his men, formed them, and advanced into the work. One of the workmen approached the sentinel, cheering for the Union. He was at once checked, ordered into the fort, and all noise forbidden. Half of the command that had arrived were put at once on guard. Sentinels were placed over the main gate outside and in, and upon the ramparts, as it was apprehended that a disturbance might arise among the workmen. The boats returned at once for the remainder of the troops. At Fort Moultrie the greatest caution was used as the boats passed and returned. In accordance with the special instructions of Major Anderson two of the heavy guns bearing upon the channel towards Fort

Sumter, had been loaded, and orders given to Captain Foster, who had been left in charge at Fort Moultrie, that if there should be any attempt to interfere with the passage of the boats upon the part of the guard-boat, he was to fire upon her. As the guard-boat approached she was recognized at once. It was the Nina, and her appearance was familiar to us. It was a moment of suspense, as those who were left immediately manned the guns, which were trailed directly upon a point she must pass. Directing our glasses upon her, the writer discovered, as she crossed the broad belt of moonlight that stretched across the channel, that she was in the act of towing a vessel. This was at once made known, and she was allowed to pass. Captain Doubleday's boat crossed her bow within 100 yards, and rising and sinking upon the swell of the sea, she was soon lost to view in the dark shadow of the fort. Three trips were made by the boat, including one for the bedding and other articles for immediate use. The last boat had now passed over without molestation, when in accordance with the previous instructions of Major Anderson, two signal guns were fired from Fort Moultrie, the writer firing the second. The report of these guns was to announce to Lieutenant Hall—who, in command of the lighters with the women, children and stores on board, was now off Fort Johnson—the transference of the command to Fort Sumter and his duty to make all sail for that work. Lieutenant Hall acted with promptness, although not without the opposition of a captain of one of the lighters, who refused to proceed to Fort Sumter and only yielded to force. All had now been accomplished, and by eight o'clock the entire command at Fort Moultrie had been successfully transferred within the walls of Fort Sumter. Immediately after the transfer of his command Major Anderson made the following report to his Government:

"FORT SUMTER, South Carolina,
"December 16, 1860.
"8 P.M.

"COLONEL:

"I have the honor to report that I have just completed, by the blessing of God, the removal to this fort of all my garrison, except the surgeon, four non-commissioned officers and seven men. We have one year's supply of hospital stores and about four months' supply of provisions for my command. I left orders to have all the guns at Fort Moultrie spiked, and the carriages of the 32-pounders, which are old, destroyed. I have sent orders to Captain Foster, who remains at Fort Moultrie, to destroy all the ammunition which he cannot send over. The step which I have taken was, in my opinion, necessary to prevent the effusion of blood.

"Respectfully, your obedient servant,

ROBERT ANDERSON,

"Major First Artillery.

"Colonel S. COOPER, *Adjutant-General;"*

But the firing of the signal guns was not the only duty confided to the officers left at Fort Moultrie. When the command had crossed, the further instructions of Major Anderson were complied with. The guns in the entire battery were spiked and rendered temporarily useless, and the flag-staff was so cut as to break in its fall upon the parapet and fall into the ditch. The writer then left the work and crossed to Fort Sumter. Lieutenant Davis, who with the remainder of Captain Doubleday's company had followed the command, returned to Fort Moultrie for some personal effects and remained with Captain Foster during the night. A detail of four non-commissioned officers and seven men were left to assist Captain Foster in carrying out the instructions of Major Anderson. The night passed without incident. Soon after the transference of this command, the guard-boat Emma, with its armed force on board, made its appearance, long after its accustomed hour, and took up its position near the forts. It remained during the night, apparently unaware that its mission had ended.

Early on the morning of the 27th the writer returned to Fort Moultrie for the purpose of directing the transfer of the hospital department to Fort Sumter. Upon approaching the work a heavy column of smoke appeared above the parapet. Upon entering, it was found that in accordance with the orders of Major Anderson the gun-carriages which supported the heavy armament in the southwest angle of the work, and which bore directly upon Fort Sumter, were in process of destruction. Two had already been set on fire under the direction of Captain Foster and Lieutenant Davis, who were assisted by the writer in the destruction of the remainder, five of the guns thus falling from their beds upon the parapet. The day was passed in transferring to the lighters which had returned to Fort Moultrie a large supply of ammunition, and the entire hospital department with its one year's supply of stores, leaving one month's and a half supply of provisions, the entire supply of fuel, a small quantity of ammunition and some personal effects of the men. As the seizure of the arsenal in Charleston and the forts in the harbor by the troops of the State was in progress, great anxiety arose for the safety of the lighters. One of them, with the ammunition and the hospital property on board, had left the wharf before noon, but had been becalmed, and it was feared that she would be seized, when Major Anderson directed Lieutenant Hall to proceed in one of the boats with a few men to remove her freight. The boat's crew of work-men refused to take him on such an errand, when shortly after the lighter arrived safely at the fort.

Meantime, it soon became known that some extraordinary action upon the part of the garrison at Fort Moultrie had taken place. An intense excitement followed, which soon spread to Charleston and through the State. It was some time before what had exactly occurred was known to the inhabitants of Sul-livan's Island, but the deserted parapet, the barred entrance, the missing flag-staff, the heavy smoke-cloud hanging over the fort, and the sudden suspension of the work, all indicated some change of an unusual character. A rumor had been spread that Fort Moultrie was in flames, and every boat that came to the island brought crowds of excited people. Men connected with the lead-ing papers came down, anxiously inquiring as to the truth of the many rumors, until now unbelieved; crowds hung around the work all day, commenting upon the action of Major Anderson and threatening immediate attack.

In Fort Sumter the sudden arrival of the command produced a decided impression among the workmen. On the 15th of December a meeting had been held among themselves, and they had determined that they would take no part in any contest with the troops of the State. The sudden seizure of the fort con-vinced them that a struggle was imminent, and many of them left the work and returned to Charleston.

Meantime, the fact of the evacuation of Fort Moultrie by Major Anderson was soon communicated to the authorities and people of Charleston, creating intense excitement. Crowds col-lected in the streets and open places of the city, and loud and violent were the expressions of feeling against Major Anderson and his action. Military organizations paraded the streets, and threats were made that they would be heard from before twenty-four hours, and that bloodshed was now unavoidable. Anderson was pronounced a traitor, and it was claimed that his act would concentrate the South. The Governor of the State was ready to act in accordance with the feeling displayed. On the morning

MAJOR ANDERSON'S QUARTERS, FORT SUMTER.

of the 27th he despatched his aide-de-camp, Colonel Johnson Pettigrew, of the First South Carolina Rifles, to Major Anderson. He was accompanied by Major Ellison Capers, of his regiment. Arriving at Fort Sumter, Colonel Pettigrew sent a card inscribed,

"Colonel Pettigrew, First Regiment Rifles, S. C. M., Aide-de-camp to the Governor, Commissioner to Major Anderson. Ellison Capers, Major First Regiment Rifles, S. C. M." Major Anderson, with his officers, was in a small room in the second story of the officers' quarters in the gorge of the work, where they had passed the night. Colonel Pettigrew and his companions were ushered into the room. The greeting was reserved and formal, when, after declining seats, Colonel Pettigrew immediately opened his mission.

"Major Anderson," said he, "can I communicate with you now, sir, before these officers, on the subject for which I am here?"

"Certainly, sir," replied Major Anderson; "these are all my officers; I have no secrets from them, sir."

The Commissioner then informed Major Anderson that he was directed to say to him that the Governor was much surprised that he had reinforced "this work." Major Anderson promptly responded that there had been no reinforcement of the work; that he had moved his command from Fort Moultrie to Fort Sumter, as he had a right to do, being in command of all the forts in the harbor.

To this Colonel Pettigrew replied that when the present Governor (Pickens) came into office, he found an understanding existing between the previous Governor (Gist) and the President of the United States, by which all property within the limits of the State was to remain as it was; that no reinforcements were to be sent here, and particularly to this post; and that there was to be no attempt made against the public property here by the State; and that the status in the harbor should remain unchanged. He was directed, also, to say to Major Anderson that it had been hoped by the Governor that a peaceful solution of the difficulties could have been reached, and that a resort to arms and bloodshed might have been avoided; but that the Governor thought that the action of Major Anderson had greatly complicated matters; and that he did not now see how bloodshed could be avoided; that he had desired, and intended, that the whole matter might be fought out politically and without the arbitration of the sword, but that now it was uncertain, if not impossible.

To this Major Anderson replied that, as far as any understanding between the President and the Governor of the State was concerned, he had not been informed; that he knew nothing of it, that he could get no information or positive orders from Washington, and that his position was threatened every night by the troops of the State. He was then asked by Major Capers, who accompanied Colonel Pettigrew, "How?" when he replied, "By sending out steamers armed and carrying troops on board; that these steamers passed the fort going north; and that he feared a landing on the island and the occupation of the sand-hills just north of the fort; and that one hundred riflemen on that hill, which commanded his fort, would make it impossible for his men to serve their guns; and that any man with a military head must see this. To prevent this" (said he, earnestly) "I removed on my own responsibility, my sole object being to prevent bloodshed."

Major Capers replied that the steamer was sent out for patrol purposes, and as much to prevent disorder among his own people as to ascertain whether any irregular attempt was being made to reinforce the fort, and that the idea of attacking him "was never entertained by the little squad who patroled the harbor." Major Anderson replied to this, that he was totally in the dark as to the intentions of the State troops, but that he had reason to believe that they meant to land and attack him from the north; that the desire of the Governor to have the matter settled peacefully and without bloodshed was precisely his own object in transferring his command to Fort Sumter; that he did it upon his own responsibility alone, and because he considered that, the safety of his command required it, and as he had the right to do. "In this controversy" said he, "between the North and the South, my sympathies are entirely with the South. These gentlemen," said he (turning to the officers of the post who stood about him), "know it perfectly well." And he added that his sense of duty to his trust as commander in the harbor was *first* with him, and had influenced his determination to do his duty to the Government. Colonel Pettigrew then replied, "Well, sir, however that may be, the Governor of the State directs me to say to you, courteously but peremptorily, to return to Fort Moultrie." "Make my compliments to the Governor, and say to him that I decline to accede to his request; I cannot and will not go back," said Major Anderson. "Then, sir," said Colonel Pettigrew, "my business is done;" when both of the officers, without further ceremony or leave-taking, left the fort.

The statement of Major Anderson as to his sympathies made a strong impression upon the officers who had borne the message of the Governor, and to whom they repeated his words. The manner of Major Anderson, while earnest, was courteous throughout the interview, and he entirely impressed the messengers that he was really most anxious to prevent bloodshed, and that the movement had been made, upon his part, with that view.

At fifteen minutes before noon the command at Fort Sumter was ordered to parade. The band was placed upon the ramparts; the command and guard were drawn up near the flag-staff, forming one side of a square, the workmen of the fort, 150 in number, forming the other sides; Major Anderson by the flag-staff with the halyards in his hand. The chaplain of the post stood in front, near the centre. When all was ready the command was brought to a "parade rest" and everyone uncovered. The chaplain made a prayer, in which, after expressing gratitude to God for our safe arrival in the work, he prayed that our flag might never be dishonored, but soon float again over the whole country, a peaceful and prosperous nation. When the prayer was finished, Major Anderson, who had been kneeling, arose, the battalion presented arms, the band played the National Air, and the flag went to the head of the flag-staff, amid the loud and earnest huzzas of the command.

CHAPTER XI.

UPON the return of his messenger with the refusal of Major Anderson to return to Fort Moultrie, the Governor of the State at once proceeded to seize and occupy by military force the forts in the harbor and the arsenal in the city of Charleston. His aide-de-camp who had carried his demand to Major Anderson was ordered by him to assemble the Washington Light Infantry and the Meagher Guards at the citadel in the city, to arm them there, and to take measures for occupying Castle Pinckney. He was to proceed under the following instructions:

"HEADQUARTERS,
"CHARLESTON, December 27, 1860
"To COLONEL J. J. PETTIGREW,
"*Sir:* You are ordered to take possession of Castle Pinckney. You are to act with the greatest discretion and prudence, and to let it be known that you take possession in the name of the Governor of South Carolina, and in consequence of the extraordinary orders executed last night in relation to Fort Moultrie, and with a view at present to prevent further destruction of public property, and as a measure of safety also.
(Signed)   "F. W. PICKENS."

A similar order was issued to Lieutenant-Colonel W. G. De Saussure, of the First Regiment of Artillery, instructing him to take possession of Sullivan's Island immediately after the seizure of Castle Pinckney. In accordance with his instructions, Colonel Pettigrew embarked a force consisting of the Washington Light Infantry, Captain Simonton, the Carolina Light Infantry, and the Meagher Guards upon a small transport and proceeded to Castle Pinckney, where, under the engineer officer in charge, Lieutenant

113

R. K. Meade, the work of repair was steadily going on. About four o'clock in the afternoon the boat approached the work, when the officer in charge immediately closed and barred the main gate. The workmen, in alarm, rushed to the parapet, but were at once ordered to their quarters. Meantime, the force had landed, a portion of them proceeding to the main gate, which they found closed. A party with their rifles stood watching the parapet, while the remainder, placing the ladders they had brought against the walls, commenced an escalade. The commanding officer, Colonel Pettigrew, led the ascent; stepping upon the parapet he encountered Lieutenant Meade, who approached him, when he demanded to know who was the commanding officer of the work. Lieutenant Meade replied that he was that officer, when Colonel Pettigrew informed him that he had been commanded by the Governor of South Carolina to take charge of the work in the name of the State.

Producing his orders, he commenced to read them, when he was interrupted by Lieutenant Meade, who said to him that he did not acknowledge the authority of the Governor to take possession of the work; that he had no means of resistance, and could but enter his protest against any such proceedings. Colonel Pettigrew informed him that he was acting under the orders of the Governor, and would give receipts for the public property. Lieutenant Meade replied that as he did not acknowledge the authority of the Governor he declined to accept his receipts. Colonel Pettigrew, accompanied by Lieutenant Meade, then descended into the parade. Meanwhile, the wall had been scaled by others, who had unbarred the gate, when the troops immediately entered and were formed upon the parade.

A sentinel was posted at once over the entrance, when Lieutenant Meade asked if his movements were to be restrained. Colonel Pettigrew replied, that while he did not propose to restrain his movements, he would not be permitted to return to the post if he left it that night; that he did not mean to expel him from the post, and should ask for further instructions. Lieutenant Meade declined to give his parole, as he did not consider himself a prisoner of war. After stipulating for considerate treatment of the old ordnance sergeant and his family, until they could be removed elsewhere, Lieutenant Meade left the work at once for Fort Sumter. All of the Government property was

FORT SUMTER WHEN ENTERED BY ANDERSON'S TROOPS.

seized and appropriated, including one month's provisions. With the exception of two or three heavy guns on the barbette tier, and one 42-pounder in casemate, the armament of the fort was complete; the magazine was well supplied, as the powder from the-arsenal had been stored there; and in this condition Castle Pinckney passed under the flag of the State.

Shortly after its occupation Lieutenant-Colonel De Saussure, in accordance with the orders received; having assembled 200 picked men of the First Regiment of Artillery, S. C. M., proceeded to Sullivan's Island. The command approached Fort Moultrie by the main streets.

Approaching the work upon the west side, Colonel De Saussure and a small guard entered it and unbarred the gate, which had been closed by the sergeant or overseer of the engineer force, the solitary guardian of the work. A report had been spread, and generally believed, that the work was mined, and this became a subject of sensitive inquiry at every interview held with the State officials. With the exception of Colonel De Saussure himself and a few of his men, the troops of the State did not occupy Fort Moultrie on the night of its seizure. In the morning it was occupied permanently, and its armament, consisting of fifty-six" pieces of ordnance, including heavy and light guns, Columbiads and mortars, with their carriages and implements and a large supply of ammunition passed into the hands of the State.

Both forts had now been seized and occupied by the State troops; and, as if to complete the seizure of the Government property, the officers attached to the United States Custom House, in obedience to an ordinance passed by the Convention on the 26th of December, entered into the service of the State and the flag of South Carolina was raised over the building.

Mail communication had been as yet undisturbed, and it was deemed important, that the General Government should perform that service as long as possible.

Two days after the Ordinance of Secession had been passed by the Convention, an order for $450 worth of postage-stamps was received at Washington from the Postmaster at Charleston for the use of that office, and at a later date the same official

---

* Sixteen 24-pounders, nineteen 32-pounders, ten 8-inch Columbiads, one 10-inch seacoast mortar, four 6-pounders, two 12-pounders, four 24-pound howitzers.   Lieutenant-Colonel De Saussure's report, December 31, '60.

reported to the Postmaster-General at Washington, to say that he held himself responsible to the Federal Government for the revenue accruing to his office.

The rapidity and secrecy of his movement from Fort Moultrie had compelled Major Anderson to leave, temporarily, many of the private effects of the officers and the clothing of the men. The necessity of securing these at once, as well as to provide for the safety of the women and children of the command in case of an attack upon him, induced him to send a special messenger to the Governor. Accordingly, early on the morning of the 30th of December, Lieutenant Snyder was sent to the city with a communication from Major Anderson. His boats were seized by the police as soon as he had landed. He found the Governor at the Executive office amid a party of gentlemen who appeared to be acting in the capacity of a council. Lieutenant Snyder announced the object of his visit. He had come, he said, from Major Anderson, commanding Fort Sumter, to say that he hoped, if an attack was to be made upon him, that he should be informed, in accordance with civilized warfare, in time to remove the women and children and the non-combatants of his garrison to a place of safety. He desired to know, too, whether the private effects of the officers yet remaining at Castle Pinckney and Fort Moultrie would be returned to them. The Governor replied that Major Anderson was at liberty to remove the women and children to Sullivan's Island, and he offered them on his own part complete protection; that the private effects of the officers might be removed to the city, and would be respected; but that for the present no other communication would be allowed between the garrison of Fort Sumter and the city except to carry and receive the mails, and that he exacted this to prevent any irregular collision or the unnecessary effusion of blood.

A memorandum in writing and signed by Governor Pickens was handed to Lieutenant Snyder, of which the following is a copy

"HEADQUARTERS,
"December 30, 1860.
"In reply to Major Anderson's request, made this morning verbally through First Lieutenant Snyder from Fort Sumter, I hereby order and direct that free permission shall be given to him to send the ladies and camp women from Fort Sumter, with their private effects, to any portion of Sullivan's Island, and that entire protec-

tion shall be extended to them. It is also agreed that the mails may be sent over to the officers at Fort Sumter by their boats, and that all the ladies of Captain Foster's family shall be allowed to pass, with their effects and the effects of any kind belonging to Captain Foster, from the Mills House to Fort Sumter, and the kindest regard shall be paid to them. Of course, Lieutenant Meade's private effects can be taken possession of, but for the present there shall be no communication of any other kind allowed from the city to the fort, or any transportation of arms or ammunition, or any supplies to the fort; and this is done with a view to prevent irregular collisions, and to spare the unnecessary effusion of blood.

"F. W. PICKENS."

The Governor then asked if Lieutenant Snyder was of the opinion that Major Anderson would return to Fort Moultrie if ordered by the President. Lieutenant Snyder replied that Major Anderson would promptly obey any order of the President. Would his second in command, if ordered by himself (the Governor)? Lieutenant Snyder thought not, and expressed the opinion that there was no officer there who, if it devolved upon him, would return to Fort Moultrie if ordered by the Governor.

In the city there was great excitement. Upon returning to the boats nothing was allowed shipment but the baggage. The fresh meats and stores which had been put on board in Charleston were removed.

Upon the same day Lieutenant Hall was sent by Major Anderson to the officer in command of Fort Moultrie. He was to demand by what authority he had occupied that work. He was to ask, also, if any obstacle would be-opposed to the removal of the private effects of the officers and the clothing of the men, with the wood and coal left there.

The commanding officer, Colonel W. G. De Saussure, replied that he occupied that work in the name of the sovereign State of South Carolina and by the authority of its Governor. He declined to permit the removal of any of the public property, but all private property would be respected, and he would assist in its removal. The public property he was ordered to secure, make an inventory of and protect. It would all be preserved and submitted to the Commissioners to negotiate upon, except the provisions left, and these he should use.

Colonel De Saussure carried out his intentions in a kindly spirit, allowing no one to enter the fort until the property had been collected together and an inventory made, with the expectation of their removal. But a box of clothing had already been broken open and its contents scattered, the men appropriating the great-coats of the soldiers which had been left. The movement of Major Anderson was remarked by Colonel De Saussure as being one of "consummate wisdom," in a military point of view, but that it would greatly complicate matters. Meantime, owing to continued stormy weather, no communication was held with Fort Moultrie for a few days, when Lieutenant Hall again visited that post for the purpose of securing the clothing and personal effects of the men. He was accompanied by Captain Foster, who crossed for the purpose of paying off the employees that had been at work under his control at Fort Moultrie. The commanding officer, Colonel De Saussure, had not changed his intention in regard to the subject, and suggested that these officers should return the next day, when Captain Foster might complete his payments and the articles in question be removed.

Meantime, Colonel De Saussure had been relieved by order of the Governor, that he might attend to his civil duties as a member of the Legislature, then in session at Charleston. Lieutenant-Colonel R. S. Ripley had succeeded him at Fort Moultrie. Brigadier-General Dunovant was in command of the island, and upon the following morning, when Captains Foster and Seymour went to the island, they were arrested by General Dunovant's order. They were subsequently released and permitted to return to Sumter, when no further communication with Fort Moultrie took place.

Having now taken possession of Castle Pinckney and Fort Moultrie; the Governor proceeded to seize the United States arsenal situated in the midst of the city of Charleston, with its large and valuable supply of ordnance and ordnance stores.

The early possession of the arsenal had long been regarded as essential to the success of the movement now made by the State. Its defenseless condition, with its important and valuable stores, was well known to the Government, and as early as the month of November the War Department had ordered Brevet-Colonel Benj. Huger, of the Ordnance Department, to proceed to Charleston and assume command of the arsenal. Colonel Huger was a native of South Carolina, and from his ability, high standing and prominent social relations, he was deemed, under the existing circumstances, to be a suitable appointment. He was aware of the views of the Secretary of War, and it was believed that while he would maintain peaceable relations; he would at the same time protect the interests of the Government. Before assuming command on the 20th inst., he had visited Columbia, where he had held repeated conferences with the Governor of the State.

Upon the 1st of December Major Anderson was directed to confer with Colonel Huger upon matters which had been confided to each of them, as the latter had been recalled temporarily to Washington by the Secretary of War. For some unexplained reason Colonel Huger, who had been in command of the arsenal in Charleston but ten days, did not return to it, but, under instructions from the Secretary of War, resumed his duties at Pikesville, N. C.; and thus the United States arsenal in the city of Charleston, with its large and valuable supply of stores, was left without a commissioned officer of Ordnance, and under, the charge of a military storekeeper and enlisted men, until its final and easy seizure by the troops of the State."

The attempt of Colonel Gardiner to obtain stores from the arsenal, and the sending of an officer to secure them, had greatly excited the people. Numbers gathered in the vicinity. Threats were made of an attack upon it, and a collision between the populace and the agents of the Government seemed to be unavoidable and imminent. The State authorities became anxious to prevent any premature act of violence, and yet were unwilling to repress actively the public feeling, in view of its political effect. It was under such circumstances that the Governor of the State (Gist), after an understanding with Colonel Huger, determined to establish a guard of State troops over the arsenal, and upon the 9th of November, after the election of Mr. Lincoln had become known, a guard, consisting of an officer and twenty men of the Washington Light Infantry, was tendered by the Governor and was accepted by the military storekeeper, who thus reported to his chief.

---

* "Colonel Huger joined the Confederacy. In a conversation with General De Saussure, during the war, he recalled the above circumstances, and said that he came to Charleston in the nature of an envoy from Mr. Buchanan and General Scott, whose 'plighted faith' he had that the status should not be changed, that General Scott had mislead him and compromised him with his people."–*General De Saussure to Author.*

"CHARLESTON ARSENAL, S. C.,
"November 12, 1860.

"Col. H. K. CRAIG,
 "Chief of Ordnance, U. S. A., Washington, D. C.

"Sir: In view of the excitement now existing in this city and State, and the possibility of an insurrectionary movement on the part of the servile population, the Governor has tendered, through General Schnierle, of the South Carolina Militia, a guard, of a detachment of a lieutenant and twenty men, for this post, which has been accepted. Trusting that this course may meet the approval of the Department, I am, sir,
 "Very respectfully, your most obedient servant,
 "F. C. HUMPHREYS,
 "Military Storekeeper Ordnance,
 "Commander."

* The guard was stationed within the arsenal enclosure, and sentinels were posted guarding every approach from all sides to the buildings. And this was continued until the night of the age of December, when they were relieved by the German Riflemen, Captain Small.

While the presence of this guard might be relied upon to protect the arsenal and its valuable stores from popular violence, it gave equal assurance that neither arms nor ammunition could now be moved from the arsenal to any of the forts in the harbor of Charleston.

On the 28th of December the guard at that time on duty was increased in numbers, and closed around the arsenal, refusing ingress or egress to any one without the countersign, the officer in command disclaiming any "intention of occupancy." The military storekeeper in charge at once telegraphed the fact to his chief, sending the details by mail and asking instructions.

None were sent to him. He had on the 29th protested against the indignity offered to him and his command, and had informed his Government that, if upon a proper request to the State authorities the troops were not removed, he would consider their action as an occupancy of the arsenal, and should haul down his flag and surrender. This communication was submitted by the

---

*It was the posting of this guard that led Governor Pickens to assume that it was done with the acquiescence of the President, and which induced him to send a special messenger to Washington the day after his inauguration to ask that the same authority be given to him in reference to Fort Sumter. The President had not given such authority.

chief Ordnance officer in Washington to the Secretary of War on the 1st of January. But meanwhile, the Governor of the State had determined to take entire possession of the arsenal. On the morning of the 29th of December; having selected Colonel John Cunningham, of the Seventeenth Regiment Infantry, S. C M., for the service, he directed him to take a detachment of select men, in the "most discreet and forbearing manner," and proceed to the United States arsenal in Charleston, and there demand in his name its "entire possession." He was to state "distinctly" that this was done with a view to prevent any destruction of public property that might occur in the present excited state of the public mind, and also as due to the public safety. He was to take an inventory of the stores and of the condition of the arms. He was to read his orders to the military storekeeper who was in charge. If he refused to deliver the arsenal to him, he was to take it, using as much force as might be necessary. Great discretion and liberality were to be used towards Captain Humphreys, who was at liberty to remain, and indeed was requested to remain, in his present quarters as long as it might be agreeable to him.

On the 30th, within half an hour after the receipt of the order, Colonel Cunningham, with a detachment from the Union Light Infantry, Captain Ramsay, which was on duty near the arsenal, proceeded to the quarters of Captain Humphreys and demanded, in writing, an immediate surrender of the arsenal under his charge and the delivery to him of the keys and contents of the arsenals, magazines, etc. He informs Captain Humphreys that he was already proceeding to occupy it with troops, and that he occupied it in the name of the Governor, and by virtue of orders from him. Captain Humphreys replied to this demand, in writing, that he was constrained to comply with his demand for the surrender of the arsenal, as he had no force for its defense, but that he did so under protest. He demands as a right to salute his flag, and that his men be allowed to occupy their quarters until instructions could be obtained from the War Department. This was accorded by Colonel Cunningham, whose men at once occupied the arsenal grounds and buildings, opened the arsenals and magazines, and commenced an issue of the property. In his report* to Governor Pickens, Colonel Cunningham states that "the dignity, courtesy, frankness and

---

* Official report of Colonel Cunningham.

conduct of Captain Humphreys" enabled him "to establish the most pleasant and even confiding relations with him," and that Captain Humphreys had facilitated his operations in every way consistent with his duties. Some of the employees passed into the service of the State. The value of the stores seized was estimated by the officer who occupied the work at $400,000. On the morning of the 30th the military storekeeper reported by telegram to his chief in Washington, that the arsenal in his charge had that day been seized by force of arms.

On the same day, and by the same authority, "Fort Johnson and the adjacent grounds" were seized and occupied by a detachment of State troops under the command of Captain Jos. Johnson, Jr.; and a large supply of fuel belonging to the Government, and whose want was greatly felt by the garrison at Fort Sumter, passed into the hands of the State. The destruction or removal of any of the public stores was forbidden by the Governor in his orders to the officer in command, and he was also to intercept any parties from Fort Sumter and to prevent any communication with that work. Nothing but the mails was allowed to be sent.

Having now obtained possession of the unoccupied forts and arsenal, the Governor proceeded immediately to establish batteries for the control of the harbor. On the morning of the 29th of December orders were issued to his chief engineer officer to proceed to some suitable point on Morris Island beyond Fort Sumter, to associate himself with the ordnance officer, Colonel Manigault, and to select a location for a battery to bear upon the ship channel, and to erect "the same as soon as possible;" two 24-pounders were to be sent at once, and the number was to be increased. A point upon Sullivan's Island was also to be selected by the same officers, and a battery established beyond Fort Moultrie and out of the range of guns from Fort Sumter," to guard the harbor and to prevent reinforcements to the garrison.

The orders of the Governor were carried into immediate execution and Major P. F. Stevens, commanding the Citadel Academy, with a detachment of forty cadets and two 24-pounders, was ordered to Morris Island to assist in the erection of the battery. The Vigilant Rifles, under Captain Tucker, numbering ninety-men, were sent at once to the assistance and protection of Major Stevens. The work was soon done, and two 24-pound guns were after some difficulty mounted, protected by the natural sand-

FORT JOHNSON, AS SEEN FROM FORT SUMTER.

hills from the guns of Sumter. Another gun was added, making a battery of three guns, and it was the intention of the Governor to replace them by heavy Columbiads as soon as it was possible to do so. It was this battery, thus constituted, that fired upon the *Star of the West.* But the defensive measures of Governor Pickens were not yet completed. On the same day that orders were issued for the establishment of the batteries on Morris and Sullivan's islands, he directed a force under Colonel Charles Alston, commanding the Thirty-second Regiment, S. C. M., to proceed immediately to the most exposed points between the harbor of Charleston and the North Carolina line, and there, with the assistance of the engineer force, to establish batteries to protect the entrances to the bays and rivers on the coast.

His work was now complete; and he transmitted to the Convention the following communication:

"EXECUTIVE DEPARTMENT,
"28th December, 1860.

"To the Hon. D. F. JAMISON
"President of the Convention.
"Sir: As the Convention sent for me yesterday to be informed upon important matters, I take occasion to say that under my order Castle Pinckney was taken last evening, and the United States flag hauled down, and the Palmetto banner run up in its place; and I also ordered a detachment from an artillery regiment to occupy Sullivan's Island, and, if it could be done without any immediate danger from mines, or too great loss of life, to take Fort Moultrie and run up the Palmetto flag, and to put the guns in immediate preparation for defense. I have now full possession of these two forts. I considered the evacuation of Fort Moultrie, under all the circumstances, a direct violation of the distinct understanding between the authorities of the Government at Washington, and those who were authorized to act on the part of this State, and bringing on a state of war.

"I therefore thought it due to the safety of the State that I should take the steps I have. I hope there is no immediate danger of further aggression for the present.

"Respectfully,
(Signed) "F. W. PICKENS."

Later, in his message to the Legislature on November 5, 1861, he says: "In taking Castle Pinckney, Fort Moultrie and the late United States arsenal, we acquired large supplies of heavy ordnance, arms and munitions of war. As we took the responsibility of acting alone, and of risking all, we were fairly entitled to all we acquired."

CHAPTER XII.

FROM the moment of his entry into Fort Sumter, Major Anderson found himself surrounded by difficulties which he had not anticipated. His movement had been made with so much secrecy and despatch that he was without any supply of fuel; and many minor articles essential to him were wanting. He confesses that there was yet something to do before he should feel independent, as the work was not impregnable, as he had understood it to be. The memorandum of the Governor dissatisfied him, as he considered that he treated him as an enemy; and the suspension of all intercourse with the city, except in the transmission of his mails, in thus depriving him of the opportunity of purchasing fresh provisions, added to his embarrassment. Still, he deemed himself "safe," and he thanked God that he was now where the Government might send him additional troops at its leisure, and that he could command the harbor as long as the Government wished to keep it;

It was now the 6th of January, and Anderson had already begun to assume definite position. He thought that he could hold Fort Sumter against any force which could be brought against him; he was daily increasing the strength of his position, and his command "was in excellent health and in fine spirits." He would not ask for any increase of his command, as he did not know the ulterior views of the Government; but he no less pointedly repeated that he was, or soon would be, cut off from all communication unless the batteries at the mouth of the harbor should be carried by a powerful fleet. His communication was as follows:

126

"FORT SUMTER, S. C., January 6, 1861.
"Col. S. COOPER, *Adjutant-General:*

Colonel: Through the courtesy of Governor Pickens I am enabled to make this communication, which will be taken to Washington by my brother, Larz Anderson, Esq. I have the honor to report my command in excellent health and in fine spirits. We are daily adding to the strength of our position by closing up embrasures which we shall not use, mounting guns, etc. The South Carolinians are also very active in erecting batteries and preparing for a conflict, which I pray God may not occur. Batteries have been constructed bearing upon and, I presume, commanding the entrance to the harbor. They are also to-day busily at work on a battery at Fort Johnson intended to fire against me. My position will, should there be no treachery among the workmen, whom we are compelled to retain for the present, enable me to hold this fort against any force which can be brought against me, and it would enable me, in the event of a war, to annoy the South Carolinians by preventing them from throwing supplies into their new posts except by the out-of-the-way passage though Stono River. At present it would be dangerous and difficult for a vessel from without to enter the harbor, in consequence of the batteries which are already erected and being erected. I shall not ask for any increase of my command, because I do not know what the ulterior views of the Government are. We are now, or soon will be, cut off from all communication, unless by means of a powerful fleet, which shall have the ability to carry the batteries at the mouth of this harbor.

"Trusting in God that nothing will occur to array a greater number of States than have already taken ground against the General Government,

"I am, Colonel, respectfully, your obedient servant,
"ROBERT ANDERSON,
"Major, First Artillery, Commanding."

He explains, too, the reason for his movement to Fort Sumter. "Many things convinced" him that the authorities of the State designed to proceed to a hostile act, and he deemed it to be his solemn duty to move his command from a position which could not have been held more than forty-eight or sixty hours, to one where his power of resistance was greatly increased, and the more he reflected upon the movement he had made, the stronger were his convictions that he was right in making it; that his safety in Fort Moultrie depended only upon the forbearance of the State, while Fort Sumter might have been seized at any moment, and he would then "have been in their power;" and he made the unanswerable argument that if such understanding as was alleged or claimed to have existed between the "two Governments" had any force, the fact of the Governor having ordered armed steamers to keep watch over him, would have released the Government at Washington "from any obligation to remain quiescent." He was convinced, too, that upon the failure of the mission to Washington, an attack would have been made upon him and his command sacrificed. But besides the report to the Government, Major Anderson in private letters has freely set forth the sentiments that controlled his action. Upon the day after his movement to Fort Sumter, he addressed to Mr. Robert N. Gourdin, a prominent citizen of Charleston, a member of the Convention, and with whom he was upon terms of personal intimacy, the following communication, which was read by Mr. Gourdin to the Convention, then in session:

"FORT SUMTER, Charleston, S. C., December 27, 1860.
"My dear Sir : I have only time to say that the movement of my command to this place was made on my own responsibility and not in obedience to orders from Washington. I did it because in my opinion it was the best way of preventing the shedding of blood. God grant that the existing condition of affairs may be adjusted without any resort to force.
"Truly your friend, ROBERT ANDERSON.
The Hon. ROBERT N. GOURDIN."

His friend, however, strongly objected to and condemned the movement, as calculated to complicate and embarrass the condition of things, and so informed Major Anderson; when on the 29th of December Major Anderson replied to him, as follows:

"FORT SUMTER, South Carolina, December   29, 1860.
"My dear Sir: No one will regret more deeply than I shall, should it prove true that the movement I have made has complicated rather than disembarrassed affairs. There is an unaccountable mystery in reference to this affair. I was asked by a gentleman within a day or two, if I had been notified by your Government that I would not be molested at Fort Moultrie, and when I replied that I had not been so notified, he remarked that he was glad to hear it, as it convinced him that I had acted in good faith, having just told him that I had not received such an intimation from my own Government. Now if there was such an understanding, I certainly ought to have been informed of it.
"But why, if your Government thought that I knew of this agreement, was everything done which indicated an intention to attack? Why were armed steamers kept constantly on the watch

for my movements? The papers say that I was under a panic. That is a mistake; the moment I inspected my position I saw that the work was not defensible with my small command, and recommended, weeks ago, that we ought to be withdrawn, I remained, then, as long as I could under the fearful responsibility I felt for the safety of my command, and finally decided on Christmas morning that I would remove the command that day; and it would have been attempted that day if the weather had not proved inauspicious. Not a person of my command knew of my determination until that morning, and only on that day. The captains of the lighters are, I am sorry to see, threatened by the Charlestonians for what they did. I do hope that they will not disgrace themselves by wreaking their wrath upon these men. They were employed to take the women and children, and food for them, to Fort Johnson, and were as innocent in the matter as any one. Another lighter was filled with commissary stores for the workingmen here, and her captain certainly is not blamable for bringing them. Not a soldier came in either of these vessels except the married men with their wives for Fort Johnson, and there was not an arm of any kind permitted to be taken on board those boats.   Only one person on board those boats knew that Fort Johnson was not their final destination, until the signal was given that the command was in Fort Sumter. My men were transferred in our *own* boats, and were all, with the exception of those attached to the hospital, in the fort before 8 o'clock. So much in exoneration of the captains

"I regret that the Governor has deemed proper to treat us as enemies, by cutting off our communication with the city, permitting me only to send for the mails.   Now this is annoying, and I regret it. 'We can do without going to the city, as I have supplies of provisions, of all kinds, to last my command about five months, but it would add to our comfort to be enabled to make purchases of fresh meats and so on, and to shop in the city. The Governor does not know how entirely the commerce and intercourse of Charleston by sea are in my power. I could, if so disposed, annoy and embarrass the Charlestonians much more than they can me. With my guns I can close the harbor completely to the access of all large vessels, and I might even cut off the lights, so as to seal the approach entirely by night. I do hope that nothing will occur to add to the excitement and bad feeling which exists in the city.   No one has a right to be angry with me for my action.   No one can tell what they would have done unless they were placed in the same tight place. . . . I write this note hurriedly, as I wish to acknowledge the receipt of your kind note, and to assure you that I am firmly convinced that, had you been in my place, and known no more of the political bearing of things than I did, you would have acted as I did. I know that if my action was properly explained to the people of

Charleston, they would not feel any excitement against me or my command.

"Praying that the time may soon come, etc.,

"ROBERT ANDERSON."

Upon the following day he wrote to his former rector at Trenton, N. J., the Rev. R. B. Duane, informing him of his movement and of his reasons for making it. His letter was as follows:

"FORT SUMTER, S. C,
"December 30, 1860.

"My dear Sir: Your most welcome letter of the 26th of December, received to-day, finds me, as you see, at Fort Sumter. God has been pleased to hear our prayers, and has removed me to this stronghold. Perhaps at the very moment you were writing to me I was by His guidance leading my little band across to this place. I left Fort Moultrie between 5 and 6 P. M., and had my command here by 8 o'clock the same evening. You say that you had marvelled that I had not been ordered to hold Fort Sumter instead of Fort Moultrie. Much has been said about my having come here on my own responsibility. Unwilling to see my little band sacrificed, I determined, after earnestly awaiting instructions as long as I could, to avail myself of the earliest opportunity of extricating myself from my dangerous position. God be praised! He gave me the will and led me in the way. How I do wish that you could have looked down upon us when we threw the stars and stripes to the breeze, at 12 o'clock on the 27th! . . .

"I am now, thank God, in a place which will, by His helping, soon be made so strong that the South Carolinians will be madmen if they attack me. There are some alterations and some additions which I wish to have made. The Governor of this State has interdicted all intercourse with the city except that of sending and receiving letters, so that you see we are *quasi* enemies. Were I disposed to declare myself independent of, to secede from, the General Government and retaliate, I could cut Charleston off from her supplies, but I will show him that I am more of a Christian than to make the innocent suffer for the petty conduct of their Governor.

"ROBERT ANDERSON.

"You see it stated that I came here without orders. Fear not! I am sure I can satisfy any tribunal I may be brought before, that I was fully justified in moving my command."

Work upon the fort was at once resumed, the mounting of the guns commenced, and the closing of the embrasures in the second tier rapidly pushed forward.

When occupied by Major Anderson's command on the night

of the 26th of December, Fort Sumter was in no condition for defense.

There were but three 24-pounders mounted on the left of the upper or barbette tier, which however was ready for its armament. The second tier was wholly incomplete, without embrasures, and with forty-one openings eight feet square left in the wall. Twenty were closed with one-inch boards; twenty-one were open, or partially closed only by dry brick. There was but one gun, and that for experimental purposes, yet mounted on that tier. On the lower tier, eleven 32-pounders had been mounted, and the posterns in the angles closed. The barracks for the men were unfinished, but, where tenable, were occupied by workmen. The officers' quarters were completed, and were occupied by the garrison. A large number of wooden structures crowded the parade. They were of the most temporary character and served as storehouses for the tools and material of the workmen, while all over the parade lay sand and rough masonry, and sixty-six guns with their carriages and 5,600 shot and shell. The main entrance was closed by double gates secured by bars, but they were insecure and weak. The seven loop-holed doors in the gorge were closed, as were also twelve ventilators of the magazine.

Material for the construction of the work around the wharf and esplanade greatly obstructed the movements of the garrison. Work, however, was at once pushed with great vigor, and especially with reference to the armament. Under the instructions of Major Anderson, the defense was to be limited to the upper and lower tiers, where guns were to be immediately mounted. On the lower tier, guns were to be mounted at the angles only, and the remaining openings and those of the entire second tier were to be "permanently and securely" closed. The transferrence of the command of Fort Moultrie to Fort Sumter produced an alarm among the workmen. It was supposed by them that an attack upon the fort was imminent. They had previously resolved that they would take no part in any conflict, and many claimed their discharge. Of the laborers at work when the command occupied Fort Sumter, many were discharged within a few days. The report had spread that an attempt had been made to force these men into the military service of the Government, and to detain them against their will at Fort Sumter, and the Governor of the State had asked for information upon the subject. No such course had been pursued or been contemplated at Fort Sumter, although Major Anderson had felt himself compelled to retain some of them. The employees of the Engineer Department remained or were discharged, as they elected to do. Many that left the work added to the excitement in the city, by false representations of what was transpiring in Fort Sumter. The force now under the command of Major Anderson consisted of ten officers, seventy-six enlisted men, forty-five women and children, and with a gradually lessening force of laborers, their number was reduced to fifty-five, at which point it remained until the work

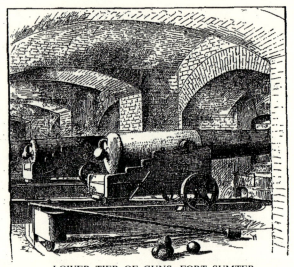

LOWER TIER OF GUNS, FORT SUMTER.

fell. Intercourse with Charleston had not yet been officially suspended; and on the 29th of December Captain Seymour visited the city. There was no opposition to the landing of his boat. He described the feeling, of the people as intensely excited against Major Anderson, and expressed his conviction that we would he at once attacked. On the 30th all communication with the city was cut off, and no supplies of any description allowed to go to the fort, the Governor having declined to change or modify his order. Storm and rain had now set in, and for several days the fort was enveloped in fog, and under its cover and concealment the work was pushed rapidly on. Every effort was made to hasten its armament. Three guns were mounted in the angles of the work on the 30th, and Major Anderson considered that in a "week longer" he would he fully prepared for any attack that might be made.

Meantime, increased activity was visible in the harbor. Small steamers with troops and laborers were passing to and fro, and men and material landed on Morris Island and preparations made for remounting the guns at Fort Moultrie and strengthening its parapet towards Fort Sumter. The harbor lights on Sullivan's and on Morris islands were put out on the night of the 20th, leaving the one upon Sumter and that upon the light-ship in the offing the only lights in the harbor.

On the 5th of January the wife of Captain Foster, with her sister, left the work to proceed to Washington. There was no detention at the island, to which they had crossed in a small boat. No communication was allowed with them, and they were told that they must decide upon remaining either at Fort Sumter or at the island altogether. To the surprise of the garrison, the wife of Major Anderson came down to the fort, with the permission of the authorities, accompanied by her brother, Mr. Bayard Clinch, Mr. Larz Anderson, and Mr. Robert Gourdin, a member of the Convention. She was still an invalid, and had left New York alone to come to Charleston. The intelligence they brought impressed the garrison with the fact that the secession of South Carolina was about to be followed by that of other Southern States. The fact of the vote in the House of Representatives sustaining Major Anderson, was greatly gratifying to him. At 4 o'clock the party returned to Charleston.

Upon the return of his brother to Washington, Major Anderson was permitted by Governor Pickens to communicate with his Government.

On the morning of the 8th of January, by a boat that brought down some men of the Engineer Department, a newspaper was received, and in it was the announcement that the *Star of the West* was to sail with reinforcements for Fort Sumter, and would arrive on the night of the 8th. The information was not credited, as it was believed that any reinforcements for the work would necessarily be sent in a vessel of war, and in this view Major Anderson coincided.

The greatest activity was meanwhile manifested. The

defenseless and exposed condition of the work so plainly invited an assault, that the earlier efforts of the garrison were directed to meet it, should one be made.

Projecting galleries (Machicouli) were erected upon the parapet, to be used in dropping shells and hand-grenades. Stands of grape and canister were carried to the parapet, and barrels containing fragments of rock in which a loaded shell had been embedded, to be used in repelling an assault, were placed at intervals near the galleries.* The scarcity of fuel began already to be felt, and it became at once necessary to restrict its issue. But one fire was allowed to the officers and one to the hospital; none were permitted in the quarters. The mess of the officers was moved to the kitchen, where they were to be served last. To add to the restrictions imposed upon the garrison, the mail of the 1st of January brought an order from the Governor withdrawing the permission heretofore given for the transmission of the mails, and prohibiting all communication between the fort and the city. Events now followed each other with rapidity. The inspector of light-houses, Captain Hunter, of the United States Navy, was ordered to leave the State and his vessel seized.

On the 1st of January a large force of men were landed on Cumming's Point, the part of Morris Island nearest Fort Sumter, and distant only 1,200 yards. The light-ship was towed in on the same day, thus leaving the harbor in darkness, except the solitary light upon Fort Sumter.

The light upon Rattlesnake Shoals, which was burning until 3 o'clock on the morning of the 1st, was at the signal of rockets extinguished.

It was reported that the steamer *Harriet Lane* was coming to Charleston to collect the revenue, and that reinforcements were also to be sent, and it was mainly upon the strength of this report that the lights were extinguished in the harbor by the authorities. Major Anderson, to whom the writer carried the report, was greatly cheered by it: we were not to be returned to Fort Moultrie, and he was sustained in his action. There was also great unanimity of sentiment among the officers, who, in the activity and energy dis-played, were ready to do their whole duty.

The position was gradually growing stronger. Where no guns

*A suggestion of Captain Seymour.

were to be mounted, the embrasures were filled with masonry and the shutters secured by strong iron bars, and such of the loop-holes for musketry as were not to be used were closely planked up. Heavy guns, 32 and 42 pounders, were now in position in the pan coupes, at either flank of the gorge. The men worked cheerfully and willingly from morning till night. Inside of the fort a feeling prevailed that an attack was imminent, while upon the part of the State authorities it was anticipated that an attempt would be made by the Government to reinforce the work, and immediate preparations were made by each with reference to their special convictions. Sentinels were placed on the parapet and over the batteries

CLOSING AN EMBRASURE WHERE GUN NOT USED.

below, and every effort was made by Major Anderson to place in position a heavy Columbiad. But the want of sufficient or proper tackle greatly delayed the work, and it soon became apparent that the neglect to transfer the proper material for moving and equipping the large ordnance would seriously embarrass and delay the prompt and efficient arming of the work. On the 2d of January assignments of the officers to command the batteries now mounted were made. The guns, consisting of three 32-pounders at the southeast angle, were placed under the command of Captain Doubleday, while the battery at the southwest angle was assigned to Captain T. Seymour. Preparations were now made to hoist the heavy guns to the parapet.

The excitement in the city seemed to increase, and every one that came to the fort brought reports of its existence and intensity. The Governor had determined to isolate the fort entirely, and its garrison was subjected to many petty annoyances. A brother of Major Anderson had come to Charleston to visit him at the fort. He was permitted to go to Fort Sumter accompanied by Mr. Robert Gourdin and Mr. Alfred Huger, with the understanding that the interview should take place in the presence of these gentlemen. This interview produced a depressing effect upon Major Anderson, who thought that nothing could now prevent a conflict. A fact, too, was made known that caused him great anxiety. It was discovered that there were short rations of sugar and coffee, and but thirty or forty barrels of flour on hand. The effect of the hasty movement from Fort Moultrie was still felt. The private property of Captains Foster and Seymour had not yet been permitted to come to them, although a promise to that effect had been made, both by the Governor and the commanding officer of the island. In order to secure it these officers crossed directly to Fort Moultrie on the 4th instant, where they were arrested by order of General Donovant, and it was proposed to send them to the Governor. Representing that this would be an act of war, as force must be used, they were finally allowed to return without accomplishing the object of their mission, the officer in command informing them that his orders were positive.* The contents of the Engineer office, with the record-books, instruments, and maps containing detailed information of the forts and the harbor, were seized in Charleston, while the former clerk of the engineer in charge, J. Legare, having been appointed one of the construction engineers on Morris Island, passed into the service of the State, with much of the valuable information acquired in his former position. Great energy was now displayed upon all sides.

On the 6th there was increased activity at Fort Johnson, and a mortar battery was commenced in front of the old barracks, on the western shore, belonging to the Government, to bear directly upon Fort Sumter.

Traverses were begun on the parapet of Fort Moultrie, and

---

* The effects of these officers were not removed until the 23d of March. Charleston *Mercury,* March 25, 1861.

experimental firing commenced at that work and from the battery on Morris Island. Steamers were plying between the fort and the batteries at all hours, conveying men and ammunition. A code of signals had been adopted, which was put in constant practice. Permanent garrisons were at once provided for the forts that had been seized. A detachment of infantry and twenty men of an artillery company under Captain King occupied Castle Pinckney, and Lieutenants Gibbs and Reynolds, graduates of West Point, who had resigned their positions in the army, were also assigned to that post to instruct the men. Lieutenant-Colonel De Saussure, with a detachment of 170 men from an artillery regiment and thirty men from Colonel Pettigrew's rifle regiment, occupied Fort Moultrie, with a force of engineers, to protect the heavy guns that commanded the Maffit Channel from the fire of Fort Sumter. Points for batteries on Sullivan's and Morris islands for heavy guns had been selected, and the work vigorously pushed forward to guard the harbor" at those points, and "to prevent reinforcement to the garrison in Fort Sumter."* Officers (Lieutenant I. R. Hamilton, Wade H. Gibbes, H. S. Farley, James Hamilton, George N. Reynolds, Jr.), and among them cadets of West Point, who had entered the service of the State, were sent down to assist in directing and managing the guns of large calibre to be placed in these batteries; and they were also authorized, in connection with the commanding officer of Fort Moultrie, to procure and sink any vessels in a proper place in the channel, that might aid and assist in preventing reinforcements from entering the harbor.†

But before taking this important step, however, it was deemed advisable to consult the Board of Pilots on duty in the harbor, and a conference was held between them and the Executive Council on the 3d of January. The Board advised that at least six vessels or hulks should be sunk in the channels, effectually to obstruct the entrance of vessels drawing twelve feet or over, which was done on the 11th of January.

In the midst of the execution of these orders intelligence was received by the Government from the South Carolina Commissioners at Washington, that the *Harriet Lane* had sailed, that

---

* Pickens's orders to General Schnierle, December 21, 1861. Record of Fort Sumter. Columbia, 1862.

† Pickens to Lieutenant-Colonel De Saussure, December 31, 1860.

her destination was probably Fort Sumter, and that she would be off the bar on the night of the 1st. The Governor was prompt to act. Despatching a competent officer with a force of artillerists to the commanding officer of Fort Moultrie, he informs him that he had anticipated his want as to the management of the large guns, and had sent this force to his assistance, as the time was short, and that he deemed it of the *last* importance to sustain themselves in the first fight.

Upon the same day the Governor communicates with Major-General Schnierle, the commandant of the forces in the harbor and vicinity, directing him to order Captain N. L. Coste or other officer in command of the cutter *Aiken* to proceed to such point as may be expedient, to overhaul all vessels, and to arrest all those that attempted to bring reinforcements or supplies of any kind for the United States troops at Fort Sumter; and he was to "deliver such vessel, reinforcements and supplies to Lieutenant-Colonel W. G. De Saussure or other officer in command of Sullivan's Island." On the following day the chief pilot (Carnagan) was ordered to take a vessel and occupy a position off or near the bar of Charleston immediately, and in case of the approach of any public vessel of the United States or any vessel bearing aid or supplies to the United States garrison at Fort Sumter, or in any way intending to exercise authority or jurisdiction in any manner in the waters, he was to warn them off in the most decided manner," and to hand them the following proclamation.

"HEADQUARTERS, 1st January, 1861.

"Be it known, to all concerned, that a state of things exists which makes it my duty to warn all public vessels of the United States or any vessel bearing aid and supplies to the garrison at Fort Sumter, or in any way directed to exercise any authority whatever in the waters of South Carolina, that they are hereby forbid to do so, and to abstain from entering especially the harbor of Charleston.

"Given under my hand and the seal of the State, the day and year aforesaid:
(Signed)   "F. W. PICKENS,
*Gov. and Comm'r in Ch'f in and over
the State of South Carolina.*"

The destination of the *Harriet Lane* was not Fort Sumter, nor the harbor of Charleston; but the conviction that an expedition of some kind, either hostile or pacific, was on foot, and that its object was to change or modify the existing condition of things in the harbor of Charleston, remained, and the greatest anxiety was manifested by the Governor of the State and his subordinates, and the greatest vigor shown in pushing forward to completion the works undertaken to prevent the success of such expedition.

Men and material were moved daily from point to point in the harbor without any attempt at concealment. On the 3d of January the Governor of the State again addressed the commandant of Fort Moultrie. He informed him that "recent news seemed to indicate" that a vessel of war of the United States would enter the harbor; that she might not have reinforcements on board, and her object might be pacific, and that she might be intended to collect the revenue only. If this could be ascertained, "the immediate necessity of firing upon her" might not be so great, but if she had reinforcements, "there could be no doubt that there must be all proper exertions made to prevent the reinforcements — *let the consequences be what they may.*"

General Donovant was directed to put himself in communication with the pilot captain on watch at the bar, and to ascertain the facts in regard to the vessel. An expedition, however, had meantime been prepared, and had sailed from New York on the night of the 5th inst. Information had been communicated by telegram to Governor Pickens, who considered that every precaution had been taken, and who awaited the result. To complete, however, his arrangements, and to leave no step untaken, he finally transmitted orders to Colonel John Cunningham, commanding the arsenal in Charleston, to take 300 picked riflemen "fully armed with the best rifles and at least 100 best artillery sabres," to proceed to the steamship *Marion,* and put his men under the hatches until he passed Fort Sumter. He was to proceed to the bar, and if possible prevent the *Star of the West* or any other vessel from passing reinforcements to Fort Sumter, and in consultation with Captain Hamilton, of the South Carolina Navy, they were to settle the proper time for boarding. Captain Hamilton received similar instructions, and was required to exercise the greatest precaution, and "the most decided and prompt action" that might be necessary to prevent supplies to Fort Sumter. A constant exchange of signals was made by day and night between the city, the temporary batteries and the vessels on duty in the harbor, and every means at the disposal of the State was resorted to in order to prevent relief from reaching the garrison of Fort Sumter.

CHAPTER XIII.

Washington–Effect of Anderson's movement–False report of reinforcement–
Telegram of Governor–Reply of Secretary of War–Commissioners appointed by Convention–Arrive in Washington–President appoints day to
receive them–Arrangement made by agent of South Carolina–News of
Anderson's movement changes the relations–Statement in detail of agent
of the State–President urged to restore the status–He declines–Anderson's movement without his orders–Secretary of War telegraphs to Anderson–Anderson's reply confirming report–President's action–Cabinet
convened–Discussion–Copy of order by Major Buell sent for–South Carolina Commissioners–Interview with the President–They transmit their
letter of authority from the Convention–Demand explanation of Anderson's movement–President receives Commissioners–Promises reply–President submits draft of letter to his Cabinet, who are divided in opinion–
Northern members threaten resignation–No conclusion reached–Secretary of War Floyd tenders his resignation–Correspondence with the
President–Secretary of State, Judge Black, determines to resign if letter is
sent–President informed–Interview with Judge Black–Question of personal honor urged by the President–Commits draft of letter to Judge
Black, who comments upon it–President's letter to Commissioners–Their
action–Mr. Trescot, the agent of the State, interviews the President–Subsequently sees Mr. Hunter, of Virginia–Offers through him that the State
would withdraw from the forts if the President would withdraw Anderson
from Sumter–President declines–Attorney-General Stanton's opinion–
President yields, and sides with the Union sentiment.

THE news of Anderson's movement had been promptly carried
to Washington, and, as might have been anticipated, produced
an effect immediate and startling. Unexpected as it was to the
President or his Cabinet, it forced the issue upon them so strongly
as to define their individual positions finally, and with great
distinctness.

Meanwhile the difficulties continued to increase. The Assistant Secretary of State, having resigned his position, had consented,
upon the urgent request of the Governor, to become the agent of
the State, and he was soon called upon to act in that capacity.
On the 23d a telegram from Governor Pickens was received by
him to the effect that Governor Pickens had been informed that
thirteen men had arrived in Charleston and reported that they

140

were sent to Fort Moultrie, and were a part of a body of 150 who were to follow; and he desired to know immediately if it was intended to reinforce the forts or to transfer any force from Fort Moultrie to Fort Sumter. He asked for a "clear answer immediately;" and he says, "Until the Commissioners shall negotiate at Washington, there can be no change here." The agent at once called upon Governor Floyd. "The Governor was evidently becoming impatient under the embarrassments of his position, for it was difficult to be accountable to the President on the one hand and to the State of South Carolina on the other. He had done everything that a man in his situation could do to prove his good faith, and he felt, very naturally, that the difficulties of his position ought to be appreciated, and that explanations and pledges, perhaps inconsistent with his duties, should not be pressed except under the very gravest necessity. It was, moreover, a matter of great moment that in this juncture Governor Floyd should retain his place in the Cabinet as long as possible, and every step he took or did not take was watched and misrepresented, for no man at the South was more cordially detested by the Black Republican party. Governor Floyd told me to reply to the Governor that there was not the slightest foundation for any alarm, that he knew nothing of any such men, and any statement to such an effect was a sheer fabrication, made, he must suppose, for purposes of mischief. As for the removal of troops to Sumter, he could not see any likelihood of it; that he did not think it necessary to send special orders to that end to Major Anderson, for he could not consider it at all probable; and that, in fact, he thought any such contingency provided against by orders already sent, to which he did not feel at liberty to refer more specially; that the Commissioners must soon be in Washington, and that he could see no rational ground for anticipating premature difficulty. I thought this as far, really, as he could go, and that to press upon him or the President more positive action was to risk the advantage that continued delay on the part of the Government was giving to the State. I therefore telegraphed the Governor the contradiction he authorized, and waited with anxiety the arrival of the Commissioners."

The expressions of the Secretary of War were transmitted to Governor Pickens, and everything now awaited the anticipated arrival of the Commissioners from South Carolina. On the 20th the Convention had passed the Ordinance of Secession, and on the 22d of December the Governor of the State transmitted the following telegram to his agent in Washington:

"Sir: The Hon. R. W. Barnwell, the Hon. J. H. Adams and the Hon. James L. Orr have been appointed Commissioners by the Convention to proceed immediately to Washington to present the Ordinance of Secession to the President, and to negotiate in reference to the evacuation of the forts and other matters growing out of the Act of Secession. They will probably arrive on Tuesday next. Please inform the President of this. Answer this,   (Signed)   "F. W. PICKENS.
"Hon. W. H. TRESCOT."

The information was immediately carried to the President by Mr. Trescot. The President inquired as to the character of the appointments, expressed his readiness to receive them, and his determination to refer them to Congress.

On Wednesday, the 26th of December, the Commissioners arrived in Washington, and their arrival was communicated at once to the President by the agent of the State. Judge Black, who had now entered upon his duties as Secretary of State, was present, and the subject was spoken of informally, and the President appointed 1 o'clock on the following day, the 27th of December, as the hour when it would be agreeable to him to receive the Commissioners.

He was told by the agent of the State that the Commissioners proposed to present their credentials and have an informal conversation with him, but that if it was his intention to submit the question of their reception to Congress, they wished to submit a written communication to accompany his message. If, however, the President should agree in thinking it the better course, the Commissioners would not prepare the paper until after the interview with him, when they would better understand one another, but in that case it was to be considered that the communication was submitted at the interview. To this the President consented, and matters were approaching some definite solution, when Anderson made his sudden and unexpected movement from Fort Moultrie to Fort Sumter. The news arrived in Washington, at once wholly changing the relations of the parties and altering the whole character of the negotiation.

"The next morning early, I was at the residence of the Commissioners, and while talking over the condition of affairs, Colonel Wigfall, one of the Senators from Texas, came in to inform us that the telegraph had just brought the news that Major Anderson had abandoned Fort Moultrie, spiked his guns, burned his gun-carriages, cut down the flag-staff and removed his command to Fort Sumter. We all expressed our disbelief of the intelligence, and after a good deal of discussion as to its probability I said, 'Well, at any rate, Colonel, true or not, I will pledge my life, if it has been done, it has been without orders from Washington.' Just as I made the remark Governor Floyd was announced. After the usual courtesies of meeting I said, 'Governor, Colonel Wigfall has just brought us this news—repeating it—and as you were coming up-stairs I said I would pledge my life it was without orders.' 'You can do more,' he said, smiling, 'You can pledge your life, Mr. Trescot, that it is not so. It is impossible. It would be not only without orders, but in the face of orders. To be very frank, Anderson was instructed in case he had to abandon his position to dismantle *Fort Sumter,* not Fort Moultrie.' I asked him, if his carriage was at the door, to let me take it and go home, as there might be telegrams there. I went, and in a few minutes returned with two telegrams for Colonel Barnwell, which he read and handed to Governor Floyd, saying, 'I am afraid, Governor, it is too true.' Floyd read them, asked the Commissioners if the authority was sufficient, and made no comment, but rose, saying, 'I must go to the Department at once.'

"As soon as he had left I drove to the Capitol, communicated the intelligence to Senator Davis, of Mississippi, and Senator Hunter, of Virginia, and asked them to accompany me to the President. We drove to the White House, sent in our names, and were asked into the President's room, where he joined us in a few moments. When we came in he was evidently nervous, and immediately commenced the conversation by making some remark to Mr. Hunter concerning the removal of the consul at Liverpool, to which Mr. Hunter made a general reply. Colonel Davis then said, 'Mr. President, we have called upon an infinitely graver matter than any consulate.' 'What is it?' said the President. 'Have you received any intelligence from Charleston in the last few hours? asked Colonel Davis. 'None,' said the President. 'Then,' said Colonel Davis, 'I have a great calamity to announce to you.' He then stated the facts, and added, 'And

now, Mr. President, you are surrounded with blood and dishonor
on all sides." The President was standing by the mantel-piece,
crushing up a cigar in the palm of one hand—a habit I have seen
him practice often. He sat down as Colonel Davis finished, and
exclaimed, 'My God, are calamities (or misfortunes, I forget
which) never to come singly! I call God to witness, you gentlemen,
better than anybody, *know* that this is not only without but against
my orders. It is against my policy.' He then expressed his
doubt of the truth of the telegram, thought it strange that nothing
had been heard at the War Department, said he had not seen
Governor Floyd, and finally sent a messenger for him. When
Governor Floyd came, he said no news had come to the Department, that the heads of the Bureaus there thought it unlikely, but
that he had telegraphed Major Anderson to this effect himself.
'There is a report here that you have abandoned Fort Moultrie,
spiked your guns, burned your carriages and gone to Fort Sumter.
It is not believed, as you had no orders to justify it. Say at once
what could have given rise to such a story.'

"The President was urged to take immediate action; he was
told the probability was that the remaining forts and the arsenal
would be seized and garrisoned by South Carolina, and that Fort
Sumter would be attacked; that if he would only say that he
would replace matters as he had pledged himself that they should
remain, there was yet time to remedy the mischief. The discussion was long and earnest. At first he seemed disposed to
declare that he would restore the status, then hesitated, said he
must call his Cabinet together; he could not condemn Major
Anderson unheard. He was told that nobody asked that; only
say that *if* the move had been made without a previous attack
on Anderson he would restore the status. Assure us of that
determination, and then take what time was necessary for consultation and information. That resolution telegraphed would
restore confidence and enable the Commissioners to continue
their negotiation. This he declined doing, and after adjourning
his appointment to receive the Commissioners until the next day
we left. On our way out we met General Lane, Senators Bigler,
Mallory, Yulie, and some others on their way to make the same
remonstrance, for the news was over the city. Later in the day I
saw him again, to show him some telegrams fuller in details.
Senator Slidell was with him, but all that he did was to authorize

me to telegraph that Anderson's movement was not only without but against his orders."

The following is the actual text of the telegrams that passed:

"WAR DEPARTMENT,
"ADJUTANT-GENERAL'S OFFICE,
"December 27, 1860.

"Intelligence has reached here this morning that you have abandoned Fort Moultrie, spiked your guns, burned the carriages and gone to Fort Sumter.

"It is not believed, because there is no order for any such movement. Explain the meaning of this report.

(Signed) "J. B. FLOYD,
"Secretary of War."

The reply of Major Anderson was immediate. He said:

"CHARLESTON, December 27, 1860.

"The telegram is correct. I abandoned Fort Moultrie because I was certain that, if attacked, my men must have been sacrificed, and the command of the harbor lost. I spiked the guns and destroyed the carriages to keep the guns from being used against us. If attacked, the garrison would never have surrendered without a fight.

(Signed) "ROBERT ANDERSON,
"Major First Artillery.
"Hon J. B. FLOYD, *Secretary of War."*

What had just been made known had occasioned the President astonishment and regret. He had believed that Major Anderson was safe in his position, and that the coming of the Commissioners would determine the solution of the difficulty, by whatever action Congress should see fit to take. The movement of Major Anderson would, he feared, so excite the sympathy of the cotton and border States, that South Carolina would no longer be alone in her act of secession; that the measures of compromise yet pending before the Committee of Thirteen of the Senate would be suspended or defeated, and that in his hope to confine secession to the State of South Carolina alone he would be disappointed. But before he would take any positive action, he determined to await "official information" from Major Anderson himself. He could not, under his instructions, have made such a movement as was attributed to him unless he had the "tangible evidence" of an impending attack upon him, and of this there was as yet no proof.

The Cabinet was called together immediately. As the members assembled, Major Buell, who had carried the orders to Major Anderson, and who had been sent for by the Secretary of War, now joined him in the hall of the President's mansion. The Secretary at once accosted him. "This is a very unfortunate move of Major Anderson," said he; "it has made war inevitable." "I do not think so, sir," replied Major Buell; "on the contrary, I think that it will tend to avert war, if war can be averted." "But," said the Secretary, "it has compromised the President." But little else was said, and Major Buell was left uncertain as to the object of his summons. As the members proceeded to the room the criticisms upon Anderson's movement were severe and general.

All seemed to think that he had acted without orders. Secretary Floyd was loudly condemnatory of Anderson's action. He had disobeyed his instructions; there was no reason for his movement, and he had broken a definitely understood agreement without any authority for it. The existence of the orders of the 11th of December, transmitted to Major Anderson by Major Buell, seemed to be ignored or forgotten, when the attention of the Cabinet was promptly called to them by the Secretary of State, Judge Black. He claimed, as he clearly stated, that Anderson had acted wholly within the purview of his instructions, and in accordance with his orders; referring pointedly to the orders sent to him on the 11th of December. He suggested that the order should be sent for to the War Department, when it was produced and again read in the presence of the President and Cabinet. The paper itself contained the endorsement of the Secretary of War, affirming its correctness; and so completely had it been forgotten by the President, who possibly had regarded it as a matter of routine only, that in his reply to the letter of the Commissioners on the 31st of December he stated that the order had been issued to Major Anderson on the 11th of December, but that it had not been brought to his notice until the 21st of that month. Although this important order involved to a greater degree than any other consideration the question of peace or war to the country, the President of the United States was for ten days wholly ignorant of its existence.

On the 20th of December the Commissioners had their first and only interview with the President. He received them courteously and as private gentlemen alone. He listened to their statement, but informed them that it was to Congress they must look, at the same time expressing his willingness to lay before Congress any "propositions" they might make to him. They were excited during the interview, the action of Major Anderson having added greatly to the feeling already existing. They had come to Washington to find the Cabinet divided upon the question most important to themselves.

A letter had been prepared setting forth the authority for their mission, their purposes and views, but in accordance with a previous understanding, already stated, this letter was not presented at the interview with the President, but transmittted to him on the morning of the following day, the 29th. In this letter they transmitted to him a copy of the full powers from the Convention of the people of South Carolina, under which they were: "Authorized and empowered to treat with the Government of the United States for the delivery of the forts, magazines, lighthouses, and other real estate; with their appurtenances, within the limits of South Carolina, and also for an apportionment of the public debt, and for a division of all other property held by the Government of the United States as agent of the confederated States, of which South Carolina was recently a member." They were also to negotiate in reference to all proper measures and arrangements required by the existing relations of the parties, and for the "continuance of peace and amity." In the performance of their trust, they presented an official copy of the Ordinance of Secession, by which, as their letter stated, the State of South Carolina had resumed the powers delegated by her to the General Government, and had declared her "perfect sovereignty and independence."

They would have been ready to enter upon the negotiation of all questions thus raised, with the desire of an amicable adjustment, but the events of the last twenty-four hours rendered such assurance impossible. An officer of the United States, acting not only without but against the orders of the President, had dismantled one fort and occupied another, which could at any time during the last sixty days have been taken by the State "but which, upon pledges given in a manner that they could not doubt," determined to trust to the "honor of the President, rather than its own power."

Until an explanation should be made which should relieve them from all doubt as to the spirit in which the negotiations should be conducted, they would suspend all discussion as to an amicable adjustment, and they closed their communication by urging upon the President the immediate withdrawal of the troops from the harbor of Charleston, "as they were a standing menace which rendered negotiations impossible and threatened a bloody issue."

This interview between the President and the Commissioners from South Carolina lasted nearly two hours, and is important, as showing the wavering position of the President at that time, as well as the determined course of the State. "The Honorable R. W. Barnwell acted as the chairman of the Commission. He brought to the attention of the President the arrangement which had been made early in December, between him and the South Carolina delegation; that it had been observed in good faith by the people of South Carolina, who could at any time, after the arrangement was made, up to the night when Major Anderson removed to Sumter, have occupied Fort Sumter and captured Moultrie with all its command; that the removal of Anderson violated that agreement on the part of the Government of the United States, and that the faith of the President and the Government had been thereby forfeited. The President made various excuses why he should be allowed time to decide the question whether Anderson should be ordered back to Moultrie and the former status restored. Mr. Barnwell pressed him with great zeal and earnestness to issue the order at once. Mr. Buchanan still hesitating, Mr. Barnwell said to him, at least three times during the interview:* "But, Mr. President, your personal honor is involved in this matter; the faith you pledged has been violated; and your personal honor requires you to issue the order." Mr. Barnwell pressed him so hard upon this point that the President said: "You must give me time to consider—this is a grave question." Mr. Barnwell replied to him for the third time: "But, Mr. President, your personal honor is involved in this arrangement." Whereupon Mr. Buchanan, with great earnestness, said: "Mr. Barnwell, you are pressing me too importunately; you don't give me time to consider; you don't give me time to say my prayers. I always say my prayers when required to act upon any

---

*Letter of the Hon. James L. Orr to writer, September 21, 1871. Mr. Orr was one of the Commissioners, and was present at the interview.

great State affair." The interview terminated without eliciting an order from the President to restore the status of the troops in Charleston Harbor.

The President received the letter of the Commissioners courteously, and promised a reply, which he wrote, and the draft of which he presented to his Cabinet the same day. He had early called his advisers together on the 27th, after the intelligence of Anderson's movement had reached Washington, and their sessions were repeated by day and night, but they were so divided in sentiment, that they were upon the point of separation themselves. The Cabinet at this period consisted of Judge Black, Secretary of State; Phil. F. Thomas, Secretary of the Treasury; Jacob Thompson, Secretary of the Interior; Joseph Holt, Postmaster-General; John B. Floyd, Secretary of War; Toucey, Secretary of the Navy; and Edwin M. Stanton, Attorney-General. But the differences of opinion were as conspicuous in the new as in the old Cabinet, and when the President, on the evening of the 29th of December, submitted to his advisers the paper he had prepared in reply to the Commissioners from South Carolina, but one member, Mr. Toucey, wholly approved it. Of the six remaining members, three, Judge Black, Mr. Holt and Mr. Stanton, suggested changes in the paper, holding that, from its unguarded language, it was open to the criticism of seeming to make concessions, which it could not be the purpose of the President or his Cabinet to make. The President made no reply, but, as was his custom, took the suggestions under consideration. The three remaining members, Mr. Thompson, Mr. Thomas and Mr. Floyd, opposed it because it yielded too little to the demands of the Commissioners. Such consideration as was then given to the paper having led to no special determination before the adjournment of the Cabinet, the Secretary of War, Mr. Floyd, produced a paper that he had prepared, and, in a "discourteous and excited tone," read in the presence of the President and his Cabinet a recommendation that the troops in Charleston Harbor should be withdrawn.

The tenor of this paper caused the President great astonishment. The Secretary followed it by his resignation on the following morning, the 30th, offering at the same time to continue in office until the appointment of his successor. His resignation, which had been called for by the President as long before as the 23d of December, was at once accepted without reference to the offer made, and Postmaster-General Holt was appointed Secretary of War, and entered at once upon the duties of his office.

The change was at once reported to Charleston by Senator Wigfall, of Texas, who telegraphed on the 2d of January to the Hon. M. L. Bonham, Charleston, South Carolina: "Holt succeeds Floyd. It means war. Cut off supplies from Anderson and take Sumter as soon as possible."*

The correspondence with the President was as follows:

"WAR DEPARTMENT,
"December 29, 1860.

"Sir: On the morning of the 27th inst. I read the following paper to you in the presence of the Cabinet, in the Council Chamber of the Executive Mansion.

"'Sir: It is evident now, from the action of the commander of Fort Moultrie, that the solemn pledges of the Government have been violated by Major Anderson.

"In my judgment but one remedy is now left us, by which to vindicate our honor and prevent civil war. It is in vain now to hope for confidence on the part of the people of South Carolina in any further pledges as to the action of the military. One remedy only is left, and it is to withdraw the garrison from the harbor of Charleston altogether. I hope that the President will allow me to make that order at once. This order, in my judgment, can alone prevent bloodshed and civil war.

(Signed)   " 'JOHN B. FLOYD,
"'*Secretary of War.*

" 'TO THE PRESIDENT.'

"I then considered the honor of the administration pledged to maintain the troops in the position they occupied, for such had been the assurance given to gentlemen of South Carolina who had the right to speak for her.   South Carolina, on the other hand, gave reciprocal pledges that no force should be brought by them against the troops or against the property of the United States. The sole object of both parties to these reciprocal pledges was to prevent a collision and the effusion of blood, in the hope that some means might be found for a peaceful accommodation of existing troubles, the two Houses of Congress having both raised Committees looking to that object. Thus affairs stood until Major Anderson's step—unfortunately taken while Congress was striving, while Commissioners were on their way to this Capital on a peaceful commission looking to the avoidance of bloodshed—has complicated matters in the existing manner. Our refusal or even our delay to place affairs back as they stood under our agreement, invites a collision and must inevitably inaugurate civil war. I can-

* War of the Rebellion, page 252. Telegram.

not consent to be the agent of such a calamity. I deeply regret to feel myself under the necessity of tendering to you my resignation as Secretary of War, because I can no longer hold the office under my convictions of patriotism, nor with honor, subjected, as I am, to a violation of solemn pledges and plighted faith.

"With the highest personal regard,

"I am, most truly yours,

(Signed)   "JOHN B. FLOYD.

"TO HIS EXCELLENCY THE PRESIDENT OF THE UNITED STATES."

To this the President made the following reply:

"WASHINGTON, December 31, 1860.

"*My Dear Sir:* I have received and accepted your resignation of the office of Secretary of War, and not wishing to impose upon you the task of performing its mere routine duties, which you have so kindly offered to do, I have authorized Postmaster-General Holt to administer the affairs of the Department until your successor shall be appointed.

"Yours very respectfully,

(Signed)   "JAMES BUCHANAN,

"TO HON. JOHN B. FLOYD."

The differences of opinion in the Cabinet, on the paper submitted by the President as his reply to the South Carolina Commissioners, were so irreconcilable as to threaten its dissolution.

The President seemed to be firm in the position he had taken, and it was thought that his mind could not be changed. But the member of the Cabinet that seemed more impressed by the erroneous view contained in the reply of the President was the Secretary of State, Judge Black. When the Cabinet had adjourned their session he sought the Postmaster-General, Holt, with whom he conferred, and who fully agreed with him as to the necessity of making important changes in the President's letter before its transmittal to the Commissioners.

He then sought an interview with Mr. Toucey, the Secretary of the Navy, and informed him of his intention, in case the letter of the President was insisted upon, to submit his resignation. He had known nothing of the alleged understanding between the President and the South Carolina delegation until now, and he had no reason to believe that the views of the President would be modified or changed, and he shrank from the interview which he knew was now inevitable. The Secretary of the Navy at once communicated the fact to the President, who sent immediately for his Secretary of State, when a long and earnest conference took place.

"Do you, too, talk of leaving me?" said the President, with feeling, as he stated the information that had just been communicated to him by the Secretary of the Navy. He referred to their association and mutual respect, that had so long existed, while he at the same time assured the Secretary that his intention was to submit the paper to his judgment before transmitting it to the Commissioners. The Secretary of State replied that he was not aware of the course the President intended to pursue; that he could not know it; and that he felt that it would be impossible for him, holding the views that he did, to remain in the Cabinet and to appear to endorse the positions stated in the reply which the President contemplated making to the South Carolina Commissioners.

The President then proposed to amend, at the suggestion of his Secretary, the paper in question. This was declined by Judge Black, as was also the proposal that he should there and then make, himself, the proposed modifications. "If what I propose," said he, "is adopted, the whole paper must be recast." The position of the President involved, was the subject of an earnest discussion.

In regard to any "understanding," or "agreement," the President had acknowledged it, and claimed that he was affected by it personally. "You do not seem to appreciate, Judge Black," said he, "that my personal honor as a gentleman is involved." "Such an understanding," said Judge Black, "is impossible. You could not make it, or any agreement with any one that would tie your hands in the execution of the laws, and if you did make it, you must retire from it." Finally, the President yielded his objections, and committed the paper which he had submitted to his Cabinet into the hands of his Secretary of State.*

---

* During the reign of George IV. it became desirable that Mr. Canning should enter the Cabinet. The King was opposed to him on account of "the sympathy and friendship which he had always shown for the Queen." The Duke of Wellington essayed to make the conversion, but His Majesty told him that he had pledged his honor, as a gentleman, never to receive Mr. Canning again as one of his ministers. "You hear, Arthur, on my honor, as a gentleman." The Duke, as Sir H. Bulwer relates, told the King that he was not a gentleman; and upon the King starting back in surprise, the Duke added that he was "not a gentleman, but the Sovereign of England, with duties to his people, and that those duties rendered it imperative to call in the services of Mr. Canning." The King drew a long breath and said, "Well, if I must I must."—"The Croker Papers." Vol. I, p. 222.

Judge Black immediately went to the Office of the Attorney-General, Stanton, and there proceeded to make the following amendments to the letter of the President. As fast as the sheets were written they were handed to the Attorney-General, who copied them in his own hand, the original being sent directly to the President.

The amendments of Judge Black were as follows:

"Memorandum for the President on the subject of the paper drawn up by him in reply to the Commissioners of South Carolina:

"1st. The first and the concluding paragraphs both seem to acknowledge the right of South Carolina to be represented near this Government by diplomatic officers. That implies that she is an independent nation, with no other relations to the Government of the Union than any other foreign power. If such be the fact, then she has acquired all the rights, powers, and responsibilities of a separate government by the mere Ordinance of Secession, which passed her Convention a few days ago. But the President has always, and particularly in his late message to Congress, denied the right of secession, and asserted that no State could throw off her Federal obligations in that way.

"Moreover, the President has always very distinctly declared that even if a State could secede and go out of the Union at pleasure, whether by revolution or in the exercise of a constitutional right, he could not recognize her independence without being guilty of usurpation. I think, therefore, that every word and sentence which imply that South Carolina is in an attitude which enables the President to treat or negotiate with her, or to receive her Commissioners in the character of diplomatic members or agents, ought to be stricken out, and an explicit declaration substituted which would reassert the principles of the message.

"It is surely not enough that the words of the message be transcribed, if the doctrine there announced be practically abandoned by carrying on a negotiation.

"2d. I would strike out all expressions of regret that the Commissioners are unwilling to proceed with the negotiation, since it is very clear that there can legally be no negotiation with them, whether they are willing or not.

"3d. Above all things it is objectionable to intimate a willingness to negotiate with the State of South Carolina about the possession of a military post which belongs to the United States, or to propose any adjustment of the subject or any arrangement about it.

"The forts in the harbor of Charleston belong to this Government, are its own, and cannot be given up. It is true they might be surrendered to a superior force, whether that force be in the service of a seceding State or a foreign nation. But Fort Sumter is impregnable, and cannot be taken if defended as it should be. It is a thing of the last importance that it should be maintained, if all the power of this nation can do it; for the command of the harbor and the President's ability to execute the Revenue laws may depend on it.

"4th. The words, 'coercing a State by force of arms to remain in the Confederacy'—a power which I do not believe the Constitution has conferred upon Congress—ought certainly not to be retained. They are too vague, and might have the effect (which I am sure the President does not intend) to mislead the Commissioners concerning his sentiments.

"The power to defend the public property, to resist an assailing force which unlawfully attempts to drive out the troops of the United States from one of their fortifications, and to use the military and naval forces for the purpose of aiding the proper officers of the United States in the execution of the laws—this, as far as it goes, is *coercion,* and may very well be called 'coercing a State by force of arms to remain in the Union. The President has always asserted his right of coercion to that extent. He merely denies the right of Congress to make offensive war upon a State of the Union, as such might be made upon a foreign Government.

"5th. The implied assent of the President to the accusation which the Commissioners make, of a compact with South Carolina by which he was bound not to take whatever measures he saw fit for the defense of the forts, ought to be stricken out and a flat denial of any such bargain or pledge or agreement asserted. The paper signed by the late Members of Congress from South Carolina does not bear any such construction, and this, as I understand, is the only transaction between the South Carolinians and him which bears upon the subject, either directly or indirectly. I think it deeply concerns the President's reputation that he should contradict this statement, since, if it be undenied, it puts him in the attitude of an executive officer who voluntarily disarms himself of the power to perform his duty, and ties up his hands so that he cannot, without breaking his word, 'preserve, protect and defend the Constitution,' see the laws faithfully executed. The fact that he pledged himself in any such way cannot be true. The Commissioners, no doubt, have been so informed. But there must be some mistake about it. It arose, doubtless, out of the President's anxious and laudable desire to avoid civil war, and his often expressed determination not even to furnish an excuse for an outbreak at Charleston by reinforcing Major Anderson, unless it was absolutely necessary.

"6th. The remotest expression of a doubt about Major Anderson's perfect propriety of behavior should be carefully avoided. He is not only a gallant and meritorious officer, who is entitled to a fair hearing before he is condemned: he has saved the country, I solemnly believe, when its day was darkest and its peril most extreme.'*

"He has done everything that mortal man could do to repair the fatal error which the administration have committed in not sending down troops enough to hold *all* the forts. He has kept the strongest one. He still commands the harbor. We may still execute the laws, if we try. Besides, there is nothing in the orders which were sent him by the War Department which is in the slightest degree contravened by his act of throwing his command into Fort Sumter. Even if those orders, sent without your knowledge, did forbid him to leave a place where his men might have perished, and shelter them under a stronger position, we ought all of us to rejoice that he broke such orders.

"7th. The idea that a wrong was committed against South Carolina by moving from Fort Moultrie to Fort Sumter ought to be repelled as firmly as may be consistent with a proper respect for the high character of the gentlemen who compose the South Carolina Commission. It is a strange assumption of right on the part of that State to say that the United States troops must remain in the weakest position they can find in the harbor. It is not a menace of South Carolina or of Charleston, or any menace at all: it is simply self-defense. If South Carolina does not attack Major Anderson, no human being will be injured, for there certainly can be no reason to believe that he will commence hostilities. The apparent objection to his being in Fort Sumter is, that he will be less likely to fall an easy prey to his assailants.

"These are the points on which I would advise that the paper be amended. I am aware that they are too radical to permit much hope of their adoption. If they are adopted, the whole paper will need to be recast.

"But there is one thing not to be overlooked in this terrible crisis. I entreat the President to order the *Brooklyn* and the *Macedonian* to Charleston without the least delay, and in the meantime send a trusty messenger to Major Anderson to let him know that his Government will not desert him. The reinforcements of troops from New York or Old Point Comfort should follow immediately.

"If this be done at once, all may yet be, not well, but comparatively safe. If not, I can see nothing before us but disaster, and ruin to the country."†

Unexpectedly, the paper presented by his Secretary produced

---

* On this subject Judge Black wholly changed his opinion.
† From original paper, in Mr. Stanton's handwriting.

an effect upon the President that could not have been anticipated. He now entirely changed his ground upon many points on which he had heretofore been determined. He had ever felt the weight of the great responsibility resting upon him, and he believed that in avoiding a collision in the harbor of Charleston war could be avoided, the border States tranquilized and a peaceful arrangement of the difficulties made possible. Upon one point he was inflexible, and from it he never wavered, and that was his determination never, under any pressure of circumstances, to surrender the forts at Charleston, and to this resolve he adhered to the last. He had thought of returning Anderson to his former position at Fort Moultrie, and thus restoring the status in the harbor, as far as he was concerned, and the greatest pressure, both within and without the Cabinet, had been brought to bear upon him; and had it not been for the prompt course of his Secretary of State, as well as the fact that the State had seized the vacant forts in the harbor, there is every probability that such would have been his course. But he yielded to the arguments so forcibly placed before him, and prepared and transmitted to the Commissioners, on the 3d of December, a reply to their communication so clear in its statement and so positive in its terms as to leave no longer any illusion as to either his conclusions or his purpose.

He referred the Commissioners to his message of the 3d of December, in which he had stated that the Executive had no authority to decide as to the relations between the Federal Government and South Carolina, and that it was his "duty to submit to Congress the whole question in all its bearings," and that they were aware that such was still his opinion. His earnest desire was that Congress, who alone possessed the power, might so dispose of the subject as to prevent the inauguration of a civil war in regard to the possession of the forts in the harbor of Charleston. He deeply regretted that, in the opinion of the Commissioners, "the events of the last twenty-four hours" rendered this impossible. In regard to the alleged "pledges" referred to in the letter of the Commissioners and their violation, the President again referred to his message to Congress in regard to the property of the United States in South Carolina, and the tenure under which it was held. He recalled the interview of the 8th of December, between himself and some of the members of the delegation of South Carolina in Congress, and quoted *in extenso,* the memorandum left with him by those members; and he pointedly refers to his objection at the time to the word "provided," as capable of a construction into an agreement upon his part which he "never would make;" and he stated, also, the reply of the delegation, that nothing was further from their intention, they did not so understand it, and that he, the President, should not so consider it. He denies, too, that the delegation could enter into any reciprocal arrangement with him, and that they did not profess to have authority to do this, and were acting in their individual characters; and he states that he "considered it as nothing more than the promise of highly honorable gentlemen" to exert their personal influence in the matter. It was his "determination not to reinforce the forts in the harbor until they had been actually attacked," or until he had certain evidence that they were about to be attacked.

He assures the Commissioners that he acted in the same manner that he would have done had he entered into a positive and formal agreement with parties capable of contracting, although such an agreement would have been, on his part, impossible. He had never sent reinforcements, and he had never authorized any change in the "relative military status."

He then recites the orders sent to Major Anderson by the Secretary of War on the 11th of December, but which were not brought to his notice until the 21st instant, at a meeting of his Cabinet, and which the President had forgotten. He claims that it was "clear that Major Anderson acted upon his own responsibility and without authority, unless, indeed, he had tangible evidence of a design to proceed to a hostile act;" that such act had not yet been alleged, but that Major Anderson "should not be condemned without a fair hearing."

He further states to the Commissioners that his "first promptings" were to restore the status, so far as Anderson was concerned, with the concurrence of the South Carolina authorities, "but before any steps could possibly be taken in this direction," the vacant forts in the harbor of Charleston had been seized by the State authorities, who, although they knew that Anderson's movement was not only without but against his orders, proceeded, without any demand or request for information or explanation, to take possession not only of the forts, but upon the same day to raise the flag of the State over the United States Custom House and Post Office, and subsequently to seize and occupy the United States arsenal, with its stores valued at half a million of dollars. It was under these circumstances that he was urged to withdraw the troops from the harbor of Charleston, as a step essential to the opening of negotiations. "This," said he, "I cannot do; this I will not do. Such an idea was never thought of by me. No allusion to it has ever been made in any communication between myself and any human being."

Nor did he admit the inference that because the officer in command of all the forts had, without instructions, changed his position from one to another, that therefore he was bound to withdraw the troops from the only fort in Charleston Harbor in the possession of the United States. He informs the Commissioners of the intelligence he had just received, of the seizure of the arsenal in Charleston, with its valuable stores, by the troops of the State, and he closes his communication with the statement that, while it is his duty to defend Fort Sumter against hostile attacks, he does not "perceive how such a defense can be construed into a menace against the city of Charleston."

The reply of the President left little hope for negotiation. He had declined to disavow the act of Major Anderson, or to interfere with his movement. But even under these circumstances the Commissioners did not yet abandon hope that some temporary solution of the difficulty might be found, which would enable them to open the negotiation with which they were charged.

After a careful and full consideration of the responsibility involved, they determined upon one more step, which would be the extreme exercise of their discretionary powers, however unlimited might be those powers as conferred by the Convention. They believed that the President was sincere in his desire to meet and deal fairly with them, but the movement of Major Anderson, made upon the day of their arrival, had involved the whole subject in doubt and complicated it beyond solution.

"On the 30th the President replied to the letter of the Commissioners. On the same day I again saw the President, and found Mr. Toucey, the Secretary of the Navy, with him. I told him that with his permission I would like to have a half-hour's conversation, to which he very courteously assented. I then, as temperately as I could, commenced a review of the whole transaction. He stopped me, saying, 'You, of all persons, ought to know that it is exceedingly irregular and improper for the President to discuss such matters with the secretary of the Commissioners.' I told him that I was not secretary, nor had I any sort of official connection with the commission; that I came to him, simply because he himself had established my connection with these events, and in such a way that I thought I had a claim to be heard. 'In that case,' he said, 'proceed;' and I then had a long, very earnest and very interesting conversation with him. He showed a good deal of feeling, and seemed much worn and distressed. I inferred from all that passed that his difficulty consisted in this: that the seizure of the other forts by South Carolina rendered the restoration of the former status impossible, for if he ordered Anderson from Fort Sumter he had nowhere to send him, unless he withdrew him altogether from the harbor; and this 'lowering of the flag,' in the face of an armed rebellion, both Mr. Toucey and himself thought was impossible in the face of Northern sentiment. Under this impression I went to Mr. Hunter, of Virginia, and told him that if that *was* the difficulty, to say to the President that if he would withdraw from Sumter, the State would withdraw from the other forts, and that Major Anderson would be as safe in Fort Moultrie as if he were here; the Commissioners would accept this return to the status and guarantee his safety Mr. Hunter immediately went to him, and when he returned—I was waiting at his rooms —said: 'Tell the Commissioners it is hopeless. The President has taken his ground. I *can't* repeat what passed, but if you can get a telegram to Charleston, telegraph at once to your people to sink vessels in the channel of the harbor;' and this message he sent the next morning again by his colleague, Mr. Mason. A messenger had, however, been sent the night before to Richmond to forward the telegram from that point. There is no doubt that at that time orders for reinforcement had been issued, although afterwards countermanded. In this condition of affairs, the Commissioners addressed their second letter to the President and left Washington."*

Anderson's action, while not inconsistent with the position of his message nor the official action of his Cabinet, was wholly in violation of the policy that the President had pursued. For a time he was undetermined as to what course to take, but he had

---

* Trescot's narrative.

eventually prepared a draft of an answer to the South Carolina Commissioners which yielded the point at issue, when, by the firm and decided action of his Secretary of State, the consequence of such action upon his part was presented in so clear a light as to induce him to change his purpose and his action completely, and to commit himself so positively as to leave henceforth no illusion as to his course. The alternative was forced upon him, either to sustain Major Anderson or to condemn him. "For a moment he wavered. But he could take no other course. Cass had left him, Cobb had gone, and Floyd was about to go. Neither Thompson nor Thomas could remain. South Carolina had seized the unoccupied forts and public property in her limits, and the excitement had spread through the South, arousing fierce and pronounced feeling. His Secretary of State and his Attorney-General said to him, 'Decide; whatever you may have done, we are uncommitted. Keep the word which the South says you have pledged, and we resign. We believe in the Union, and we will not betray it.' "*

The Cabinet had resolved upon their action, and the Attorney-General, Mr. Stanton, thus forcibly expressed himself to the late Assistant Secretary of State, Mr. Trescot, who was acting as the agent of South Carolina: "You say the President has pledged himself. I do not know it. I have not heard his account, but I know you believe it. For the present, I will admit it. The President was pledged. Anderson's conduct has broken that plege. You had two courses to choose: you had a right to either. You could have appealed to the President to redeem his pledge, or you could have said the circumstances under which the President has acted prove bad faith, we will not trust you any further, and then have acted as you saw fit, but you have no right to adopt both. Stand on the President's pledge and give him the chance to redeem it, or take the matter in your own hands. Now you have chosen, you have, by seizing the remaining forts and arsenals, undertaken to redress yourselves. The President's pledge may be broken or not, that *now* concerns him individually—as to the Government, you have passed by the pledge and assumed, in vindication, a position of hostility; with that alone I have to deal."

His friends were leaving him with the secession of every State, as the party opposed to him grew daily in strength. He was to

---

* Trescot's narrative.

end his days in the North, as his character was to stand or fall by Northern opinion. He yielded finally to the determined instance of his Secretary of State, and put himself in harmony with the Union sentiment.

CHAPTER XIV.

WHILE the correspondence between the President and the
South Carolina Commissioners was pending, the subject of rein-
forcing Fort Sumter was under daily discussion in the Cabinet.
Various plans had been proposed, and among them one from the
General-in-Chief himself.

Lieutenant-General Scott was still at the head of the army.
He was now over seventy-four years of age, and had grown old in
the service of his country. The infirmities of age were upon him,
and he was a prey to many physical disabilities, which wholly
incapacitated him for active service. He was now, as he had long
been, the highest military authority in the country. Mexico and
its brilliant campaign were still remembered by the generation
who had witnessed it, and the minds of his countrymen were yet
filled with gratitude for services, many of which, without involving any great issues, were at the time and by circumstances
important.

And there were sagacious and patriotic men who, while still

earnestly working for a peaceful solution of the difficulties, were not disturbed at an issue of war, under the conscious assurance that General Winfield Scott still commanded the army.

Nature had denied to him the power of a critical discrimination, and when his mind had been directed to the consideration of political subjects or upon matters of State, his conclusions and expressions were oftentimes characterized by weakness. And hence while there was every disposition to receive and to consider with respect any suggestion of a purely military nature that he might make, so far as it was uninfluenced by controlling questions of State, the political and civil recommendations with which they were often mingled, afforded an opportunity to an administration not in harmony with him to reject both. For many reasons his relations to the President were not cordial. During the war with Mexico, the President had been the Secretary of State of Mr. Polk's administration, and had taken sides against General Scott in his controversy with General Taylor. He opposed, at all times, his aspirations for the Presidency, and criticized the action of Congress in conferring upon General Scott, the brevet of lieutenant-general in the army.* The wounds had not healed, and through preference the General had maintained his headquarters permanently in the city of New York. As early as the 29th of October he had submitted, voluntarily, to the Secretary of War a paper entitled "Views Suggested by the Imminent Danger (October 29, 1860) of a Disruption of the Union by the Secession of one or more of the Southern States." At this time the elections had not yet taken place, and no State had passed an Ordinance of Secession.

The views of the General contemplated only "a gap" in the Union by the withdrawal of an interior State or States, and which the Federal Government might re-establish by force in order to preserve the continuity of its territory; and in support of which he quotes from "Paley's Moral and Political Philosophy." But the falling off "of all the Atlantic States from the Potomac south, was not within the scope of General Scott's provisional remedies." A lesser evil than to unite the fragments of the Union by the sword would be, "he thought," to allow the fragments of the great Republic to form themselves into new confederacies, probably four,

---

* Letter to J. W. Forney, December 15, 1852. *Forneys Progress.*

Private & Confidential.

Wheatland, near Lancaster
14 June 1862

My good old friend,

I felt happy, once more to receive a letter from you; & although it informed me of the abuse poured upon my head in New York, this did not disturb my tranquillity. After a careful review of all my public conduct since the election of Mr. Lincoln I would not change any part of it if I now had the power. Every step was well considered & I never was deceived by any member of my cabinet. I knew them all well. It will not be long before the public mind will be disabused of the slanders against me; & I have not the least apprehension of the award of posterity. I would be the happiest old man in the country were it not for the civil war; but I console myself with the conviction that no act or

omission of mine has produced this
terrible calamity. After the attack on
Fort Sumter war became inevitable & so
I warned the South in advance. I trust
that Divine Providence may speedily
bring it to a successful conclusion &
that the Constitution & the Union may
be re-established.

I should be much gratified to see
you at Wheatland & would give you
a cordial welcome. I cannot ask you
to incur the trouble & expense of coming
here for no other purpose than to see me;
but if you should have business at
Philadelphia, I hope you will not fail
to come here & see your old friend.

Yours sincerely
James Buchanan

John Griffin Esquire

165

to each of which he assigns their proximate boundaries, "after many waverings and conflicts."*

In the formation of one of these confederacies, he thought that but little if any coercion, beyond moral force, would be necessary to embrace seven slave-holding States, with parts of Virginia and Florida, in a new confederacy with Ohio, Indiana, Illinois, etc., when the overwhelming weight of the great northwest was taken in connection with the laws of trade, contiguity of territory, and the comparative indifference to Free-soil doctrines on the part of Western Virginia, Kentucky, Tennessee, and Missouri. He appeals to Virginia, and quotes the Declaration of Independence, that prudence dictated that governments should not be lightly changed, and also from "Paley's Moral Philosophy," that national honor was not to be pursued as distinct from national interest.

The military point of the communication was embodied in a short statement that, from his knowledge of the Southern population, it was his solemn conviction that, preliminary to secession, there was danger of a seizure of some or of all of a number of Southern forts, then destitute of or without sufficient garrisons; and he recommends that all these works should be immediately so garrisoned as to make any attempt to take any one of them, by surprise or *coup de main*, ridiculous.† After some suggestions in regard to exports and the collection of imports upon ships of war, the "Views" conclude with the statement that they eschewed "the idea of invading a seceded State."

This paper was published upon the authority of General Scott, in a daily journal in the city of Washington,‡ on the 18th day of January, 1861, without either "the consent or previous knowledge of the President," and for the assigned reason that it was necessary to correct misapprehensions "that had got abroad" in pub-

---

*1. The Potomac River and the Chesapeake Bay to the Atlantic; 2. From Maryland along the coast to the Alleghany (perhaps the Blue Ridge) range of mountains, to some point on the coast of Florida; 3. The line from, say the head of the Potomac to the west or northwest, which it will be most difficult to settle; 4. The crest of the Rocky Mountains. And to the confederacies thus formed, he alleges their probable capitals. The New England Confederacy was to be formed of the New England and Middle States, and the Capitol at Washington to be removed to Albany.

† Forts St. Philip, New Orleans; Morgan, Alabama; Pickens and McRae, Pensacola, Fla.; Pulaski, Georgia; Moultrie and Sumter, South Carolina.

‡ *National Intelligencer*, Washington, January 18, 1861.

lic prints and speeches in regard to the "Views."* The President received the paper with surprise. He regarded that such an open expression of opinion from so distinguished a source as the General-in-Chief would be used by "disunion leaders" to mislead as well as to incite the people of the cotton States and "drive them to extremities." He thought, too, that in a report from the commanding general of the army to the Secretary of War, the political portion of the "Views" being speculative and prospective in their character, and unconnected "with military operations, was out of time and out of place." He considered, also, that a recommendation to garrison the nine Southern forts should have been accompanied by a "practical plan" for doing it, and its detail submitted to the President. The attention of General Scott was called to this omission, when on the following day, October 30, in a communication to the Secretary of War, entitled "Supplemental Views," he simply stated that "there is one regular company at Boston, one here (at the Narrows), one at Pittsburg, one at Augusta, Ga., and one at Baton Rouge—in all five companies only, within reach, to garrison or reinforce the forts mentioned in the "Views."

The regular force at the disposal of the President was widely scattered upon the distant frontier, where its whole force, amounting at the maximum to 18,000 men, was required, he thought, for the protection of the border settlements.† General Scott, impressed with the necessity of giving reasonable security to the settlers, and considering this force as inadequate, had in 1857 asked for an increase to the regular army of four regiments. His request had been approved by the President, who had recommended to Congress to raise five additional regiments, which, however, was not acted upon.‡

The President believed it to be "impossible to garrison the numerous forts in the United States in time of peace." Destitute as he was of military force, and without power, as he conceived, under the laws to call out the militia, or to accept the service of volunteers, he believed that to scatter the five companies among the nine forts in the Southern States "would have been a con-

* Floyd at Richmond, upon his return in January, 1861.
† Report of the Military Committee of the House of Representatives, February 18, 1861.
‡ United States Senate Documents, 1857-58.

fession of weakness," as they were absurdly inadequate to the object in view, and that it would have done but little to have prevented secession, but would have tended rather to provoke it. It would have precipitated civil war, for which Congress had made no preparation, and it would have exasperated the border States and probably driven them into hostilities, and all hope of compromise would have been destroyed.* But his Attorney-General believed that Fort Sumter should have been relieved under any circumstances, and with part of the five companies which General Scott had reported as available. He thought that General Scott's report of the force available was not a correct one, as we had no Indian disturbances at that time, and more troops might have been had from the frontier.

He therefore considered it to be his duty "to refrain from any act which might provoke or encourage the cotton States into secession, and to smooth the way for congressional compromise.†

The "Views" submitted by General Scott were considered, by themselves, so impracticable in their nature, and so strange and inconsistent in character, that the President dismissed them from his mind without further consideration."

But General Scott was thoroughly alive to the dangers which threatened the country. On the 31st of October he suggested to the Secretary of War that a circular be sent to the forts warning the garrisons against sudden assaults, but this permission was not granted.

On December 12 he arrived in Washington, and in a personal interview with the Secretary of War he urged the same views, and points out the organized companies and the recruits at the principal depots available for the purpose.

The Secretary did not agree with him; nor could he have done so without putting himself in opposition to the announced policy of the President; but in accordance with the request of General Scott an interview for the 15th of December with the President was arranged. At this interview the whole subject was discussed, and General Scott renewed his recommendation for reinforcement. His recommendation was unexpected. The President gave his opinion that no immediate secession beyond South Carolina was to

* "Buchanan's Administration."
† Conversation with Judge Black at his residence, November 17, 1880.

be apprehended, and he declined to reinforce Fort Moultrie or to garrison Fort Sumter, as the proper time had not in his judgment arrived. He determined to await the action of the South Carolina Convention and the arrival of Commissioners to him, which he would refer to Congress, and if Congress should decide against them, he would then reinforce the forts in Charleston Harbor and direct the commanding officer to defend them. He had at this time defined his policy, if indeed he had a policy. In opposition to the opinion of General Scott, he thought that there was no present necessity of any reinforcements to secure the forts in the harbor of Charleston, and he believed in the possibility of an adjustment. He desired, too, to separate South Carolina from the other Southern States, and he was convinced that any attack made by her upon Fort Moultrie would be condemned by them. When the Secretary of War referred to the fact that the sloop of war *Brooklyn*, with 300 men, lay in readiness at Norfolk to sail at any moment to Charleston, an objection was at once made by General Scott to taking so many men from Fortress Monroe, but that they might be taken from New York. He thought, however, that it would be then too late, as the South Carolinians would have the game in their hands," and that as Fort Sumter was not garrisoned, any handful of men might seize it. At a later period, the General thought that if the 300 men had been sent then or later, both forts would have remained in the possession of the Government; no batteries could have been erected, and the access to the sea been preserved.*
How Mr. Buchanan regarded these statements and comments of General Scott when long afterward (October, 1862) they first fell under his observation, will be seen in a subsequent part of this narrative.†

General Scott now became persistent in his efforts to relieve the situation. Upon the 28th of December, after the movement of Major Anderson to Fort Sumter, he urged upon the Secretary of War that Fort Sumter might not be evacuated, but that 150 recruits might "'instantly" be sent to Fort Sumter, with ample supplies of subsistence and ammunition; and he renews his recommendation in regard to the forts upon the Southern coast. It was upon the same

* Scott's autobiography, p. 615.
† General Scott was burned in effigy January 12, at the University of Virginia, by the students, amid cheers for the seceding States and groans for Anderson, who was called the American Sultan.

day that the Commissioners from South Carolina held their first and only interview with the President. On the following day (the 29th) he addressed a communication to the brother of Major Anderson, and informed him that the War Department had kept secret from him (General Scott) the instructions sent to Major Anderson, but that he, in common with the whole army, had admired and indicated as a defensive measure the masterly transfer of the garrison to Fort Sumter.

Meantime, the feeling that relief should be sent to Fort Sumter began, to manifest itself among the people, and proposals of every character for relieving Fort Sumter were made by patriotic citizens throughout the country to the President and to General Scott. Among these, on the 29th of December, a proposal was made to Lieutenant-General Scott by Mr. James A. Hamilton, of New York, that Major Anderson should at once be reinforced by a force of from 100 to 400 volunteers; and he asks a letter of introduction to Major Anderson, that these volunteers were to be guests of Major Anderson, but subject to his command. The patriotic feeling that suggested this extraordinary proposition was approved by General Scott, who read it to the President, who also approved the spirit; but they equally agreed that the immediate military needs of the country required no appeal to militia or volunteers in aid of the regular force.

Impatient at the apparent delay, General Scott again addressed the President, on the 30th, and requested permission to send, as secretly as possible and without reference to the War Department, 250 recruits from New York Harbor, to reinforce Fort Sumter, and that a sloop of war and a cutter may be ordered for that purpose as early as to-morrow. For some time the sloop of war *Brooklyn,* under the command of Captain Farragut, had been lying off Fortress Monroe, with secret instructions to hold herself in readiness to proceed with 300 men to Fort Moultrie in case "of its attack or danger of attack." In view of the movement of Major Anderson and the seizure by the State authorities of the forts and public property in the city and harbor of Charleston, the President had determined upon sending reinforcements, but he deemed that a ship of war with experienced troops was preferable to a sloop of war and a cutter with 250 recruits. She could not cross the bar: and overruling the suggestion of Lieutenant-General Scott, he determined to send the *Brooklyn* to the relief of Major Anderson.

On the following morning he gave the necessary orders to his secretaries. His course was endorsed by General Scott, who called upon him on the evening of the 31st to congratulate him that the orders had been issued and were in his possession.* Upon the same day an order was issued by Lieutenant-General Scott to the commanding officer of Fort Monroe to prepare and put upon the *Brooklyn* four companies, making at least 200 men, destined to reinforce Fort Sumter, with twenty-five spare stands of arms and subsistence for the detachment for ninety days, and that everything was to be managed "as secretly and confidentially as possible." During the interview between the President and General Scott, it was agreed that before issuing the orders an opportunity should be given to the South Carolina Commissioners to reply to the President's letter sent to them a few hours before; and it was the President's opinion that as "this letter would doubtless speedily terminate their mission," the delay could not exceed forty-eight hours. General Scott deemed this as only "gentlemanly and proper," and the orders were withheld temporarily. The delay gave rise to "a prolonged and heated discussion in the Cabinet," when it was finally determined to send an officer to Major Anderson to inquire of him whether he needed reinforcements, or desired that they should be sent to him.† Fearful of further delay the Secretary of State inquired: "Does the sending of a messenger imply that no additional troops are to be sent until his return?" "It implies nothing," replied the President. The tone of the President's letter to the Commissioners, and the determination evinced, satisfied them that negotiation was impossible, and they prepared to return to South Carolina. The interview between the President and Senator Hunter had taken place on the 30th of December. On the 1st of January the Commissioners prepared their final answer, and it was upon the 2d–when, at a Cabinet meeting and at the moment when in accordance with the plan determined upon, that the Postmaster-General, Mr. Holt, was writing down the questions to be put to Major Anderson–that this communication was handed to the President, when it was at once read in the presence of the Cabinet. It began by a reference to his declaration that he possessed no power to change the existing relations between the State

* In his "pocket," as he expressed himself.
† C. F. Black, manuscript.

and the Government, to acknowledge the independence of the
State, nor to recognize the official character of the gentlemen who
had addressed him. To this they replied, that the State of South
Carolina having exercised the great. right of self-government, they
had no special solicitude as to the character in which he might
recognize them, and that they were willing to waive any formal
considerations which his constitutional scruples "might have prevented him from extending."'

His willingness to receive them and submit the propositions which they should make to Congress was to them ample
recognition of the condition of public affairs which rendered
their presence necessary. They recall a portion of the President's
letter in which he had expressed his desire that the whole subject
might be referred to Congress, and his regret that in the opinion
of the Commissioners "the events of the last twenty-four hours
render this impossible;" and they assert that the language which
had been quoted as theirs by him "is altered in its sense by the
omission of a most important part of the sentence;" that what
they did say was, "But the events of the last twenty-four hours
render *such an assurance* impossible." An assurance that they
were ready to enter upon the negotiation, with an earnest desire upon
their part to avoid all unnecessary collision. In their communication they review the acts of the President from the passage of
the Ordinance of Secession by the Convention, which manifested a
desire upon his part to settle the difficulties without collision; the
ground taken in his annual message, that he had no right to coerce
a seceded State; his refusal to send reinforcements to Charleston
Harbor; his return of the arms taken from the arsenal to arm the
employees of the engineer; his understanding with the South
Carolina delegation; and his pledge, to return to them the paper
they had given him, should he determine to send reinforcements.
The facts of their mission to him were stated, their arrival, and
the news of Major Anderson's movement, which was at once
communicated to him, and their call upon him to redeem the
"pledge" that he had made. That he did not deny it then, nor did
he now, but that he sought "to escape from its obligation" on the
ground that the Commissioners terminated all negotiation by demanding as a preliminary the withdrawal of the United States
troops from the harbor of Charleston, and from the action of the
State authorities, who, instead of asking an explanation of Ander-

son's movement, "took possession of other property of the United States."

They deny that any such demand was made by them; that there was nothing in their letter which could have prevented him from declining to withdraw the troops, "and offering the restoration of the status" to which he was pledged, if he had desired to do it; that, whatever might be his assertion, "such an idea was never thought of" by him. His conversation left upon their minds the distinct impression that he did "seriously contemplate the withdrawal of the troops from Charleston Harbor," and that he had discussed the subject with gentlemen of the highest possible public reputation," and whose testimony was beyond cavil; and that it was the knowledge of this fact that induced them to urge upon him a policy that had the weight of such authority.

They deny that the action of the State authorities availed him for defense, for the opportunity of decision was afforded him before these facts occurred. That on the very day that the news of Major Anderson's movement came, men who had striven successfully to lift him to his great office, who had been his tried and true friends through his troubles, entreated him "to act" and "to act at once." He was told that every hour complicated his position, and he was only asked to give the assurance that if Anderson had acted "without and against his orders and in violation of his pledges," he would restore the "status" which he had pledged his "honor to maintain." The letter recalled his refusal to do this, the action of the Secretary of War, and the fact that "more than twelve hours passed and the Cabinet meeting had adjourned before you (he) knew what the authorities of South Carolina had done," and that even if he had known it he should have kept his faith. That as to Fort Sumter, "the people were with difficulty restrained from securing, without blood, the possession of this important fortress," but that they thought kindly of the President, believed him true, and were willing to spare him unnecessary collision; but that the Commissioners had hardly left Charleston before Anderson waged war. "No man could have believed," said they, "that any officer could have taken such a step, not only without orders, but against orders;" that the State acted in simple self-defense, for the act of Major Anderson was as much war as firing a volley. All this was done, they allege, without the slightest provocation, and that no evidence in justification of the movement had yet been alleged. They recognize his decision: he had resolved to hold by force what he had obtained through their "misplaced confidence," and, by refusing to withdraw Anderson, had "converted his violation of orders into a legitimate act of your (his) Executive authority." And they conclude their letter by an assertion that, by his course, he had probably rendered civil war inevitable; that if he chose to force the issues upon them, the State of South Carolina would accept it, and, relying upon the "God of Justice as well as the God of Hosts," would endeavor to perform the duty which lay before her, hopefully, bravely and thoroughly.*

The Commissioners; convinced that the troops would not be withdrawn from Fort Sumter, and apprehensive that reinforcements were about to be sent to the garrison, transmitted their letter at once to the President and left the city on the afternoon of the 2d of January.

The effect produced by this communication was immediate and decided. It excited so much indignation as to leave no illusion as to the disposition to be made of it.

The President, taking his pen, wrote across the manuscript:

"EXECUTIVE MANSION, 3:30 o'clock, Wednesday.

"This paper, just presented to the President, is of such a nature that he declines to receive it;" and at once caused its return to the Commissioners.

The discussion in the Cabinet was an open one; and the decision of the President was announced in as "emphatic terms" as he probably ever addressed to one of his Secretaries. Turning to his Secretary of War, he said, "It is now over, and reinforcements must now be sent."

There was now no longer either reason or excuse for delay, when, upon the same day that the letter of the Commissioners was returned to them by the President, he was informed by the Secretaries of War and of the Navy that Lieutenant-General Scott, upon conferring with an expert in naval affairs, had become convinced that both secrecy and success would be best secured by sending a "mercantile steamer" with the recruits from New York. The President yielded with great reluctance to the "pressing instance" of Lieutenant-General Scott himself, and

* Commissioners' letter. Executive Doc. H. R. Vol. 6, No. 26.

the *Star of the West,* a side-wheel merchant steamer, was substituted for the sloop of war *Brooklyn.* *

The detail of the despatch of the expedition was entrusted to General Scott. Proposals in view of such action had previously been submitted by Mr. A. C. Schultze, a merchant of New York, who was at once informed by General Scott that his proposals were entertained, and who despatched Lieutenant-Colonel Thomas, the Assistant Adjutant-General upon his staff, to New York to superintend the detail of the expedition. Colonel Thomas was directed to satisfy himself that Mr. Schultze's agency was reliable, and he was then to forward the expedition secretly and with all despatch. That officer proceeded at once to New York, and on the 4th of January he reported to the General-in-Chief that he was satisfied that the movement could be made with the Star of the West without exciting suspicion; and that through the agency of Mr. Schultze he had chartered her at $1,500 per day from Mr. Marshal O. Roberts, who, as Colonel Thomas reported, "looked exclusively to the dollars," while Mr. Schultze was "acting for the good of his country." The troops were to be concealed upon reaching the harbor of Charleston, and Major Anderson was to be warned against all telegrams, and informed that his conduct met with the approbation of the highest authority, and that further reinforcements would be sent to him, if necessary.

The ship was to clear for New Orleans without formal notice, and as if for her regular trip. The provisions necessary were to be bought on the ship's account, so that no public agency should be used. The arms and ammunition were to be put on board the next day by means of tugs from Governor's Island, when all communication with the island and the city was to be cut off temporarily. The orders to the proper officers were promptly executed, and First Lieutenant C. R. Woods, of the Ninth United States Infantry, assisted by two lieutenants and a medical officer, was placed in command of the military force.

Major Anderson was also informed by letter of the character and composition of the expedition on the day that it sailed, and special instructions were communicated to him that, if fire should be opened upon any vessel bringing reinforcements or supplies

* "Buchanan's Administration," p. 189.

within reach of his guns, "they may be employed to silence such fire;" and he was also to act in like manner in case that his fort was fired upon.

The three months' supply of subsistence was promptly transferred on board the vessel, and at 5 P. M. of the 5th of January the *Star of the West* left her wharf and proceeded down the bay. When near Staten Island she stopped, and received on board from a steam-tug four officers and 200 men, with their small-arms and ammunition, and at 9 P. M. she crossed the bar at the mouth of the harbor and steamed to the southward. In spite, however, of the efforts to conceal the movement, a New York journal announced the fact in its afternoon edition of the 5th of January.

Colonel Thomas had informed the General-in-Chief by telegram, on the morning of the 4th of January, that the arrangements were made as proposed, and that the expedition would leave the following evening. Meantime, intelligence had reached Washington from Major Anderson that he felt himself to be secure in his position, and he thanked God that "we are now where the Government may send us additional troops at their leisure."

Information had reached the Government on the 5th inst. of the establishment of the battery on Morris Island, which would in all probability destroy any unarmed vessel attempting to pass it. Influenced by these considerations, and opposed as he was to the use of an unarmed vessel for such service, and deeming it not absolutely necessary at that time that reinforcements should be sent, the President, with the acquiescence of General Scott, countermanded the order for the sailing of the *Star of the Week*. On the evening of the 5th of January a telegram was despatched by the General-in-Chief to his son-in-law and A. A. C., Colonel H. L. Scott, at New York, to retain the ship. It reached that officer at too late an hour, as the ship had then left the harbor.

Later, upon the 7th of January, an order was sent by the Secretary of the Navy to the commander of the *Brooklyn* to escort and protect the *Star of the West,* and the officer in command of the expedition was informed by General Scott that the *Brooklyn* would "aid and succor" him in case of disaster to his ship. If he could not land at Fort Sumter he was to return to Fortress Monroe and discharge his ship.

On the 10th of January the Secretary of War *ad interim,* Mr.

Holt, addressed a communication to Major Anderson acknowledging the receipt of his letter announcing that the Government might reinforce him at its leisure, and that he felt secure in his position; and he informed him that the *Star of the West* had been ordered to him with reinforcements, that the probability was that she had been fired into and had not been able to reach him.

The letter was as follows:

"WAR DEPARTMENT,
"January 10, 1861.

"Major ROBERT ANDERSON,

    "First Artillery, Commanding at Fort Sumter, S. C.:

    "SIR: Your dispatches to No. 16, inclusive, have been received. Before the receipt of that of 31st December,* announcing that the Government might re-enforce you at its leisure, and that you regarded yourself safe in your present position, some two hundred and fifty instructed recruits had been ordered to proceed from Governor's Island to Fort Sumter on the *Star of the West,* for the purpose of strengthening the force under your command. The probability is, from the current rumors of to-day, that this vessel has been fired into by the South Carolinians, and has not been able to reach you. To meet all contingencies, the *Brooklyn* has been dispatched, with instructions not to cross the bar at the harbor of Charleston, but to afford to the *Star of the West* and those on board all the assistance they may need, and in the event the recruits have not effected a landing at Fort Sumter they will return to Fort Monroe.

    "I avail myself of the occasion to express the great satisfaction of the Government at the forbearance, discretion and firmness with which you have acted, amid the perplexing and difficult circumstances in which you have been placed. You will continue, as heretofore, to act strictly on the defensive; to avoid, by all means compatible with the safety of your command, a collision with the hostile forces by which you are surrounded. But for the movement, so promptly and brilliantly executed, by which you transferred your forces to Fort Sumter, the probability is that ere this the defenselessness of your position would have invited an attack, which, there is reason to, believe, was contemplated, if not in active preparation, which must have led to the effusion of blood, that has been thus so happily prevented. The movement, therefore, was in every way admirable, alike for its humanity [and] patriotism, as for its soldiership.

"Very respectfully, your obedient servant,

"J. HOLT,
"Secretary of War ad interim."

---

* Received January 5, 1861.

As the members were leaving the Cabinet session on the 3d inst., when the determination of the President had been announced, the Secretary of the Interior had been asked by the Secretary of State, Judge Black, "in a spirit of kindness and friendship," if in case troops should be sent to Charleston, would he feel bound to resign.* His reply was, that he would so feel bound, when the Secretary of State requested that he might have an opportunity to talk with him before he acted. To this the Secretary of the Interior agreed, assuring Judge Black at the same time that he had no thought that his purpose could be changed, and he asks Judge Black if, at the time of that conversation, *he* knew that troops had been ordered with the knowledge of the President. In order to restrain the South Carolinians from coming in contact with the Government, an event which he believed would only be disastrous to both sections of the country, and in order to keep his correspondents apprised of the action of the Government, the Secretary of the Interior had opened and continued a correspondence, both by letter and telegram, with Judge A. B. Longstreet, a distinguished citizen of South Carolina. On the morning of the 5th of January, the day upon which the Star *of the West* left New York, he had answered a direct inquiry of his correspondent as follows:

"I cannot speak by authority, but I do not believe any additional troops will be sent to Charleston while the present status lasts. If Fort Sumter is attacked, they will be sent, I believe."

And to a Mr. A. N. Kimball, of Jackson, Miss., he had telegraphed on the previous day, "No troops have been sent to Charleston, nor will be, while I am a member of the Cabinet."

When, therefore, he was apprised of the fact by a telegram in the *Constitution* newspaper of the 8th inst., that an expedition had actually sailed and was then on its way to Charleston Harbor, he was surprised and affected by the intelligence. He had every reason to think that his assurances, made in good faith, had done much to maintain the peaceful status which until now had prevailed in the harbor and to save Sumter from an attack. He at once determined to resign his position, and while so engaged in the presence of the Secretary of State, a telegraphic inquiry in regard to the sailing of the *Star of the West* reached him from

---

* Mr. Thompson to Judge Black, January 14, 1861.

Judge Longstreet. He considered that he had been trifled with, if not deceived, and claimed it to be his duty, although in so doing it might imperil the Star *of the West* and her mission, to remove the delusion into which he had unconsciously led his correspondent; and that in informing him, while still a member of the Cabinet, that reinforcements had actually been sent, but without his knowledge or consent, he was not violating his official duty or taking improper advantage of his position, but that "honor, truth and justice" to Judge Longstreet and himself required of him a reply."

He accordingly prepared the despatch at his house and exhibited, it to Judge Black, the Secretary of State, who had gone there in order to persuade him from the act. It was to the effect that the *Star of the* West, with 250 troops aboard, had sailed (by order of the Hon. J. Holt, the then Secretary of War) on Monday morning to reinforce Major Anderson at Charleston. The Secretary had fully made up his mind, and entrusting the despatch to William W. Cowling, the messenger of his Department, he directed him to cause its transmission by telegraph to his correspondent in South Carolina. But the messenger had been present, and had heard the discussion that took place between the Secretary of the Interior and the Secretary of State, the former insisting that it was a matter in which his honor was involved, and that the course he proposed to pursue, was a "sacred duty," while the latter "kindly but firmly protested against Mr. Thompson's action, and attempted to dissuade him from taking such a course."† He had been present, too, at other conversations between the Secretary of the Interior and Southern Members of Congress and other distinguished Southern men, and he was prepared to expect that at any moment hostilities might commence. Uncertain as to what course to pursue, the messenger proceeded to the office of the chief clerk, Mr. Moses Kelly, to whom he submitted the despatch, and who assured the messenger that he should do what he thought would be right, and it would be right. The messenger then tendered his

---

* Mr. Thompson's letter, March 11, to the *National Intelligencer,* Charleston *Mercury,* March 21, 1861.

† Cowling's statement, Judge Black's papers.

resignation, as he had resolved to disobey the order of the Secretary and not to deliver the despatch.

Shortly afterward, meeting the Hon. John Sherman, then a Member of Congress from Ohio, he submitted the message to him and informed him that he intended to detain it. In this resolve he was sustained by Mr. Sherman, with a promise of protection in case that trouble should arise from his action.

The message intrusted to Cowling was not sent; but whether from suspicion of his agent or from an anxiety to ensure the transmission of the information, or whether he had again heard from his correspondent, the Secretary again telegraphed, on the morning of the 8th of January, that the *Star of the West* had sailed for Charleston with 250 troops on board, and that she ought to reach the city on that day. The Secretary was not alone in thus informing the South Carolina authorities, for upon the same morning similar information was forwarded by Senator Wigfall, of Texas, and L. Q. Washington, from the city of Washington, and also by Mr. W. S. Ashe, from Wilmington, N. C. On the 7th a telegram signed Jones, and to the same effect, had been communicated to the Convention at its evening session. The telegram of L. Q. Washington was important; it informed Governer Pickens that "Secretary Thompson has resigned. Government troops were sent on Saturday night from New York to Charleston. Mr. Thompson has been deceived by the administration. These facts I derived from Mr. Barksdale, of Mississippi, who has left Secretary Thompson. (Signed) L. Q. Washington."

These telegrams reached Charleston before 5 o'clock P. M. of the 8th, thus warning the authorities, but barely in time for them to complete their preparations of resistance.

The action of the Secretary of the Interior was made the subject of severe criticism. The Secretary of War, Mr. Holt, in communication to a daily journal in Washington, on the 5th of March, asserted that the Secretary of the Interior, while yet a member of the Cabinet, disclosed to those who were in open rebellion against the United States information which he had derived from his official position, and which he held under the seals of a confidence that from the beginning of our history as a nation had not been violated.

This met with the earnest and emphatic denial of Mr. Thompson, who insisted that the information came to him through the public prints, and was known to every well-informed man in the city of Washington as soon as to him.*

Secretary Holt, however, maintained the opinion that, from whatever source the information was derived, the Secretary of the Interior was bound as a Secretary of the President to keep it secret—a position that was unassailable.

Upon the same day he transmitted his formal resignation to the President as follows:

"WASHINGTON, January 8, 1861.

"Sir: It is with extreme regret I have just learned that additional troops have been ordered to Charleston. This subject has been frequently discussed in Cabinet council; and when on Monday night, 31st of December, ult., the orders for reinforcements to Fort Sumter were countermanded, I distinctly understood from you that no order of the kind would be made without being previously considered and decided in Cabinet. It is true that on Wednesday, January 2, this subject was again discussed in Cabinet, but certainly no conclusion was reached, and the War Department was not justified in ordering reinforcements without something more than was then said. I learn, however, this morning, for the first time, that the steamer *Star of the West* sailed from New York last Saturday night with 250 men, under Lieutenant Bartlett, bound for Fort Sumter. Under these circumstances I feel myself bound to resign my commission as one of your constitutional advisers into your hands.

"With life regard, your obedient servant,
(Signed) "J. THOMPSON.

"HIS EXCELLENCY JAMES BUCHANAN,
"President of the United States."

From the fact that reinforcements were determined upon, the President had anticipated the resignation of his Secretary, and in accepting it he tells him that he (the Secretary) had been so emphatic in opposing reinforcements that his resignation was expected in consequence of the President's decision.

The letter of the President was as follows:

"WASHINGTON, January 9, 1861.

"Sir: I have received and accepted your resignation yesterday of the office of Secretary of the Interior.

"On Monday evening, 31st December, 1860, I suspended the orders which had been issued by the War and Navy Departments to send the *Brooklyn* with reinforcements to Fort Sumter. Of

---

* Mr. Thompson's reply, March 21, 1861.

this I informed you on the same evening. I stated to you my reasons for this suspension, which you knew, from its nature, would be speedily removed. In consequence of your request, however, I promised that these orders should not be renewed 'without being previously considered and decided in Cabinet.'

"This promise was faithfully observed on my part. In order to carry it into effect, I called a special Cabinet meeting on Wednesday, January 2, 1861, in which the question of sending reinforcements to Fort Sumter was amply discussed, both by yourself and others. The decided majority of opinions was against you. At this moment the answer of the South Carolina 'Commissioners' to my communication and others of the 31st December was received and read. It produced much indignation among the members of the Cabinet. After a further brief conversation, I employed the following language: 'It is now all over; reinforcements must be sent.' Judge Black said, at the moment of my decision, that after this letter the Cabinet would be unanimous, and I heard no dissenting voice. Indeed, the spirit and tone of the letter left no doubt on my mind that Fort Sumter would be immediately attacked, and hence the necessity of sending reinforcements there without delay. Whilst you admit that on Wednesday, January 2, this subject was again discussed in Cabinet, you say 'but certainly no conclusion was reached, and the War Department was not justified in ordering more than what was then said.'

"You are certainly mistaken in alleging that no conclusion was reached.

"In this, your recollection is entirely different from that of your four oldest colleagues in the Cabinet. Indeed, my language was so unmistakable that the Secretaries of War and the Navy proceeded to act upon it; without any further intercourse with myself than what you heard or might have heard me say. You had been so emphatic in opposing these reinforcements that I thought you would resign in consequence of my decision. I deeply regret that you have been mistaken in point of fact, though, I firmly believe, honestly mistaken. Still it is certain you have not the less been mistaken.

"Yours very respectfully,
(Signed)   "JAMES BUCHANAN."

After severing his connection with the Cabinet the Secretary proceeded to his State, and there, in a speech to an assemblage that had met to greet him, he announced that as he was writing his resignation he sent a despatch to Judge Longstreet that the *Star of the West* was coming with reinforcements. "The troops," said he, "were thus put on their guard, and when the *Star of the West* arrived, she received a warm welcome from

booming cannon, and soon beat a retreat. I was rejoiced the
vessel was not sunk, but I was still more rejoiced that the concealed trick, first conceived by General Scott and adopted by
Secretary Holt, but countermanded by the President when too
late, proved a failure."*

Meantime, the *Star of the West* pursued her course towards
Charleston.† The weather was fine, and off the coast of North
Carolina she stopped to fish. A skilled pilot accompanied the
ship. At 1:30 on the morning of the 9th she arrived off the
Charleston bar. At first there were no lights to be seen.
Extinguishing her own, she groped in the dark until near dawn,
when the solitary light at Sumter became visible. Checking her
course, she steamed slowly along under careful soundings, until
she arrived off the main ship channel, where she hove to, to await
the dawn. At daylight a steamer was discovered a short distance in-shore. Upon seeing the ship, she immediately commenced signalling by colored lights and rockets, and steamed
rapidly in for the bar. A pilot-boat had come in and had raised
and lowered a large American flag, and then stood out again to sea.

In order to get the proper range for crossing the bar, the
ship remained hove to until there was sufficient light to see the
light-house on Morris Island. All of the buoys that marked the
channel had been taken up, rendering careful soundings necessary. At 6:20 A. M. the national flag was run to the peak, and the
ship crossed the bar at high water and continued along the Morris
Island side up the ship channel; the steamer before noticed keeping on her course toward Moultrie, about a mile distant and
constantly signalling.

When opposite to a group of houses near the shore, a red
Palmetto flag was seen, and immediately and without warning a
gun-battery opened upon the ship. The battery was concealed amid the sand-hills near the shore, and its existence had been
unsuspected. Its first shot had been fired across the bow of the
ship, which, however, continued on its course, when a rapid and
continuous fire was opened by the battery. The firing was wild
and unskillful, narrowly missing the pilot-house and machinery.
One spent shot struck the ship aft near the rudder, while another

---

* *National Intelligencer,* March 2, 1861.
† Captain McGowan's report.

struck just aft the port channels, about two feet above the water-line, passing through one of the guards. As soon as the battery had opened fire, a large garrison flag was run up at the fore, low-ered, and again run up as a signal to Major Anderson, whose flag was flying at Sumter. Just before leaving New York this flag had been sent on board by Assistant Adjutant-General Thomas, who accompanied the officers and men to the ship, and who com-municated to the captain definite orders to the effect that he was to hoist it "at the fore, in case the batteries fired" upon him, "and that Major Anderson would understand it and protect the ship with the guns of Sumter."

The *Star of the West* had now almost passed the battery, and continued her course against a strong ebb tide, up the main ship channel. Her draft of water rendered this necessary, and she would soon be within the range of the guns of Fort Moultrie, then distant about one and a half miles. Seeing her approach, the commanding officer of that work determined to gratify the anxiety of his men "to try a shot,"* and changing the elevation of her guns, opened at long range with four Columbiads and two 32-pounders, the shots falling wildly and in all directions. Fort Sumter was silent. It was then determined, both by the officer in command of the troops and the captain of the ship, that it was impossible to reach Fort Sumter. Had she continued upon her course it would have been necessary to have gone bows-on to a buoy in the channel 1,100 yards from the fort, where, to enter the inner harbor, she must have exposed her broadside to the direct and close fire of the entire battery of Fort Moultrie bearing on the channel, and whose fire would have been, in all probability, fatal. Lessening her speed she came round in a narrow part of the channel, lowered the flag from her fore, and putting on all steam headed down the channel for the bar, the battery on Morris Island continuing its fire as long as the ship was within range, but without injury. The strong ebb-tide carried the ship swiftly out of range to the bar, upon which the tide had so fallen that she struck three times in crossing it. A steamer from Charleston followed the retiring ship for some hours, but finally returned. There was no communication with any vessel or boats, or with any persons, nor was any warning

* Colonel Ripley's official report

not to enter the harbor given to the ship from any source whatever that was understood. Upon the evening of the day upon
which the firing took place, Captain Carraghan, a pilot, who was
stationed with his boat off the bar to warn vessels bearing the
United States flag not to enter, was summoned before the Executive Council in Charleston. He stated that he saw the *Star
of the West* that morning, "and made every effort to hail her,
and hoisted a white flag, but that she took no notice of it."*

The garrison of Fort Sumter was not without warning, although
unofficial and accidental, that an effort to relieve and reinforce
them was about to be made. By a boat which came to the fort
on the 8th of January with some employees of the Engineer
Department, a newspaper was received which announced that
the *Star of the West* was to sail with reinforcements for the fort,
and would be down that night. The news in its unofficial shape
was not credited by the garrison. Major Anderson thought that
Lieutenant-General Scott would not send troops except by a vessel of war, and in consequence no especial arrangements were
made nor orders given, in anticipation of such a contingency;
while at the same time the cheering which was distinctly heard
from Fort Johnson and at Cummings Point convinced the garrison
of Fort Sumter that something unusual was anticipated.

At 6 o'clock on the morning of the 9th of January the writer
was aroused by the announcement that the Carolinians were firing
from Morris Island upon a vessel bearing the national flag, that was
attempting to enter the harbor. He went at once to the parapet at
the southeast angle of the work. A large steamer was coming in
with the flag flying at her peak. Major Anderson, who had been
aroused by Captain Doubleday upon the firing of the first gun
from the battery, had given orders to beat the long roll, and the
men had fallen in, had reached the parapet and had manned the
guns. Three 24-pounders and one 8-inch seacoast howitzer were
the only guns mounted on the gorge of the work, and no ammunition had yet been served to them. The grape with which they
had been loaded was taken out and they were loaded with solid shot.
They were of the lighter calibre, and, encumbering the parade,
they had been mounted on the parapet to clear the way for the
heavier guns, the main object of the garrison being to transfer the

* Minutes of the Executive Council.

large amount of ordnance material, besides the provisions and stores which obstructed the entrances to the work, to the interior, and to prepare at once to resist an assault which the exposed and unfinished condition of the fort too evidently invited. All was soon in readiness, and the gunner (Oakes) stood with the lanyard in his hand at the 8-inch seacoast howitzer and ready for the word.   The battery was nearly 1,000 or 2,000 yards distant, and had been built under a sand-hill wholly safe from any direct shots and almost secure from shells, owing to the difficulty of exploding a shell over a fixed point. Major Anderson, with Lieutenants Davis and Meade and the writer, was in the angle of the parapet, the latter with his glass upon the steamer and reporting her movements. Major Anderson was excited and uncertain what to do.   The steamer, in the midst of the fire upon her, had hoisted and lowered a large national flag to her fore, when the writer reported to Major Anderson that she was making signals to the fort.   Major Anderson turned to his flag, but the halliards had become twisted about the staff and the flag could not be used. Fort Moultrie had now opened, when Lieutenant Davis called the attention of Major Anderson to the fact, and suggested that it was upon that fort that our fire should be opened, and that to fire upon the battery would be useless. Major Anderson seemed for a moment to acquiesce, and directed Lieutenant Davis to go down to the lower tier, to take command of a battery of two 42-pounders which were mounted in the angle and which bore on Fort Moultrie, and to await his orders.

Lieutenant Meade earnestly advised that fire should not be opened at all, as it would at once initiate civil war, and that the Governor would probably repudiate the act. Meantime, the *Star of the West* had passed the battery, when Moultrie opening upon her, she turned and left the harbor. Seeing her turn, Major Anderson said, "Hold on; do not fire. I will wait. Let the men go to their quarters, leaving two at each gun-I wish to see the officers at my quarters."*

* Personal notes.

CHAPTER XV.

THE officers assembled in Major Anderson's quarters at once.
All were present. The sight they had just seen seemed to
impress each one individually. The flag of the country had been
fired upon under the very guns of their work, and no helping
hand had been extended. Major Anderson stated to them that
he had called them together to hear their views in relation to the
act of the State, and to say to them that he proposed to close the
harbor with his guns, and to fire upon any vessel that might
attempt to enter.* He desired to receive any recommendations
they might have to make. He began with asking the junior officer,
Lieutenant Hall, who was his adjutant. Lieutenant Hall stated
that he thought the harbor should be closed by our guns. Lieutenant Meade, of the Engineer Department, thought that we
should wait: to close the harbor would be an act of war; that
we would thus inaugurate civil war in the country, and as we had
been directed to act upon the defensive strictly, we had no right
to take such a step. Lieutenant Snyder was for immediate action;
he was in favor of closing the harbor to all vessels and firing upon
all steamboats that were engaged in carrying reinforcements.
Lieutenant Davis thought that we should wait, and send to the

* Personal notes.

Governor, informing him of what had occurred, and ask if he avowed the act. If he sanctioned it we were then to close the harbor with our guns. Captain Seymour's opinion not recorded.

Captain Doubleday advised immediate action. He thought that every day's delay would add to the strength of their position and that they would finally shell the fort. Assistant Surgeon Crawford thought that as the battery was not fired upon when it opened upon the ship, we had suffered the opportunity to go by for immediate action, and that it would be better now to send to the Governor and let him know our determination. Major Anderson acquiesced in the suggestion of the officers, that the Governor should be advised of the course he proposed to take in case the action of his subordinates in firing upon the ship should be avowed by him, and he at once addressed the following despatch to the Governor of the State:

FORT SUMTER, South Carolina, January 9, 1861.

"Sir: Two of your batteries fired this morning upon an unarmed vessel bearing the flag of my Government. As I have not been notified that war has been declared by South Carolina against the Government of the United States, I cannot but think that this hostile act was committed without your sanction or authority. Under that hope, and that alone, did I refrain from opening fire upon your batteries. I have therefore respectfully to ask whether the above-mentioned act, one I believe without a parallel in the history of our country or of any other civilized government, was committed in obedience to your instructions, and to notify you, if it be not disclaimed, that I must regard it as an act of war, and that I shall not, after a reasonable time for the return of my messenger, permit any vessel to pass within range of the guns in my fort. In order to save, as far as lies within my power, the shedding of blood, I beg that you will have due notice of this, my decision, given to all concerned. Hoping, however, that your answer may be such as will justify a further continuance of forbearance upon my part, I have the honor to be,

"Very respectfully, your obedient servant,
"ROBERT ANDERSON,
"Major First Artillery, Commanding.
"To HIS EXCELLENCY the GOVERNOR of South Carolina,"

This despatch was submitted by Major Anderson to a council of his officers, and approved of by them, with the insertion of the clause that he would await a reasonable time for the return of his messenger before opening fire, which was not part of the original

despatch. The delivery of the despatch was entrusted to Lieutenant Hall, who in full uniform and under a white flag bore it
to Charleston. Upon landing, he was surrounded by a crowd of
citizens. Making his way with difficulty through them and followed by them, he finally found the Governor in council at his
office. At the door he met an aide, who invited him to enter. He
declined, but requested that his card be taken to the Governor,
with the statement that he had come under a white flag to see
him in person. The council was dissolved, and he was introduced
to the Governor. In the meantime, a report had been spread
through the city that the object of Lieutenant Hall's visit was to
announce that the city would be bombarded, and statements to
that effect were posted upon the bulletins.

The boat's crew were at once beseiged by the crowd, but were
ordered to hold no communication with any one. After reading
the communication of Major Anderson, the Governor called his
Cabinet together and submitted the letter to them. After some
delay an answer to the communication was handed to Lieutenant
Hall by Governor Pickens in person. As a matter of prudence,
in the excited state of the people, Lieutenant Hall was returned
to his boat by carriage, accompanied by one of the aides of the
Governor and an escort.

The reply of the Governor was clear and decided. He infers
that Major Anderson had not been informed fully of the "precise
relations" which existed between the General Government and
the State of South Carolina. That the State had seceded and had
resumed all of her delegated powers, and had communicated the
fact officially to the Government, and that the right thus exercised
did not now admit of discussion. That it was understood by the
President that the sending of any reinforcements to the troops in
the harbor would be regarded, equally with any change in the
occupation of those forts, as an act of hostility. That the occupancy of Fort Sumter had been regarded as the first act of
positive hostility committed by the troops of the United States
within the limits of the State, and that it occasioned the termina-
tion of the negotiations then pending at Washington. The
attempt to reinforce Fort Sumter or to retake the other forts
which were abandoned, could only be considered by the authorities as an attempt to coerce the State by armed force, and to repel
such an attempt was only "too plainly its duty." Special agents

had been stationed off the bar to warn all approaching vessels having troops on board to reinforce the forts not to enter this harbor, and special orders had been communicated to the officers in command not to open fire upon such vessels "until a shot thrown across their bows should warn them of the prohibition of the State." "Under these circumstances," said he, *"the Star of the West,* it is understood, this morning attempted to enter this harbor with troops on board, and having been notified that she could not enter, was fired into. The act is perfectly justified by me." He informs Major Anderson, also, that his position in the harbor had been tolerated by the authorities; that while the act he complained of was in perfect consistency with the rights of the State, the course he proposed to follow was only reconcilable with "that of imposing upon the State the condition of a conquered province."

This communication was read in the presence of the officers, who thought it rather an extraordinary answer to the note of Major Anderson. It defined, however, so clearly the position of the Governor, that the immediate commencement of hostilities was anticipated. Indeed, it now seemed that there was but one course to pursue.

Shortly afterward, however, Major Anderson again called the officers together and stated to them that he had, upon reflection, determined that it was but right to send a messenger to Washington, and he desired to hear the opinion of the officers upon the subject. It was generally conceded that it would be but right, although some of the officers thought that we should at once pursue the course that we had laid down. Lieutenant Talbot was selected by Major Anderson to go to Washington, and, in advance, to bear the following letter to the Governor.

"HEADQUARTERS, FORT SUMTER, S. C.,
January 9, 1861.
"To HIS EXCELLENCY F. W. PICKENS,
   "Governor of the State of South Carolina.
   "Sir: I have the honor to acknowledge the receipt of your communication of to-day, and to say that, under the circumstances, I have deemed it proper to refer the whole matter to my Government and that I intend deferring the course indicated in my note of this morning, until the arrival from Washington of the instructions I may receive. I have the honor, also, to express a hope that no obstructions will be placed in the way of, and that you will do me the favor to afford every facility to, the

departure and return of the bearer, Lieutenant T. Talbot, United States Army, who has been directed to make the journey.

"I have the honor to be, very respectfully,

(Signed) "ROBERT ANDERSON,

Major U. S. A., commanding."

Later in the day, Lieutenant Talbot, in citizen's dress, accompanied by the writer in uniform, left the work under a white flag and proceeded to Charleston. Upon arriving in Charleston, they were followed by a crowd to the Charleston Hotel, where it was thought that the Governor was to be found. A card was sent, when, after a long delay, an aide-de-camp of the Governor conducted the officers to the executive office, where the Governor was engaged in session with his Cabinet, and where, apparently much business was being transacted. The letter of Major Anderson was handed by Lieutenant Talbot to the Governor, who, upon reading it, expressed his gratification at receiving it, that he was "very glad indeed," and that of course Lieutenant Talbot could go to Washington, and that he would afford him every facility. From the marked courtesy shown by the Governor and those around him, as well as from the expressions used in the conversation that ensued, it was inferred by the officers who carried the letter, that the suspension of his decision to open fire upon the shipping, and his determination to submit the matter to his Government upon the part of Major Anderson, was gratifying to the authorities of the State. The officers were then presented to the members of the Cabinet. The Governor then gave a safeguard to Lieutenant Talbot to proceed through the State, and also a permit to Assistant Surgeon Crawford to obtain the mail matter for the fort, the transmission of which had been prohibited. The officers returned to the boat accompanied by one of the aides of the Governor in a carriage, to avoid the crowd. Some seventy or eighty persons had collected at the boat. No opposition was made to the removal of Lieutenant Talbot's baggage to the station, and the boat returned to the fort.

The threat of Major Anderson to close the harbor to all vessels had brought the possibility of his being able to execute that threat so plainly before the State authorities that it was determined to renew the demand upon him for the delivery of Fort Sumter to the authorities of the State. Accordingly, shortly after noon on the 11th of January, the same day upon which the hulks of four vessels were sunk across the channel at the entrance of the harbor, a small steamer under a white flag was seen approaching the work. She grounded near the fort, when, upon being hailed, she replied "Messenger from the Governor." A boat was sent to her and brought Judge A. G. Magrath, the Secretary of State of South Carolina, and General D. F. Jamison, the State Secretary of War, messengers from the Governor to Major Anderson. They were met by Major Anderson at the wharf and conducted by him into the room of the officer of the guard, within the sally-port of the work, where they remained for some time in close consultation, when Captain Doubleday, Captain Seymour and Captain Foster were called into the room. After some conversation the rest of the officers were sent for as a council of war, and to them was submitted the letter of the Governor. It was as follows:

"STATE OF SOUTH CAROLINA, Executive Office,
"Charleston, January 11, 1861

"To MAJOR ANDERSON,
    "Commanding Fort Sumter.
    "Sir: I have thought proper, under all the circumstances of the peculiar state of public affairs in the country at present, to appoint the Hon. A. G. Magrath and General D. F. Jamison, both members of the Executive Council and of the highest position in the State, to present to you considerations of the gravest public character, and of the deepest interest to all who deprecate the improper waste of life, to induce the delivery of Fort Sumter to the constituted authorities of the State of South Carolina with a pledge on its part to account for such public property as is under your charge.
                "Your obedient servant,
                        (Signed)   "F. W. PICKENS."

The conversation in the guard-room was general, and with special reference to the consideration involved in the proposition of the Governor. Judge Magrath was the principal speaker. He set forth the reasons for the demand in an argument of great force from the standpoint assumed by the State. Upon the assembling of the officers, the question was submitted to Major Anderson, "Shall we accede to the demand of the Governor, or shall we not?" when it was unanimously decided that the demand of the Governor should not be acceded to under any circumstances. Lieutenant Meade, the junior officer, suggested that, as a messenger had been sent to Washington, it would be proper to await his return, and in this view all the officers coincided. The officers then separated, after some conversation, and returned to the room of the officer of the guard, where a long conversation ensued with the messengers from the Governor. A marked impression was made upon them by the statements made. They were told that the Government at Washington was almost dissolved, that a Senator, from his seat in the Senate, had asked who was *de facto* Secretary of War,* and that the President had denied that reinforcements had been sent to us by his authority; that Mississippi had left the Union, and that all Virginia was in a blaze; that Senator Davis, in taking leave of the Senate, had delivered a speech which had made the most profound impression in the country. In reference to the fort, General Jamison stated that there were 20,000 men in the State that were ready to come and would come down and take them, and that they would tear the fort to pieces with their fingers, and that the waters of the harbor would be stained with blood; and that the people in the interior could hardly be restrained from coming down now. Major Anderson now re-entered the room, and stated that he would not be able to comply with the request of the Governor. General Jamison had remarked that he regretted it very much, as God only knew what the consequences would be, when Judge Magrath then said, deliberately and with feeling: "I desire you to understand, Major Anderson, that it is not an alternative that is offered to you by the Governor, it is not peace or war that he offers in making this communication to you: it is done more to give you an opportunity, after understanding all the circumstances, to prevent bloodshed."† Major Anderson at once replied: "I am very glad to know this; I did not so understand it; but I cannot do what belongs to the Government to do. The demand must be made upon them, and I appeal to you as a Christian, as a man, and as a fellow-countryman, to do all that you can to prevent an appeal to arms. I do not say as a soldier, for my duty is plain in that respect. Let it be the last and not the first resort. Why not exhaust diplomacy, as on other matters? I assure you that I am ready to assist you in every way in my power to settle the matter peaceably. I will send an officer with a messenger from the

---

* Senator Slidell.
† Personal notes.

Governor to Washington. I will do anything that is possible and honorable to do to prevent an appeal to arms." An impressive silence followed, when the messengers shortly afterward took their leave. The action of the Governor was considered by Major Anderson as a demand upon him for the surrender of the fort. Although he had received instructions as to his course should he be attacked in his position—which, however, he had reported as secure—he deemed it proper to transfer the responsibility of any decision to Washington, and he prepared and handed to the messengers of the Governor the following letter as they were leaving the work:

HEADQUARTERS, FORT SUMTER, S. C.,
January 11, 1861.

"To HIS EXCELLENCY F. W. PICKENS,
  "Governor of South Carolina."
  Sir: I have the honor to acknowledge the receipt of your demand for the surrender of this fort to the authorities in South Carolina, and to say in reply that the demand is one with which I cannot comply. Your Excellency knows that I have recently sent a messenger to Washington, and that it will be impossible for me to receive an answer to my despatch forwarded by him, at an earlier date than next Monday. What the character of my instructions may be, I cannot foresee.

Should your Excellency deem fit, prior to a resort to arms, to refer this matter to Washington, it would afford me the sincerest pleasure to depute one of my officers to accompany any messenger you may deem proper to be the bearer of your demand. Hoping to God that in this and all other matters in which the honor, welfare and life of our fellow-countrymen are concerned, we shall so act as to meet His approval, and deeply regretting that you have made a demand with which I cannot comply,

"I have the honor to be, with the highest regard,
"Your obedient servant,
"ROBERT ANDERSON,
"Major U. S. Army, Commanding."

Before leaving the fort General Jamison stated to the writer that the officers in the fort could have no idea of the intense feeling animating all classes in the State, and that he daily received offers of service from all quarters offering to serve the State in the humblest capacity. Upon the return of the messengers to Charleston, with a report of their mission and the decision and proposition of Major Anderson, the Governor at once determined to acquiesce in the latter, and early on the morning of the

12th a boat under a white Rag was again seen approaching the work. An aide of the Governor, accompanied by Mr. R. N. Gourdin, had come to say that the Governor had determined to send a messenger to Washington with the officers selected by Major Anderson. Lieutenant Hall was selected, and in a short time was in readiness. His instructions were not only in writing, but he was charged to lay before the Government a detailed narrative of the events that had transpired.

Meantime, the Governor of the State, having determined to send a messenger to accompany Lieutenant Hall to Washington, selected the Hon. Isaac W. Hayne, the Attorney-General of the State, and on January 11 addressed a communication to the President. He stated that he regarded the possession of Fort Sumter by the troops of the United States under the command of Major Anderson, "as not consistent with the dignity or safety of the State of South Carolina." That he had that day addressed a communication to Major Anderson to obtain possession of the forts; that Major Anderson had informed him that he had no authority to comply with his request, and had referred his demand to the President; that he, the Governor, had determined to send to the President the Hon. Isaac W. Hayne, the Attorney-General of the State, and had instructed him to demand the delivery of Fort Sumter to the State. He states also, that both his previous demands of Major Anderson and the one he now makes of the President are suggested in view of his earnest desire to avoid bloodshed, which a persistence in the retention of the fort would cause, and which would be unavailing to secure that possession to the Government. In the demand which he now made, he would secure for the State the satisfaction of having exhausted every attempt to avoid the unhappy consequences, if such should ensue. The envoy was also authorized to pledge the State to an accountability for the valuation of the public property of the United States within Fort Sumter, when the relations of the State with the United States should be adjusted.

The special instructions to the envoy were communicated to him by the Secretary of State of South Carolina from the "Executive Office, State Department, Charleston, January 12, 1861." The demand upon the President now made was stated. The interruption of the negotiations authorized by the Convention, empowering its Commissioners to enter into negotiations with the General Government for the delivery of forts and other real estate within the limits of South Carolina, was referred to; and that this interruption left all matters connected with Fort Sumter and the United States troops in the State affected by the fact "that the continued possession of the fort was not consistent with the dignity or safety of the State, and that an attempt to reinforce the fort would be resisted. A state of hostilities had, in consequence, arisen and the State placed in a condition of defense, and that while she was preparing, an attempt was made to reinforce Fort Sumter and repelled." "You are now instructed to proceed to Washington, and there, in the name of the Governor of the State of South Carolina, inquire of the President of the United States whether it was by his order that troops of the United States were sent into the harbor of Charleston to reinforce Fort Sumter. If he avows that order, you will then inquire whether he asserts a right to introduce troops of the United States within the limits of this State, to occupy Fort Sumter, and you will, in case of his avowal, inform him that neither will be permitted, and either will be regarded as his declaration of war against the State of South Carolina."

The demand of the Governor upon him having been referred by Major Anderson to the Government, the envoy was instructed to demand from the President the withdrawal of the troops of the United States from Fort Sumter and the delivery of that work to the State.

The question of property was not to be allowed to embarrass the assertion of the political right of the State to the possession of the fort. That possession was alone consistent with the dignity and safety of the State, but it was not inconsistent with a right to compensation in money upon the part of another Government, provided that the claim of such Government was a just one; but that the possession of Fort Sumter could not be compensated by any consideration of any kind from the Government, when that possession was "invasive of the dignity" and affected the safety of the State, nor could it now become a matter of discussion or negotiation. The envoy was therefore directed to require from the President a "positive and distinct answer" to his demand for the delivery of the fort. He was authorized, also, to adjust all matters susceptible of valuation in money, upon the principles of equity and justice always recognized by independent nations.

The President was to be warned that an attempt to continue the possession of Fort Sumter, would "inevitably" lead to a bloody issue, with but one conclusion; that the citizens of the State recognized it as a duty to shed their blood in defense of their rights, and that the Governor in such a cause would feel that his obligation to the State would "justify the sacrifice necessary to secure that end." And the letter concludes with the statement "that the Governor does not desire to remind the President of the responsibilities which are upon him."

The envoy of the Governor, Mr. Hayne, and the messenger of Major Anderson, Lieutenant Hall, left at once for Washington, where they arrived on the evening of the 12th of January.

CHAPTER XVI.

PREPARATIONS for the defense of the fort were pushed on vigorously under the immediate superintendence of Major Anderson himself. The armament was the most important interest. Heavy guns, unmounted, were encumbering the parade. These had to be raised to the parapet, their gun-carriages refitted, and the guns mounted *en barbette* and on the lower tier. The necessary tackle for hoisting, and the proper implements for manœuvring them had to be prepared. The means and materials at the disposition of the garrison for this purpose were limited, and in some instances wanting, but the men worked under the proper officers with the greatest energy, so that on the 21st of January Major Anderson was enabled to report to his Government that he had then fifty-one guns in position; twenty-four were *en barbette,*

198

including six 8 inch Columbiads and five 8-inch seacoast howitzers
while in the lower tier there were twenty-four 32 and 42 pounders
bearing upon Fort Johnson, Fort Moultrie and the channel.
Three 10-inch Columbiads lay upon the parade, it being impossible to raise them to their proper positions by any means at the
disposal of the garrison. Platforms were prepared, and these
heavy guns were mounted by the 5th of February, as mortars, to
bear upon Morris Island, Fort Moultrie and the city of Charleston. At the same time, four 8-inch seacoast howitzers were

HOISTING GUNS ON THE PARAPET, FORT SUMTER.

planted in the area of the parade of the work, to bear upon
Morris Island. A large number of 8-inch shell were filled and
friction-tubes inserted. Long lanyards were attached to them.
They were to be dropped from the parapet in case of assault, and
exploded by the firing of the friction-tubes upon the tension of
the lanyard. Cartridges were prepared for the Columbiads, and,
owing to a want of the proper material, the flannel shirts in the
Quartermaster's Department were used for bags. Every
practical means to strengthen the position was adopted. The

main gate was reinforced by a solid wall of masonry, three feet in thickness, a narrow passage being left for egress from the work, as well as to serve as an embrasure for an 8-inch howitzer, which had been placed in position at the entrance, and whose direct fire would sweep the wharf. Two guns were mounted outside to the right and left of the sally port, and lanyards to fire them brought inside. Their fire commanded the base of the gorge wall. The filling up of the embrasures on the second tier was continued. There being no flanking defenses, "Machicouli galleries" were made at the suggestion of Captain Doubleday and run out, overhanging the angles of the fort to command the faces of the work. They were prepared for musketry fire and for the dropping of shells. The loop-holes for musketry in the gorge wall were partially filled up. From the smallness of his force, and the fact that the lower tier was the weakest point, Major Anderson determined to fill up some of the embrasures on that tier, where he had not sufficient strength to man his guns, to close up by brick masonry the embrasures not needed, and to reduce the effective battery on this tier to three guns to each angle. The scarcity of necessary material began now to be felt. All of the cement and bricks had been used; the scarcity of the fuel forbade the burning of lime, and the substitution of dry stones was resorted to. The work of defense was pushed on uninterruptedly under the direction of the able and energetic engineer officers and their force, who alone mounted all the guns and lent their willing aid and assistance to every measure of defense. The arrangement of the disposable force gave but eight men only to each face and flank, with a general reserve of but twenty men. By the 14th of January, an arrangement was entered into in regard to the mails for the fort, the transmission of which had been suspended. An exchange was to take place at Fort Johnson, in order to avoid any risk of a collision between the boat's crew and ill-disposed persons in the city. Owing to the severity of the weather, the whole command were now quartered in the officers' quarters, which were completed.

Early on the 11th of January a small steamer was seen off the ship channel near Morris Island towing the hulks of four vessels. They were loaded with stone. After considerable movement, as if uncertain where to locate them, she finally anchored them in a line across the mouth of the channel near the bar and sank them one by one. This was to close the channel to all vessels. The hulks were towed in from without the harbor.

The firing upon the *Star of the West* was still the subject of earnest discussion among the officers, some of whom thought that, in agreeing to await the return of the messenger, an error of judgment had been committed, as the State would go on actively with her preparations, which she did. The communication of the Secretary of War of the 10th of January, commending the course of Major Anderson, had greatly encouraged him as well as his command. He felt deeply the perplexing circumstances under which he found himself, and he reported to the Government on the 29th of January that everything around him showed it to be the determination of the people to bring on a collision with the General Government. No fresh provisions had been permitted to come to the fort, nor was he allowed to procure his usual supplies in Charleston. This prohibition had been made the subject of remonstrance at Washington, and earnest representation had been made by prominent Southern men to the Governor, who determined, finally, to permit the transmission of such supplies. On the 9th of January General Jamison, the State Secretary of War, informed Major Anderson that the Government had directed that an officer of the State should procure and carry over to him, with his mails, such supplies of meats and vegetables as he might require.

Major Anderson replied that he was at a loss to understand the Governor's action, as he had made no representation that he was in need of such supplies; that the manner in which a military post was supplied was prescribed by law; and if he was allowed to procure his supplies by contract, as he had been in the habit of doing, and as it was his "right" to do, he would go on, but if the permission was "founded on courtesy and civility," he was compelled to decline it; and he hopes also that the course he deemed proper to pursue in the matter would allay the "excitement" which, he inferred from the papers, was growing in the city. Meantime, without waiting for a reply from Major Anderson, the Quartermaster-General of the State, in accordance with the orders of the Secretary of War of the State, sent down in connection with the mail on the morning of the 19th, a quantity of "fresh meat and vegetables to last the garrison of Fort Sumter for forty-eight hours," informing Major Anderson that he would purchase and take down every day such provisions from the city market as he might indicate. The boat arrived at the fort at noon on the 20th. Its arrival and the sight of fresh provisions created an excitement among the men, who had been without such supplies since the 26th of December. The provisions were seized and borne rapidly to the kitchen, when the order of Major Anderson was received to return them to the boat, as he had declined to receive them. Without complaint or hesitation they were returned. On the 21st Major Anderson reported the facts to his Government, with the statement that so many acts of harshness and incivility had occurred since his removal from Fort Moultrie, which he had not deemed it proper to notice or report, that he could not accept of any civility which might be considered as a favor or an act of charity.

On the 21st General Jamison replied that "the Governor was influenced solely by considerations of courtesy;" that if he had no other reasons he would have been moved by prudential reasons for the safety of Major Anderson's "people" in preventing a collision; that the Governor was indifferent to the manner in which the supplies were procured, provided that they were carried over under an officer of the State. On the 24th a letter was accordingly written, by Major Anderson's direction, to the former contractor, renewing the terms of the old contract and requesting that it should go at once into effect, and specifying at the same time the supplies that he required. Time passed and the contractor made no reply; and Major Anderson in his report to the Government of the 31st of January presumed that the contractor dared not send any provisions for fear that he would be "regarded as a traitor to South Carolina for furnishing comfort and aid to her enemies."

On that day, however, Major Anderson had renewed his application through a member of the Convention, Mr. Gourdin, who informed him that the Governor was desirous that he should receive the supplies regularly, "and thought that there could be no difficulty in reference to groceries also."

The action of Major Anderson was largely influenced by erroneous statements made in regard to his being daily in receipt of these supplies. The principal journal in Charleston had published a statement on the 19th of January that provisions were daily sent to the fort, and in his reply to the Southern Senators in Washington who, on the 15th of January, had addressed to Colonel Hayne a letter suggesting that Major Anderson should be allowed to obtain these supplies, he had answered: "Major Anderson and his command, let me assure you, *do* now obtain all necessary supplies of food (including fresh meat and vegetables), and I believe fuel and water."

In his report of the 27th of January to his Government, Major Anderson referred to the "false reports" originating "in Charleston and elsewhere" about him, and that it was "apparent enough" that the object of one of them—which was that he was getting fresh provisions from the Charleston market—was to show that they were treating him courteously, "which was not a fact," and that up to that moment "he had not derived the least advantage from the Charleston markets."

The reason for the action of the contractor was simply that he had not been paid for seven months. His account was at that time over $500, and he feared, from the condition of things, that all relations between the fort and the city might be at any moment interrupted and his money lost. Lieutenant Hall had returned from Washington, neglecting to bring with him a treasury draft for his Department. The contractor was afterward paid, when he renewed his contract and resumed his dealings with the fort.

The result of the hasty movement from Fort Moultrie began already to show itself in the deficiencies in the small stores. Upon the departure of Lieutenant Hall to Washington the writer was directed to assume the duties of quartermaster and commissary of the post temporarily, during the absence of that officer. An inspection and inventory of the stores on hand on the 15th of January showed a limited supply of some of the articles of the ration, that instead of a six months' supply there was scarcely four, and that it would be necessary to place the command upon half-rations of coffee and sugar, and to deprive the officers temporarily altogether. There were neither candles nor soap for issue, and but half a barrel of salt, and the batteries and guard were lighted by using the oil of the light-house, in bowls in which wicking was placed and a taper made.

Strict guards were placed over the batteries, which were examined at every relief during the night under the immediate direction of the officer of the day. The workmen of the Engineer

Department were affected by the firing upon the *Star of the West* and the fear of an approaching conflict, and many left, largely reducing the force. This, however, did not continue, and forty-three remained, working with alacrity at any work required of them, almost exclusively mounting all of the guns and remaining faithful and enthusiastic in the discharge of their duty till the last. Efforts were made to dissatisfy them, as well as the soldiers, whenever opportunity offered; and various reports, many of them wholly without foundation, were published and circulated. It was reported that the men were retained in Fort Sumter by force, and had attempted to escape from the windows; it was also reported that a boat from Fort Sumter, in making a reconnoissance of a battery on Morris Island, had been fired into and one man wounded. On the 19th Lieutenant Davis, who had gone to town in charge of four enlisted men who had been summoned by the civil court as witnesses, was informed that his men had become seditious and were threatening him, and that he ought to arm himself, as the men intended to desert. Arms were offered to Lieutenant Davis, which he declined. On the 27th, the men who went for the mail to Fort Johnson, in pursuance of the arrangement made, were rudely treated, nothing but the mail was allowed to go, and a small quantity of tobacco which had been bought with money sent by the foreman was taken away, and no communication with the men allowed. Inside, the work rapidly progressed. As the heavier guns were mounted, experimental firing to determine the range was commenced, and continued from time to time with satisfactory results. The men of the command and the workmen had been lodged in the completed officers' quarters, and were thus protected from the constant rain and fogs that prevailed during the month of January, and which permitted the necessary work to go on without observation.

Meantime, Lieutenant Talbot, who after the firing upon the *Star of the West* had been sent to Washington by Major Anderson, returned to the fort on the 19th of January, bringing despatches to Major Anderson and to Governor Pickens. The news that he brought was greatly encouraging to the garrison: Major Anderson's course was approved by the Secretary of War and the Cabinet, and by Union men generally. The different departments all applauded the course taken by Major Anderson, and the administration would support him.

The following is the letter of the Secretary of War:

"WAR DEPARTMENT, January 16, 1861.
"MAJOR ROBERT ANDERSON,
    "*First Artillery, Commanding Fort Sumter.*

"Sir: Your dispatch No. 17, covering your correspondence with the Governor of South Carolina, has been received from the hand of Lieutenant Talbot. You rightly designate the firing into the *Star of the West* as "an act of war," and one which was actually committed without the slightest provocation. Had their act been perpetrated by a foreign nation, it would have been your imperative duty to have resented it with the whole force of your batteries. As, however, it was the work of the Government of South Carolina, which is a member of this confederacy, and was prompted by the passions of a highly-inflamed population of citizens of the United States, your forbearance to return the fire is fully approved by the President. Unfortunately, the Government had not been able to make known to you that the *Star of the West* had sailed from New York for your relief, and hence, when she made her appearance in the harbor of Charleston, you did not feel the force of the obligation to protect her approach as you would naturally have done had this information reached you.

"Your late dispatches, as well as the very intelligent statement of Lieutenant Talbot, have relieved the Government of the apprehensions recently entertained for your safety. In consequence, it is not its purpose at present to re-enforce you. The attempt to do so would, no doubt, be attended by a collision of arms and the effusion of blood—a national calamity which the President is most anxious, if possible, to avoid. You will, therefore, report frequently your condition, and the character and activity of the preparations, if any, which may be being made for an attack upon the fort, or for obstructing the Government in any endeavors it may make to strengthen your command.

"Should your dispatches be of a nature too important to be intrusted to the mails, you will convey them by special messengers. Whenever, in your judgment, additional supplies or re-enforcements are necessary for your safety, or for a successful defense of the fort, you will at once communicate the fact to this Department, and a prompt and vigorous effort will be made to forward them.

                "Very respectfully, your obedient servant,
                                        "J. HOLT."

In regard to the firing upon the *Star of the West,* the Secretary of War, in his despatch of the 16th of January, informs Major Anderson that the Government had not been able to make known to him that the *Star of the West* had sailed to his relief, and that in consequence he had not felt "the force of the obligation to protect her approach" as he would otherwise have done; that the firing upon her was an act of war, committed without the slightest provocation, and had it been committed by a foreign nation his imperative duty would have required him to resent it with the whole force of his batteries. As it was, however, "the work of the Government of South Carolina, which is a member of this Confederacy," and prompted by passions of American citizens, the Secretary informed him that his forbearance to return the fire is fully approved by the President.

He also says that his late despatches had greatly relieved the Government of their apprehensions for his safety. "In consequence," he says, "it is not their purpose at present to reinforce you; that the attempt would be attended with bloodshed—a national calamity which the President was most anxious, if possible, to avoid. He was to report his condition frequently, and also the character and activity of the preparations about him to attack the fort or to obstruct the Government in its endeavors to strengthen him." And he concludes his despatch by assuring Major Anderson that whenever, in his judgment, additional supplies or reinforcements should be necessary for his safety, or for a successful defense of the fort, he should at once communicate the fact, "and a prompt and vigorous effort will be made to forward them." The reception of this despatch greatly sustained and encouraged the garrison. Besides the despatch of January 10, from the same authority, it was the only indorsement the garrison had received that their course was approved by the Department, and anything like definite instructions as to the future furnished for their guidance. This, in connection with the sentiments of Lieutenant-General Scott, which were announced to the men at parade, and which were received with enthusiasm by them, greatly encouraged the garrison, who renewed their work with increased energy and vigor.

The presence of so large a number of women and children, besides drawing largely upon his supplies, embarrassed Major Anderson in carrying on the defensive preparation of his work; and in view of possible hostilities, he determined to send them to the North. Accordingly, on the 19th of January, in a communication to General Jamison, the Secretary of War of the State, he asks that, as an act of humanity and great kindness, the Governor would permit a New York steamer to transport the women and children of his garrison to New York, that he could not furnish them with proper food, and that it was an indulgence always granted "even during a siege, in time of actual war." The Governor at once expressed his willingness, and offered every facility in his power to enable Major Anderson to remove them from the fort. An agent of the New York line of steamers was permitted to come to Fort Sumter, with whom arrangements were concluded, and on the 1st of February, forty-two women and children were embarked upon a lighter and left the fort for the steamer.

At noon on the 3d the steamer passed under the guns of the fort on her way northward. The men had crowded to the parapet, and with the consent of Major Anderson one gun was fired as the vessel passed—amid the loud cheers of the men—which was answered from the steamer. The number of women sent on was much larger than the legal allowance, but Major Anderson thought that under the present excited state of feeling towards his command, it would not do to send to the city or to Sullivan's Island any of the soldiers' wives or their relatives who had been living with them. The men lingered upon the parapet until the vessel was lost to view on the horizon, and all felt that the departure of their women and children, while relieving the garrison from embarrassment and responsibility, did not the less clearly define to them their own position.

While within the fort the work of defense was carried on steadily and with energy, the authorities and troops of the State were no less active, and works for the defense of the harbor, as well as for the ultimate reduction of Fort Sumter, were begun, and pushed forward with the greatest industry and vigor. The means at their command were crude and inappropriate at this early period, their officers and men inexperienced and new, and often differing widely in their views, but they worked with an enthusiasm and unanimity of purpose that largely compensated for many deficiencies and amply sustained them in their purpose until the last.

The retention of Major Anderson and his command at Fort Sumter by the Government, its attempt to reinforce and provision him, and the open repulse of that attempt had more clearly defined the relation existing between the Government and the State. The one determined to hold the fort as its property and to maintain the garrison; the other claimed its possession as a right arising from its new political position, and demanded its surrender, and it prepared to assert that right by force. Upon the 9th of January, the day upon which the *Star of the West* was fired upon, the Governor of South Carolina addressed a communication to three engineer officers* directing them to come together immediately to consider and report upon the most favorable plan for operating upon Fort Sumter, so as to reduce it, by batteries or other means, and they were to include Colonel Manigault, the State Ordnance officer, in their consultation.

MOUNTING GUNS WITH THE GIN.

This military board, or Ordnance Board, exercised more or less control over military operations. They objected to the firing upon the *Star of the West,* as they had also done to the occupancy of the forts on the 27th of December.†

The persons designated met promptly, and upon the following date reported to the Governor that they were decidedly and unanimously of the opinion "that surprise, assault or stratagem

---

* Colonels Walter Gwynn, White and Trapier.
† Ordnance Board: General James Jones, General Gab. Manigault, General Jamison, Major Walter Gwynn, Thos. F. Dayton.

were not to be depended upon, as uncertain in their results and involving much probable sacrifice of life, and that their dependence and sole reliance must be upon batteries of heavy ordnance" until "an incessant bombardment and cannonade" had made such an impression that an assault would be easy, and they submitted the following plan: that the dismantled battery "at Fort Moultrie should be restored, and protected by merlons and made an embrasure battery;" that mortar batteries should be erected at a point west of Fort Moultrie on Sullivan's Island nearest to Fort Sumter; and that at Fort Johnson and Cummings Point a battery of three 8-inch Columbiads should also be established. As germain to the plan of attack upon Fort Sumter, they recommend the erection forthwith of "a gun-battery of heavy guns" at 1,400 yards east from Fort Moultrie to command the Maffit Channel, and which, by blocking up all the other channels to the city, could be defended in case of failure in their attack upon Fort Sumter and the destruction of Fort Moultrie, and enable them to get possession of Fort Sumter by "the slow (but sure) process of starvation." The plan was approved, and preparations immediately made and continued to carry it into effect. Whatever of hesitancy or uncertainty may have prevailed before the *Star of the West* was fired upon, there was no illusion as to the purpose of the State after that event had occurred. The preparations for defense and for the reduction of the fort were carried on openly and without disguise, and the garrison witnessed, from day to day, the gradual construction of works intended to close the harbor to all relief to them and to be used in their destruction.

On every side there was the greatest activity manifested. Steamers laden with troops and munitions and material of war were passing and repassing by day and night. Large bodies of negroes were employed without interruption in constructing the new works and in repairing and strengthening the old. Signalling between the town, the forts and the vessels was in constant practice. At daylight on the 12th it was discovered that the parapet of Fort Moultrie had been lined with merlons during the previous night. Three large traverses were subsequently erected on the sea front, and one begun by our own engineers was enlarged, and solid merlons, formed of timber, sand-bags and earth were raised between all the guns that bore on Fort Sumter, as well as others, to protect the guns on the sea front from an enfilading fire. These merlons were run up solidly to the height of five feet, and completely covered the quarters and barracks of Fort Moultrie to the eaves. The guns dismounted by the burning of the gun-carriages upon the abandonment of the fort by Major Anderson were all remounted by the 27th of January. Rapid progress was made upon the battery at Cummings Point. A large quantity of material was landed, and a strong force of workmen kept constantly employed. Heavy guns were landed, and although from the isolated position of Fort Sumter it was impossible to determine with positive accuracy the exact nature of the work going on around it, it was yet evident that every energy was being brought to bear upon the construction of their batteries in preparation for an attack upon and the reduction of the fort. Work was often carried on by night, and heavy timbers, formed into rafts, floated down and stranded near the sites of the batteries begun.

On the 15th the Fresnel light and the light-house on Morris Island were taken down, and the strictest watch kept upon vessels attempting to enter the harbor. A steamer, thought to be of the New York line, in coming in on the morning of the 12th, had a shot fired across her bow, when she ran up the Palmetto flag and was allowed to pass.

On the 18th of January the Executive Council determined upon the construction of a "floating battery," and for which $1,200 was appropriated and the work at once begun. The public press seemed determined to maintain a hostile feeling and to bring on a collision with the Government. A feverish expectation that reinforcements would again be sent seemed to pervade the community, while within the fort a feeling prevailed that an attack upon it was inevitable. On the 29th firing from the batteries on Morris Island took place. Rockets were sent up, and answered from the steamers. The guard-boats came in from outside, with two tugs from the bar, and after midnight two guns were fired from Moultrie. It was supposed by those in the fort that a steamer was approaching. No vessel could be seen. In reporting the circumstances to his Government, Major Anderson, whose anxiety had been clearly manifested, says that he hopes no effort would be made by friends to throw supplies in, and that their doing so would do more harm than good.

So closely was the work upon Fort Moultrie watched by the

engineer officer, that he was enabled from his observations to criticize the construction. He reported to his chief on the 21st of January, in a general summary of the work going on, that he thought the timber cheeks to the embrasures at Fort Moultrie, set on end like pallisades, were "objectionable"; that "the exterior slope of the merlons is too great to resist the pressure of the earth, and that the sand-bags are pressed out in one or two places."

Of the battery at the east end of Sullivan's Island, nothing could be reported, as it was beyond the reach of our glasses and shielded from our fire. The existence of an additional battery, said to contain guns or mortars and located about 300 yards west of Fort Moultrie, was reported, but being masked by houses and fences, could not be seen sufficiently to be described accurately.

Two batteries at Fort Johnson were established, one for three guns and the other for the same number of mortars. The battery on Morris Island, which fired upon the *Star of the West* and which now mounted four guns, was also reported, as well as the progress made upon the formidable battery in construction upon Cummings Point, and upon which a powerful fire from Fort Sumter from four 8-inch Columbiads, three 42-pounders, one 8-inch seacoast howitzer and six 24-pounders *en barbette* and two 32-pounders in the lower tier could be brought to bear.

On the 31st of January, a further report of the work done around the fort was made by the same officer, who stated that "the batteries on the island above Fort Moultrie are two in number. The first is only a short distance above the Moultrie House, and about 1,460 yards above Fort Moultrie. It is armed with three guns, either 24-pounders or 32-pounders. It is not in sight of this fort. Its position is opposite that portion of the Maffit Channel which comes closest to the island. The second battery is at the upper or east end of the island and is armed with two guns, 24 or 32 pounders. The last information from the island gave the number of men there as 1,450."

A failure to comply with his instructions in regard to the provisions had resulted in a deficiency of small-stores, and on the 27th of January, Major Anderson reported to the Government that his supplies now consisted of 38 bbls. pork; 37 bbls. flour, 13 bbls. hard-bread, 2 bbls. beans, 1 bbl. coffee, ½ bbl. sugar, 3 bbls. vinegar, 10 lbs. candles, 40 lbs. soap, ½ bbl. salt.

The envoy of the Governor had meanwhile arrived in Washington and opened negotiations with the Government, but as far as could be determined from our position, there was no interruption whatever in the prosecution of the works undertaken by the State.

CHAPTER XVII.

IN order to a full and just understanding of the course pursued by the Secretary of War, Governor Floyd, at this juncture,
his relations to the President, and his final action, a résumé of his
connection with these events is necessary.

The President had not known Governor Floyd personally
before tendering to him a position in his Cabinet. He had,
like his father, been Governor of Virginia, and the fact that he
had declined a recommendation from the Electoral College of
Virginia, urging him for a position in the Cabinet, believing as he
did, that the President should be left free in his 'choice, brought
him under the favorable notice of Mr. Buchanan, who appointed'
him Secretary of War. He was at this time, and up to nearly the
close of Mr. Buchanan's administration, an avowed Union man
and a "consistent opponent of secession." He had supported
the President in his determination not to send reinforcements to
Charleston Harbor, and he was resolved, as far as it lay in his own
power, to maintain the existing status in the harbor until an effort
at negotiation should have been fairly tried. He thought secession unnecessary, but recognized it as a right of the State, and
he fully sympathized with the South in whatever action she might
see fit to take, while at the same time he was ever opposed

to coercion. His position at the head of the War Department gave him especial prominence as the events developed themselves and daily became more threatening.   But developments of another nature began to be known, which very seriously affected the character of the Secretary, and largely altered his relations to the President.   In the early autumn of the year 1860, and before the return of the President to Washington, a large claim had been presented to the War Department by one De Groot. The Secretary was anxious that this claim should be paid. The papers had been presented at the Treasury Department, but upon examination the Secretary, Mr. Cobb, determined to suspend the payment until the return of the President to Washington.   Upon his return, the papers were sent by his direction to the Attorney-General, Judge Black, and while in his hands, he was called upon at his office by the Secretary of War. The claim was refused. The confidence of the President in his Secretary had been shaken; but while he believed that he was without judgment in financial matters, or ability to manage them, he was not wanting in personal integrity. But shortly afterwards, an exposure was made of a serious fraud occurring in the office of the Secretary of the Interior directly, and involving the personal character of the Secretary of War. It was reported to the President on the night of the 22d of December, that eight hundred State bonds for $1,000 each, which had been held in trust by the Government for different Indian tribes, had been removed from the safe in the office of the Secretary of the Interior, and had been delivered by Goddard Bailey, the clerk in charge of them, to William H. Russell, of the firm of Russell, Majors & Waddell. Bailey had, from time to time, received from Russell bills corresponding in amount to the bonds abstracted, and which he had substituted for them in the safe in the office of the Secretary of the Interior, transferring the bonds to Russell.

These bills were drawn by the firm of Russell, Majors & Waddell on John B. Floyd, Secretary of War. They had been drawn in anticipation and accepted in violation of the law. The acceptances were thirteen in number, and it was remarked "that the last of them, dated on the 13th of December, 1860, for $135,-000, had been drawn for the precise sum necessary to make the aggregate amount of the whole number of bills exactly equal to that of the abstracted bonds." This exposure produced a profound effect in the country. A commission "to investigate and report" upon the subject was appointed by the House of Representatives, at the instance of the Secretary of the Interior, Mr. Thompson, who in their report of the 12th of February, 1861, wholly exonerated that officer by a declaration that they had discovered "nothing" to indicate that he had any complicity in the transaction "or knowledge of it, or anything to involve him in the slightest degree in the fraud." In pursuing their investigation the Commissioners had summoned before them for examination as witnesses both Wm. H. Russell and John B. Floyd. An act of Congress had provided that a witness examined before a committee of either House, should not be held "to answer criminally in any court of justice for any fact or act" touching which he shall have testified.

The action of the Committee thus prevented any further investigation of a judicial character, but the connection of the Secretary of War with this "fraudulent transaction" concentrated upon him so much of public feeling that the President determined to remove him from his Cabinet. Sending for his Secretary of State, Judge Black, he mentioned to him his determination, and requested him to see the Secretary of War and ask him to tender his resignation. This the Secretary of State declined to do; while stating to the President his willingness to do all that lay in the line of his duty, he considered that 'this was a matter so entirely between the President and his Secretary of War alone, that he preferred not to interfere. In this the President acquiesced, saying that he would "find some one."* Shortly afterward he sought the Vice-President, Mr. Breckenridge, who was a kinsman of Secretary Floyd, and communicated to him his wishes. The Secretary had entertained at the time no thought of resigning, and he so stated to the Vice-President, qualifying his statement at the same time that he would only resign in case the President should express such a wish. "The President does wish it," replied Mr. Breckenridge. But that cannot be," said the Secretary, "for he has not so intimated to me." "He has requested me to say so to you," said the Vice-President, who then informed the Secretary that in case he should not resign he would be removed. The Secretary then stated that he would resign his office.

---

* Judge Black to writer.

But he did not resign at that time, although the President considered him as virtually out of his Cabinet as he was and had been for any purpose of advice or counsel, although he presented himself at the Cabinet meetings so constantly held at the time that the South Carolina Commissioners were in Washington, and Anderson had made his movement from Fort Moultrie to Fort Sumter. On the 29th of December the formal resignation of his office was sent to the President. It was immediately accepted without reference to the offer of the Secretary to continue in the discharge of the duties until his successor could be appointed, and he left the Cabinet, giving way to the Postmaster-General, Holt, who was appointed Secretary of War, *ad interim.*

On the 20th of December, the day upon which the Ordinance of Secession was passed by the Convention of South Carolina, the Secretary of War, without the knowledge or consent of the President, directed the Chief of the Ordnance Bureau, Captain Maynadier, to forward to the forts on Ship Island and at Galveston the heavy guns necessary to their armament. The usual form in transmitting orders in such case was not observed, and the order was given verbally and was not recorded. It was in every way premature, for the forts were in no condition to receive their armament.

The order of the Secretary was obeyed by Captain Maynadier, who in his letter of the 3d of February; 1862, to the Council of Representatives, stated that it never entered into his mind "that there could be any improper motive or object in the order," as the Secretary was then regarded throughout the country as a strong advocate of the Union, and an opponent of secession." In accordance with the order, and under the regular routine of the service, towards the close of December the armament was made, ready for shipment on board of the *Silver Wave,* then awaiting the transfer. The Engineer Department had informed the Chief of Ordnance that the number and character of the guns required was 113 Columbiads and eleven 32-pounders. The news of the order that a number of the large guns at their foundry were about to be sent South, soon spread among the community of Pittsburg, and caused immediate and great excitement. Secretary Floyd had now left the Cabinet. A committee of gentlemen of the city of Pittsburg had meantime communicated the facts to the President, who, through his then Secretary of War, Mr. Holt, promptly countermanded the order. The guns were not moved, the excitement was allayed, and on the 4th of January, 1861, a formal vote of thanks from the select and common councils of the city was tendered to the President, his Secretary of State, Judge Black, and the Secretary of War, Mr. Holt.

Previously to this affair public rumor had connected the name of the Secretary of War with a transaction involving the transmission of a large amount of small-arms to the South "for the use of insurgents." It was stated, and at the time generally credited, that the Secretary of War, with the knowledge of the President, had taken from the Northern arsenals in December, 1859, 15,000 stand of arms of superior quality, with their accoutrements and supplies of ammunition, and transferred them in excessive quantities to the arsenals at Fayetteville, Charleston, Augusta, Mount Vernon and Baton Rouge in the South, "so that on the breaking out of the maturing rebellion they might be found without cost, except to the United States, in the most convenient positions for distribution among the insurgents."

So important a charge could not pass unnoticed, and the Committee on Military Affairs of the House of Representatives was instructed to inquire and report to the House into all the circumstances connected with the charge made; and the Committee were authorized not only to send for persons and papers, but "to report at any time in preference to all other business."

While the report of the Committee of the House wholly relieved the Secretary of War from any criminal intent in the transmission of these arms, his course had been such that it was necessary for him, as he thought, to propitiate those with whom he had now thoroughly identified himself; and upon his arrival at Richmond he announced "that he had, while Secretary of War, supplied the South with arms in anticipation of the approaching rebellion" —a confession that he had proved treacherous to his former high official trust. And he succeeded. He was taken into favor and was subsequently appointed to the rank of brigadier-general in the Confederate Army, although in opposition to the wishes of Mr. Jefferson Davis, who only yielded to the solicitations of Virginia in his behalf.

CHAPTER XVIII

THE envoy of the Governor of South Carolina arrived in Washington on the 12th January, and on the 14th held an "informal and unofficial" interview with the President. He had already been informed that what was of an official nature should be conducted by written communications. He did not present his credentials, but informed the President verbally that he bore a letter from the Governor of South Carolina in regard to the occupation of Fort Sumter, and which he would deliver to him with a communication from himself the next day. His arrival, however, and the object of his mission had become known.

On the 15th of January the envoy was waited upon by a Senator from Alabama, representing all the Senators from the States which had then seceded or were about to secede, who were then in Washington. He represented to the envoy that all of these Senators felt interested in the object of his mission equally with South Carolina; that initiation of hostilities now between South Carolina and the. General Government would necessarily involve their States; and that the action of South Carolina might complicate the relations between her and the seceding States and interfere with a peaceful solution of the difficulties existing.

218

They therefore requested that he would defer for a few days the delivery of the letter of the Governor to the President, until the suggestions they had to make should be considered by both To this the envoy agreed, when on the same day the Senators referred to addressed to him a communication informing him that they were apprised of his arrival with the letter to the President, but that without knowing its contents they yet requested him to defer its delivery. That the possession of Fort Sumter, and the circumstances under which it was taken, was a "just cause of irritation and apprehension" upon the part of the State, and the chief if not the only source of difficulty, but that they had assurances that it was only held as "property," without any hostile or unfriendly purpose. They desired an amicable adjustment, and, representing States which had already seceded or would soon do so, and whose people felt that they had a common destiny with South Carolina and were looking forward to meet her in the coming Convention of the 15th of February, to form a new confederation and provisional Government, they thought that it was due from South Carolina to the other slave-holding States that she should avoid initiating hostilities, as far as she could do so consistently with her honor. They also asserted that "we have the public declaration of the President, that he has not the constitutional power to make war in South Carolina, and that the public peace shall not be disturbed by any act of hostility towards your State." Hence, they saw no reason why a settlement of existing difficulties might not be arrived at, if time were given for calm and deliberate counsel, and they trusted that an arrangement would be agreed upon between him and the Presidents "at least until the 15th of February next." They urged, too, that the State should suffer Major Anderson to obtain necessary supplies "of food, fuel or water," and enjoy free communication by post or special messenger with the President, upon the understanding that the President would not send him reinforcements during the same period; and their proposition, with the answer of the envoy, they proposed to submit to the President. These suggestions they hoped might be submitted to the Governor if the envoy himself was not clothed with the power to act, and that until his response was communicated to the President, "of course" Fort Sumter would not be attacked and the President would not offer to reinforce it. The letter was signed by Louis T. Wigfall, John Hemphill, D. L.,

Yulee, S. R. Mallory, Jeff. Davis, C. C. Clay, Jr., Benj. Fitz-patrick, A. Iverson, John Slidell, J. P. Benjamin.

The envoy felt the force of the appeal made to him, and, as far as he felt justified, complied with the request. As he stated in his communication of the 17th inst., he was not clothed with power to make the arrangements they suggested, but he offered to withhold the communication with which he was charged and to await further instructions, provided that the Senators who addressed him could get satisfactory assurances "that *no* rein-forcements would be sent to Fort Sumter in the interval," and that there should be no act of hostility towards the State. He assures the Senators, also, that Major Anderson was then obtain-ing "all necessary supplies," which was erroneous, and he closed his communication by authorizing the Senators to assure the President that in case of their proposition being acceded to, no attack would be made upon Fort Sumter until the response of the Governor had been received and communicated to him. On the 19th of January the correspondence between the "Senators of the United States" and Colonel Hayne was presented to the Presi-dent, who was asked to "take into consideration the subject, of said correspondence." This letter was dated in the Senate Chamber, and signed by Benj. Fitzpatrick, S. R. Mallory and John Slidell. To these Senators the Secretary of War, upon the part of the President, addressed a reply on the 22nd of January, three days after the receipt of their letter. The Secretary acknowledges the receipt of the letter by the President, and recapitulates the circumstances under which it had been sent. He considered it unnecessary to refer specially to the suggestions made by the Senators, because the letter addressed to them by Colonel Hayne of the 17th inst. presents a clear and specific answer to them, which he recites. He informs the Senators that it was the fixed purpose of the President, then, as it had been heretofore, "to perform his executive duties in such a manner as to preserve the peace of the country and to prevent bloodshed;" to act upon the defensive and to authorize no movement against the people of South Carolina, unless clearly justified by a hostile movement on their part; and he alleges that his forbearance to use force when the *Star of the West* was fired upon, was a proof of that desire. But, that to give "assurances" that no reinforce-ments would be sent to Fort Sumter in the interval, or that the public peace would not be disturbed by any act of hostility towards South Carolina, as proposed by Colonel Hayne, was "impossible." "The President," said the Secretary, "has no authority to enter into such an agreement or understanding." That as an executive officer, he was bound to protect the public property, and that he could not violate his duty by evading that obligation, either for an indefinite or a limited period. It was not deemed necessary to reinforce Major Anderson, because he had made, no such request, and felt secure in his position. "Should his safety, however, require reinforcements, every effort will be made to supply them."

He also informs the Senators that to Congress alone belongs the power to make war; and for the Executive to give an assurance, as requested by Colonel Hayne, that the public peace would not be "disturbed by any act of hostility towards South Carolina" upon the part of Congress, would be an act of usurpation upon his part, however strongly the President might be convinced that no such intention existed. He expresses his gratification that Major Anderson is permitted to obtain supplies from Charleston, and expresses his conviction that the happiest result which could be attained would be the continuance of the present amicable footing between Major Anderson and the authorities of South Carolina, "neither party being bound by any obligation whatever, except the high Christian and moral duty to keep the peace and to avoid all causes of mutual irritation."

The President had anticipated that this "peremptory refusal" to enter into the agreement proposed to him would have terminated the mission of the envoy and released him from the obligation imposed by the truce. In this he was disappointed.

On the following day seven of the Senators who had signed the previous communication to Colonel Hayne again addressed him, informing him of the receipt of the letter from the Secretary of War, and which they enclosed to him. Although its terms were not as satisfactory as they could have desired, they expressed their entire confidence that no reinforcements would be sent to Fort Sumter, nor the public peace disturbed within the period requisite for full communication between the envoy and his Government; and they trusted that he would feel justified in applying for further instructions before delivering to the President "any message" with which he had been charged. They again expressed the earnest hope that the State would take no step tending to produce a collision, until their States, which were to share the fortunes of South Carolina, should join their counsels with hers.

To this proposition, thus submitted to him, the envoy agreed. In his reply to the Senators who had addressed him, the envoy, in communicating his determination to withhold the letter entrusted to him, took occasion to express his regret that the President thought it necessary to keep a garrison of troops "at Fort Sumter to protect it as the property of the United States;" that South Carolina would scorn to appropriate to herself the property of another, "without accounting to the last dollar for everything" which she might deem necessary to take into her own possession for her protection and in vindication of her honor; that as "property," Fort Sumter was in far greater jeopardy occupied by a United States garrison than it would be if delivered to the State authorities, with a pledge that they would fully account for it "upon a fair adjustment;" that the occupation of a fort in the midst of a harbor, with its guns bearing on every point, by a Government no longer acknowledged, could not be else than an occasion of irritation, excitement and indignation, and as creating a condition of things which he feared was but little calculated to advance the observance of the "high Christian and moral duty to keep the peace," recommended by the Secretary of War in his communication.

In his judgment, to continue to hold Fort Sumter by United States troops was the worst possible means of protecting it as "property," and the worst possible means of effecting a peaceable solution of the difficulties.

The correspondence between the envoy and the Senators, including the reply of the President through the Secretary of War, was at once transmitted to the authorities of South Carolina, and 'on the 26th of January a reply upon the part of the Governor through A. G. Magrath, the Secretary of State, was returned to the envoy.*

The communication was lengthy, but at once clear and unequivocal It reviewed all of the facts as stated and the points at

---

* Judge Magrath's letter of January 26, 1861, to Hayne. P. 21, Appendix to Convention of South Carolina.

issue; in reference to the intervention of the Senators from the seceding States and the suggestions made by them, he informs the envoy that no such communication was anticipated by the Governor in the instructions which were furnished to him; but that the discretion exercised in the delay of the delivery of his letter to the President, under the circumstances, commended itself to the approval of the Governor, as due from the State of South Carolina to the representatives of her sister States expecting to act with her.

The reply of the President through his Secretary of War, and especially that part of it in regard to his purpose to hold Fort Sumter as "property" of the United States; his declaration in response to the expressed desire of the Senators that the State should avoid the initiation of hostilities, and also the impossibility of giving any assurance that reinforcements would not be sent, to Fort Sumter, and that they would be sent should Major Anderson's safety require it—were all carefully restated by the Governor's Secretary of State, who in his communication replied to them all. He thought that the letter of the Senators and the envoy's reply presented a "marked and agreeable contrast" to the President's letter; that the Governor appreciated the feeling which that letter must have excited in those Senators, as well as their forbearance and their generosity in still continuing to hope that a collision might be avoided until their States should equally share the dangers. It was intended that the acquiescence of the President in the "arrangements or understanding" by which he would be prevented from sending reinforcements to Fort Sumter, should be binding upon him, and it was so declared by the Senators in their letter to the envoy of the 15th of January. With the concession from the State in certain measures, a concession from the President was "evidently expected" by them. The reply of the President, and his refusal to agree to abstain from action either until the 15th of February, the day named by the Senators, or even until the envoy could communicate with the Governor of the State, although the President knew that such attempt would be regarded by the State as an act of war, was commented upon. What the State had been desired to do by the Senators, she had done, not in acknowledgment of any right on the part of the United States, but as an act of courtesy; with the supplies Major Anderson was receiving and the facilities, he was enjoying, no pretext for interference with the harbor could be found, except in connection with the *right* claimed to reinforce the fort, and which, "involved in a duty," carried with it the necessity that he should determine when that duty should be discharged. As to the President's intimation that no reinforcements would be sent, because Anderson had not asked for them and felt secure in his position, it should be remembered that on a previous occasion, when he had not asked for reinforcements and possibly felt as secure as now, they were nevertheless sent, and it was not the fault of the Government "that they did not reach him." The proposition thus made by the Southern Senators was "unsolicited and unexpected." "It was the evidence of a generous impulse" and an exhibition of an anxious desire to avoid collision and strife, and the moderation of their terms would long be remembered. Under these circumstances it was now not only "important" but "indispensably necessary" that the Governor should "correctly understand" the position of the General Government towards the State of South Carolina. The correspondence and the letter of the President served to dispel much of whatever doubt may have existed, and the Governor concluded that, stripped of all disguise, the "real purpose of the President" was to retain Fort Sumter as a military post; that the position of the President in regard to South Carolina was the same in reference to the other States which had seceded; and the Governor considered it to be his duty to regard all hostile attempts by the General Government upon any State which had seceded as "attempts made directly upon South Carolina."

The envoy is further informed by the South Carolina Secretary of State, that it was regarded as a "happy circumstance" by the Governor that, in deferring to the wishes of the Senators, their good intent had been rewarded by "leading to that declaration from the President," which would be regarded in every seceding State as "his declaration of war against them," In reference to the firing upon the *Star of the West,* the Governor did not wish to be understood as acquiescing in the correctness of that construction of the President's conduct, which the President was "pleased to consider a proof of his forbearance," but which the Governor considered under the circumstances of the case, wholly unjustifiable, and more than aggravating." The repulse of the steamer was not to be considered by the President as the attack of the State upon an unarmed vessel. If it was not a vessel intended for war, it was less excusable to attempt to introduce armed men to execute the orders of the President "under the shield of a peaceful trader." It was not only a hostile demonstration, but one attempted under a disguise, and which, had it been successful, would have had nothing but the success attending it "to compensate for the sacrifice of the proprieties with which it had been purchased."

The propriety of the demand with which the envoy was charged had not only been confirmed in the opinion of the Governor, but he had now become convinced of its necessity. The safety of the State required "that the position" of the President should be "distinctly understood," and the safety of all of the seceding, States was equally, involved. To hold Fort Sumter as a military post within the limits of South Carolina "will not be tolerated." The envoy was to say to the President that if he asserted the right to send reinforcements to Fort Sumter, South Carolina would regard such a right, when asserted, or an attempt at its exercise, as a declaration of war. If the President intended that it should not be so understood, it was proper that he should know how the Governor felt "bound to regard it."

If the President should refuse to deliver the fort upon the pledge the envoy was authorized to make, he would at once communicate that fact to the Governor. If the President, however, should not be prepared to give an immediate answer, he was to be informed that his answer might be transmitted to the Governor. The envoy was not to remain longer than to execute this as his closing duty, and when he should receive the reply of the President, the Governor would then consider the conduct which would be necessary upon his part. Finally, the Senators who had "generously interposed" were thanked by the Governor, who expresses the feeling that if other counsels should prevail, his own efforts and those of the Senators interested were earnestly made to avert them, and that he had no further communication to make to his envoy, except to thank him for the manner in which the duty entrusted to him had been discharged.

CHAPTER XIX.

Envoy Hayne presents his letter to the President–Subsequently addresses President directly–Comments upon the letter of Secretary of War–Receives further instructions, and communicates as special envoy–Offers to make compensation for Fort Sumter–Comments upon the President's letter to the Southern Senators–Justifies the firing upon the *Star of the West*– Able response of Secretary of War for the President–Fort Sumter as "property"–Answers propositions of envoy–Right of "eminent domain" cannot be asserted–No constitutional right in President to "cede or surrender" Fort Sumter–Right to send reinforcements "unquestionable"– President will send them, if necessary–Fort held as property and for no unfriendly purpose–Envoy replies directly to the President and leaves Washington–His letter–The President declines to receive it–Letter returned to Colonel Hayne by mail.

UPON the receipt of the communication of the Secretary of State of South Carolina, the envoy of the Governor lost no time in presenting the letter with which he had been charged to the President. On the 31st of January he addressed to the President a communication, in which he rehearsed the steps that had been taken since his personal interview with him, the part taken by the Southern Senators, their address to him, and his reply to their letter through his Secretary of War. This reply is commented upon by the envoy at some length, who pronounces it as "unsatisfactory" to him. It appeared to him that not only was the main proposition of the Senators rejected in advance, but that there was also in the Secretary's letter a distinct refusal to make any stipulation on the subject of reinforcement, even for the short time requisite for him to communicate with his Government. The reply was unsatisfactory to him, and would be so also to the authorities he represented. But as the reply was not addressed to him or to those authorities, and as South Carolina had addressed nothing to the Government or asked anything at the hands of the President, he had looked only to the note addressed to him by the Senators of the seceded and seceding States. Further instructions had arrived on the 30th, for his guidance, and he had now the honor to make to the

226

President his first communication as "Special envoy from the Governor of South Carolina."

The letter of the Governor of the 12th of January was enclosed to the President, the envoy at the same time stating to him that the Governor was not only confirmed in his opinion as to the propriety of the demand, but that the circumstances developed by his mission had increased that opinion into a conviction of its necessity. If Fort Sumter was not held as property, but as a military post, such a post within the limits of South Carolina could not be tolerated. He did "not come as a military man to demand the surrender of a fortress," but as the legal officer of the State, its Attorney-General, to claim for the State the exercise of its undoubted right of "eminent domain," and to pledge the State to make good all injury to the right of property which might arise from the exercise of that claim. The right assumed by the State "to take into her possession everything within her limits essential to maintain her honor and her safety, she would not permit to be drawn into discussion. She would make compensation, "upon a fair accounting, to the last dollar." And the envoy informs the President that the proposition now was that he, her law officer, should pledge the faith of the State under the authority of the Governor and Council, "to make such compensation in regard to Fort Sumter" to the full extent of the money-value of the property of the United States delivered to the authorities of the State.

The view that a continued armed possession of the fort would put it in jeopardy and lead to a collision, was again expressed to the President. In the opinion of the envoy, "no people not completely abject and pusillanimous, could submit, indefinitely" to an armed occupation of a fort commanding the harbor of its principal city; where "the daily ferry-boats that ply upon the waters" moved "but at the sufferance of aliens." This armed occupancy was not only unnecessary, but it was manifestly the "worst possible means" which could be taken to accomplish the object. The reply of the President to the Senators on the subject of reinforcements was referred to and quoted by the envoy. That part of the President's message of the 28th of January, where he expresses himself that it would be a "usurpation" upon his part to attempt to restrain the action of Congress by entering into any agreement in regard to matters over which he, as President, had no constitutional control, as Congress might pass laws which he would be bound to obey, was quoted by the envoy, who replied that the proposition was addressed to the President under the laws as they then were, and had no reference to new conditions under new legislation. "It was addressed to the Executive discretion, acting under existing laws." If Congress should in any way legislate so as to affect the peace of the State, "her interests or her rights," she would have timely notice, and would endeavor, he trusted, to meet the emergency.

In regard to the assertion of the Secretary of War, that should Anderson's safety require it, every effort would be made to send him reinforcements, the envoy thought that this seemed "to ignore the other branch of the proposition made by the Senators," in reference to the suspension of any attack upon Fort Sumter during the period suggested. It was the imperative duty of the State, and as an absolute necessity of her condition, and in consideration of her own dignity as a sovereign and the safety of the people, "to demand that this property should not longer be used as a military post by a Government she no longer acknowledges."

The President's expressed opinions as against coercion and for a peaceful solution of the difficulties, were invoked by the envoy, who expressed the hope that he would not, upon further consideration "and mere question of property, refuse the reasonable demand of South Carolina." If this hope should be disappointed the responsibility would not rest with the State. He urges, too, that if war was to be made, it should be made as of deliberate device, and entered upon as war and of set purpose," and not "as the incident or accident" of a policy professedly peaceful.

He justifies the firing upon the *Star of the West,* and informs the President that the interposition of the Senators who addressed him was unexpected by his Government, and unsolicited by him, but that while the Governor of his State appreciated their high and generous motives, he felt that his demand upon the President should no longer be withheld.

The President, upon the receipt of the letter of the envoy, once more availed himself of the able pen of his Secretary of War, Mr. Holt, to reply, and on the 6th of February that officer transmitted to the envoy of the Governor of South Carolina a response of great force, in which the whole subject was reviewed and the conduct of the President explained and justified.

The demand of the Governor, as contained in his letter of January 12, was referred to and its terms quoted, as well as the subsequent instructions of the Governor, through his Secretary of State, that the right in Fort Sumter as "property" could be ascertained and satisfied. The modification of his demand, in view of these instructions, presumably under the influence of the Senators, was noticed, as well as the expression of the envoy under the "full scope and precise purpose" of his instructions as thus modified, that he did "not come as a military man to demand the surrender of a fortress," but as the Attorney-General of the State to assert its undoubted right of "eminent domain," and to pledge the State to make good, all injury to the rights of property,

The proposition to make compensation for Fort Sumter to the full extent of its money value, which the envoy, as the law officer of the State, should pledge the faith of the State to make, was also stated by the Secretary of War, as well as reference made to the suggestion of the envoy that an attack upon the fort, which must result if continued to be held, would not improve it as property, and if taken, "would no longer be the subject of account." "The proposal, then," said the Secretary, "now presented to the President, is simply an offer upon the part of South Carolina to buy Fort Sumter and contents, as property of the United States, sustained by a declaration, in effect, that if she is not permitted to make the purchase, she will seize the fort by force of arms." The proposal under the circumstances impressed "the President as having assumed a most unusual form," but that he had investigated the claim made, apart from the declaration that accompanied it. "Property" and "public property" were the most comprehensive terms that could be used in such connection, and when used in reference to a fort, they embraced the entire and undivided interest of the Government. The title to Fort Sumter upon the part of the Government was incontestable. Its interest "might probably be subjected to the exercise of the right of eminent domain," were it "purely proprietary" only, but its political relations gave it "a much higher and more imposing character" than mere proprietorship. Its jurisdiction and the power to "exercise exclusive legislation" over it, was absolute and was therefore incompatible with the claim of "eminent domain" now claimed by the State. And this authority was derived from the peaceful cession of South Carolina itself, and in accordance with law, and South Carolina could no more assert the right of "eminent domain" over Fort Sumter than Maryland could assert it over the District of Columbia, the "political and proprietary rights" in each case, being precisely the same.

But whatever might be the claim of the State, the President had no constitutional right to cede or surrender the fort. As the head of the executive branch of the Government, the President could "no more sell and transfer" the fort to the State of South Carolina, than he could sell the Capitol of the United States to Maryland. The question of sending reinforcements, the Secretary considered as having been fully disposed of in his letter to the Senators. He declined to renew its discussion, but repeats the determination of the President to send them if needed and Anderson should ask for them, and he thought that he could add nothing to the "explicitness" of that language, which still applied. The right to send those reinforcements rested on the same "unquestionable foundation" as the right to occupy the fort itself. The suggestion contained in the letter of the Senators of the 15th of January, that it was due from South Carolina to her sister States that she should "avoid initiating hostilities with the United States or any other power," as well as the gratifying assurance now given by the envoy, that "South Carolina has every disposition to preserve the public peace," would seem to ensure the attainment of this common and patriotic object, since the President himself was animated by the same desire. But it was difficult to reconcile this assurance with the declaration of the envoy, that her dignity as a sovereign and the safety of her people prompts the State to demand that Fort Sumter "should not longer be used as a military post by a Government she no longer acknowledges," and that this occupation must lead to a collision and to war. "Fort Sumter is, in itself," said the Secretary, "a military post and nothing else, and it would seem that not so much the fact as the purpose of its use should give to it a hostile or a friendly character." The Government held it now for the same national and defensive objects for which it had been always held since its completion, and the whole force of its batteries would be at once used against an enemy which should attack Charleston or its harbor. And the President could not understand how "a small garrison actuated by such a spirit" could become a source of irritation to the people or compromise the dignity or honor of the State. Its attitude was neither menacing *nor* unfriendly, and it was under orders to stand strictly on the defensive, and unless the Government and people of South Carolina should seek its destruction and assault it, they could "never receive aught but shelter from its guns," and that Senator Davis had truthfully stated the intent with which the fort was held when, in connection with other Senators, in their letter to him of the 15th of January, he informed him that the fort was held as property only, and not for any unfriendly purpose. If the President's pacific purposes and his forbearance, so severely tried, be not received as a pledge of his policy, then neither language nor conduct could possibly furnish one. And if, after the multiplied proofs that existed of the President's anxiety for peace, Fort Sumter should be assaulted and the lives of the garrison imperilled, and the country plunged into war, upon the authorities of the State and those they represent must rest the responsibility."

The President thought that the statements and arguments of this letter were unanswerable, and that they could not but produce an effect upon the envoy personally. It was to be presumed, too, that the argument had been exhausted in the long correspondence that had taken place. Upon its receipt, however, the envoy on the 7th of February prepared a communication which the President considered an "insulting answer," and which was directed, not "as usage and common civility required," to the Secretary of War, but directly to the President. The envoy "then suddenly left Washington, leaving his missive behind him, to be delivered after his departure."

As no mere extract from this unusual communication could give a proper idea of its character, it is inserted in full, and is as follows:

"WASHINGTON, February 7, 1861.
"TO HIS EXCELLENCY JAMES BUCHANAN, President.

"*Sir:* Your reply through your Secretary of the War Department to my communication of the 31st of January, covering the demand of the Governor of South Carolina for the delivery of Fort Sumter, was received yesterday. Although the very distinct and emphatic refusal of that demand closes my mission, I feel constrained to correct some strange misapprehensions into which your Secretary has fallen.

---

* "Buchanan's Administration."

"There has been no modification of the demand authorized to be made, and no change whatever in its character, and of this you were distinctly informed, in my communication of the 31st of January. You have the original demand as delivered to me by Governor Pickens on the 12th of January, and you have an extract from the further instructions received by me, expressly stating that he, the Governor, was confirmed in the views he entertained on the 12th of January, by that very correspondence which you assign as the cause of the alleged modification. You assume that the character of the demand has been modified, yet you have from me but one communication, and that asserts the contrary, and you have nothing from the Governor but the very demand itself, which you say has been modified. What purpose of peace or conciliation your Secretary could have had in view in the introduction of this point at all, it is difficult to perceive.

"You next attempt to ridicule the proposal as simply an offer on the part of South Carolina to buy Fort Sumter and contents as property of the United States, sustained by a declaration, in effect, that if she is not permitted to make the purchase, she will seize the fort by force of arms. It is difficult to consider this as other than intentional misconstruction. You were told that South Carolina, as a separate, independent sovereignty, would not tolerate the occupation, by foreign troops, of a military post within her limits, but that inasmuch as you, in repeated messages and in your correspondence, had 'laid much stress' upon the character of your duties, arising from considering forts as property, South Carolina, so far as this matter of property suggested by yourself was concerned, would make compensation for all injury done the property, in the exercise of her sovereign right of eminent domain. And this your Secretary calls a proposal to purchase. The idea of purchase is entirely inconsistent with the assertion of the paramout right in the purchaser. I had supposed that an 'interest in property' *as such,* could be no other than 'purely proprietary,' and if I confined myself to this narrow view of your relations to Fort Sumter, you at least should not consider it the subject of criticism.   Until your letter of yesterday, you chose so to consider your relations, in everything which you have written, or which has been written under your direction.

"It was precisely because you had yourself chosen to place your action upon the ground of 'purely proprietary' right, that the proposal of compensation was made, and you now admit that in this view 'it (Fort Sumter) would probably be subjected to the exercise of the right of eminent domain.'

"In your letter of yesterday (through your Secretary) you shift your position. You claim that your Government bears to Fort Sumter 'political relations of a much higher and more imposing character.'

"It was no part of my mission to discuss the 'political relations' of the United States Government to anything within the territorial limits of South Carolina. South Carolina claims to have severed all political connection with your Government, and to have destroyed all political relations of your Government with everything within her borders. She is unquestionably at this moment *de facto* a separate and independent Government, exercising complete sovereignty over every foot of her soil except Fort Sumter. Now that the intention is avowed to hold this place as a military post, with the claim of exclusive jurisdiction on the part of a Government foreign to South Carolina, it will be for the authorities to determine what is the proper course to be pursued. It is vain to ignore the fact that South Carolina is, to yours, a foreign Government, and how with this patent fact before you, you can consider the continued occupation of a fort in her harbor a pacific measure and parcel of a peaceful policy, passes certainly my comprehension.

"You say that the fort was garrisoned for our protection, and is held for the same purposes for which it has been ever held since its construction. Are you not aware, that to hold, in the territory of a foreign power, a fortress against her will, avowedly for the purpose of protecting her citizens, is, perhaps, the highest insult which one Government can offer to another? But Fort Sumter was never garrisoned at all until South Carolina had dissolved her connection with your Government. This garrison entered it at night, with every circumstance of secrecy, after spiking the guns and burning the gun-carriages, and cutting down the flag-staff of an adjacent fort, which was then abandoned. South Carolina had not taken Fort Sumter into her own possession, only because of her misplaced confidence in a Government which deceived her. A fortress occupied under the circumstances above 'stated, is considered by you not only as no cause of irritation, but you represent it as held for our protection!

"Your Excellency's Secretary has indulged in irony on a very grave subject. As to the responsibility for consequences, if indeed, it does rest on us, I can assure your Excellency we are happily unconscious of the fact.

"I return to Charleston to-morrow. With considerations of high regard,

"I am, very respectfully,

"J. W. Hayne,

"Special Envoy."

The President thought that from the conduct of the envoy, he had evidently anticipated the fate of his letter; and upon the same day upon which it was received, he caused its return to him, having placed upon it the following endorsement: "The character of this letter is such that it cannot be received. Colonel Hayne having left the city before it was sent to the President, it is returned to him by the first mail."

The President retained no copy of the letter, nor did he again hear of it.

CHAPTER XX.

THE action of Major Anderson in referring the demand for the surrender of Fort Sumter to Washington, and the establishment, in consequence, of a "truce" until the return of the messengers, occasioned surprise and embarrassment to the President. He thought that Major Anderson had thus placed it out of his power to ask for reinforcements, and also beyond the power of the Government to send them until the President "should again decide against the surrender of the fort." Although the President

235

might have annulled the truce, it would have cast, as he thought, a "serious reflection" upon Major Anderson for having concluded it, and he therefore determined to respect it. But he at the same time thought that his instructions would have justified Anderson in "peremptorily informing" the messengers of the Governor that he would not surrender the fort, but would defend it, and that such action upon his part would have been in accordance with the "explicit determination" of the President, as announced to the South Carolina Commissioners.

From his letters and reports to the War Department, it was confidently believed that Major Anderson felt himself to be wholly equal to his position, and although the President and his Cabinet had determined that reinforcements should be made ready, and promptly sent to him in case of need, they were at this time under no immediate anxiety as to his safety.

But with the departure of the envoy, the President felt that he was no longer bound by the obligation imposed by the "truce," and he proceeded to put on foot an expedition for immediately reinforcing Fort Sumter, and in regard to which a council consisting of the Secretaries of War and the Navy, accompanied by General Scott, had been requested to meet the President on the 30th of January, the day upon which the demand of the Government for the surrender of Fort Sumter had been made upon him.

But the subject of reinforcing Fort Sumter immediately had earnestly engaged the attention of certain members of the Cabinet whose influence with the President was potential.

On the 16th of January, six or seven days after the firing upon and repulse of the *Star of the West,* the Secretary of State Judge Black, addressed to Lieutenant-General Scott a letter in which, while deferring to his better judgment in "such a matter," and informing him that while his opinion would be conclusive upon him, he yet desired more clearly to understand the subject, in view of his own responsibilities; and in a communication of singular clearness and power he reviews the position of Major Anderson in Fort Sumter, the necessary steps to his relief, the comparatively trifling character of the obstacles existing, and presents in strong light the unmistakable and immediate duty of the Government; and if he should have erred in the views he presents, he asks that the General-in-Chief should correct him. This important and almost unknown letter is given in full:

"DEPARTMENT OF STATE; January 16, 1861.
"LIEUTENANT-GENERAL WINFIELD SCOTT:

"*Dear General :*   The habitual frankness of your character, the deep interest you take in everything that concerns the public defense, your expressed desire that I should hear and understand your views—these reasons, together with an earnest wish to know my own duty and to do it, induce me to beg you for a little light, which perhaps you alone can shed, upon the present state of our affairs.

"1. Is it the duty of the Government to re-enforce Major Anderson?

"2. If yes, how soon is it necessary that those re-enforcements should be there?

"3. What obstacles exist to prevent the sending of such re-enforcements at any time when it may be necessary to do so?

"I trust you will not regard it as presumption in me if I give you the crude notions which I myself have already formed out of very imperfect materials.

"A statement of my errors, if errors they be, will enable you to correct them the more easily.

"I. It seems now to be settled that Major Anderson and his command at Fort Sumter are not to be withdrawn. The United States Government is not to surrender its last hold upon its own property in South Carolina. Major Anderson has a position so nearly impregnable that an attack upon him at present is wholly improbable, and he is supplied with provisions which will last him very well for two months. In the meantime Fort Sumter is invested on every side by the avowedly hostile forces of South Carolina. It is in a state of seige. They have already prevented communication between its commander and his own Government, both by sea and land. There is no doubt that they intend to continue this state of things, as far as it is in their power to do so. In the course of a few weeks from this time it will become very difficult for him to hold out. The constant labor and anxiety of his men will exhaust their physical power, and this exhaustion, of course, will proceed very much more rapidly as soon as they begin to get short of provision.

"If the troops remain in Fort Sumter without any change in their condition, and the hostile attitude of South Carolina remains as it is now, the question of Major Anderson's surrender is one of time only. If he is not to be relieved, is it not entirely clear that he should be ordered to surrender at once? It having been determined that the latter order shall not be given, it follows that relief must be sent him at some time before it is too late to save him.

"II. This brings me to the second question: When should the re-enforcements and provisions be sent? Can we justify ourselves in delaying the performance of that duty?

"The authorities of South Carolina are improving every moment, and increasing their ability to prevent re-enforcement every hour, while every day that rises sees us with a power diminished to send in the requisite relief. I think it certain that Major Anderson could be put in possession of all the defensive powers he needs with very little risk to this Government, if the efforts were made immediately; but it is impossible to predict how much blood or money it may cost if it be postponed for two or three months.

"The fact that other persons are to have charge of the Government before the worst comes to the worst has no influence upon my mind, and, I take it for granted, will not be regarded as a just element in making up your opinion.

"The anxiety which an American citizen must feel about any future event which may affect the existence of the country, is not less if he expects it to occur on the 5th of March than it would be if he knew it was going to happen on the 3d.

III. I am persuaded that the difficulty of relieving Major Anderson has been very much magnified to the minds of some persons. From you I shall be able to ascertain whether I am mistaken or they. I am thoroughly satisfied that the battery on Morris Island can give no serious trouble. A vessel going in where the *Star of the West* went will not be within the reach of the battery's guns longer than from six to ten minutes. The number of shots that could be fired upon her in that time may be easily calculated, and I think the chances of her being seriously injured can be demonstrated, by simple arithmetic, to be very small. A very unlucky shot might cripple her, to be sure, and therefore the risk is something. But then it is a maxim, not less in war than in peace, that where nothing is ventured nothing can be gained. The removal of the buoys has undoubtedly made the navigation of the channel more difficult. But there are pilots outside of Charleston, and many of the officers of the Navy, who could steer a ship into the harbor by the natural landmarks with perfect safety. This, be it remembered, is not now a subject of speculation; the actual experiment has been tried. *The Star of the West* did pass the battery, and did overcome the difficulties of the navigation, meeting with no serious trouble from either cause. They have tried it; we can say *probatum est;* and there is an end to the controversy.

"I am convinced that a pirate, or a slaver, or a smuggler, who could be assured of making five hundred dollars by going into the harbor in the face of all the dangers which now threaten a vessel bearing the American flag, would laugh them to scorn, and to one of our naval officers who, has the average of daring, 'the danger's self were lure alone!'

"There really seems to me nothing in the way that ought to stop us except the guns of Fort Moultrie. If they are suffered to open a fire upon a vessel bearing re-enforcements to Fort Sumter, they might stop any other vessel as they stopped the *Star of the West.* But is it necessary that this intolerable outrage should be submitted to? Would it not be an act of pure self-defense on the part of Major Anderson to silence Fort Moultrie, if it be necessary to do so, for the purpose of insuring the safety of a vessel whose arrival at Fort Sumter is necessary for his protection, and could he not do it effectually? Would the South Carolinians dare to fire upon any vessel which Major Anderson would tell them beforehand must be permitted to pass, on pain of his guns being opened upon her assailants? But suppose it impossible for an unarmed vessel to pass the battery, what is the difficulty of sending the *Brooklyn* or the *Macedonian* in? I have never heard it alleged that the latter could not cross the bar, and I think if the fact had been so it would have been mentioned in my hearing before this time. It will turn out upon investigation, after all that has been said and sung about the *Brooklyn,* that there is water enough there for her. She draws ordinarily only sixteen and one-half feet, and her draught can be reduced eighteen inches by putting her upon an even keel. The shallowest place will give her eighteen feet of water at high tide. In point of fact, she has crossed that bar more than once. But apart even from these resources, the Government has at its command three or four smaller steamers of light draught and great speed, which could be armed and at sea in a few days, and would not be in the least troubled by any opposition that could be made to their entrance.

"It is not, however, necessary to go into the details, with which, I presume, you are fully acquainted. I admit that the state of things may be somewhat worse now than they were a week ago, and are probably getting worse every day; but is not that the strongest reason that can be given for taking time by the forelock?

"I feel confident that you will excuse me for making this communication. I have some responsibilities of my own to meet, and I can discharge them only when I understand the subject to which they relate. Your opinion, of course, will be conclusive upon me, for on such a matter I cannot do otherwise than defer to your better judgment. If you think it most consistent with your duty to be silent, I shall have no right to complain.

"If you would rather answer orally than make a written reply, I will meet you either at your own quarters or here in the State Department, as may best suit your convenience.

"I am, most respectfully, yours, &c.,

"J. S. BLACK."

This communication of Judge Black, from its able grasp of

the military situation and its earnest view of the plain duty of the Government, is, in view of its source, remarkable,

To this communication of the Secretary of State, General Scott made the following endorsement: "Lieutenant-General Scott received the Hon. Mr. Black's most interesting communication yesterday, at too late an hour and in the midst of too perplexing engagements to attend to it. The moment he is released by the War Department this morning, General Scott will seek Mr. Black, and repeat his efforts till he has had the pleasure of finding him at the Department of State Thursday morning.*

But the General-in-Chief did not meet the Secretary, nor was there any official reply or notice, upon his part, or of the Secretary's letter.†

The subject, however, and its increasing complications, was the constant theme of discussion in the Cabinet now working in harmony. On the 22d of January, the day upon which the President, through his Secretary of War, had communicated to the Senators of the seceding States his intention in regard to reinforcing Fort Sumter, a Cabinet meeting was held. Prevented by sickness from being present, the Secretary of State addressed a letter to the President in regard to the prospective deliberation. His communication was not to be laid before the heads of Departments, but was for the eye of the President alone. He warns the President that they had been grossly imposed upon recently, by statements that the reinforcement of the forts would result in civil war, an idea now ridiculed; that there was a large military force in Charleston; that Fort Sumter could not be occupied; that the *Brooklyn* could not cross the bar, and that no ship could pass the battery on Morris Island; and that South Carolina would not make war upon us if we were weak, but would, should we make ourselves strong. And the Secretary urged upon the President that these things, being taken for true, led to disastrous consequences, to the discredit of the administration and even the Union itself.

---

* From the original paper of General Scott.

† Shortly afterward, the Secretary and General-in-Chief met casually, when the latter complimented the Secretary upon his letter, and said that it was worth) of a Field-Marshal. "Judge Black," he asked, "where did you get your military education?" Judge Black replied, "I was first lieutenant of the Bloody Mountain Cavalry in Somerset County."

His letter was as follows:

FRANKLIN Row, January 22, 1861.

"MY DEAR MR. PRESIDENT: A slight attack of rheumatism will prevent me from leaving my room to-day, and of course I shall not be at the Cabinet meeting. But the deep interest I feel in the result of your deliberations induces me to write this note, not to be laid before the heads of Departments, but for your own eye alone. If I am wrong in my interpretation of the past or in my expectations concerning the future, you can correct me as well as anybody else, and if I am right the suggestions I make may possibly be of some value.

"You must be aware that the possession of this city is absolutely essential to the ultimate designs of the Secessionists. They can establish a Southern Confederacy with the Capital of the Union in their hands, and without it all the more important part of their scheme is bound to fail. If they can take it and *do not* take it, they are fools. Knowing them, as I do, to be men of ability and practical good sense, not likely to omit that which is necessary to forward the ends which they are aiming at, I take it for granted that they have then eye fixed upon Washington. To prove their desire to take it requires no evidence at all beyond the intrinsic probability of the fact itself. The affirmative presumption is so strong that he who denies it is bound to establish the negative. But there are additional and very numerous circumstances tending to show that a conspiracy to that effect has been actually formed, and that large numbers of persons are deeply and busily engaged in bringing the plot to a head at what they conceive to be the proper time. I do not mean now to enumerate all the facts. They form a body of circumstantial evidence that is overwhelming and irresistible. I know that you do not believe this, or did not when I saw you last. Your incredulity seemed then to be founded upon the assurances of certain outside persons in whom you confided, that nothing of that kind was in contemplation. The mere opinion of those persons is worth nothing apart from their own personal knowledge. They can have no personal knowledge unless they are themselves apart of the conspiracy. In the latter case fidelity to their fellows makes treachery to you a sort of moral necessity. In short, the mere declarations of uninformed persons who are not in the secrets of the Secessionists amount to very little, and well-informed persons who are admitted to their counsels can hardly be expected to communicate their schemes to the head of the nation.

"Suppose it to be doubtful whether any hostile intentions against the Capital are entertained, what is the duty of the administration? Shall we be prepared for the worst, or leave the public interests unguarded, so that the 'logic of events' may demonstrate our folly? Preparation can do no possible harm in any event, and in the event which to me seems most likely, it is the country's only chance of salvation.

"Let us not forget the lessons we have learned in the past three months. The gross impostures practiced upon us recently ought to make us very slow about believing assurances or taking advice which comes from the enemies of the Union. *Timeo Danaos.* They told us that civil war would be the result of manning the forts at Charleston: Now they laugh at all who believed that prophecy. They told us about the eight regiments of artillery in South Carolina; the twenty thousand other troops; the battery that could take Castle Pinckney; the impossibility of occupying Fort Sumter; that the *Brooklyn* was the only ship of war fit to be sent down there, and that she could not cross the bar; that the little battery on Morris Island would prevent a ship from going up the channel; that South Carolina would not make war upon us if we were weak, but would if we should make ourselves strong—all these things were taken for true, and you know how disastrous the consequences were? not merely to the credit of the administration, but to the Union itself,

"'Upon whose *property* and most dear *life* a damn'd defeat was made.'

"I understand that the Secretary of the Navy has promised the Secessionists that he will withdraw the ships from the Florida and Alabama harbors. I hope and believe that he has no authority from you to make such promise: and if he has done it of his own head, I am sure he will receive a signal rebuke. You know how much I honor and respect Toucey, but I confess I find it a little difficult to forgive him for letting it be understood that the *Brooklyn* could not get into the harbor of Charleston; and the order which he gave to that ship, by which her commander felt himself compelled, after he was in sight of Fort Sumter, not to go in, is making this Government the laughter and derision of the world.

"I hope it will soon be decided what our policy is to be, with reference to the relief of Major Anderson. There certainly would be no hurry about it, if it were not for the fact that the South Carolinians are increasing their means of resistance every day, and this increase may be such as to make delay fatal to his safety. But how that is I do not pretend to know at present. Certainly, however, the facts ought to be ascertained.

"In the forty days and forty nights yet remaining to this administration, responsibilities may be crowded greater than those which are usually incident to four years in more quiet times. I solemnly believe that you can hold this revolution in check, and so completely put the calculations of its leaders out of joint that it will subside after a time into peace and harmony. On the other hand, by leaving the Government an easy prey, the spoilers will be tempted beyond their power of resistance, and they will get such an advantage as will bring upon the country a whole illiad of woes. The short official race which yet remains to us, must be run before a cloud of witnesses, and to win we must cast aside every weight, and the sin of state-craft which doth so easily beset us, and look simply upon our duty and the performance of it as the only prize of our high calling.

"I am free to admit that in this hasty note I may have been much mistaken. I do not claim to be more zealous in the public service nor more patriotic than my neighbors; certainly not wiser than my colleagues. To your better judgment I defer implicitly. But my absence from the Council to-day annoyed me, supposing, as I did, that some of the matters here referred to might be discussed in it. I took this mode of saying what I probably would have said if I had been with you.

"I am, most respectfully yours, etc.
"THE PRESIDENT."

Meanwhile other influences had been at work. The General Assembly of Virginia had instituted the "Peace Convention," and by a concurrent vote had appointed Ex-President John Tyler a commissioner to the President of the United States, and Judge John Robertson to South Carolina and other seceding States, to request that, pending the proceedings of the Convention, they should abstain from all acts calculated to produce a collision of arms. When Ex-President Tyler arrived in Washington, the President, in anticipation of his visit to him, requested his Secretary of State to call upon him informally. Accompanied by Mr. Stanton, Judge Black called upon the Ex-President. He found him anxious and excited. Scarcely were the ordinary greetings over when the Ex-President said: "What are you doing here with all these preparations; are you going to make war? Nothing could be more exciting to the Southern people than these preparations. I have come here for peace." The conversation was interrupted, and the visit soon after terminated, Judge Black thinking that what Mr. Tyler had to say had better, in his frame of mind, be said to the President himself."

On the 23d of January the Commissioners arrived in Washington, and upon the following day presented the resolution of Virginia to the President, urging upon him at the same time "to become a party" to the proposed agreement. The President declined. He informed the Commissioner that he had in "no manner changed his views," that he could give no pledges; it was his duty to

*Judge Black to writer.

enforce the laws; and that the whole power rested with Congress. On the 28th of January he transmitted a message to Congress at the same time with the Virginia resolution. The same views in regard to the powers of the Executive that he had expressed to the Senators from the seceding States, and also to the envoy from the Governor of South Carolina, were repeated, and he again asserted that "defense, and not aggression" had been the policy of his administration from the beginning. That while he could not enter into the engagement as proposed, he cordially recommended to Congress to abstain from passing any law producing a collision of arms whilst the proceedings contemplated by the General Assembly of Virginia were in progress. But Congress took no action whatever in the matter, which impressed unfavorably the people of Virginia. In the Senate the question of printing them was discussed until the 21st of February, when the subject was dropped, and in the House, after a motion "to refer and print" them, they were not again noticed.

The Commissioner to South Carolina proceeded at once upon his mission, and on the 28th of January the Governor, in a message to the South Carolina Legislature, presented the resolutions of Virginia. The object of the resolutions was to induce the State to send on Commissioners to meet others from Virginia and from the other States who might agree to send them, on the 4th of February, at Washington, for the purpose of agreeing upon some suitable adjustment of the "great issues" made in the Confederacy. The proposition was coldly received by the authorities, and with violent feeling by the press. The Governor recalls the failure of Virginia to respond to a similar call made by South Carolina through a Commissioner sent by her, making an urgent appeal upon Virginia to step forward and "devise some plan upon which the States immediately concerned might act together," save their rights, and yet preserve the common Constitution as a blessing for all the States. Had this been done at that time, he thought, something might have been accomplished to secure new guarantees and protection in a common Union. A general indictment against the Northern States was recited by the Governor, who asserted that the result of the recent election was to put into power a party and a President, "with open and avowed principles of deep and settled hostility" and pledged to the final extermination of institutions essential to them and to the peace of their society.

With the most profound respect for the State of Virginia, he does not see how South Carolina could agree to send Commissioners to Washington to meet Commissioners from the Northern and Southern States, as it might result in only greater difficulty and confusion. But he submits the matter to the wisdom and decision of the Legislature, at the same time calling their attention to the fact that delegates had been appointed by the State Convention to meet, on the 4th of February, with similar delegates appointed by other seceding States. He thought that it would thus "be obviously impolitic" to send delegates to Washington appointed for the same day to meet the States of the North, with any view to preserve or to reconstruct the Federal Union with them, when South Carolina had agreed first to meet the seceding States, to whom she owed her deepest obligation, and to whom she was bound by every tie to make no compromises until a separate and independent Union with them had been formed.

The action of the South Carolina Legislature was immediate. On the 28th of January the Senate resolved, unanimously, while acknowledging the friendly motives which had inspired the mission to the State, that candor which was due to Virginia induced the General Assembly to declare, with frankness, that they did not deem it advisable to "initiate negotiations, when they had no desire nor intention to promote the ultimate object in view," which was to procure "amendments or new guarantees to the Constitution of the United States;" that the separation of the State was final, and that she had no further interest in the Constitution of the United States, and that the only appropriate negotiations were as to their mutual relations as foreign States; that the most solemn pledges of the Government had been disregarded, and an attempt made to introduce troops into one of the forts, "concealed in the hold of a vessel of commerce," and with a view to the subjugation of the people of the State, and that another vessel with troops and munitions of war had been sent South "since the authorities at Washington had been informed of the present mediation of Virginia."

Under these circumstances the General Assembly declined to enter into the proposed negotiations. These resolutions were

---

* Resolutions of the Legislature, Executive Document No. 4. Governor's message and correspondence. Charleston, 1861.

at once sent to the House of Representatives of South Carolina, and were concurred in by that body the same day,

On the 29th of January, the Commissioner informed the Governor that the news of the sailing of the Brooklyn had determined him not to press a reply to his note; that it had been arranged between Ex-President Tyler and himself that they should endeavor to get from the Government at Washington and the authorities of the seceding States "mutual assurances" that would be reciprocally binding, that no act should be committed which was calculated to produce hostilities during the period indicated by Virginia. He had, on the 28th, received from Ex-President Tyler a despatch informing him that the President declined to give a written pledge, nor did he understand that he proposed to give a verbal one."

It seemed wholly unnecessary, under the circumstances—as the State has declined to send delegates—if not unreasonable, to make such request of the State. He considered his mission as terminated, but would willingly be the bearer of any response the State might see fit to make.

On the same day, the Secretary of State of South Carolina, in inclosing a copy of the resolution passed by the General Assembly to the Commissioners, informs him that the refusal of the President was not unexpected by the Governor, and that he might now understand thoroughly the motives of the authorities of the State in not relying upon assurances. To that evidence it was not necessary for the Governor to add anything, and he was satisfied that the State of Virginia would receive his report in the proper spirit.

But the Commissioner of Virginia to the President did not cease in his efforts to accomplish the object of his mission. Although some days had passed since the President had declined to enter into any pledges restricting his action in regard to Fort Sumter, the Commissioner on the 7th of February despatched to the Governor of South Carolina the following telegram:

"WASHINGTON, 7th February.
"To GOVERNOR PICKENS: Can my voice reach you? If so, do not attack Fort Sumter. You know my sincerity. The Virginia delegates here earnestly unite.
                    (Signed)   "JOHN TYLER."

---

* Executive Document No 4 Charleston, 1861.

And again on the same date, to Judge Robertson, at Montgomery, Ala.: "Hayne has returned. Prevent, if possible, collision. It is of great importance to results here."

The answer of the Governor was immediate. In consequence of the appeal of Virginia, he was willing to await the result as long as he could consistently, but while Sumter was held with a view to their subjugation, even Virginia would refuse. He would decide when he knew the exact grounds upon which the President acted.

Not satisfied, however, with the response of the Governor, Mr. Tyler again telegraphed, on the 9th, that the President directed him to say that the letter to Colonel Hayne was designed to be both respectful and kind, and that he so considered it, but that he "complained much" of Colonel Hayne's last letter and manifested "great solicitude" on the point. And he repeats his inquiry as to the assurance to be given by the Governor that no attack should be made, provided that the President would give a like assurance that no reinforcements would be sent.

On the same day, the Governor again responds. He acknowledges the receipt of the telegrams sent him, and says that the letter of Secretary Holt was then under consideration; that no pledge could be given unless officially informed of some proposal from the President, but that his course might be controlled by the direction given by the provisional Government at Montgomery, should they assume such direction in reference to Fort Sumter; and that everything that could consistently be done to avoid collision and bloodshed would be the purpose of the authorities in South Carolina.

On the 18th of February, Mr Tyler again telegraphs to Governor Pickens. He informs him that the President is startled by information, considered to be reliable, and coming indirectly from a former Member of Congress from South Carolina, assuring him that Fort Sumter would be taken on or before the 4th of March, "without reference to what the Montgomery Government might advise or order on the subject;" and Mr. Tyler asks that the Government would quiet the President by his reply.

Meantime, the Governor was kept constantly advised of what was transpiring in Washington in reference to Fort Sumter. On the 20th of February, Senator Wigfall telegraphed to him as follows: "Attempt to reinforce Anderson by stealth at night in small boats determined." And such information, oftentimes mistaken, was sent constantly to Charleston.

The Governor had long felt the weight of the responsibility resting upon him and the necessity for action, and towards the close of February he sent the following telegram to the Confederate Secretary of the Treasury at Montgomery:

"Received your telegram to-day. But am sure if you do not act immediately and appoint a commander-in-chief to take charge, it will be too late. Act quickly, now, or I shall be compelled to act. Send your Commissioners on to Washington now, right off, and telegraph me, or it will be beyond your control. Things look bad in Washington.   "F. W. P."

The mission of Mr. Hayne had terminated in such fashion that the Governor sent a message to the House of Representatives on the 19th of January, saying that as the Convention had expressly reserved to itself the power to make treaty and to declare war, the final report of Hayne might render it proper for him to reconvene the Convention. Meantime, the question of reinforcing Fort Sumter was under constant discussion in the Cabinet at Washington. A council consisting of Secretaries Holt and Toucey, Lieutenant General-Scott, and Commander Ward of the Navy, after several consultations, had, with the knowledge of the President, determined upon a plan approved by General Scott, which seemed to offer the best chances of success. It was to be quietly prepared under the direction of the Secretary of the Navy; it was to consist of four small steamers to be borrowed from the Treasury Department, and was to sail from New York under the command of Commander Ward of the Navy, an intimate friend of the Secretary. This officer was empowered to select his officers and men, and the expedition was to sail the following night after the receipt of the telegram from the Secretary directing the movement. He was to enter the harbor of Charleston in the night and anchor under the guns of Fort Sumter, if possible.

Another proposition for the relief of Sumter was made by Captain Gustavus V. Fox, who early in January, after the result of the expedition of the *Star of the West* had become known, had submitted a plan in writing, for the relief of Fort Sumter, to a friend of Lieutenant-General Scott, to whom it was shown, and who at once gave it his approval.

Captain Fox had been an officer of the Navy for nineteen years. A thorough and accomplished sailor, he had early seen the necessity of prompt and vigorous action, and he submitted a plan of relief which, had it been promptly resorted to, would at that time have had every chance of success. The sole reward asked by Captain Fox was to be assigned to the command of the expedition. His plan was at once simple and efficient. The troops and provisions were to be placed on board a large sea steamer, preferably the Collins steamer *Baltic,* which was to carry three hundred extra sailors and enough armed launches to land all the troops in one night. Two powerful light-draught tug-boats, their machinery protected by cotton-bales or hay, which would shield it from grape or fragments of shells, were to be used to transport the troops and provisions from the bar; the men below, the provisions on deck. The whole to be convoyed by the United States sloop of war *Pawnee,* drawing twelve feet of water and carrying seven guns, the only available steam vessel north of the Gulf of Mexico. As a steamer, she was a failure, but Captain Fox thought she might answer in the emergency, as she was "unfortunately the only resource." She was to protect the transports and tugs from any attack of the enemy, and to serve as a base of operations. The batteries were to be run at night by the tugs, and the barbette guns of the work were relied upon to keep the channel between the islands free from hostile vessels while entering. If perfectly calm, boats were to be used. The plan of Captain Fox was also endorsed by Mr. G. W. Blunt, Mr. Chas. H. Marshall and Russell Sturgis of New York, and Mr. Marshall agreed to furnish or provision the vessels without publicity.

On the 4th of February Captain Fox was summoned to Washington by General Scott by telegram, as he had also been by letter that failed to reach him. The whole subject was fully discussed in the General's presence on the following day. The proposition made by Lieutenant N. J. Hall, one of Major Anderson's officers, who had been sent to Washington by Major Anderson after the demand for the surrender of the fort on the 11th of January, that a steamer should go in protected by a vessel on each side loaded with hay, was pronounced impracticable.

The plan of Captain Fox was approved by General Scott, who presented him to the Secretary of War on the 7th of February, to whom Captain Fox explained his project and who agreed to submit it to the President that evening. On the 20th of February Lieutenant-General Scott directed his aide-de-camp in New York (Lieutenant-Colonel H. L. Scott) to put himself into communication with Commander Ward, to see what recruits and what stores he would want, and to see that everything was supplied for Major Anderson's needs. At the same time, a memorandum made by Lieutenant Hall, of the articles required at Fort Sumter, was sent to Colonel Scott with directions to supply them, and as large a supply of subsistence as Commander Ward could take. All was prepared and the expedition made ready for sea. But Mr. Buchanan had again changed his purpose. On the 8th the news of the formation of a provisional Government at Montgomery by the seceding States had reached Washington. While the President declined to enter into any pledges in regard to the sending of reinforcements to Fort Sumter, he considered "the truce" established by Major Anderson as binding, and as restraining him from sending such reinforcements. He determined also to respect the appeal made by the General Assembly of Virginia. The negotiations between the envoy and the Government were yet in progress, and Major Anderson had not asked for reinforcements, and the authorities of the State seemed equally inclined to suspend immediate action. He therefore deemed it to be his duty to, refrain from any action which might precipitate a crisis, and the expedition under Commander Ward, which had been determined upon, was in consequence not sent. This determination of the President was the cause of "great disappointment and astonishment" to General Scott, who so expressed himself to Captain Fox on the 8th of February. General Scott believed that up to the 12th of February it was easy to relieve Fort Sumter, and that the expedition of Commander Ward would have been successful, and that he would have been able to reach Sumter "with all his vessels." In a communication to the incoming President on the 3d of March, it was stated by General Scott that the expedition under Commander Ward "was kept back" by something like a truce or armistice, which was established between President Buchanan and the "principal seceders," and which lasted until the end of Mr. Buchanan's administration. To this the President took exception, and asserted that the truce was made by Major Anderson himself, and that it expired on the 5th of February, when the Secretary of War, Mr. Holt, announced to the South Carolina. Commissioner, Mr. Hayne, the refusal of the President to sur- render Fort Sumter under any circumstances.* The President characterized the strictures of General Scott as "unfounded and unjust." In his communication no reference is made by General Scott to the existence of the truce between Major Anderson and the Governor of South Carolina."

On the 21st of February it was announced in the public press that it was determined by the Government to relieve Fort Sumter by boats at night, although in a telegram to a friend Lieutenant- General Scott had expressed his belief that this plan of Captain Fox had been "adjourned."

This statement was made the subject of a communication to the Hon. Montgomery Blair by his relative, Captain Fox, in which the impracticability of the plan by open boats, its danger and the publicity given to it, were shown. It would now be anticipated, and he renews and specifies more particularly his own proposition.

On the 1st of March it was discovered that the Charleston authorities had opened negotiations in New York for the pur- chase of two of the same tugboats that Captain Fox had selected as the only suitable ones for the work in the city, and he thought that the probability of the reinforcement of Fort Sumter would be greatly lessened by this action. The tugs had been put in order, although his plan had been suspended, but relying upon the endorsement of General Scott, Captain Fox again urged the consideration of his plan.

---

* "Buchanan's Administration."

CHAPTER XXI.

A DISCIPLE of the school of Madison and of Jackson, the President believed that the union of the States could not be preserved by the mere exertion of the coercive powers confided to the General Government, and he felt it to be his duty, as it was his earnest wish, to exert all of his constitutional as well as his personal power to avert the danger so imminently threatening the nation.

Congress had met on the 2d of December, and to it he transmitted a carefully prepared message, in which he reviews the actual political situation, and makes certain recommendations for its action.* He asserts that "the long-continued and intemperate interference of the Northern people with slavery in the South had produced its natural effect;" that the sovereign States of the South were alone responsible for the existence of slavery within their limits; and that the North was not responsible, and had no right to interfere. He denies that the rights of the South are in

---

* President's message, December, 1860.

danger, and affirms that Congress had never at any time, by legislation, impaired in the slightest degree the "rights of the South to their property in slaves, nor their equal rights in the Territories to hold such property; that the action of different State Legislatures to defeat the execution of the Fugitive-slave law, was unconstitutional, and thus null and void; but that the Southern States had a right to demand the repeal of these "obnoxious enactments," and if refused, the injured States, after using all peaceful means or redress, would be justified in "revolutionary resistance."

He claims that, as the Executive, he had no power to decide the relations which should exist between the Federal Government and South Carolina, much less to acknowledge its independence; that while a State had no right to secede from the Union at its pleasure, Congress had no constitutional power to coerce such State which was attempting to withdraw or had actually withdrawn from the Union.

He argues, too, that the property of the United States in South, Carolina had been bought with the consent of the Legislature of the State, and that the Constitution of the United States gave to it executive control; that he did not believe that any forcible attempt would be made against that property, but that if such should be made, the officer in charge had orders to act defensively.* And he recommends, as the one mode of arresting the "headlong career" of the cotton States, that an explanatory amendment be presented to the States, recognizing their property in slaves, protecting that right in the Territories, while Territories, under the decision of the Supreme Court.

In regard to the performance of his duty, in whole or in part, under the acts of 1795 and 1807, it was rendered nugatory by the demolition of the whole machinery of the Federal Government necessary for the distribution of remedial justice, and that it would be difficult if not impossible to replace it, but that he should collect the revenue and defend the public property against all assaults. The position assumed by the President in his message, and for which the country had so anxiously waited, gave

---

* No money was paid for the forts or sites for forts in South Carolina, and this statement of the President gave rise to much comment both in and out of Congress. After the cession of the forts in 1805, South Carolina advanced money to assist in making repairs upon Fort Moultrie and Castle Pinckney.– Charleston *Mercury,* December 22, 1860.

rise to very diverse sentiments. It satisfied neither of the great
parties now definitely formed in the country. The Southern
leaders in Washington became reserved in their intercourse with
the President, at learning his views on the right of secession; and
although his course had hitherto met their approval and they had
implicitly trusted him to act in their interest, his message disappointed them, as not going far enough in the direction of their
views, and one by one they left him, until his refusal to restore
the status by the return of Anderson to Fort Moultrie severed all
relations with him at once and finally.   The ground laid down by
the President in his message of the 3d of December, while denying the right of secession to the State, and denying equally the
right of the General Government to coerce a State, was popularly
but erroneously attributed to the Attorney-General, Judge Black,
who, however, was not the writer of it.   The sentiments of the
message of the 8th of January, however, expressed the views of
the Attorney-General, which were adopted by the President.

Meantime, Congress was in daily session, but it seemed to be
impossible to obtain its consent to any measure, either upon the
recommendation of the President or as originating among themselves, which would meet the impending revolution by conciliatory measures or oppose it by force.

Impatient at the delay, recognizing the fact that the cotton
States were following each other into secession, and conscious of
his own want of power, either to check or prevent it, the President again, on the 8th of January, addressed a special message
to Congress, reciting the actual condition of affairs as in a worse
state that at the time of his first message.

He states that "recent reflections" had only confirmed him
in the conviction that no State had a right by its own act to
secede from the Union; that he, as the President, had no power
to recognize the exercise of such right even if it existed, and that
neither he nor Congress had any right to make war upon a State,
but. that the military force might be used defensively against
those who resisted federal officers or who assailed the Government property; that the power and the responsibilities to make
war or to secure peace rested with Congress alone. A delay to adopt
some practical proposition to conciliate, might render any adjustment impossible. And he concludes by stating that he had determined that no act of his should contribute to the excitement; that

his purpose was not to commence a civil war, nor even to furnish an excuse for it, and that he had thus "refrained" from reinforcing Major Anderson in Charleston Harbor, lest it might be unjustly regarded as a menace of military coercion, and especially as "no necessity for these reinforcements seemed to exist."

In this special message the important correspondence between the President and the South Carolina Commissioners was submitted.

The President's message contained nothing new, and it was considered by Senator Jefferson Davis, as stated in his speech the following day, as containing very little indeed beyond that which the world, less indeed than reading men generally, knew before it was communicated. And he characterized the message of December as one from which "it was not within the power of man to reach any fixed conclusion."

By a singular omission in the only act passed by Congress involving the question, that of 1795, no provision was made to resist insurrection against the General Government upon the part of the States. Even this important consideration received no attention from Congress during its entire session. A bill enabling the President to call out the militia for the purpose of retaking the forts already seized, or that might hereafter be seized, was presented to the House of Representatives, but immediately withdrawn and recommitted, and not again referred to,

On the 18th of February a bill was introduced, extending the powers of the President to employ the militia in suppressing insurrection against the Government, and to accept volunteers. It made no provision for repossessing the forts, and its consideration was purposely postponed until too late to be acted upon, and it was thus defeated; and this action only too plainly demonstrated to what an extent the United States Senate was affected by the secession sentiment. The Senate neglected to confirm the nomination of a collector of customs for the port of Charleston, S. C., Senator Jefferson Davis having played a conspicuous part in preventing any action. Nor was any measure looking to the collection of the revenue outside of the closed ports by means of the Navy considered or passed during the entire session.

It was not denied that the President was powerless. No one claimed that he could, by virtue of his office, make war, or that, without additional and special legislation, he could properly or efficiently act; and yet the Congress of 1860-61 simply and per-sistently refused to pass any act, or to adopt any resolution, either to preserve the Union by peaceful measures or to grant to the Executive the power of aggression, or to increase and define his power of defense.

The "Crittenden amendment," which was a proposition to recognize the existence of slavery in the Territories south of the old Missouri Compromise line, was introduced early in the session. It forbade any interference with slavery by Congress in such Territories, and left the question of its continuance to be decided by the Constitution of the new State, formed from such Territory, upon its admission as a State into the Union. The compromise thus offered seemed to meet the approval of a large majority of those who still clung to the Union of the States.

It was, however, rejected by the committee to whom it was referred, who reported on the 31st of December that they had not been able to agree upon any plan of adjustment. It tolerated slavery in New Mexico, and no Republican supported it at any time. But the patriotic author of the proposition was not discouraged, and he substituted for it a joint resolution referring his amend-ment to a direct vote of the people. Although this seemed to meet popular approbation, and received also the endorsement of the President, its consideration was again and again postponed, and when finally introduced, after much opposition, it was so amended by the substitution of another and wholly different reso-lution, in accordance with the Chicago platform, that the original proposition was destroyed by it, and the substitute was carried by the fact that six Northern Senators had failed to vote against it. And at the end of the session the original proposition itself, when presented, was defeated upon a direct vote.

Meantime, the Peace Convention called by Virginia, in a noble effort to adjust the difficulties and to preserve the Union, had met at Richmond on the 4th of February. It was composed of commissioners from States North and South that were willing to unite in an effort to preserve the Union. The hopes of every patriot were turned to it, and it was felt that nothing remained but a rupture of the Union, should it fail to accomplish its object. But the cotton States had already separated themselves from the Union, and were about to form a provisional Government of their own. After much discussion and the loss of valuable time, a series of amendments were reported of the same tenor and purpose, with the compromise measures proposed by Mr. Crittenden, save that it limited the provisions to the present Territories.

This amendment was at once communicated to Congress, and an effort made by the Commissioners in charge of it to induce the Senate, by joint resolution, to propose it as an amendment to the Constitution. This failed of accomplishment, when Mr. Crittenden adopted it in preference to his own proposition, and in consideration of its origin, offered it to the Senate, which rejected it by a large majority.

The House of Representatives refused to permit its Speaker to present the Amendment proposed by the Convention for its consideration, and no copy of it appears upon its Journal. The fate of the original proposition of this earnest statesman has been already seen, and Congress finally adjourned without passing a single measure calculated to tranquilize or assure the dissatisfied, or to meet by force the revolutionary spirit now threatening the integrity and peace of the country.

But long ere this, the people of the Southern States had ceased to look to Congress for any conclusive measure of prevention or reconciliation. Their resolution to go into convention of their States and to solve the difficulties for themselves, had been quite determined upon, and when, upon the 31st of December, the Committee of Thirteen reported themselves as unable to agree upon any plan of adjustment, they would wait no longer. On the 7th of January action was taken by Florida, and by the end of the month four more of the cotton States had passed the Ordinance of Secession by overwhelming majorities. They were joined by Texas on the 5th of February. The public property within the limits of these States was seized, and, in the case of Louisiana, a large amount of public money was removed from the Mint at New Orleans before the passage of the Ordinance; nor has the General Government ever received any offer of indemnity for this spoliation.

Congress adjourned, leaving the status unaltered by statute, and the President, with his peculiar views, helpless. But there was a belief, notwithstanding the threatening nature of the difficulties, that a peaceable solution might yet be attained; and without confidence in the action of the President, and uncertain of the views of the incoming administration, and unwilling to tie its hands or to anticipate its action by initiating hostile measures, Congress seemed to trust alone to time and to the new administration shortly to assume power.

CHAPTER XXII.

WHILE inaction and hesitation seemed to characterize the proceedings of Congress, and which the President regarded as favorable to him in the position he had taken, there was no illusion as to the course of those States that, as far as their own act could accomplish it, had now separated- themselves from the Federal Union. Hardly had the last of the cotton States passed the Ordinance of Secession, when on the 4th of February the Commissioners appointed by the several State conventions, met in session at Montgomery, Ala. These State conventions had sent their ablest men, many of them well known to the country at large, and whose lives were characterized by devotion to Southern sentiment and to Southern interest. An abundant material was thus supplied, from which was drawn an array of executive ability that gave life to every department of the new Government, and that in determined and deliberate concert did not hesitate to act.

The provisional Congress had no sooner assembled than it at once began the passage of resolutions and of acts entitled "By the Confederate States of America in Congress assembled." The varied and complicated machinery of an established government was promptly organized and the officers to direct it chosen. The executive, legislative and judicial departments were provided for and set in motion, and the salaries of the Cabinet officers regulated.

To a Congress thus composed, the United States of America became a "foreign country," and a measure enforcing the "existing revenue laws against all foreign countries" except the State of Texas was promptly adopted.*

A resolution for the appointment of three commissioners by the "President-elect," to be sent to the Government of the United States of America, "to settle questions of disagreement between the two Governments," was adopted on the tenth day of the session. A department of State was organized, and a "great seal" provided for, and its uses prescribed. On one and the same day the Treasury, War and Navy departments were called into existence. and a Department of Justice authorized. The establishment and organization of a general staff for the Army of the Confederate States was resolved upon, and before the month of February had closed provision had been made to raise money for the support of the Government, and to provide for the defense of the Confederate States, to raise provisional forces, and to accept the service of volunteers.

Early in March, acts were passed to provide for the public defense, so as to maintain the rightful possession of the Confederate States in every portion of territory belonging to each State. The President was authorized to accept the service of 100,000 volunteers. On the 6th of March, the establishment and organization of an army was provided for, and in a subsequent act provision was made for its support. And thus within a month from the time at which it had assembled at Montgomery, a Government fully officered, and with every attribute of national power and supported by its people, had sprung into existence within the limits of the old Union, prepared to defend to the last extremity the position it had taken. "Jefferson Davis has created a nation," said Mr. Gladstone in his place in Parliament, and a nation was thus seemingly formed, "because each State

---

*Acts of the Provisional Congress, 1861.

possessed within itself an established and organized Government, under the influence of which right was maintained and wrong redressed. A remarkable change in the political government of this people was thus accomplished without the slightest disturbance of their social condition, and without the slightest exhibition of license or tendency to anarchy."* The secret strength that lies in the complete and distinct organization of the States as separate communities, and upon which our whole Federal system of government relies, was appealed to, and used to whatever success was attained in the new movement. But from its nature, as well as from its organization, the Congress found itself at once obliged to assume the immediate control of questions whose solution involved the question of peace or war to the Confederacy, and accordingly, upon the 12th of February, within one week of its organization, it took under its charge the "questions and difficulties" existing "between the several States of this Confederacy and the United States of America relating to the occupation of forts" and other public establishments. Upon the 28th of February, in the act to raise provisional forces and "to enable the Government of the Confederate States to maintain its jurisdiction over all questions of peace and war," the "President" was authorized to assume control of all military operations in every State, in questions between them and powers foreign to them. Under this act, provision for the support of 3,000 men for twelve months, to be called into service at Charleston, was made, as well as an appropriation for 2,000 additional troops whenever in the discretion of "the President" their services might be required at Charleston.

The action of the provisional Congress in thus assuming the control of the "questions and difficulties" existing between any State and the Government of the United States, had immediate reference to the actual condition of affairs at Charleston and in Florida. Although the probability of such action had been anticipated by some of those in power in South Carolina, if not invited directly by the Governor, the passage of the resolution by the provisional Congress gave rise to considerable feeling, and to an extended discussion in the Convention and among the people.

In sending their delegates to Montgomery, it was understood

---

* "Representative Men of the South."–*Sketch of Magrath.*

to be the wish of the Convention of South Carolina that a provisional Government should be first promptly organized and set in motion; to be followed at once by the establishment of a permanent Government, and that this being accomplished, the delegates should return to their State conventions. It was to be understood that the assembled delegates were not the Legislature, nor were they to administer the Government, but to remain a Convention only."

The presentation of these views was met by earnest opposition from the deputies from Alabama, Louisiana and Georgia, who urged that a return of the deputies to their Convention "or to the people" would hazard the fate of the whole movement; that they had not so interpreted the resolution of South Carolina, and that their Conventions had conferred full power. This view was supported earnestly also by Florida, thus rendering it probable that Mississippi would be the only State that would support the peculiar view taken by South Carolina. Under these circumstances, the deputies from South Carolina yielded, and so reported to the Governor of their State, expressing the concurrent opinion of the entire delegation except two (Mr. Barnwell and Mr. Rhett).

It soon became manifest that the general Convention, as such, was not competent to meet the exigencies of the situation, nor to grapple successfully with the events now pressing upon them with startling rapidity. It was therefore determined "that the Convention should declare itself the Congress of a provisional Government," that it should act and should so exercise the powers of such Government until a permanent establishment under a new Constitution could be organized and a new Government inaugurated under it. It was in fact "the Constituent Assembly," and meantime the provisional Congress was the sole power for the "embryo Confederacy." "It exercised all the functions of Government, executive as well as legislative, and it held back and restrained the State of South Carolina from an attack on Fort Sumter, until the Confederate Government was in a condition to act."†

It was during this transition state that a very general impression if not a conviction prevailed, that an immediate assault upon Fort Sumter was threatened by the authorities of South Carolina;

---

* Letter of Mr. Percher Miles, February 10, 1861.

† Judicial decision. Judge I. M. Clayton, 7th Judicial District, 1866.

Even since the entrance of Major Anderson into that work, and the refusal of the General Government to transfer his command to Fort Moultrie, the question of its reduction and possession had presented itself incessantly and with accumulated force to the people and authorities of South Carolina. Distrusting his own judgment, impatient of the pressure brought upon him, the Executive of the State had sought counsel from without, and having previously addressed a communication to Senator Jefferson Davis, then in *his seat as* a Senator from Mississippi, he received from him a reply on the 13th of January.

He says that he was unable to place any confidence in the adherence of the administration to a "fixed line of policy;" that the general tendency was to hostile measures, and that it was necessary to prepare to meet them; and that he took it for granted that the time allowed to the garrison of Fort Sumter had been diligently employed by "yourselves," "so that before you could be driven out of your earthworks, you will be able to capture the fort which commands them." He argues against the shutting up of the garrison with the view to starve them into submission, as such action would create a sympathy much greater than any which could be obtained on the present issue. He doubted, too, the loyalty of the garrison, and as he supposed that the entrance of the harbor was closed to any reinforcements, he thought that there could be no danger to the freest intercourse between the garrison and the city. His letter was as follows:

"WASHINGTON, D. C.,
January 13, 1861.

"GOVERNOR F. W. PICKENS,

"*My dear sir:* A serious and sudden attack of neuralgia has prevented me from fulfilling my promise to communicate more fully by mail than could safely be done by telegraph. I need hardly say to you that a request for a conference on questions of defense had to me the force of a command; if, however, found me under a proposition from the Governor of Mississippi, to send me as a commissioner to Virginia, and another to employ me in the organization of the State militia. But more than all, I was endeavoring to secure the defeat of the nomination of a foreign collector for the port of Charleston, and at that time it was deemed possible that in the Senate we could arrest all hostile legislation such as might be designed either for the immediate or future coercion of the South. It now appears that we shall lack one or two votes to effect the legislative object just mentioned, and it was decided last evening, in a conference which I was not able to attend, that the Senators of the seceded States should promptly withdraw upon the telegraphic information already received.   I am still confined to my bed, but hope soon to be up again, and, at as early a day as practicable, to see you.   I cannot place any confidence in the adherence of the administration to a fixed line of policy. The general tendency is to hostile measures, and against these it is needful for you to prepare. I take it for granted that the time allowed to the garrison of Fort Sumter has been diligently employed by yourselves, so that before you could be driven out of your earthworks you will be able to capture the fort which commands them. I have not sufficiently learned your policy in relation to the garrison at Fort Sumter, to understand whether the expectation is to compel them to capitulate for want of supplies, or whether it is only to prevent the transmission of reports and the receipt of orders.   To shut them up with a view to starve them into submission would create a sympathetic action much greater than any which could be obtained on the present issue. I doubt very much the loyalty of the garrison, and it has occurred to me that if they could receive no reinforcements-and I suppose you sufficiently command the entrance to the harbor to prevent it—that there could be no danger of the freest intercourse between the garrison and the city. We have to-day news of the approach of a mixed commission from Fort Sumter and Charleston, but nothing further than the bare fact. We are probably soon to be involved in that fiercest of human strifes, a civil war.   The temper of the Black Republicans is not to give us our rights in the Union, or allow us to go peaceably out of it.   If we had no other cause, this would be enough to justify secession, at whatever hazard.   When I am better I will write again, if I do not soon see you.

(Signed)   "Very sincerely yours, JEFFERSON DAVIS."*

Upon the 20th of January he again wrote that his quiet hours were mostly spent in thought of Charleston Harbor; that the opinion of the friends of Governor Pickens was adverse to the presentation of a demand for the evacuation of Fort Sumter; that the little garrison in its present position pressed upon nothing but a point of pride; that war was made up of real elements, and that it was a physical problem from the solution of which all sentiment must necessarily be excluded; that he hoped that they should soon have a Southern Confederacy, should soon be ready to do all which interest or even pride demands, and that an indemnity would be found for any chafing they had now to endure. That there was much preparation to

---

* From original letter.

make, both in civil and in military organizations, and that the time which served for their preparation, by its moral effect tended toward a peaceful solution. He thought, too, that the "occurrence" of the *Star of the West* seemed to put the Governor in the best condition for delay, so long as the Government permits that matter to rest where it is; and that if things should continue as they were for a month, they would then "be in a condition to speak with a voice that all must hear and heed." He wrote:

"WASHINGTON, 20th January, 1861.
"GOVERNOR F. W. PICKENS.

"*Dear Sir:* I wrote you a note yesterday announcing to you my disappointment at the circumstances which prevented me from meeting you on my way home. You will not be surprised when I say to you that my quiet hours are mostly spent in thoughts of Charleston Harbor, and may therefore pardon the frequency of my letters.

"Colonel Hayne has doubtless informed you of the condition in which he found matters here. The opinion of your friends, which has been communicated to him, is adverse to the presentation of a demand for the evacuation of Fort Sumter. The little garrison in its present position presses on nothing but a point of pride, and to you I need not say that war is made up of real elements. It is a physical problem from the solution of which we must need exclude all sentiment. I hope we shall soon have a Southern Confederacy, shall soon be ready to do all which interest or even pride demands, and in the fullness of a redemption of every obligation. The more impatient will find indemnity for any chafing, in the meantime, they would have to endure. We have much of preparation to make, both in military and civil organization, and the time which serves for our preparation, by its moral effect tends also towards a peaceful solution. Secure of ourselves, walking steadily onward to the purpose we have avowed, if any should misunderstand us, it will be only to awake from their delusion to the realization of the virtues and powers which will seem all the greater for their sudden development.

"I learn but vaguely the progress of your works, but rest content in the conviction that all is done which is possible.

"The occurrence of the *Star of the West* seems to me to put you in the best condition for delay, so long as the Government permits that matter to rest where it is. Your friends here think you can well afford to stand still, so far as the presence of a garrison is concerned, and if things continue as they are for a month, we shall then be in a condition to speak with a voice which all must hear and heed.

"I should be very happy to hear from you at Jackson, Miss.;

and hoping to meet you soon, permit me to assure you that my heart will be with you, and my thoughts of you.

"Very respectfully and truly,

"Yours,

(Signed)   "JEFFERSON DAVIS"

A letter of similar import had been addressed by Governor Pickens to the Executive of Georgia, Governor Jos. E. Brown, who replied to him on the and of February that he fully appreciated the difficulties by which he was surrounded, and the irritation which his people must feel while menaced by a hostile force. That there were political considerations which induced him to believe that it would be bad policy to make an attack, or commence actual war during Mr. Buchanan's administration. He urged that if war was commenced during Mr. Buchanan's administration, the Democratic party of the North would sustain the President, and would be put in the front of the attack; that Mr. Lincoln would take it up as "unfinished business actually commenced," and bring the Republican party with him against the South. But that if a rupture with Buchanan was avoided, and Mr. Lincoln should commence the war, the Northern Democracy would oppose the measure and divide the people upon the issue; that Mr. Lincoln must commence the attack at once, if at all, when he would be weak, and when he would have offended a large number of the leaders of his party in the distribution of patronage. He therefore thought it unwise to make any attack at present, unless the interest and honor of South Carolina required a different course."

But the report of the alleged intention of Governor Pickens in regard to the assault upon Fort Sumter had reached Montgomery and engaged the attention of the leaders of the new movement. On the 9th of February a communication was addressed to the Governor of South Carolina by the Hon. Robert Toombs, then or immediately afterward the Secretary of State of the new Confederacy, urging that Sumter might not be attacked "without the sanction and jurisdiction of our joint Government."

To this Governor Pickens replied that, under "your Constitution" he supposed that he had no jurisdiction unless, in case of defense or invasion, but that he considered the occupation of Fort Sumter now, after the rejection of his demand at Washington, and

---

* Governor Pickens's files.

the grounds upon which such rejection was made, as an act of invasion.

The garrison was not in the same fort as when the State seceded; and their action in deserting Fort Moultrie and the destruction they committed was, he thought, only justifiable in the face of a public enemy, and certainly inaugurated a state of active hostilities if not war." "But of course," continues the Governor, "if the President of our Republic will come on here or send a commander-in-chief immediately, or if your Congress will by any public or specific declaration, indicate jurisdiction, either by request or otherwise, then I could not hesitate to abide most cheerfully by your control," unless an act of aggression or insult would require "immediate action."

The idea that the Government at Montgomery, might interfere had been for some time entertained, if not desired, by Governor Pickens, who, on the 9th of February, in a communication to the Hon. John Tyler, stated that, "if the provisional Government at Montgomery assume the direction of this State in reference to Fort Sumter, our course may be controlled by such direction." This, in view of the determined feeling of the people, was as far as the Governor could go without involving himself directly with the sentiment so often and so earnestly expressed by the Convention and by the Legislature. But it was no less an open suggestion, if not a solicitation, the object of which was to transfer a responsibility pressing upon him with daily increasing weight, and from which if not ostensibly, he not the less really shrank. But the Governor still continued to plead the necessity for an attack at the earliest possible moment, and in his communication to Mr. Toombs of the 12th of February, the day upon which the resolution was passed, he says, "I hope to be ready by Friday night, and think I am prepared to take the fort or to silence it." The fact that an immediate attack was contemplated, was telegraphed to the South Carolina delegation and created "deep concern." It was thought that the Governor was not informed as to the powers of the Congress. It was believed, too, that the attack would be premature, that it would interfere with the arrangements then in progress to establish a Government, and would put an end to any hope of a peaceful solution of the difficulties. It was at once determined that the Congress, being now the master, should interfere. A resolution assuming control of the difficulties was promptly offered and at once passed, and the whole question of Fort Sumter passed into the hands of the provisional Government. Upon the evening of the same day, the President of the provisional Congress (Mr. Cobb) announced the action of the Congress in a telegram to the Governor of South Carolina, who made on the following day a lengthy reply. The whole subject of the "questions and difficulties" was discussed, as well in its political as its military relations. The claim of the United States to hold Fort Sumter as a military post, and the denial of the right of the State to have possession of the fort, was in fact a denial of its independence.

But the assertion of the rightful independence of the State carried with it necessarily the right to reduce a fort into its own possession, when that fort was held by an unfriendly power for a hostile purpose. It was therefore proper and necessary for the State to take possession of "that fort" as soon as it was prepared to do it.   With the completion of the preparation which was near, and certain of the object, it had ever been the purpose of the State authorities to take the fort.   It was the right of the State, and her resources were equal to the exercise of that right; that whatever solution might be adopted upon the part of the Convention in regard to the "questions and difficulties," the position of South Carolina as to them should be regarded, and that as soon as her preparations were completed, the fort should be reduced. As to the time the attack should be made, he thought, with the best lights he could procure in guiding him, he was perfectly satisfied that the welfare of the new Confederation, as well as the necessities of the State required "that Fort Sumter should be reduced before the close of the present administration at Washington." To delay the attack until after the inauguration of Mr. Lincoln, the troops which were then quartered in the Capital might be employed in attempting that which they could not now be spared to do.

"Mr. Lincoln," says the Governor, "cannot do more for this State than Mr. Buchanan has done. Mr. Lincoln will not concede what Mr. Buchanan has refused, and Mr. Buchanan has based his refusal upon grounds which determine his reply to six States as completely as to one. If war can be averted it will be by making the capture of Fort Sumter a fact accomplished during the continuance of the present administration, and leaving to the incoming administration the question of an open declaration of war. If, however, the attack upon the fort is made during Mr. Lincoln's administration, it would be an act of present hostility; and a declaration of war would not be a question to be considered by him, but would be inevitable.   Mr. Buchanan cannot resist because he has not the power; Mr. Lincoln may not attack because the cause of quarrel may be considered by him as past."*

This assumption of the war power by the Convention, and the control of the external relations of the States composing the new Confederacy, was effected before the new Government under the provisional constitution was organized. There was as yet no executive, no Cabinet, and the single House of the Congress was the entire Government. And it was feared by many in South Carolina that the result of the transfer of the matter of Fort Sumter to the Montgomery Government would be the postponement of the possession of that work, and the assault upon it now confidently expected as soon to take place, would be entrusted to other hands, and that thus a reflection would rest upon the State.

Although at this period the preparations for an assault upon the fort were incomplete, if not inadequate, no sooner had the transfer of the responsibility in regard to it been made to the provisional Congress, than the people of the State became more clamorous, and the authorities of the State more urgent, that the attack upon it should be made. The situation had become more complicated everywhere. According to a statement in the Southern press on the 1st of February, sixteen forts had now been seized whose united armament consisted of 1,262 guns, and whose construction had cost the Government over six million and one half of dollars.† Seven remained. As early as the 12th of February, however, Governor Pickens had deemed himself prepared, and he wrote to Mr. Toombs, who shortly afterward became the Secretary of State of the new Confederacy, that he thought he was prepared to take Fort Sumter, or to silence it.   He had, he said, in his most powerful battery, 1,240 yards from the fort, three 8-inch heavy Columbiads and three heavy mortars, and

---

* Pickens to Cobb, February 13 1861.

† Charleston *Mercury,* February 1, 1861.

that two more were to be placed there. He had also a floating battery, which was to be placed under the weakest part of the work. "Besides these," he says, "I have mortars and Columbiads at Fort Moultrie, and plenty of 32-pounders as well as mortars at Fort Johnson. If the attack was commenced, the fort, should be taken at every hazard; and if resisted, the slaughter of the garrison was inevitable." The channel was well guarded, and no ship could enter without being sunk, and this should be done, "let the consequences be what they may." If reinforcements were attempted, he would not wait an hour. He did not desire that the border

HAMILTON FLOATING BATTERY.

States should patch up a miserable and disgraceful Union with the North, and he thought that perhaps the immediate possession of the fort might be necessary to open a gulf between the border States and the North, so deep that it could never be closed, and that perhaps it would be politic to do this, even at the expense of bloodshed. Such things had been done in great revolutions.

On the 22d of February, the provisional President had forwarded to Governor Pickens the resolution of the Congress, taking into their own charge the military operations in progress in the several States of the Confederacy. To this the Governor replied on the 27th of February, by a recital of the steps he had taken. That in order to consult him on military matters he had asked him to come to Charleston; that he had sent to the Governor of Georgia for General Twiggs, and to him (Davis) for a military engineer. That nothing should be done to involve the States in a permanent war by any separate act of theirs, unless it was necessary in self-defense, or to prevent reinforcements. But in the meantime, he proposed to go on with the same authority as ever in preparing his defenses and his men for any event that may arise. And he asks to be informed if, when he is ready to assault the fort, should he do so or await "your order," and also if he should demand the surrender, or would it be made, by the executive, and he asked that an answer be sent him by telegraph. The Congress at Montgomery had meantime organized a provisional Government, and an executive in the person of Mr. Jefferson Davis had been chosen, who, upon the 9th of February, proceeded to Montgomery and at once entered upon the duties of his office. Among the earlier acts of his administration was the appointment of a brigadier-general for the army of the Confederacy, and to assign him at once to the command of the operations in the harbor of Charleston. Previous to this appointment, the Governor of South Carolina had been urgent that a skilled engineer should be sent to him at Charleston. Captain W. H. C. Whiting, a former officer of engineers of the United States Army, and who, having vacated his commission, was now in the service of the State of Georgia, was sent to report to him. On the 22d of February he received his orders from the provisional President directly. He was to proceed to Charleston, to confer with the Governor of the State, and to enter at once upon a reconnoissance of the harbor; he was to inspect the works, and was to gain such knowledge of Fort Sumter as circumstances would permit. He was to make an inventory of the armament and munitions, and note particularly the different qualities of cannon powder, and he was generally charged with the examination of the works and the preparation for active operations. Captain Whiting proceeded to Charleston, and entered at once upon the service required of him. The result of his inspection was soon attained. He disapproved of much which had been done, and gave an "alarming description of affairs" in the harbor of Charleston. This official decision deeply wounded the susceptibilities of the officials and people in Charleston, many of whom demanded his removal. The efforts of the State authorities had been almost exclusively directed to the reduction of Fort Sumter. With a view to the accomplishment of this purpose, the work upon Fort Moultrie, Fort Johnson and the iron-clad battery upon Cummings Point seemed to receive their principal attention. It was evident that a breaching fire was contemplated from the batteries at Cummings Point. The labor there was unremitting, and it soon attracted the earnest attention of Major Anderson and his officers. It was to meet the fire from these batteries and to resist the contemplated assault, that the gorge of Fort Sumter was protected and strengthened by every available means, and the strongest batteries upon the parapet made to bear upon the works at that point. The recommendations of their Board had been carefully carried out. All through January and February the work was prosecuted, and often continued late into the night. On the 22d of February Major Anderson reported to his Government that, "one of the works on Cummings Point appeared to be bomb-proof, and was possibly intended to defilade their guns bearing on the channel from our fire," and that it was evident that they considered them as important. The shape and appearance of the battery, and the use of bars of railroad iron in its construction, was on the 4th of February first made known. The guns which were intended to fire directly upon Sumter were first mounted, placed in position and covered with bomb-proof roofs and the embrasures closed with iron shutters. On the 9th of February an additional battery of three heavy guns, three hundred yards eastward of the iron-clad battery, and connected with it by a covered way, apparently was recognized and reported. Work went on steadily upon these batteries from day to day. Meantime, on the 12th of February, the action of the provisional Congress in assuming the control of the military operations of the seceded States had become known, and it seemed to those who watched the operations from Fort Sumter to be followed by a lack of activity in the work going on about the fort. But from whatever cause it may have arisen, the suspension was but temporary, and work was soon actively renewed. By the middle of February a third breaching battery was established at Cummings Point, and the three embrasures for its guns commenced.

CHAPTER XXIII.

Salutes upon Washington's birthday in Charleston Harbor–Scenes in Washington–president countermands order for parade of troops–Representative Sickles protests–Interview with the President at the War Department –President yields–Parade takes place–Makes explanation to Ex-President Tyler–His letter–Major G. T. Beauregard selected as Brigadier-General of the new Confederacy–His character and history–Proceeds to Charleston–Makes thorough inspection–Unfavorable result–Absence of systematic organization and control–Operations around Sumter changed –Detached batteries located on shores of harbor–Fort Sumter to be enveloped by a circle of fire–Defenses of Fort Moultrie rebuilt–Chief engineer's accurate observations and reports–His letter to his chief–Major Anderson clearly reports his condition; and the work going on around him.

It was now the 22d of February, and Castle Pinckney had opened early with a salute of thirteen guns in honor of the birthday of Washington. At noon the guns upon the barbette were manned and Sumter fired a national salute. On that morning a different scene was enacting at Washington.

In accordance with custom a parade of the troops stationed there had been ordered by the Secretary of War in celebration of the day, and its execution committed to General Scott on the 21st inst. Upon the evening of that day the President, hearing of the order, went in person to the residence of the Secretary of War and asked if such parade had been ordered by him.

He was replied to affirmatively, and informed that it was in accordance with custom, when the President at once countermanded the order. The Secretary replied to him that it would be difficult now at so late an hour to countermand it, as a copy of the order had already gone to the public press, but that he would make the effort to obey his instructions. Upon the morning of the 22d, knowing nothing of the countermand, and having seen the published order, large crowds had assembled to witness the parade, and with an especial interest, as it was believed that troops had been assembled in Washington with reference to the approaching inauguration on the 4th of March. The President

273

had gone to the War Department, and was in the office of the Secretary of War, who had preceded him, when Daniel E. Sickles, then a Member of Congress from New York, and who had made his way into the closed Department, appeared at the door of the Secretary's office and demanded to see the President. When cautioned by the Secretary that the President wished to be alone, he insisted; when, hearing the noise, the President inquired the reason of the disturbance. His relations with the Representative had been close for a long period. While minister to England the latter had been the Secretary of Legation, and as a Member of Congress he had been an ardent supporter of Mr. Buchanan's administration, and the relations existing were now taken advantage of by the latter to bring the subject of the suspension of the parade before the President with great force. It would be misunderstood, there was no reason for it, and would be productive of great harm. It must go on, and any orders for its suspension must be at once revoked. The President reluctantly yielded, when the Representative went at once to the office of Lieutenant-General Scott, who feared that it was then too late, as his officers were now "unbelted," as he expressed it. Word was, however, promptly sent; those organizations that had not yet been dismissed were assembled, and a parade was made without any knowledge upon the part of the people that it had been interrupted. Hardly had the Representative left the department when the President addressed the following communication to ex-President John Tyler, the President of the Peace Convention then. in session in Washington, and which was at once copied by the Secretary of War. It was as follows;

"WASHINGTON, February 22, 1861.
    "My Dear Sir: I found it impossible to prevent two or three companies of the Federal troops from joining in the procession to-day with the volunteers of the District, without giving serious offence to the tens of thousands of people who have assembled to witness the parade.
    "The day is the anniversary of Washington's birth, a festive occasion throughout the land, and it has been particularly marked by the House of Representatives.
    "The troops everywhere else join such processions in honor of the birthday of the Father of our Country, and it would be hard to assign a good reason why they should be excluded from the privilege in the Capital founded by himself. They are here simply as a *posse comitatus,* to aid the civil authorities in case of

need. Besides, the programme was published in the *National Intelligencer* of this morning without my personal knowledge, the War Department having considered the celebration of the national anniversary by the military arm of the Government as a matter of course.

"From your friend, very respectfully,

"JAMES BUCHANAN.

"PRESIDENT TYLER."

Renewed activity was soon manifested about the fort. The area to include all the batteries from Cummings Point was enlarged, and the batteries themselves connected by curtains, and work progressed upon these curtains, which the engineer officer, who carefully watched their progress, thought was "a magazine or a bomb-proof of timber to be used as a battery." The work at Moultrie and at Fort Johnson was steadily pursued, and it was while thus in progress that the officer appointed by the Government at Montgomery reported in Charleston. Major G. T. Beauregard, late of the United States Army, was the officer selected, who, in personal character and professional attainment fully merited the distinction. A native of Louisiana, he had graduated from the Military Academy at West Point in the Corps of Engineers of the class of 1838, with Hardee and McDowell, and had been justly considered one of the most accomplished members of that corps. By a singular coincidence Major Anderson was his instructor of artillery, and upon his graduation retained him as his assistant instructor of artillery and artillery practice. He had made a record of faithful service to the Government, which but a short time before had appointed him to the superintendency of the Military Academy at West Point, which position had been tendered to him the previous year.

In the war with Mexico he had distinguished himself by his engineering ability, and especially in his proposal and advocacy of the attack upon the city by its western approaches, and in support of which he stood almost alone, but which was finally successfully adopted. He was twice wounded, and was brevetted a captain, and again a major, in the army "for gallant and meritorious conduct at Contreras and at Cherubusco." He reported at the Academy, but, in accordance with his orders, postponed

---

*November 8, 1860.

assuming command until after the January examinations had closed, when he relieved the then superintendent, Major Delafield. His object in postponing action arose from the anticipated course of Louisiana, his native State, and which would decide his position, and in regard to which he was open in expression, having communicated his intentions to the chief of his corps. Major Beauregard remained in command but a few days, when he was relieved by an order from the Secretary of War, Mr. Holt, who, upon examining into the nature of the appointment, and discovering that it had been made without reference to the claims of older officers, and deeming that the appointment of an officer with such views and sympathies to the command of the military school at West Point an unsuitable one under the circumstances, and one which could not but produce a demoralizing effect upon the cadets, relieved him by his own order. Major Beauregard returned to Louisiana, when he at once tendered his resignation, and where by his counsel and advice he materially assisted the Governor in his preparations for the defense of the State and the approach to its valuable harbor. He declined the offer of a colonelcy in the State service, as he deemed himself, from his position and services, entitled to the brigadier-generalcy, which had been offered to and accepted by another (Bragg). The appointment of Beauregard to West Point was due to Senator John Slidell, of Louisiana, his brother-in-law. When his relief from command became known, Senator Slidell, upon the 27th of January, addressed a note to the President, asking him if this had been done with his approbation. His influence with the President was at this time potential. Soon after the Secretary of War received a summons to the White House, and on entering the President's room he found him seated at his official table with Mr. Stanton at his side. On approaching him he handed to the Secretary an open paper, saying to him, "Read this." It proved to be the note from Senator Slidell just referred to, and was in these words:

"WASHINGTON,
"January 27, 1861.
"MY DEAR SIR: I have seen in the *Star,* and heard from other parties, that Major Beauregard, who had been ordered to West Point as superintendent of the Military Academy, and had entered on the discharge of his duties there, had been relieved

from his command.   May I take the liberty of asking you if this has been done with your approbation?

"Very   respectfully   yours,

"JOHN   SLIDELL."

* Upon reading it the Secretary, indignant at its tone, said: "Mr. President, we have heard this crack of the overseer's whip over our heads long enough.   This note is an outrage; it is one that Senator Slidell had no right to address to you."   "I think so myself," replied the President, "and will write to him to that effect." "No," continued the Secretary, "I feel that I have a right, Mr. President, to ask that you will do more than this; that you will say to Senator Slidell, without qualification and without explanation, that this is your act, for you know that as Secretary of War I am simply your representative, and if my acts, as such, are not your acts, then they are nothing."   The President assented to this view, and without delay sent the following answer to Senator Slidell.

"WASHINGTON, January 29, 1861.

"MY DEAR SIR: With every sentiment of personal friendship and regard, I am obliged to say in answer to your note of Sunday, that I have full confidence in the Secretary of War; and his acts, in the line of his duty, are my own acts, for which I am responsible.

"Yours   very   respectfully,

(Signed)   "JAMES   BUCHANAN."

This terminated Senator Slidell's social relations with the President; he never appeared at the White House again.   Upon the 22d of February, Major Beauregard was summoned to Montgomery. He had meanwhile resigned his commission in the army of the United States, upon the 8th of February, but until its acceptance by the Government he abstained from entering the service of the Confederacy, when the appointment of brigadier-general was first tendered to him at Montgomery.   At the suggestion of Mr. Jefferson Davis, a telegram was sent by Major Beauregard to Washington, asking for action upon his resignation, when a reply was received formally accepting it, to take effect upon the 7th of February, and he at once passed into the service of the Confederate States. On the 1st of March, he was directed by his War Department to proceed to Charleston and

* Secretary Holt to writer.

report to the Governor of South Carolina for "military duty in that State." He was authorized to receive into the service of the Confederacy, a force not exceeding 5,000 men, as might be tendered, or who might volunteer. A sum of $20,000 was placed at his disposal, other sums arranged for, and the services of a competent staff suggested. Upon the same day, the Confederate Secretary of War* informed Governor Pickens of the appointment of General Beauregard and of the confidence in him, and he at the same time informed him that the President of the Confederacy shared the feeling the Governor had expressed, that Fort Sumter should, as early as possible, be in their possession. This natural and just feeling, however, must yield to necessity. "The first blow must be successful both for its moral and physical consequences, and thorough preparations must be made before an attack was attempted; otherwise the result would be disastrous and would demoralize our people,"† and injuriously affect them in the opinion of the world as reckless and precipitous. General Beauregard proceeded at once to his post. In order to become acquainted with the actual condition of things in the harbor, the progress of the works and the object proposed by the State authorities, General Beauregard abstained for a few days from assuming command. Soon afterwards, accompanied by the engineer officer, Captain Whiting, he proceeded to a thorough inspection of the system of works then in process of construction on Morris Island by the local engineers, for the reduction of Fort Sumter. The result of the inspection was unfavorable to the system, which, as engineers, was condemned by them. There was an absence of systematic organization or control; the guns and merlons at or about Cummings Point had been injudiciously crowded. Work had been confined to measures looking to the reduction of the forts, while the channel entrances had been almost overlooked, and it was deemed of the highest importance while keeping in view the reduction of Fort Sumter, to isolate it immediately from any possibility of reinforcement. A marked change in the operations around them soon became visible to those who watched from Fort Sumter. Under the instructions of the new commander, a system of detached batteries along the

* L. P. Walker.

† Letter book of the Confederate War Department, 1860-61.

shores of both Morris and Sullivan's islands was at once commenced.   Mortar batteries were to be located as far as practicable
beyond the range of the guns of the fort, "at every available
point on the bay around a circumference of which the fort should
be the centre, in order to concentrate thereon the fire of all my
batteries"* The position to be taken by the floating battery when
completed, was indicated, and a mortar battery located upon
Mount Pleasant closed the circle of fire intended to envelop the
fort. Additional mortars were brought from Savannah and Pensacola and placed at Fort Johnson and at Mount Pleasant in
strong works. They were within effective range, but beyond the
reach of the guns of Fort Sumter.   The character of the work at
Fort Moultrie was not thought to be effective. The defenses
were rebuilt; the merlons between the guns bearing on Sumter
were raised and supported by heavy timbers, and greatly increased
in strength. Renewed activity was soon manifested at every
point in the harbor of Charleston; new batteries sprang up along
the shore, steamers carrying men and materials passed and
repassed by day and night under the guns of Fort Sumter. A
large force of laborers was kept at work daily, including Sunday,
and the new object to be attained was steadily prosecuted. There
was no attempt at disguise.   Trials for range were made as soon
as any new work was completed and had received its armament,
and the artillery practice constantly going on soon manifested to
the garrison the steady improvement in firing and the accuracy
of range attained, and which they watched from their walls with
increasing interest. Daily reports, careful and minute in their
character, were made to Washington by Major Anderson, and the
engineer officer, Captain Foster, and the reports of Major Anderson were often accompanied by accurate sketches of the works
going on, made by Captain Seymour. Necessarily, these were
limited to what could be seen from the work by the medium of
glasses, as well as what appeared in the daily journals and what
could be learned from occasional messengers to the fort. Much
was inference and what seemed to be the probable intention, but
there was singular accuracy in the reports, and the Government
was kept as fully advised of the progress of the works around the
fort as the garrison itself. Through the months of February

*Beauregard's letter to writer, July 16, 1872.

and March, these reports were regularly made and the progress of the works reported, and especially upon the works at Cummings Point, which were nearest to the fort and deemed by the garrison as the most prominent. The transfer of mortars to the different works, the establishment of new batteries and the probable effect of their guns, their trials for range, the extension of their batteries to Morris Island bearing on the channel, as well as their changes at Moultrie to strengthen its defensive arrangement, were all carefully and promptly reported; also the arrival of General Beauregard and the immediate extension of the work for the defense of the harbor. So minute were the observations of the engineer officer, that he was enabled to report to his chief on the 6th of March, as follows:

"FORT SUMTER, S. C.,
"March 6, 1861.

"GENERAL: I have the honor to report that during the day, and especially towards night, unusual activity was observed among the South Carolinians around us; several steamer loads of men were landed on Cummings Point. The number was greater than the arrangements for shelter, apparently, for I observe quite a large number grouped about their bivouac fires this morning. Their suffering must have been considerable during the night, for the weather suddenly changed from the warm temperature of the preceding days to a high degree of cold, for this climate, the wind blowing fresh from the north.

"I learn that portable hot shot furnaces have been furnished to several, and probably all, of the batteries. The mortar battery on James Island, south of Fort Johnson, is armed, but the number of mortars is not ascertained. The magazine in the flank of this battery is also finished. The mortar battery on Sullivan's Island, west of Fort Moultrie, is also armed. All the batteries on Morris Island are armed. The guns range from 32-pounders down, with the exception of the iron bomb-proof, which is (I think, from all reports and observations) armed with 8-inch Columbiads—three of them.

"The raft does not meet expectations. It is being covered with railroad strap iron instead of the T rail. This has a cross-section of about three-fourths or one inch by two inches or two and a half inches.

"They are now ironing the top portion, the front not being yet commenced. Two 8-inch Columbiads are lying on the wharf ready to be put on board. I do not think this floating battery will prove very formidable.

"We have not yet received the inaugural address of President

Lincoln, although it is reported from town that it is coercive in its character, and that much excitement prevails.

"Very respectfully, your obedient servant,

"J. G. FOSTER,

"Captain Engineers.

"GENERAL JOS. G. TOTTEN,

"Chief Engineer U. S. Army, Washington, D. C."

Anderson, too, wholly alive to the fact that the harbor was being rapidly closed to all relief to him, and that any vessel coming to his assistance would be under fire from the harbor bar to the walls of his fort, clearly reported his condition to the new administration on the 9th of March as follows:

"FORT SUMTER, March 9, 1861.

"(Received A. G. O., March 12.)

"COLONEL S. COOPER,

"Adjutant-General, United States Army.

"Colonel: I have the honor to report that we can see the South Carolinians engaged this morning strengthening and extending considerably what we supposed to have been intended for a mortar battery at Fort Johnson. Small parties are also working at Nos. 9 and 10, and a very heavy force at the bend of the island, this side of No. 1. Whether they are constructing another battery there or strengthening one that is already there I cannot tell. One of my officers reports that he has counted nine 24-pounders which have been landed at Cummings Point within a week. Yesterday he saw several shot or shells which appeared to be about eight inches in diameter. They are certainly busy strengthening the batteries already constructed, and probably adding others. It appears to me that vessels will, even now, from the time they cross the bar, be under fire from the batteries on Morris Island until they get under the walls of this work. I do not speak of the batteries which have been constructed on Sullivan's Island, as I am not certain of their positions. Fort Moultrie will, of course, be a very formidable enemy.

"I am, Colonel, very respectfully,

"Your obedient servant,

"ROBERT ANDERSON,

"Major First Artillery, Commanding.

"COLONEL S. COOPER, *Adjutant-General United States Army."*

CHAPTER XXIV.

Close of President Buchanan's administration–Condition of the country–Anderson's letter of February 28–Its character–Estimate of himself and officers–Relieving force necessary–Letter delivered to President on 4th of March–Transmitted to incoming President by Secretary of War Holt on 5th of March–Resume of President Buchanan's course in dealing with the seceded States–His failure to recognize the real condition of affairs–His policy and action–Secretary Holt's letter accompanying Anderson's communication–Misled by Anderson's statements–Believed Anderson safe–Line of policy not to reinforce, unless called upon by Anderson, adhered to –Anderson's previous report–Main statements of his condition–Impossible to relieve him without large force–Anderson's views in private correspondence–Important letter to a Rhode Island correspondent–Good condition of the garrison–Annoyances from without–Irritation of the people –Floating battery–Anderson asks for instructions in regard to it–Reply of Secretary of War–Destruction of the temporary wooden buildings on the parade–Ammunition furnished to the batteries–Rearrangement of the guns–Gorge protected and strengthened–Anderson mines the wharf.

THE 4th of March had now come, and with it the close of the administration of Mr. Buchanan. The garrisons of Forts Sumter and Pickens had not been withdrawn, and these works still remained in the possession of the Government. The seceding States had not been recognized, either in the representative character of their Commissioners, or in their corporate capacity, or in any way whatever. The National Government had failed to assert itself. Congress had adjourned, and had left the situation unaltered by statute and uninfluenced by action. The status had been apparently preserved; bloodshed had been thus far avoided; the border States yet remained in the Union, but no settlement of the difficulties had been determined upon, and the country was steadily drifting towards a condition of things of which war seemed to be the inevitable conclusion.

The Commissioners from the Confederate Government had arrived in Washington, and were only waiting a change in administration to open negotiations with the Government, and to present their demands. The sounds of active preparation were heard in Charleston Harbor, and Fort Sumter was being rapidly surrounded by batteries to effect its reduction, while the shores and islands of the harbor were lined with works to prevent its reinforcement or relief, and this without hindrance from any quarter. The little garrison, unsustained by official sympathy and unsupported by material aid, were laboring, with the limited means at their disposal, to place the work in their charge in a state of efficient defense. Six States had severed their connection with the Union as far as their own act could accomplish it, and had established a Government of their own in full operation. But the friends of a peaceful solution of the questions at issue were active and confident; and it was believed by those in control that such solution was yet possible, as long as either side should abstain from any hostile act. The firing upon the *Star of the West* failed to arouse the nation, and the expedition was succeeded by the preparation of another and more elaborate scheme, but which, in view of the earnest efforts of the friends of peace, and the absence of any active hostility, was held until Major Anderson at Fort Sumter should call for relief.

It had been arranged that the expedition under Commander Ward, before alluded to, which had been made ready under the immediate direction of Lieutenant-General Scott himself, upon receiving a telegraphic despatch from the Secretary of the Navy, should on the night following the receipt of the despatch, set sail at once for Charleston Harbor.

It was at this crisis that the letter of Major Anderson, containing the estimate of himself and his officers as to what force was now necessary, in their judgment, to relieve the fort, was received at the War Department on the 4th of March. On the 28th of February Anderson had called suddenly upon his officers to submit in writing to him what force, in the estimation of each of them, would now be necessary to relieve the work. They were not to consult with each other, and their replies must be immediate. The opinions of the officers were varied as to the number of men required, but all agreed that the co-operation of the Navy was essential. The estimate of Major Anderson was that he would not risk his reputation with less than 20,000 men. That of his officers was as follows:

Captain J. G. Foster, United States Engineers, 6,000 regulars or 20,000 volunteers to take the batteries, and 10,000 regulars or 30,000 volunteers to hold them; First Lieutenant G. W. Snyder,

United States Engineers, 4,000 men with four vessels of war: Second Lieutenant R. K. Meade, United States Engineers, Assistant Surgeon S. W. Crawford, Medical Staff, 4,000 men supported by naval vessels; Captain Doubleday, First Artillery, 1,000 men with naval vessels; Brevet Captain T. Seymour, First Artillery, First Lieutenant T. Talbot, First Artillery, 3,000 men with naval vessels; First Lieutenant J. C. Davis, First Artillery, 3,000 men and six war vessels; Second Lieutenant N. J. Hall, First Artillery, 3,500 men and seven war vessels.*

On the morning of the 4th of March the President, with some of the members of the Cabinet, had gone to the Capitol for the purpose of acting upon bills presented to him, when the Secretary of War appeared with the letter just received from Major Anderson. The contents of the letter were made known to the President and to his Cabinet. There was at that time no discussion in regard to it, the President merely remarking, upon learning its contents, that it was "now a matter for the new administration."

It was at once perceived that the Government had been under an erroneous impression, arising from the statements of Major Anderson, from which it was believed that Fort Sumter could at any time be relieved by the expedition under Captain Ward, which had been made ready under the immediate direction of Lieutenant-General Scott himself. The "seeming extravagant estimate" now made by Major Anderson was wholly unanticipated by the President or his Cabinet. In accordance with custom, the President had vacated the Executive mansion on the 3d of March, and had removed with his family to a private residence, where, upon the evening of the 4th of March, the letter of Major Anderson was the subject of conversation between him and his Cabinet, who had called to take their leave of him. Meantime the Secretary of War, Mr. Holt, had prepared a letter to President Lincoln to accompany that of Major Anderson, and, upon the morning of the 5th of March, read it to the Ex-President and such members of his Cabinet as had come to the War Department. Mr. Buchanan expressed himself as gratified with the answer as prepared by the Secretary of War, and in this the members of his old Cabinet concurred. The parting of the

---

* "War of the Rebellion." Vol. I, Series I, p. 202.

President with his associates took place soon after, and the administration of Mr. Lincoln took charge of the Government, the Secretary of War having continued in his position until the qualification of his successor in office. On the afternoon of the 5th of March the Secretary of War transmitted his letter accompanied by that of Major Anderson to President Lincoln at the Executive mansion. Shortly afterward the President sent for the Secretary, and taking him. into a private apartment, asked him if at any time in his intercourse with Anderson he had occasion to doubt his loyalty. The Secretary replied that he had not, when the subject was dropped.

The failure upon the part of the President to reinforce the Southern forts, or any of them, in accordance with the repeated suggestions of Lieutenant-General Scott and the urgent recommendations of his Secretary of State, Judge Black, and others, had produced its legitimate result. No restraint had been placed upon such hostile measures as those in control in the seceded States had seen fit to inaugurate and to perfect, and it was now, in the judgment of those best fitted to decide the important question, too late to attempt such relief without precipitating a conflict, become in the very nature of the situation inevitable.

Had such relief been promptly sent when Anderson, from Fort Moultrie, clearly defining his position and his necessities, had urged with an earnestness carried to the verge of military propriety, that they should be sent to him; when two of the most distinguished members of his Cabinet, who from the beginning of the difficulties had tendered to him but one advice and besought him to act; when no State had yet attempted to secede from the Union-the situation might have been far different. It is true that the organized force legitimately under his control, as reported by Lieutenant-General Scott, was small, but it was at the time, at least, sufficient to show the purpose of the Government and to hold Fort Sumter until Congress could come to the rescue of the country. But the President did nothing. His fear that by his own act he might inaugurate hostilities and so bring on civil war, sustained by his political convictions that the Union could not be preserved by a war between the States, his overwhelming desire for peace and his hope to keep the border States, amounted to a timidity which "wholly incapacitated him for action." Launched into political power in Pennsylvania, by an abandonment of his previous political principles, he had, throughout a long public career, remained the politician, and had rarely risen to the level of practical statesmanship. Mr. Buchanan knew that the war was coming; he saw it in every feature of those who approached him, he heard it in their every tone. In addition, he was, up to the moment when Anderson moved the command of Fort Moultrie to Fort Sumter, largely influenced by Southern sentiment and controlled by Southern men. As far as his constitutional obligations permitted, he yielded to the pressure so constantly brought to bear upon him, and accorded to them their every demand. They were his constant associates. In his Cabinet they were, to an almost exclusive extent, his advisers, and they ruled him with an inflexible purpose. He had agreed with them that the status then existing should not be disturbed, and, until Anderson's movement, it was not disturbed, nor then by his consent or even with his knowledge. His policy was to protract, not to meet the issue, which, in the face of the country, was precipitated by his officer in command at Charleston. He had until then ever failed to realize the real nature and extent of the revolution, accustomed as he was to use "State politics merely as counters in the game for Federal power;" he recognized the present popular excitement as nothing more than another of the many agitations by which men had come into power, and reckoned that, like the others, it would run its course and be followed by a reaction and peace. His public life as President had not won the affections of his fellow-men. Indirect in his ways of action, wary and full of statecraft, with a cynical estimate of men from party experience, Mr. Buchanan had utterly misunderstood the real nature of the crisis and had compromised "a great position by feeble acts;" and when at last he did come to appreciate his position, his instinct was to save his administration and to protect himself. He had come into his high office at a time when the antagonism between the sections had attained its highest point of development. The various compromises that had been adopted had proved but lulls in the storm, and two phases of civilization, wholly at variance with each other, had developed to a point of opposition without hope of adjustment. And yet Mr. Buchanan desired and strove to serve his country. He had asked Congress for those powers necessary to meet the unprecedented condition of things, but whose exercise without the action of Congress he deemed impossible. To all of his appeals for such powers Congress treated him with indifference if not with contempt. His able message against the right of secession, his declaration that he was resolved to maintain the laws of the nation, protect its property and to collect its revenue, had its offset, unfortunately, in his diplomacy with those whom he could not control, in his promises to preserve the status, to receive Commissioners, and to refer them to Congress. The policy was an individual one and not that of his Cabinet, whose Northern members he had not consulted, but which arose from suggestions and promises of the Southern members, both of his Cabinet and of Congress, as well as from unauthorized and indirect communication with the South Carolina authorities. And in this policy he persevered, uninfluenced by the resignation of his Secretary of State, General Cass, unmoved by the urgent entreaties of the Attorney-General, Judge Black, until the movement of Major Anderson and the seizure of the forts in Charleston Harbor forced upon him the necessity of immediate and decided action beyond the possibility of evasion.

His decision in regard to Anderson, and the result of that decision, forced from him at last the acknowledgment that he believed there was a revolution. It placed him wholly upon the side of Northern sentiment and largely determined his future action. The vacant places in his Cabinet were now filled by earnest and patriotic men, with whom he worked in harmony until the last. But it was too late, and he saw his Southern friends whose advice had influenced him, and whose suggestions he had followed, condemn him for having followed their counsel, suspend even their personal relations with him, and leave him one by one. And thus, with the issues postponed from day to day, with no approach to any settlement, with the country torn by dissension, with an entire section revolutionary and defiant, with a Treasury impoverished and despoiled designedly for a preconceived purpose, with a Congress wholly distrustful of him, and with a large proportion of his countrymen attributing to him and his official course the responsibility of the impending ruin, the administration of James Buchanan passed into history; and when history shall come to pen the record of the close of his career, it will judge him not from what he did, but what, from his great opportunities and grave responsibilities, he utterly failed to do.

The new administration had hardly undertaken the direction of the Government, when the subject of Fort Sumter in its various phases was forced upon their attention, and under circumstances that rendered immediate and effective action necessary. At any moment hostilities might commence at Charleston; the Southern Commissioners were in Washington to inaugurate negotiations looking to a positive settlement of the questions arising out of the action of the seceded States, and with especial reference to the Government property within the limits of the Confederacy. It was at this crisis, and on the 5th of March, that the letter of Major Anderson with its enclosures was laid before the President by the Secretary of War, Mr. Holt, in a letter of singular distinctness and power. The Secretary recalled the statements of Major Anderson received from time to time, "that he was where the Government might reinforce him at its leisure; that he was safe; that he could command the harbor as long as the Government wished to keep it." His communication of the 6th of January was also referred to, in which he had reported that he could hold the fort against any force which could be brought against him. These, said the Secretary, as well as the "intelligent statements" of Lieutenant Talbot, who had been sent to Washington, had relieved the Government of any apprehension for his safety, and on the 16th of January Major Anderson had been so informed, and also that it was not the purpose of the Government at that time to reinforce him, but that whenever in his judgment supplies or reinforcement were necessary for his safety or a successful defense, he was to communicate the fact, and a "prompt and vigorous effort" would be made to send them. Major Anderson had not since made any such request. He had reported the progress of the batteries in construction around him, but as late as the 30th of January he had urged with emphasis, that he hoped that no attempt would be made by friends to throw supplies in, and that their doing so would do more harm than good.

His letter of the 5th of February was also quoted and the suggestion made by him of "a small party successfully slipping in," had been considered carefully and rejected as impracticable.

His chief engineer officer seemed to be of the same opinion in regards to reinforcements, and in his letter to his chief, of the 14th of January, he says: "I do not consider it good policy to send reinforcements here at this time. We can hold our own as long as it is necessary to do so."

In view of these very distinct declarations of Major Anderson and the earnest desire to avoid a collision, the line of policy laid down had been adhered to by the Government; and in anticipation of a call from Major Anderson the Ward expedition, under the supervision of Lieutenant-General Scott, had been prepared and was ready to sail, but it was not upon the scale approaching the "seeming exaggerated estimate of Major Anderson." The Government were unprepared for the disclosures of Major Anderson, and were taken by surprise, as he had not before intimated any such necessity.

But however impressed the Government might have been with the statements of Major Anderson as quoted by the Secretary of War, it is not the less certain that since his entry into Fort Sumter he had been impressed with the steadily growing importance and strength of the works around him, and of the necessity of the employment of a large force in case it should be determined to relieve him, and of this he kept the Government constantly apprised. He felt himself at this time comparatively secure, and his every effort, as well as that of the officers under him, was to strengthen his position by every means in his power. His views since his entrance into Fort Sumter had undergone a change in regard to the sending of reinforcements. He did not now apply that such should be sent to him, as he felt that it would put upon him the responsibility of precipitating the conflict and inaugurating civil war. Two days after his entrance into the work he had informed his Government that, "God willing," he would in a few days be so strong that the South Carolinians "would hardly be foolish enough to attack (me) him." He thought that the city of Charleston was entirely in his power; that he could cut off its communications by sea and close its harbor by destroying its light-houses, and he believed in his ability to do it.

On the 5th of February he had reported to his Government the progress and character of the works around him as follows: "Their engineering appears to be well devised and well executed, and their works even in their present condition, will make it impossible for any hostile force other than a large and well-appointed one, to enter this harbor, and the chances are that it will then be at a great sacrifice of life. Again, upon the 14th of February he reported that "vessels will be under fire from Morris Island after they pass the first battery," and, in a subsequent communication, that they would be under such fire "until they got under the walls of this work." These opinions were early entertained by Major Anderson, and made known to his Government, and when at a later period an able and experienced head had arrived in Charleston to direct the operations against him, the increased activity soon manifested, the rapid establishment of formidable works to close the harbor, and the engineering ability everywhere displayed, soon converted the opinions of Major Anderson into a firm conviction which the result in every way justified. Yet he did not ask for reinforcements, and his reasons therefor have been set forth with great clearness in a response made by him to a lady correspondent who had written to him on the 5th of April, 1861, from Rhode Island, in sympathy with his position, as well as in reflection upon the Government for its inaction in tendering to him voluntary aid. After an acknowledgment of the offer, Major Anderson says: "Justice, however, compels me not to stop here, but to take upon myself the blame of the Government's not having sent to my rescue. Had I demanded reinforcements while Mr. Holt was in the War Department I know that he would have despatched them at all hazards. I did not ask them, because I knew that the moment it should be known here that additional troops were coming, they would assault me and thus inaugurate civil war. My policy, feeling—thanks be to God!—secure for the present in my stronghold, was to keep still, to preserve peace, to give time for the quieting of the excitement, which was at one time very high throughout this region, in the hope of avoiding bloodshed. There is now a prospect that that hope will be realized, that the separation which has been inevitable for months, will be consummated without the shedding of one drop of blood. The ladies must not then blame the latter part of Mr. Buchanan's administration, nor the present one, for not having sent me reinforcements. I demanded them under Mr. Floyd. The time when they might have been sent has passed weeks ago; and I must ask you, too, in praising me, not to do injustice to my brother officers, a vast majority of whom would, placed in the same circumstances, have acted at least as well as I have done. God has, I feel, been pleased to use me as an instrument in effecting a purpose which will, I trust, end in making us all a better and a wiser people. . . . A hope may be indulged in that our errant sisters, thus leaving us, as friends, may at some future time be won back by conciliation and justice."*

Anderson now felt strong in his position, and he frequently remarked to the writer that he controlled the situation. His whole effort was to effect, as far as it lay in his power, a peaceful solution of the difficulties. Within Fort Sumter the work yet remaining to be done was pushed on with vigor and enthusiasm. The trouble that had at one time existed among the workmen had ceased. No more of the laborers had for some time been discharged, and all were employed at any necessary work, which they accepted willingly. The enlisted men were in good spirits and worked with alacrity, every one seeming to feel the responsibility of his position. The difficulties in regard to the fresh provisions had been adjusted; the mails were sent regularly, and the garrison maintained in a high state of health. Every effort to strengthen and to prepare the work to resist an attack that all felt must sooner or later be made upon it, was made, and in the daily and detailed reports of his action, from what he could see and infer as to the works erected around him, Major Anderson kept the Government at Washington fully apprised of his condition and prospects.

The same course was followed by the engineer officer, who in his daily reports to his chief, which were often submitted to the Secretary of War and to the General-in-Chief, gave a minute and detailed journal of events. In addition, admirable sketches were made by Captain Seymour from time to time, of the work going on around the fort, as far as could be ascertained by observation through our glasses, as well as what was done inside of the work by the command.

A notice that three rifled cannon had been shipped from England to Charleston had arrested his attention, and on the 7th of February he reports to his Government that such an addition to the batteries opposed to him would make his position much less secure than he had considered it, and that it would be necessary to reinforce him in a few days after the commencement of hostili-

* From the original letter of Major Anderson, in writer's possession.

ties. His anticipations were fully realized. But one gun arrived. It was placed in position on Cummings Point, and, as will be subsequently seen, rendered efficient service.

Meantime, Lieutenant Hall had returned from Washington, bringing to Major Anderson and his command the approval of the authorities and of General Scott, which served to encourage the men and confirm them in their work. His position had subjected him to many annoyances, which he felt, and which compelled him to correspond constantly with the authorities in Charleston. On the morning of the 12th of February, one of the guard-boats that were constantly on duty around the fort, approached so near that she was hailed by the sentinel and warned off, but continuing to approach she was fired over, when she altered her course. It was considered fortunate that the battery did not open.

Upon the immediate representations made to the Secretary of War of the State, "renewed instructions" were issued to the vessels to keep at a proper distance, so as to prevent any collision. Packages for the officers that had come to their address, were retained without any just cause—the private property of Captain Foster had not been sent, and also some private property belonging to one of the men, which had been left at Fort Moultrie. The popular feeling in Charleston was wholly hostile to the retention of the work by the Government, and the principal papers kept alive that feeling by a constant succession of articles calculated to excite and alarm.*

The people were incensed against the Governor for permitting provisions to be sent to the fort, and they threatened to prevent it, but the Governor had declared that, if necessary, he would order a "company of soldiers to put them on board the boat."

The work upon the floating battery was now near completion, and in anticipation of its use, Major Anderson asks for instructions in case of its taking position near his work. To this the Secretary of War replied on the 23d. He was informed that it

---

* WASHINGTON, February 21, 6 P. M.—There is the best of reason for believing that Holt designs reinforcing secretly by boats at night. The reinforcements having already been sent, you may look out for them at any moment The whole anxiety of Scott and the coercionists centers now in Fort Sumter. There the Cabinet has determined that Lincoln shall find everything ready to his hand.—Charleston *Mercury.*

was "not easy to answer satisfactorily this important question" at such a distance from the scene of action.

The policy indicated to him in a previous communication must continue to guide him. He was to act strictly on the defensive, and to avoid, consistently with his safety, all collision with the force around him. These instructions would not now be changed, but if he had sufficient evidence that the battery was advancing to assault him, he would be justified, in self-defense, in not awaiting its arrival, but in repelling it by force. If it was only approaching "to take up a position at a good distance," and his safety was not "clearly endangered," he should act with that forbearance which had distinguished him in permitting the South Carolinians to strengthen Fort Moultrie and erect new batteries for the defense of the harbor. And this would keep the pledge of the War Department to Colonel Hayne. Despatches had been received which had impressed the President with the belief that there would be no immediate attack upon Fort Sumter, and that the labors of the Peace Congress, then in session, added to the powerful motives existing to avoid a collision. This important letter is given in full:

"WAR DEPARTMENT, February 23, 1861.
"MAJOR ROBERT ANDERSON,
"*First Artillery, Com'g Fort Sumter, Charleston Harbor, S. C.:*

"SIR: It is proper I should state distinctly that you hold Fort Sumter as you held Fort Moultrie, under the verbal orders communicated by Major Buell, subsequently modified by instructions addressed to you from this Department, under date of the 21st of December, 1860.

"In your letter to Adjutant-General Cooper, of the 16th instant, you say:

"I should like to be instructed on a question which may present itself in reference to the floating battery, viz.: What course would it be proper for me to take if, without a declaration of war or a notification of hostilities, I should see them approaching my fort with that battery? They may attempt placing it within good distance before a declaration of hostile intention.'

"It is not easy to answer satisfactorily this important question at this distance from the scene of action. In my letter to you of the 10th of January I said:

"You will continue, as heretofore, to act strictly on the defensive, and to avoid, by all means compatible with the safety of your command, a collision with the hostile forces by which you are surrounded.'

"The policy thus indicated must still govern your conduct.

"The President is not disposed at the present moment to change the instructions under which you have been heretofore acting, or to occupy any other than a defensive position. If however, you are convinced by sufficient evidence that the raft of which you speak is advancing for the purpose of making an assault upon the fort, then you would be justified on the principle of self-defense in not awaiting its actual arrival there, but in repelling force by force on its approach. If, on the other hand, you have reason to believe that it is approaching merely to take up a position at a good distance should the pending question be not amicably settled, then, unless your safety is so clearly endangered as to render resistance an act of necessary self-defense and protection, you will act with that forbearance which has distinguished you heretofore in permitting the South Carolinians to strengthen Fort Moultrie and erect new batteries for the defense of the harbor. This will be but a redemption of the implied pledge contained in my letter on behalf of the President to Colonel Hayne, in which, when speaking of Fort Sumter, it is said:

" 'The attitude of that garrison, as has been often declared, is neither menacing nor defiant nor unfriendly. It is acting under orders to stand strictly on the defensive, and the Government and people of South Carolina must know that they can never receive aught but shelter from its guns, unless, in the absence of all provocation, they should assault it and seek its destruction.'

"A despatch received in this city a few days since from Governor Pickens, connected with the declaration on the part of those convened at Montgomery, claiming to act on behalf of South Carolina as well as the other seceded States, that the question of the possession of the forts and other public property therein had been taken from the decision of the individual States, and would probably be preceded in its settlement by negotiation with the Government of the United States, has impressed the President with a belief that there will be no immediate attack on Fort Sumter, and the hope is indulged that wise and patriotic counsels may prevail and prevent it altogether.

"The labors of the Peace Congress have not yet closed, and the presence of that body here adds another to the powerful motives already existing for the adoption of every measure, except in necessary self-defense, for avoiding a collision with the forces that surround you.

"Very respectfully, your obedient servant,
"J. HOLT."

Again, on the 28th inst., the Adjutant-General at Washington informs him, by order of the Secretary of War, that a basis of settlement had been agreed upon by the Peace Convention, and that the Secretary entertained the hope that nothing of a hostile character would occur. The criticisms of their position, and of the action of the Government, in the daily journals of Charleston, discouraged the garrison; who felt that the Government had, in a measure, deserted them. Letters from all quarters flowed in upon Major Anderson and upon his officers, and he devoted a large proportion of his time in responding to them. The speeches of the President-elect as he approached Washington, from their pacific nature produced a depressing effect upon the garrison, who were disappointed in them. Major Anderson became silent and thoughtful, and said that he was "in the hands of God." The position of the garrison, their future, and the capacity of the fort to resist an attack—become now, to them, almost inevitable—was the subject of daily discussion, as the necessities of their condition became more urgent. Towards the close of February the supply of fuel ran short, and the temporary frame structures on the parade were taken down for fire-wood, as had been anticipated by Major Anderson in his communication to the War Department of the 25th of January. On the 23d it was announced by the engineer officer that he had to take down another temporary building to obtain fuel, and that a second one yet standing would furnish fuel as long as the provisions lasted. On the 26th a third building was taken down, leaving two remaining structures with twelve gun-carriages as the only material for fuel; and on the 13th of March, the supply being nearly exhausted, the apparatus from the blacksmith's shop was removed into one of the casemates, and the building used as fuel.

The parade was thus gradually cleared, and the stone flagging which encumbered it placed on end, so that shells falling upon it would be buried in the sand. Two of the enlisted men whose term of service had expired, determined to remain and share the fate of the garrison.

On the 28th of February a strong recommendation was made by all of the engineer officers, that the armament of the gorge, which now consisted of but six 24-pounders, should be at once increased by altering the casemate into barbette carriages, and mounting guns upon them. The recommendation was approved by Major Anderson, and the whole engineer force was put to work, under Lieutenant Snyder, upon carrying it out. Upon the following day one carriage was so altered and adapted to the new condition, and raised to the parapet, and one 42-pounder mounted upon it so that the gun could be used "with more effect than the others on the barbette tier."

The armament of this tier now consisted of twenty-seven guns. The parapet in front of one of the 24-pounders at the left gorge angle had been cut away, so that the gun could be depressed to eighteen degrees and cover the end of the wharf with its fire. Machicouli galleries lined with one-half inch iron plate were placed on each face and flank, and on the gorge commanding the main gate. The necessary ammunition, consisting of grape and canister and shot and shell in abundance for each gun, was placed at intervals upon the gorge. Additional 8-inch shells, to be used as grenades and to explode upon the tension of the lanyard to which they were attached, were also arranged at convenient distances for immediate use. Guns were moved, and remounted in better positions. On the 12th a second 10-inch Columbiad was raised to the parapet and placed in position upon the left flank. Large barrels filled with rocks, with an 8-inch shell in the centre—a suggestion due to Captain Seymour, and carried out by him—were placed along the parapet. Upon being rolled over, the shell was to explode by means of the friction tube attached to a lanyard of proper length.

The forty-one large openings on the second tier, and which upon the occupancy of the work had been temporarily filled, were now permanently closed. A three-foot wall of brick laid in cement, and supported by stone flagging or sand or dry bricks and refuse material, rendered them as secure as the means at the disposal of the engineer would allow.

The same number of guns as *en barbette* composed the armament of the first tier, and of these eighteen were in readiness for "instant service."

For greater security, where nine guns were mounted, but not immediately required for use, stone flagging or brick laid in mortar in addition to the outer shutter, closed the embrasure temporarily. Where there were no guns the embrasures were closed by an 18-inch brick wall in mortar, by dry stone flagging or by brick and stone in mortar. The embrasures in front of the guns for immediate service were closed by an additional inner 6-inch shutter, the two secured and fastened by an iron key. Stones were removed from the enrockment outside the fort below the embrasures, so as to increase the difficulties of an assault.

The gorge wall received the special attention of the engineers. It was the weakest part of the work, and this was increased by the large number of windows and ventilators in its structure. It was soon evident, too, that it was to be subjected to the heaviest fire from the enemy's guns, and every device that could be suggested was employed by the engineers in its protection. Its windows and ventilators were thoroughly protected by two solid iron jambs, which were placed in the recesses of each of the windows of the second tier. The doors on the lower tier were secured by thick wooden shutters against a wall of brick nine inches thick, and on the outside heavy stones were placed, made solid by wedges of

ADJUSTABLE IRON SHUTTER, LOWER TIER.

molten lead. The parade had now been cleared of encumbrance, the temporary buildings gone, and the stone flagging placed upright. To secure the hospital, splinter-proof traverses were constructed, and revetted with stone in front of the hospital and ordnance room. The main entrance to the work, another source of weakness, was now closed by a strong wall of stone and brick built against the outer gate, in which an embrasure was cut and an 8-inch seacoast howitzer mounted over it, and the wall itself loop-holed for musketry, and the gate covered with half-inch iron plates.

Anderson now determined to mine the wharf, and on the 9th of February two mines were laid containing twenty-five pounds of powder, which were completed by the 13th, with the preparations for firing them; at the same time two fougasses were located against the sea wall and upon the esplanade. They were charged with fifty pounds of powder, and were ready for firing by the 26th.   The arrangement of the mines as laid by Captain Foster was unsatisfactory to Major Anderson, who directed them to be taken up and relaid as he required, and preparations made to fire them from the inside.

CHAPTER XXV.

Work at Sumter–Reports of Anderson and Captain Foster–Work at Cummings Point–Firing for range from channel batteries–Foster reports batteries around–Inaugural of President Lincoln–Warlike construction placed upon it General Beauregard assumes command–Urged by Montgomery Government to push the work–Reports of evacuation of Fort Sumter–Confederate Secretary of War informs Beauregard–Apprehension as to mines–Correspondence of Beauregard and Anderson–Terms required-Anderson "deeply hurt" at the conditions imposed–Wigfall establishes recruiting station in Baltimore for the Confederacy–Adjutant-General Samuel Cooper, United States Army, resigns his commission–Takes similar position in the Confederacy–Peace Convention in session in Virginia–Defeats resolution of secession–President Lincoln determines to confer with some prominent Union member–J. B. Baldwin selected–Propositions said to have been made–Denials–Controversy in consequence –Baldwin returns–Convention passes the Ordinance of Secession–President's proclamation-Both sides prepare for the inevitable struggle.

ALMOST daily through the month of March both Anderson and Foster made reports to Washington, and principally with reference to the works going on around the fort, their progress and armament. In Fort Sumter the time was occupied in mounting and rearranging heavy guns at the parapet of the gorge, and in strengthening the gorge wall itself. The exterior openings of the first tier loop-holes on the gorge were filled up, a suggestion made by Captain Doubleday. The main gate was strengthened to resist the shock in firing the 8-inch howitzer in position, traverses were erected in front of the hospital and ordnance storeroom, and the parapet was cut away so as to permit the 10-inch Columbiad to be traversed. On the 27th the report made by Captain Seymour and Lieutenant Snyder, as to the exact condition of the work, was communicated confidentially to the War Department by Major Anderson. At that time the armament of the fort consisted of twenty-seven guns, *en barbette* and twenty-seven on the lower tier, eighteen of which were in readiness for instant service. On the parade were four 8-inch and one 10-inch Columbiads.

Upon the same day Captain Foster enclosed to his chief the following sketch-of the armament of the fort.

Major Anderson had early recognized the new purpose manifested in regard to him, and on the 9th of March, as previously stated, he had communicated to his Government that even then any vessels coming in by the Morris Island channel would be under fire of the batteries from the time they crossed the bar until they reached his work. "More earnestness" was now reported by Foster, as well as the landing of heavy guns on siege carriages. On the 9th a large guard-ship was anchored on the bar, and two cutters, armed with guns seized previously by the South Carolinians, took up a position near Cummings Point, on the "main ship

AN EMBRASURE OUTSIDE.

channel." As the month of March progressed, the batteries in progress at Cummings Point were closed in the rear by a line of intrenchments composed of redoubts connected by parapets and secured in the rear from our fire. Toward the middle of the month there appeared to be a lull in the operations going on around the fort. It was ascribed to the pacific news which had come on the 11th, when 150 guns were fired from the batteries around.

The report was that Fort Sumter was to be evacuated. It was in no way official, and yet the impression produced upon the garrison was so positive in its character that preparations in anticipation of orders to that effect were commenced. Under this impression the garrison labored until the last. The work around the fort seemed to be at "a standstill, and most of the men, both military and laboring, were withdrawn from them." By the 16th, however, the work was resumed and "considerable activity" exhibited in the batteries on Morris Island.

On the 15th, a gun was fired from the floating battery in Charleston, which served to show that it, too, had now received its armament. On the 18th, near midnight, one of the buoys that marked the middle ship channel, about half a mile east of the fort, was removed. Upon the same day the position of twenty-three guns was observed, as indicated by the firing that took place for range or experiment on Morris Island. Again there seemed to be a relaxation in the work, although it did not cease entirely at some points, and the engineer officer reported on the 20th that "all operations looking to an attack on this fort have ceased."

The work went on steadily upon the batteries bearing upon the channels. The new operations were soon recognized by Major Anderson. As the month progressed, more energetic action was exhibited, again to be followed by an apparent suspension of work at some points, and a lack of activity; and he reported on March 16, "The little that is being done is at the channel batteries on Morris Island, and the mortar battery on James Island." It was at this period that the messengers before mentioned arrived to consult with Major Anderson, and which seemed, to the garrison, to confirm the report that they were to be withdrawn to the North. On the 27th a new battery, not far from the Moultrie House, on Sullivan's Island was ordered, making, as Major Anderson thought, four batteries between Fort Moultrie and the eastern end of Sullivan's Island. "They practice daily," said he, "firing shot and shell in the direction of the Swash and Main channels; their practice is pretty good."

Meantime, the floating battery, with its armament on board, had been moved from its moorings to a position that could not be detected by us. There was a feverish anticipation of some immediate change, and an increased sensitiveness in regard to any dealings with the city. A boat that had come to the fort to bear a letter from the Confederate general to Major Anderson had, without the knowledge of the latter, left a small parcel.

This was made the subject of a communication to General Beauregard, with a statement that orders had been given to "prevent the recurrence of such irregularity;" and the letter concluded with an expression which showed that his removal was confidently anticipated by Major Anderson. "Trusting," said he, "that in a few days we shall be placed, in a position which will be more agreeable and acceptable to both of us than the anomalous one we now occupy, I am, &c."*

The last of March had now come. Everything was quiet as the work progressed around the fort, apparently closing up the embrasures of the breaching batteries with sand-bags laid in solidly. From the great extent of the range, as well from the reports, Major Anderson was. convinced that the three batteries on Morris Island outside of the *Star of the West* battery had certainly guns of very heavy calibre. On the last day of the month, the members of the State Convention visited the batteries on Morris Island and Fort Moultrie, when extensive firing took place.

After close observation the engineer officer reported to his chief the following, as the present armament, "very nearly," at Cummings Point. and on Morris Island..

"FORT SUMTER, S. C., March 31, 1861.
"GENERAL JOS. G. TOTTEN,
    "*Chief Engineer United States Army, Washington, D. C.:*
    "*General:* Yesterday the members of the State Convention visited the batteries on Morris Island and Fort Moultrie, and from both places extensive firing took place in honor of the event. This gave me an opportunity of observing what batteries have been increased in strength since my last report on this subject.

"The following is the present armament, very nearly, viz.:
    "Battery No. 1.—Four guns. Embrasures closed by sand-bags. Not fired yesterday.
    "Mortar battery between Nos. 1 and 2.—Three mortars. Fired yesterday. These have practiced much lately, to obtain the range and length of fuse for this fort.
    "Battery No. 2, iron-clad.—Three heavy guns. Two of them fired yesterday.
    "Battery No. 3.—Three guns. Embrasures closed with sand-bags. Did not fire.
    "Mortar battery between Nos. 3 and 4.—Two mortars. Fired yesterday.
    "Battery No. 4.—Three guns. Two fired.
    "Battery No. 5.—Four heavy guns, one Columbiad or 8-inch seacoast howitzer. Two fired yesterday. I think there are six guns in this battery, although only four have been seen to fire.

* Major Anderson, 28th March, 1861.

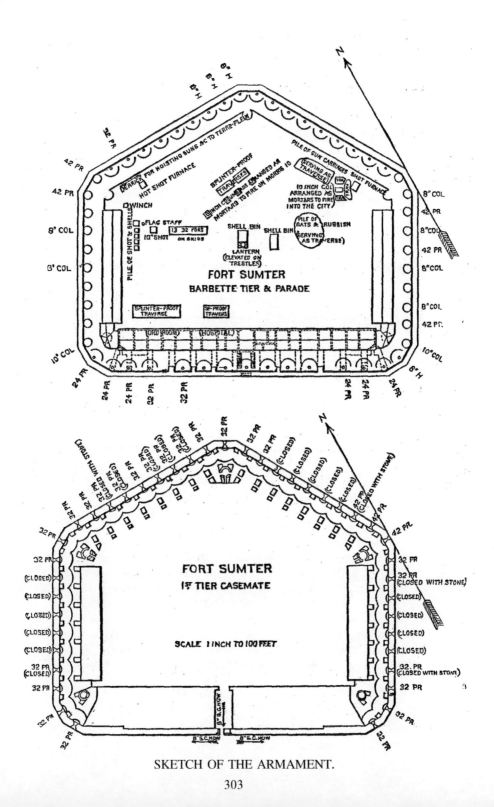

SKETCH OF THE ARMAMENT.

303

"*Star of the West* battery.—Four heavy guns, one of them an 8-inch Columbiad or 8-inch seacoast howitzer. All fired yesterday.

"Battery No. 7.—These guns are not all in the same battery, but are distributed along the beach apparently in three batteries. Eleven guns fired yesterday. All were very heavy guns except two, which I think were field-pieces in a sort of second tier.

"Above these batteries, on the sand-hills, is a line of intrenchments surrounding a house, and also several tents. The field-pieces are apparently capable of being used to defend the flanks of this intrenchment, and to fire on the channel. Their rear is covered, each with a traverse.

"It was evident in this firing that not all the guns in position were fired.

"At Fort Moultrie the firing exhibited the same complete armament as last reported.

"The provisions that I laid in for my force having become exhausted, and the supplies of the command being too limited to spare me any more, I am obliged to discharge nearly all my men to-day. I retain only enough to man a boat.

"I have the honor to be, very respectfully, your obedient servant,

"J. G. FOSTER,
"*Captain Engineers.*"

Meantime, despatches were sent from emissaries in Washington which tended to keep alive the excitement, if not to precipitate the issue daily becoming more imminent. On the 4th of March, the day of the inauguration of Mr. Lincoln to the Presidency, a telegram was sent to the Governor of South Carolina, urging him to prevent any attack without the authority of the Confederate Government;* that the inaugural meant war, and that there was strong ground for belief that reinforcements would be speedily sent. A warlike construction of the inaugural of Mr. Lincoln was placed upon it by the Southern element at Washington,† who agreed that it was the purpose of the new President to collect the revenue, "to hold Fort Sumter and Fort Pickens, and to retake the other places;" that the President was a "man of will and firmness," and that his Cabinet would yield to him, and that thus plans would be at once put into execution. It was feared, too, that Virginia would not pass a Secession Ordinance

---

* Wigfall to Pickens, March 4, 1861, p. 261.

† L. Q. Washington to Walker, Confederate Secretary of War, March 5, 1861, p. 263, "War of the Rebellion."

unless a collision took place, when public opinion would enforce such action. That there was a majority of old Federal submissionists, who had gotten into the Convention, and under the pretense that they were resistance men.

Mr. Roger A. Pryor, of Virginia, in a speech delivered at the Charleston Hotel, Charleston, S. C., on the 10th of April, 1861, stated that ever since he was capable of thinking upon political affairs, his studies had been determined by the authority of the great statesman of South Carolina, and that he could not recall any exhibition at all adequate to the action of South Carolina in the true elements of the moral and sublime. He said: "I thank you especially that you have at last annihilated this accursed Union, reeking with corruption and insolent with excess of tyranny. Not only is it gone, but gone forever. As sure as tomorrow's sun will rise upon us, just so sure will old Virginia be a member of the Southern Confederacy; and I will tell your Governor what will put her in the Southern Confederacy in less than an hour by a Shrewsbury clock. Strike a blow! (Tremendous applause.) The very moment that blood is shed, old Virginia will make common cause with her sisters of the South."

The same anticipation seemed also to prevail among the military in Charleston Harbor. On the 6th of March the commanding officer of Fort Moultrie was ordered to send immediately to the five-gun battery commanding Maffit Channel two 32 pounders, and to have them mounted. He was to "be on the lookout for the *Crusader,* a four-gun brig, reported to be on her way with 120 men for the reinforcement of Fort Sumter." But the means at the disposal of that officer were limited, and would seem to show that at that period the preparations for attack were wholly inadequate. He reports that he had no means at his disposal to send the guns, nor had he a gin to dismount or mount them; he had not a single artificer to send, and that his command consisted of some "290 indifferent artillerymen," "318 helpless infantry recruits," almost without arms, without clothing, and totally and entirely unfit to meet the enemy." He thought, however, that if the gunboats did their duty, he could attend to the "case" of the *Crusader* with the force at his disposal. At this date there were 104 companies "organized and received" under the laws passed,

---

* "War of the Rebellion," Ripley to Ferguson, A. D. C., March 6, 1861.

amounting in the aggregate to 8,835 rank and file, one division of four brigades under the command of Major-General M. L. Bonham, a former Member of Congress from the State.

On the 6th of March, by virtue of his orders, General Beauregard assumed command of all the troops, regulars, volunteers and militia, on duty in and near Charleston Harbor; announced the officers of his staff," and at once inaugurated a series of movements and changes, which were soon observable, and which greatly influenced the result. He directed "that the embrasure enfilading battery and the battery beyond Moultrie be constructed first." Guns were moved to more effective positions; the work on Cummings Point was stopped, except at the iron-clad battery and "at the condemned mortar battery," and work on the channel batteries was at once begun. The officer of Ordnance had called his attention to the condition of things in his department, and to the fact that, from the want of proper props and appropriate tackle, the guns then mounted, from a want of "inclination," would probably dismount themselves. His deficiencies in essential articles were reported, and also the fact that the cutting of the limited number of fuses at Fort Moultrie so as to multiply them, would, he feared, render the fuses of "very little use at all." Such was the incomplete condition of things, that on the 8th of March the commanding general reported to his Government that through his "cautious representation" all seemed to be aware that they were not yet ready for the contest that it was first necessary to keep reinforcements from Fort Sumter by increasing the channel defenses, and this he hoped to be able to accomplish in a week or ten days. The Government at Montgomery was no less apprehensive and anxious upon the subject of reinforcements, and on the 8th of March the Secretary of War urged upon General Beauregard the necessity of pushing forward his "contemplated works with all possible expedition;" that the reinforcement of Fort Sumter "must be prevented at all hazards" and by every "conceivable agency;" that Fort Sumter would open fire upon him if reinforcements should reach it, and that it was now silent only "because of the

* Captain D. F. Jones, Ass't. Adj.-Gen.; Captain S. D. Lee, Artillery, A. D. C., A. A. Q. M. Gen. and Com'y; Captain S. Wragg Ferguson, A. D. C.; First Lieutenant J. I. Legare, Engineer, private secretary.

† "War of the Rebellion," p. 272, Beauregard to Walker.

weakness of the garrison." He informs him, too, that there were a number of United States ships ready to start from New York, and that it was probable that an attempt to succor Sumter by whale-boats would be made at night. Friends at Washington also kept the Confederate general in command fully informed of any possible movement, and even the prevalent rumors were sent to him. On the 11th Senator Wigfall, of Texas, informs him by telegraph that it was believed that "Anderson will be ordered to evacuate Sumter in five days," and that this "was certainly informally agreed upon in Cabinet Saturday night."

At the earliest moment a reconnaissance was made to the mouth of the Stono River, by which reinforcement might enter, and field-works to "effectually guard those channels of approach" were determined upon. The General was embarrassed with the condition of things. His engineer as well as his ordnance officer had been taken away from him by the Governor of Georgia, and he was left to his own resources. "Their absence," he said, "filled him with care and grief;" and he alleged, "that while he found a great deal of zeal and energy around him, there was but little professional knowledge or experience, and that a great deal in the way of organization remained to be accomplished. Should a force land at Stono, or in that direction, he had made arrangements to meet it.

Telegrams, before referred to, had now come to the Governor of the State, in reference to the evacuation of the fort, when on the 14th of March the Confederate Secretary of War informed General Beauregard "that the steamers *Star of the West, Harriet Lane, Crusader, Mohawk,* and *Empire City* were ordered to sail from New York last night, said to carry arms, provisions and men; destination not known." From his report on the 15th, the general in command at Charleston believed that "in a very few days," he would be ready at all points." Meantime, despatches from Washington to the Confederate War Department had informed the Secretary of the mines laid at Fort Sumter, of "a purpose to destroy it and the garrison rather than be taken;" and the Secretary suggests to General Beauregard on the 15th of March, that Foster, the engineer, might be good guarantee if left in the fort, and he was directed to 'give but little credit" to the rumors of an amicable adjustment, and not to slacken his energies for a moment.

On the 21st the impression that the garrison would be shortly removed had become so strong that the Confederate Secretary again addresses a communication to General Beauregard, that the fort would shortly be abandoned, if there was any reliance to be placed upon rumors "semi-official in their character." Before this could be permitted, General Beauregard must assure himself "perfectly," that there were "no mines laid with trains within the fort;" that he was to inform Major Anderson of his intention to take immediate possession, and that he desired to do this upon an inventory to be taken by himself and one of Major Anderson's officers, properly Foster. If Anderson declined this, he was to tell him of the rumors in regard to the mines, and to demand assurance of its falsity, and if denied, he must prevent his departure. Meantime a remark of Major Anderson that if, when attacked, he found that he could not hold possession of the fort he would blow it up in preference to permitting his command to fall into the hands of the enemy, had been misunderstood and misstated in Charleston. Upon the 26th of March two of the A. A. C.'s of General Beauregard, Colonel Chisholm and Lieutenant Ferguson, came down to the fort under a white flag, bearing a communication from the General commanding at Charleston to Major Anderson. It began, "My dear Major," and was intended as a personal communication "to obtain his views first."* He stated that he had been informed that Mr. Lamon, the authorized agent of the President of the United States, had, after seeing Major Anderson, informed Governor Pickens that the command was to be transferred in a few days to another post, and that he understood that Major Anderson anticipated that a formal surrender or capitulation would be required of him. This, he informs Major Anderson, as their countries were not at war, would not be required of him, unless as the natural result of hostilities.

Whenever he was prepared to leave the fort, proper means of transportation, including baggage, private and company property, would be provided. All that would be required of him, would be his word of honor as an officer and a gentleman, that the fort, with its armament "and all public property," should remain

---

* Beauregard to Anderson, March 26, 1861. "War of the Rebellion," p. 222; Vol. I, Ser. I.

without any arrangements for their destruction; that company and side arms might be taken and the flag saluted.

Major Anderson, in responding to this communication, informed General Beauregard that he felt "deeply hurt" at the conditions which would be exacted of him, and that if he could leave the fort only upon such a pledge he would never, so help him God! "leave this fort alive." He at the same time hoped that General Beauregard did not mean what his words expressed, and in that case united with him in the wish that they might have the pleasure of meeting under more favorable circumstances. A letter was received by Major Anderson on the same date from, General Beauregard, disclaiming any intentions of wounding his feelings; that the pledge he referred to was only alluded to on account of the high source from which the rumors appeared to come, and that it might be considered a sufficient reason by "many officers of high standing" for the execution of orders which otherwise they would not approve of, and he regretted having referred to the subject. The Northern press were urgent upon the subject.

"SHALL FORT SUMTER BE DESTROYED? If, therefore, Major Anderson must abandon it, let him employ the few remaining days his provisions will hold out, in undermining inside the entire foundations, then let him make his preparations to leave, apply the fuse, and at a safe distance watch its being levelled to the ground. This would. be a gloomy but nevertheless a more worthy ending of the sad history than to leave it a stronghold in the possession of a foreign foe. If Sumter must be abandoned to the enemy, let it be a shapeless mass of ruins."—*N. Y. Commercial Advertiser.*

It was at this period that a recruiting station was established in Baltimore by the authority of the Confederate War Department by Senator L. V. Wigfall, who, had made the necessary financial arrangements with the house of Walters & Co., 68 Exchange Place; and he informed General Beauregard that by the time an officer could come for them, there would "probably be a hundred recruits to examine," and that he desired to send them to General Beauregard.

On the 18th, the Confederate War Department directed General Beauregard to order an officer to Baltimore to superintend the shipment of the men, and that he "must conceal his mission except from those in the secret." The officer indicated delayed his departure, when Senator Wigfall again telegraphed, March 21, that the number of men was increasing and that they could not be kept together much longer.   The Confederate Secretary of War promptly responded by sending an officer directly from Montgomery, who was to remain in Baltimore for some weeks under the orders of Senator Wigfall. On the 23d of March sixty-four recruits arrived in Charleston and were sent to Castle Pinckney.

On the 20th, the limits of the command of General Beauregard were increased to include the coast line of the State, but his first duty was to give his personal attention to the defense of Charleston Harbor.   Colonel Samuel Cooper, the Adjutant-General of the United States Army, a native of New York, who up to March 7 had acted in that capacity, resigned his commission and accepted the position of Adjutant-General of the Confederate States and was now in the discharge of the duties of that office at Montgomery. The works now steadily approached completion, and on the 20th of March the State Engineer reported the completion of the mortar battery on the beach at Fort Johnson, and the progress on the other works, while on the 22d, in reporting the visit of Captain Fox, and that he had reported that the supplies of Major Anderson were nearly exhausted, he announces that all of his batteries would be finished and armed in two or three days.

Meanwhile, the President at Washington looked with an anxiety that he did not conceal to the action of the Virginia Convention, still in session.

He believed that if the border States were retained in the Union, he might be able to control the action of the Gulf States. On the 17th of March a resolution was offered in the Virginia Convention, submitting an ordinance resuming the delegated powers of the State to a vote of the people in the following May. The proposition was rejected by a vote of "ninety to forty-five against the resolution," which drew the line distinctly between the Union men and the Secessionists in the Convention.   But the Convention, instead of adjourning, continued its sessions, and this the President considered as a "menace" to him. The President determined to confer with some prominent member of the Convention, and in accordance with his desire, the Secretary of State addressed a communication to Judge Sommers, who was an acquaintance of the President and who had served with him in Congress, with the request that he should come to Washington, or, in event of his inability to come, that some representative Union man should be sent to confer with him.

Soon after a messenger," sent from Washington upon the same errand, arrived in Richmond. Colonel J. B. Baldwin was selected as the proper representative, and in company with the messenger returned to Washington at once, arriving upon the morning of the 4th of April. The interview with the President was held upon the same day.

What actually transpired has been made the subject of personal controversy between a distinguished citizen of Virginia, to whom the character and result of the interview was related by the President immediately afterward, and the member of the Virginia Convention with whom the interview was held; the former asserting that the President had stated to him that he made a proposition to the messenger to the effect that, if the Virginia Convention would adjourn "sine die" without passing the Ordinance of Secession, he would withdraw the troops from Fort Sumter; while the latter asserting under oath that the early greeting of the President was, that he had come too late, and that no pledge, no undertaking, no offer, no promise of any sort was made by the President to him at that interview; and that in regard to the proposition to withdraw the troops from Sumter and Pickens, if the Virginia Convention would adjourn, that he made no suggestion and said nothing from which it could be inferred. The President repeated, in the presence of Geo. P. Smith and the members of the Committee, that he most *positively* assured Mr. Baldwin that if the Virginia Convention would adjourn without passing an Ordinance of Secession, he would abandon Fort Sumter, and in the quaint and forcible language attributed to and so characteristic of him, that he "would give a fort for a State" any time. The rejection of such a proposition at the time was considered as the assumption of a very serious responsibility upon the part of the members, and as in the interest of the minority in the Convention, who desired to separate the State from the Union.

As no witnesses were present at the time of the interview between the President and the member of the Virginia Convention the question became one of personal veracity. Circumstances of a corroborative nature were not wanting to confirm the statements

* Allan B. Magruder.

of Mr. Botts, in the testimony of persons "to whom the President had made a similar statement, as well as in that of others who heard the member say that such a proposition was made to him in the interview by the President." No report of such a proposition was made to the Convention, although the member upon his return reported to his friends that he had urged upon the President to withdraw the forces from Sumter and Pickens in the interest of peace. The Union men of the Convention were not happy in their selection of a representative. Upon his return to Richmond after the interview with Mr. Lincoln, although he cast his vote against the secession of the State, April 17, he subsequently signed the Ordinance and almost at once took office under the Confederacy, and was elected to the Confederate Congress, where he became the Chairman of the Military Committee. Upon the fall of Sumter and the appearance of the President's proclamation, in reply to an inquiry from a Northern politician as to "what will the Union men of Virginia do now," he replied, at once, "There are now no Union men in Virginia;" those who were such would now fight "in defense of their liberties."

But in order to ascertain definitely the policy of the President, a committee of prominent members was sent by the convention, after the return of the messengers, to Washington.

They reached Washington on the morning of the day that. Fort Sumter was fired upon. The President received them, and on the 14th read to them a written answer to the Resolution of the Convention. His declarations were "distinctly pacific, and he expressly disclaimed all purpose of war." The Secretary of State and the Attorney-General also gave similar assurances. They returned upon the following day, carrying with them upon the "same train" the proclamation of the President calling for 75,000 men.

On the 25th a special distribution of the ordnance was ordered by the commanding general to the batteries around the fort, and the shells specified and distributed to their appropriate service.

The delay in the actual removal of the garrison, and the absence of any official action in regard to it, soon began to excite suspicion, and on the 26th the Governor advised General Beauregard that Anderson should now say whether Colonel Lamon was authorized to arrange matters, and if he would not so state, then he, the Governor, would "begin to doubt everything." The visits of the messengers from Washington to Fort Sumter were not satisfactory to the Government at Montgomery, who, on the 29th of March, directed the general commanding to allow no further communications of that character, unless the written instructions borne by such messengers should be inspected and assurances given that there were no verbal instructions existing incompatible with them.

The month of March thus closed. But little dependence was placed upon the rumors of withdrawal of the garrison, and both sides prepared for a struggle which seemed to be unavoidable.

CHAPTER XXVI.

Confederate Congress authorizes appointment of three Commissioners to Washington–Messrs. Crawford, Roman and Forsyth selected–Their instructions–Commissioner Crawford arrives in Washington–"Fully satisfied" that to approach Mr. Buchanan would be disadvantageous–Commissioner reports to the Confederate Secretary of State–Senator W. H. Seward to be the new Secretary of State–His peaceful policy–Inauguration of Mr. Lincoln-Commissioner reports to his Government–Commissioner Forsyth arrives–Report of the two Commissioners–Senator R. M. T. Hunter–Propositions for delay made to Commissioner–Authorities at Montgomery consider a delay a doubtful policy–Evacuation of Sumter to be insisted upon–Secretary of State declines to receive the Commissioners–Associate Justice Campbell offers to mediate–Associate Justice Nelson also interests himseif–Question of the evacuation of Sumter-Associate Justice Campbell's memoranda–Further instructions from Montgomery–War like armaments–Volunteers called out at Charleston–Memorandum of Secretary of State–Its effect–The Commissioners leave Washington– Justice Campbell to Secretary of State–Writes to the President–Sumter fired upon.

ONE of the earliest acts of the provisional Congress was the passage of a resolution on the 15th of February, 1861, authorizing the appointment by the President-elect of three Commissioners for the purpose of negotiating friendly relations between the Government of the United States and the "Confederate States of America," for the settlement of "all questions of disagreement between the two Governments." Messrs. Martin J. Crawford, A. B. Roman and John Forsyth were the persons selected. Instructions for their guidance were forwarded to them on the 27th of February, from the "Department of State" at Montgomery. The leading object of their mission was to open negotiations as speedily as possible with the Government of the United States, with a view to the recognition of the independence of the Confederacy, and to conclude treaties of amity and good-will "between the two nations." They were, if possible, to obtain a personal interview with the President, and intimate to him the object of their mission. If the President should decline to receive them officially, they were to accept an unofficial interview,

314

if agreeable to him, and were to inform him verbally of the duties with which they had been charged by the President of the Confederate States.

They were to assure every one with whom they might be brought into official relation, that it was the earnest wish of the President of the Confederate States "to establish peaceful and friendly relations with the United States," and to settle all questions which had arisen by virtue of their new relations amicably. That they were determined to maintain their rights and independence at all hazards, and that nothing would induce them to assume a hostile attitude towards the United States but a refusal to acknowledge the independence of the Confederate States, accompanied by an aggressive assertion and exercise of the powers of supreme Government, which belonged to the Federal authority, under the old compact, but which had now "ceased to exist."

The policy of the Government of the United States in recognizing *de facto* governments was urged, and the right of a people to change at will their political institutions; and under it there could be no hesitation in "recognizing the independence of the Confederate States." And the action of President Buchanan was instanced, who, when Secretary of State at the time of the overthrow of the monarchy in France under Louis Phillippe in 1848-49, congratulated the minister on the promptness with which he had recognized the new Government, and remarked in his despatch that, "It is sufficient for us to know that a Government exists capable of maintaining itself, and then its recognition by the United States inevitably follows." The Commissioners were to urge that the "Confederate States form an independent nation, both de *facto* and *de jure*. They possess a Government perfect in all its branches, and richly endowed with the means of maintaining itself in every possible contingency."

If, however, the President should propose to refer the matter to the Senate or to Congress, when it should meet, no opposition was to be made, provided that they received from the President sufficient assurance that the existing status should be maintained and that the Government of the United States should make no attempt, under any pretext "to exercise any jurisdiction, whether civil or military, within the limits of the Confederacy."

To secure this was of the last importance, and the Commission-

ers were instructed to make use of every means in their power to discover, in case a delay was proposed by the United States, whether
the object was not to cover sinister designs and complete a plan
of military or naval attack.   Information as to the action and
designs of the authorities in Washington, when obtained, was to
be communicated by the most confidential agencies.   Social relations with the representatives of foreign Governments were to be
established, and such information obtained as might be useful to
the Confederate Government.

Armed with these instructions, the Commissioners proceeded to
Washington, one of them, Mr. M. J. Crawford, arriving upon the
3d of March. He lost no time in coming to his conclusions, and
upon the same day reported to the Secretary of State of the Confederacy that he had availed himself of all the means of information at his command, to learn the disposition of the United States
Government towards the Government of the Confederate States.
He had become "fully satisfied that it would not be wise to
approach Mr. Buchanan with any hope of his doing anything
which would result advantageously to our Government."*

That Mr. Buchanan had but a short time before expressed
himself as prepared to receive Commissioners "purporting" to
come from the Confederate States Government, and to submit their
"matters" to Congress, but that he had since changed his mind,
or really lost the remembrance of what he had said, and denied
having made such statement, or having ever entertained such purpose;   that he had again recalled the matter, and renewed his
intention to submit it to Congress, but that he "must first consult
his Cabinet." "His fears for his personal safety, the apprehensions for the security to his property, together with the cares of
State and his advanced age, render him wholly disqualified for
his present position." "He is as incapable now of purpose," wrote
the Commissioner, "as a child," and while he (the Commissioner)
might secure the promise of the President to receive him as a
Commissioner, his constitutional advisers "would control him the
moment he fell into their hands." He would not attempt to open
negotiation with the outgoing administration. The future must
develop the power of the peace or war element which would

---

* Correspondence of Commissioner Crawford with Confederate Secretary
of State, March, 1861.

control the incoming President, and that Governor Chase and Mr. Montgomery Blair would compose the element which would be for coercion.

The Commissioner reported also the presence of Mr. John Bell, of Tennessee, and his constant communication with the President-elect, that he had been urgent in his entreaties with Mr. Lincoln not to disturb the Confederate States. He had assured him that any attempt to collect the revenue, or to interfere with its Government, would be the signal for the secession of every border State. "He advises an indefinite truce," the withdrawal of the Government troops, except a nominal guard, from the forts, and, in order to satisfy the war party of the North, that the flag should be left flying, and that in the meantime the Confederate States were to be left alone to do as they might choose, "prepare for war, strengthen defenses, in short do whatever may seem good to them;" that the pursuance of this course was to result in favor of the United States, on account of the dissatisfaction which would arise from increased taxation upon the people of the Confederacy, which would lead to a permanent reconstruction; that these suggestions were favorably received and considered by a portion of the new administration, but that they would not, be acted upon, in the opinion of the Commissioners, if the border States remained in the Union without them; and that such coercive measures as might be safely adopted without imperilling the loss of Virginia would certainly be used.

The Commissioner concluded by stating, that "when the mob which was the controlling power at present upon the course and policy of the new President should have dispersed" and Congress adjourned, he hoped for more favorable results from his mission.

Meantime, it had become recognized as a fact, that the Hon. Wm. H. Seward, Senator from New York, was to be called to the new Cabinet as Secretary of State. On the 28th of December he had informed the President-elect, that "after due reflection and with much self distrust," he felt it to be his duty to accept the appointment of Secretary of State, if nominated, and confirmed by the Senate. He was then in his seat as Senator from the State of New York, the latest of the many honors lavished upon him by his State. His views and desires for a peaceful settlement of the troubles were well known; and his declared intention to make any consistent sacrifice for its attainment soon drew to him many from both sections who entertained similar views, either from policy or design. His matured political experience and a vision at times almost prophetic* enabled him to exert an influence that was recognized and felt as well in the South as in the North, and which induced the adoption, in the new Government, of, a peaceful intent, not as a subterfuge, but as a distinct policy of administration, until forced by the commencement of active hostilities by the South to abandon it.

His views upon every variety of political and national interest were so sought, and his opinions so desired, and his personal intimacy and influence with the President-elect so recognized, that he seemed, like Hamilton in the Cabinet of Washington, to be considered as the Premier of the new administration, and the first minister of the Cabinet of Mr. Lincoln; and however foreign to our governmental usage such an estimate might be, some of the duties he was called upon to perform would seem naturally to justify such opinion. His public career had placed him among the leaders of the great party that had now triumphed at the polls, and he was the foremost apostle of Republican doctrine. Men's minds had confidently looked to him as their chosen standard-bearer, and his failure to receive it was the occasion of wide-spread disappointment.

The President-elect had early invited him to the chief place among his counsellors, with the approbation of the country. His most formidable rival, he became his most devoted friend, and upon him, through the dark days of war, his strong arm rested mainly for support. As early as December 1, amid the vast work crowding upon him, Mr. Seward had continued a corre-

---

* In March, 1850, in a remarkable speech in the Senate of the United States, upon the admission of California, he said: "Then the projectors of the new Republic of the South will meet the question–and they may well prepare now to answer it– What is all this for? What intolerable wrong, what unfraternal injustice, has rendered these calamities unavoidable? What gain will this unnatural revolution bring to us? The answer will be: All this is done to secure the institution of African slavery! When that answer shall be given, it will appear that the question of dissolving the Union is a complex question; that it embraces the fearful issue whether the Union shall stand, and slavery, under the steady, peaceful action of moral, social and political causes, be removed by gradual, voluntary effort, and with compensation; or whether the Union shall be dissolved, and *civil war ensue, bringing on violent but complete emancipation.* We are now arrived at that stage of our national progress when that crisis can he foreseen–when we must foresee it."

spondence with his family, and from this valued source we have been permitted to draw. With the President-elect, also, he was in constant correspondence as the momentous events of that period came thronging upon the country. "The ultra Southern men mean to break up the Union," he wrote, "not really for the grievances of which they complain, but from cherished disloyalty and ambition. The President and all Union men are alarmed and despondent; the Republicans who come here are ignorant of the real designs or danger."

His laconic criticism upon President Buchanan's message of December 3 was: "It shows conclusively that it is the duty of the President to execute the laws unless somebody opposes him, and that no State has a right to go out of the Union unless she wants to!"

On the 10th, he wrote that the debates in the Senate were "hasty, feeble, inconclusive and unsatisfactory." Upon the 1st of April, in "Some Thoughts for the President's Consideration," he urged that his views were singular, but his system was built on this idea, as a ruling one, namely: "That we must change the question before the public from one upon slavery, or about slavery, for a question upon *Union or Disunion,* from one of party to one of patriotism or Union. The occupation or evacuation of Fort Sumter, although not in fact a slavery or a party question, is so *regarded.* Witness the temper manifested by the Republicans in the free States, and even by Union men in the South. I would therefore terminate it, as a safe means for changing the issue. I deem it fortunate that the last administration created the necessity. For the rest, I would simultaneously defend and reinforce all the forts in the Gulf, and have the navy recalled from foreign stations for a blockade."*

Prominent Southern men had sought him to urge the continuance of this peaceful policy, and one of them, Senator Gwynn, of California, had placed himself in communication with the authorities at Montgomery, acting as an intermediary between them and Mr. Seward, in the interest of a peaceful settlement of the difficulties until the inauguration of Mr. Lincoln. On the day preceding the inauguration, a list of the members of the Cabinet was published in the press of Washington. The name of the Hon. Salmon P. Chase as Secretary of the Treasury, had been

---

* Mr. Seward to the President, April 1, 1861.

mentioned, and had encountered determined opposition from that element now open and earnest in the effort to bring about a peaceful settlement. Mr. Chase was believed to be in favor of "a vigorous policy," and it was feared that his entrance into the Cabinet would greatly retard, if not wholly prevent, a peaceful solution, if it did not directly promote a war policy. When it was known that he had been chosen to fill the office, Senator Gwynn prepared a telegram to be sent to Montgomery, stating the fact of Mr. Chase's appointment, that the war policy was in the ascendant, and advising that the South should look out for themselves. This telegram was sent, in accordance with the understanding that prevailed, to Mr. Seward by the hands of Mr. Samuel Ward, of New York, who had been active in his patriotic efforts during the winter. After reading the telegram, Mr. Seward took his pen, and erasing all over the signature, wrote to the effect that the outlook was peaceable and that matters had never before looked so encouraging; and this altered telegram was so despatched with the original signature by Mr. Ward to Mr. Davis at Montgomery."

The new President was inaugurated in Washington on the 4th of March. He had called to his counsels men, many of whom had become conspicuous in the anti-slavery movement that had so long agitated the country. From the composition of the Cabinet, the policy it was likely to pursue was the subject of earnest speculation and anxiety. But the Commissioner had early come to a conclusion, and on the 6th reported to his Government "that the selections made of the advisers of the President would prove beneficial to the Confederate States," as it was "the *determined purpose* of the Secretaries of State and War to accept and maintain a peace policy;" that the President was not aware of the condition of the country, and that the Secretaries named were to open the difficulties and dangers to him on that day (the 6th of March).

The Commissioner, therefore, felt it to be his duty, under the instructions of his Department, as well as in accordance with his own judgment "to adopt and support Mr. Seward's policy," provided that the present status was to be rigidly maintained; that his own reasons and those of Mr. Seward were as wide apart as the poles; Mr. Seward believing that peace

* Senator Gwynn to author.

would bring about a reconstruction of the Union, while the Commissioner felt confident that it would build up and cement the Confederacy and put it "beyond the reach of either his arms or his diplomacy."

The construction which Mr. Seward "attempts" to put upon the inaugural address of the President was, that it only followed the language of every President from Washington down, as to the execution of the laws, and that it was necessary to prevent utter ruin to the party and the administration itself. That the statement, by the President, that he would "hold, occupy and possess the property and places belonging to the Government" was to be considered in connection with the qualification wherein the President deemed it to be his simple duty, and that he would perform it *unless* the American people should withhold the requisite means, or authoritatively direct the contrary. In submitting these views, the Commissioner informed his Government, "that whilst it was wise and proper to hear and note every word coming from a source so high in this Government," the main fact should never be lost sight of; that the policy of the United States Government was first to demoralize the Government of the Confederate States in the border States, then in the Confederate States themselves; and that when it was assured of support by a party in those States, "the opportune moment for coercion" would have come, should the Confederate States not submit to the national jurisdiction. It was not believed that Congress would furnish the means required by General Scott's estimate of 250,000 men to hold, occupy and possess the property of the United States, and upon this the "first minister" had based his hopes of peace for some time to come. An arrangement had been made with the Secretary of State by which the Commissioner was to be informed the afternoon of the day upon which he wrote "when and in what manner" the subject of his mission should be submitted to the consideration of the President and his Cabinet. The information contained in a recent letter of Major Anderson, reporting the insufficiency of his supplies and his inability, from a want of fuel, to hold out beyond the 1st of April, had become known to the Commissioner, who, in reporting it to his Government, said that the question of allowing or refusing this assistance to Major Anderson must soon be a question with the Government of the Confederate States, but that in the meantime the Commissioner should feel it to be his duty to use the situation of Major Anderson as a means of recognition, and for a pledge not to reinforce the forts, or to take any hostile steps against the Confederate Government, and that if the United States should consent, he should have no hesitation in stating that the Confederate Government would withhold nothing necessary for their personal comfort from Major Anderson and his command while negotiations were pending.

Meantime, Mr. John Forsyth, one of the Commissioners appointed by the Confederate Government, had arrived in Washington, and on the 8th of March communicated with his Government. He stated the belief that there was a party in the Cabinet favorable to pacific measures, and that the Secretary of State, Mr. Seward, was the head of that party, and that in order to cultivate unofficial relations with them, the Commissioners had availed themselves of the services of a late distinguished Senator of the United States (R. M. T. Hunter) to establish an understanding with the Secretary of State, who was urgent for delay. The tenor of the language used by the Secretary to the Senator was thus reported by the Commissioner: "I have built up the Republican party, I have brought it to triumph, but its advent to power is accompanied by great difficulties and perils. I must save the party, and save the Government in its hands. To do this, war must be averted, the negro question must be dropped, the irrepressible conflict ignored, and a Union party to embrace the border slave States inaugurated. I have already whipped Mason and Hunter in their own State. I must crush out Davis, Toombs, and their colleagues in sedition in their respective States. Saving the border States to the Union by moderation and justice, the people of the cotton States, unwillingly led into secession, will rebel against their leaders, and reconstruction will follow."*

In this path the Committee deemed that they could travel with the Secretary of State up to a certain point, that of fixing the peace policy of the Government. At that point a divergence would take place; and it was deemed unimportant, whatever might be the subsequent hopes or plans of the Secretary. It was well, the Commissioners thought, that he should indulge in dreams which they knew could not be realized. The Secretary had urged delay,

* Commissioners Forsyth and Crawford to Confederate Secretary of State, March 8, 1861.

and this became at once a question for discussion. While the real desire of both the Confederate authorities, as well as the Commissioners, was for delay, it was deemed the more prudent policy that this should not appear, and while yielding with apparent reluctance in their preference for peace and in the interests of humanity, they stipulated for what was of the last importance to them, and that was, that "the military status should be maintained, and no advantage taken of the delay."

The Secretary of State had urged, in his conversation with Senator Hunter, that the administration was in the most unfavorable position for action on questions so important, and if pressed for a reply to the demand of the Commissioners now, he could not answer for the result. To this, Senator Hunter, while acknowledging its force, maintained that unless the assurances required were given, the issue would be at once precipitated upon the administration, and it would be forced to define its policy. A memorandum was accordingly prepared by the Commissioners, defining the terms upon which they "would consent to and stipulate for a brief respite." In this, they agreed to postpone the consideration of the subject of their mission for a period not exceeding twenty days, provided that a positive and unequivocal pledge, binding in honor, and fully justifying the Commissioners in accepting it, that the present military status should be preserved in every respect, that there should be no reinforcements of the forts now in the possession of the United States, nor any attack upon those in possession of the Confederacy. At the same time, the Commissioners believed that the Government had not made up its mind what course to pursue, that they were "greatly concerned" at their presence, and dreaded to hear from them; that the unpleasant communication they had in store for the administration had been freely canvassed on the streets and in the press, and that their arrest and imprisonment on the charge of treason had been spoken of. They wrote that the consent to a delay upon their part was induced chiefly by the consideration that the signing of such an agreement as the memorandum contained would be a virtual recognition of them, as the representatives of a power entitled to be treated with by the General Government; and again, the instructions under which they were acting contemplated delay and authorized it, so far as the objects of their mission were to be obtained by it. While the authorities at Montgomery approved the course pursued by the Commissioners, it was thought that to accord the delay of twenty days was of extremely doubtful policy, and not unlikely to lead to embarrassing complications.   It was however acquiesced in, with the understanding that the proviso in regard to the military status should be established beyond doubt, and "of the most positive, explicit and binding character;" and to such a point was this carried, that the Commissioners were informed by their Government that they should receive assurances that a fleet of steamers, said to be then coaling and preparing for sea at the Brooklyn Navy Yard, should not only not make any hostile movement during the period of the proposed delay, but that they were not to be sent to any point adjacent to the southern borders, whence they might be employed after the expiration of the term of the delay.

The evacuation of Fort Sumter was to be insisted upon as a *sine qua non,* and no proposition to refer the subject matter of their mission to the United States Senate or to Congress was to be agreed to by them, unless some definite arrangement for the evacuation of the strong places then held by the United States within the limits of the Confederacy should be made.   During the period of delay there was no objection to the garrison of Fort Sumter receiving supplies, at short intervals and in limited quantities, this to be regulated by the proper Confederate authorities at Charleston.

The memorandum as prepared by the Commissioners was presented to the Secretary of State by Senator R. M. T. Hunter, of Virginia, who had consented to see the Secretary for them and learn if he would consent to an informal interview.

When Senator Hunter presented himself to the Secretary of State, he found him at first "perceptibly embarrassed and uneasy." He informed Senator Hunter that before he could consent to an interview, he must see the President.   He asked, too, that the request be put in writing, in order that he might submit it to the President. This was declined by Senator Hunter, who thought it inexpedient, but assented that the Secretary should state to the President the fact of his visit, and also its object and character. Upon the following day (March 12) the Senator returned to the Commissioners with a note addressed to himself, in which the Secretary of State said, "It will not be in my power to receive the gentlemen of whom we conversed yesterday."

The receipt of this paper was considered by the Commissioners as decisive of their course, and they at once prepared a formal note informing the State Department of their presence in Washington, and of the object of their mission, and asking an official interview at an early day. The Secretary of State had already determined not to recognize the Commissioners in any official capacity, nor to hold personal communication with them.

On the 13th, the note was formally delivered to the Assistant Secretary at the State Department, by Colonel J. A. Pickett, of Washington, who had consented to act as the Secretary of the Commission.   The action of the Commissioners was wholly approved and commended by their Government at Montgomery, who thought that they had acted, with "commendable promptness and becoming dignity," and had shown that they were not suppliants for the grace and favor of the United States Government, but that they were "the envoys of a powerful Confederation of sovereignties," "instructed to demand their rights" and to establish relations of "amity and good neighborhood."* The Commissioners now awaited a response to their note, which would determine their course. The Secretary of State had determined not to reply in letter form to the formal note of the Commissioners, as such might reasonably be regarded as a recognition of their official character.   In place of it he decided to prepare a "memorandum" for the files of his Department, in order to avoid the appearance of such recognition, which memorandum should define the position of the Government, and of which a copy was to be furnished, if called for.

But meantime other and powerful influences were at work. It was now the 15th of March, and the Supreme Court of the United States had ended its session.   The members were about to separate, when Associate Justice John A. Campbell announced his determination to remain in Washington, and to use his personal influence to bring about a peaceful solution of the difficulties now threatening the peace of the country.   Associate Justice Nelson had during the session of the court been engaged in a careful study of the laws bearing upon the war powers of the President and of Congress. He had consulted the Chief-Justice of the United States upon the questions involved, and had come to the

*Confederate Secretary of State to the Commissioners, March 20, 1861.

conclusion that no coercion could be successfully effected by the Executive "without very serious violation of Constitution and Statute," and in this opinion Associate Justice Campbell had, after a similar examination, agreed.*

He was convinced "that an inflexible adherence to a policy of moderation and of peace would inevitably lead to the restoration of the Union in all of its integrity; that there was an imperative obligation upon the part of the Government to display moderation and an indulgent "spirit of endurance" to prevent the spread of secession and "recompose the Union."

Impressed with the importance of his conclusions, Associate Justice Nelson had, upon the same day (March 15), in a visit to the Secretaries of State and Treasury, as well as to the Attorney-General, laid before these officials the result of his research upon the subject, and the conclusions to which he had come. He was listened to with respect and attention by these officers, and with great cordiality by the Secretary of State, who expressed himself gratified at finding "so many impediments to the disturbances of peace, and only wished there had been more;† that his policy was for peace, and that he would spare no effort to maintain it. A subject which had interested him especially was, in regard to the execution of the laws relating to "Navigation, Commerce and Revenue" without additional legislation, in consequence of secession, Congress having adjourned without action upon the subject. The Secretary was of opinion that such execution would be impossible, "except by the use of military force and the dangers of civil war." The attention of Justice Nelson had been called to a resolution introduced by a Member of Congress from New York, in regard to the coasting trade; the question involved being the validity of clearances made by State officials after secession, while the coasting trade was protected and carried on. The subject had attracted the attention of Justice Campbell, who in conference with Justice Nelson, was of the opinion that this could not go on without involving the country with the South as well as abroad. It was then that, in the consideration of the subject, Justice Campbell sought the opinion of Judge Black, formerly the Secretary of State. He addressed to him an inquiry

---

* Reply of Associate Justice Campbell to Southern Historical Society, New Orleans, December 20, 1873.

† Associate Justice Campbell to Southern Historical Society, New Orleans.

as to the policy of the Government in respect to the cotton trade of the South after secession. To this Judge Black responded, that it could not be officially acknowledged, that the United States could not recognize clearances made by State officials, or any payment of duties, unless made by the proper Federal officers; but he at the same time stated *confidentially,* and as his private opinion, that the general principle of public law was rather against the right to punish a person for doing what the local authorities who are in possession of the port and custom-house compel him to do. They agreed to examine separately, everything connected with the subject, as well as the power of the President and Congress to take any action in regard to the Confederate States.*

At this interview, the Secretary informed Justice Nelson of the demand for recognition just made by the Confederate Commissioners, and of the embarrassment it caused him, as its refusal would produce irritation and excitement in both sections adverse to a peaceful adjustment. It was then that the suggestion was made by Justice Nelson, that Justice Campbell might be of service, when, accidentally meeting him after the interview, the two retired to consult as to the proper course to be pursued. After a full discussion, the conclusion was reached that the country would be better satisfied, and the counsels of peace be promoted, by the reception of the Commissioners, and obtaining for them a full exposition of their demands, and that this could be done without any official recognition of them or of their Government. They determined to recommend to the Secretary of State to reply to the letter of the Commissioners, and announce to them the earnest desire of the Government for conciliation and peace, and a friendly adjustment, and that every effort would be made with this view, and every "forbearance" exercised, before resorting to extreme measures, and that such a course would immediately influence both the border States as well as those Southern States that had not seceded. When this counsel was laid before the Secretary of State he was "much impressed" if not "convinced" by it. He declined, however, to act in accordance with the suggestion made, asserting that the Cabinet would not acquiesce, and expressing the opinion that the Commissioners would not have been sent had the true condition of things been known at Montgomery.

---

* Letter of Judge Black in author's possession.

Mr. Seward's reply is thus described by Justice Campbell in the papers submitted by him to the Southern Historical Society, December 20, 1873.

Rising and making a forcible gesture he said: "I wish I could do it. See Montgomery Blair, see Mr. Bates, see Mr. Lincoln himself; I wish you would: they are all Southern men—convince them—no, there is not a member of the Cabinet who would consent to it. If Jefferson Davis had known the state of things here he would not have sent those Commissioners; the evacuation of Sumter is as much as the administration can bear."

A letter from Mr. Thurlow Weed was then read by the Secretary, to the effect that the surrender of Sumter would be damaging to the administration, and that he was confident that he could have made a better arrangement with the Commissioners; that Anderson, with the consent of the Commissioners, might have been allowed to remain in the fort and to purchase his supplies in Charleston.

The proposition to evacuate Sumter had not before this been made known to Associate Justice Campbell, who agreed with the Secretary of State that it was a sufficient burden upon the administration to deal with alone, and who then proposed to see the Commissioners, and to write to Mr. Davis at Montgomery.* Upon this he was authorized by the Secretary to inform Mr. Davis that before a letter could reach him he would be informed by telegram that the order for the evacuation of the fort would have been issued.†

As the administration were satisfied with the condition of things at Fort Pickens and the forts in the Gulf of Mexico, no change in reference to them was contemplated. A delay of three, and subsequently five, days was agreed upon, as more than ample to communicate with Montgomery, when after listening again to

---

* Justice Campbell's manuscript. "Facts of History."

† When Justice Campbell at this interview had informed the Secretary that he would write to Mr. Davis, he continued, "And what shall I say to him upon the subject of Fort Sumter?" "You may say to him," said the Secretary, "that before that letter reaches him—how far is it to Montgomery?" "Three days," replied Justice Campbell. "You may say to him that before that letter reaches him, the telegraph will have informed him that Sumter will have been evacuated." "And what shall I say as to the forts in the Gulf of Mexico?" He replied, "We contemplate no action as to them; we are satisfied as to the position of things there."

the renewed assurances of, the Secretary in behalf of peace, Justice Campbell at once sought the Southern Commissioners, and later upon the same morning held his first interview with Mr. Martin J. Crawford, one of the three that had been sent to Washington. He found him ostensibly impatient of delay, and disinclined to any discussion of the subject. He was full of the brilliant prospect in store for his section in the future, and urged that they were destined to form a great and prosperous nation. A reasonable delay in demanding a response to the note of the Commissioner was urged by Justice Campbell, who at the same time expressed the opinion that if a response was now pressed, a civil but firm rejection would follow. He felt confident that Sumter would be evacuated in the next five days, and that the effect of a "measure imposing vast responsibility upon the administration" should be awaited, while at the same time he felt confident that no measure changing the existing status was contemplated; and he frankly informed the Commissioner that the opinion at Washington was that "the secession movements were short-lived and would wither under sunshine." To this the Commissioner replied. that he was willing to take all the risks of sunshine, but if they could be assured of the peaceful purposes of, the United States Government, he had no doubt that the time would be allowed; but that the evacuation of Sumter was imperative, and the military status must, remain unchanged.

He required to be informed of the authority for the assertion in regard to Fort Sumter., This Justice Campbell declined to give, and informed, the Commissioner that no inference was to be made that he (Justice Campbell) was "acting under any agency," and that he was alone responsible.

Mr. Crawford at once said: "You come from Seward; those are his views?" "I declined to give him any name—and told him that he was not authorized to infer that I was acting under any agency; that I was responsible to him for what I told him; and that no other person was. I informed him that Justice Nelson was aware of all that I was, and would agree that I was justified in saying to him what I did."*

After some discussion, the Commissioner was satisfied with the assurances given him, and, influenced largely by the near

---

*"Facts of History." Justice Campbell's manuscript, in author's possession

prospect of the evacuation of Fort Sumter, he consented to the temporary delay, as his action would also be in the interest of peace. He required, however, that the information given to him should be in writing, and its accuracy endorsed by Justice Campbell personally. The following memorandum, certifying the opinions given, was drawn up by Justice Campbell, and having received the approval of Justice Nelson, and its contents having been communicated to the Secretary of State, was handed to the Commissioner, who at once advised the authorities at Montgomery.

COPY "A."*

"NOTES OF JUSTICE J. A. CAMPBELL.

"NO. I.

"I feel perfect confidence in the fact that Fort Sumter will be evacuated in the next five days, and that this is felt to be a measure imposing vast responsibility upon the administration.

"I feel perfect confidence that no measure changing the existing status of things prejudicially to the Southern Confederate States is at present contemplated.

"I feel entire confidence that any immediate demand for an -answer to the communication of the Commissioners will be productive of evil and not of good. I do not believe that it should be pressed.

"I earnestly ask for a delay until the effect of the evacuation of Fort Sumter can be ascertained—or at least for a few days, say ten days.

(Signed)   "J. A. C.

"15th of March, 1861."

Meantime the five days specified had passed, and Fort Sumter had not been evacuated. Upon the expiration of the fifth day, a telegram was sent by the Commissioners to the commanding Confederate general at Charleston, upon the request of Justice Campbell, as to what had been done looking to the evacuation of Fort Sumter. The immediate reply of that officer was, that there were no indications of any change at Fort Sumter, and that work was then going on upon its defenses. This reply was at once placed in the hands of Justice Campbell, who, in company with Justice Nelson, again sought the Secretary of State. After an assurance upon his part that all was right, an arrangement for an interview upon the following day was made, when Justice Camp-

---

* Copy from the original paper in the Treasury Department, Washington, June 10, 1873 *(the Picket purchase).*

bell again sought the Commissioners and left with them the following paper.

"COPY B.
"NOTES OF JUSTICE CAMPBELL.
"No. 2.

"My confidence in the two facts stated in my note of the 15th, to wit: that Fort Sumter is to be evacuated, and that provisions have been made for that purpose and will be completed without any delay or any disposition for delay, is unabated.

"2d. That no prejudicial movement to the South is contemplated as respects Fort Pickens. I shall be able to speak positively tomorrow afternoon.

(Signed)   "J. A. C.

"21st of March, 1861."

On the morning of the 22nd of March the interview took place, when a full and satisfactory conversation was had. The Secretary was "buoyant and sanguine." He thought that the prospect of maintaining peace was encouraging. In reply to an inquiry of Justice Campbell in regard to the delay in the evacuation of Sumter, the Secretary stated that there was no change in regard to the determination in reference to Fort Sumter; that the resolution had been come to in the Cabinet "and its execution committed to the President;" that the delay was accidental, and "that there was nothing in the delay that affected the integrity of the promise or denoted any intention not to comply." The status at Fort Pickens was not to be altered, and if any contrary purpose was determined upon, the Justice should be informed.

This assurance of the Secretary of State was repeated in writing to the Commissioners on the evening of that day, by Justice Campbell, who assured them, as the result of the interviews, that he had "unabated confidence" in regard to the evacuation of Fort Sumter, and that provisions had been made for carrying it into effect; that the delay that had occurred did not excite in him "apprehension or distrust." He counseled inaction as to any demand on the Government, assuring them that he would have knowledge of any change of determination or purpose, a fact which the Commissioners considered as of infinite importance. A memorandum of this interview was made by Justice Campbell, and after having been submitted to the Secretary of State was left with the Commissioners. It was as follows:

"No. 3.

"As the result of my interviewing, of to-day I have to say

that I have still unabated confidence that Fort Sumter will be evacuated, and that no delay that has occurred excites in me any apprehension or distrust, and that the state of things existing at Fort Pickens will not be altered prejudicially to the Confederate States. I counsel inactivity in making demands on the- Government for the present. I shall have knowledge of any change in the existing status.

(Signed)   "J. A. C.

"22d March, 1861."

The results of these interviews were at once communicated by the Commissioner to the authorities at Montgomery, and often with exaggerated comment and conclusion. On the 22nd of March, after the important interview just noticed, one of the Commissioners, in his communication to the authorities at Montgomery, stated that the attendance of Justice Nelson at the interview was for the protection of Justice Campbell against the treachery of Secretary Seward and such other members of the Cabinet as he sees, and that Justice Campbell felt sure of guarding them, as a Commissioner, against deception and fraud, and at the same time have such protection for his own honor as would ensure him against treachery on the part of the Government. The Commissioner believed that the party in favor of a peaceful issue was gaining strength, that they would be met and the points discussed; and they believed, too, that rather than appeal to the sword to restore them to the union, the seceding States would be allowed to depart.   The confident assurances that Sumter would be evacuated, as well as that the state of things at Fort Pickens would not be changed to their prejudice, had still further inclined them to any reasonable delay.   At the same time, the Commissioners, were careful to state that the friends of peace in the Cabinet were actuated, by the desire of increasing any disaffection that might exist in the South looking ultimately to an overthrow of the Confederate! Government and the reconstruction of the Union. In regard to the action of the judges, the Commissioner reported that they were used to show the exact powers of the administration under the Constitution and the laws.*

---

* "We have hitherto informed you that the judges of the Supreme Court, or these two at least, were being used to show the administration the exact power which it has under the Constitution and the laws to use the army and the navy to invade the   states or collect   the customs outside the forts." Correspondence of the Confederate Commissioners, p. 87, manuscript copy.

When the delay in regard to any action as to Fort Sumter became known, and matters seemed to be growing more serious; Justice Nelson retired from any further participation in the negotiations, and left Washington on the day of the last interview, the 22d of March. He was satisfied with the results of the efforts made by him in favor of peace, but he deemed that the affairs seemed to be going further than he had contemplated. His colleague, Justice Campbell, was likewise impressed, but being so far involved, he determined, upon the advice of Justice Nelson, to continue until the evacuation of Fort Sumter, relying upon the alleged promises of the Secretary of State, and then to withdraw from further participation in the matter.*

The reluctance manifested upon the part of the Committee to yield to any delay in prosecuting the objects of their mission, was largely assumed as their secret instructions were to retard the negotiation, and to delay until the Confederate authorities were prepared to act.†

The important interviews at Washington, and the resulting correspondence of their Commissioners, had engaged the earnest attention of the authorities at. Montgomery.

On the 28th of March, the Confederate Secretary of State replied to the communication just received from the Commissioners commending the forbearance shown in view of the hope of a peaceful adjustment. The "conciliatory consideration" which the Commissioners had shown for the United States Government, had gratified the President (Davis), as well as that proper precaution had been taken against deception and misunderstanding, a necessity obvious when the time specified had elapsed and no change was made at Fort Sumter, so confidently predicted. That while relying upon the representations of Justice Campbell, the Government does not place the same confidence in the good faith and sincerity of those from whom Justice Campbell draws his convictions. He alleged, also, that there was good reason to

---

* To an inquiry of Justice Campbell if he could rely upon the Secretary, Justice. Nelson replied, "He will not deceive you." (Southern: Historical Society, p. 24.)

† In a conversation with Colonel John Forsyth, one of the.Commissioners, the writer was told that the secret instructions from Montgomery were "to play with Seward, to delay and gain time until the South was ready." Mobile; Ala., 1870.

believe that changes have been made at Fort Pickens with a view to strengthen it, while assurances had been given that there was no intention to change its status; that the policy pursued by the United States Government tended directly to produce an impression of distrust. That it was undoubted that a spacific policy was pursued only where the Confederacy had the power to compel obedience to their demand, but not otherwise; and unless a "graceless surrender of untenable power" should be mistaken by the Confederate authorities for a voluntary evidence of peaceful and conciliatory sentiment, the means employed by the Government of the United States seemed to fail of success. They were therefore to urge, with firmness, the evacuation of all the forts now within the borders of the Confederacy, as an indispensable condition to peace or negotiation. The Commissioners were also directed to ask explanation in regard to the "unusually large naval force in the ports of the United States at this time," and they were to remark that it had attracted the serious attention of this (Confederate) Government.*

The Commissioners had not yet had a personal interview with any member of the administration when, on the morning of the 24th of March, the Russian minister, Baron Stoeckl, called upon Mr. Roman, one of the Commissioners, at his residence in Washington. He informed him that he had had a free conversation with the Secretary of State in regard to the condition of things in the country; that the Secretary had expressed an earnest desire for a peaceful settlement, and repudiated the idea of force; the peace policy would prevail in time, the Secretary thought, and the difficulties surrounding him should be considered.

In reporting the result of this interview to his Government, Mr. Roman stated that he had had cordial interviews with the Russian minister, Baron Stoeckl, from whom he received warm assurances of Mr. Seward's pacific intentions, and an invitation to meet the Secretary of State over a cup of tea at the Russian legation. This informal meeting, however, did not take place, the Secretary having found that, he could not accept. The Commissioners were still under the impression that the peace policy would be successful, and they believed that they were gaining by inactivity and delay; but they did not fail to express their anxiety

---

* Confederate State Department to Commissioners, March 28.

that the *demand* for their reception or rejection should be made upon the very first day when their Government were ready to meet the consequences.

The Russian minister had informed them of his apprehension that the Secretary of State had been overruled in his policy. But while this was not the opinion of the Commissioners, they advised "active preparations for defense by sea and land;" that a strong force should be displayed at Fort Pickens, so that the administration might "have an excuse for evacuating that fort;" "unavoidable delays have attended the evacuation of Sumter, but it will be done;" and they closed their communication of the 26th of March by stating that "it was a proposition not yet solved, whether the administration was more afraid of the Confederate States or of the radical Republicans." They again ask for instructions from the "President," but before they are sent they desire to inform him that "the British minister here said to a friend,"* that if he had been directed to state to the United States Government "that England would not recognize the Confederate States, he would not have obeyed the order, but would have requested further instructions." They also inform their Government that the Russian minister had that day said to the Secretary of State that he need not hesitate to recognize the Confederacy, for the European powers would certainly do so. In his actions in the matter, the Russian minister desired that his name and connection with it should be "considered as strictly confidential. "†

Three days afterward, one of the Commissioners again writes that the peace policy was gaining ground, but was not openly avowed by the administration, only because public opinion was not yet prepared for its announcement, as it would affect pending elections in Rhode Island and Connecticut; that the Secretary of State would shortly return to his idea of an informal interview with the Commissioner; that he dared not go so far as a final treaty of peace, but "for a truce or cessation of hostilities" until the next Congress should meet. The difficulty in the way of the administration consisted in finding means to communicate

---

* Mr. W. W. Corcoran.

† Commissioners Crawford and Roman to Confederate Secretary of State, March 26, 1861.

with the Commission without appearing to acknowledge the independence of the Confederacy. He also reported that the French minister, who had also spoken confidentially of the present and future of the Confederacy, had observed that from what he had learned from other sources, a truce maintaining the present status would be arranged. Under such circumstances, while not knowing what. France would do, he assumed that she would naturally follow the example of the Government of the United States.

The course adopted by the Commissioners was approved by their Government. Delay was now commended, as being beneficial in enabling the Confederacy to make all necessary arrangements for the public defense; and while the United States Government pursued their "hesitating and doubting" policy, no formal demand for an answer to their note was to be made, as long as they could maintain their position with honor, or unless they were specially instructed to the contrary. Nothing was to be done to compel the United States to assume a definite position; while it continued to follow its present "vacillating and uncertain course," neither declaring war nor establishing peace, "the Confederate States had the advantage of both and could better prepare themselves for the future. The motives for the policy pursued by the Secretary of State were "a matter of no importance" to them. It would redound to their advantage should a truce be proposed, as the Commission regarded as a probable event; they were instructed not to agree to such proposition unless Fort Sumter and Fort Pickens should be evacuated; and that the troops then at Forts Taylor and Jefferson, in Florida, should not be removed during the sickly season; to be subsequently returned, for, said the Confederate Secretary of State, "we want the advantages of the climate upon them."

Intimate friendly relations with the representatives of foreign Governments were to be maintained, and the Spanish minister was to be assured of the desire of the Confederacy to cultivate "close and friendly relations with Spain," as it was "fully sensible of the importance of a great European power possessing naval colonies" in its neighborhood.

While matters were thus progressing in Washington, and, as each side presumed, favorably to their especial view, the authorities of South Carolina had become impatient at the delay. The promise made to them by the agent, Lamon, that he would shortly return to remove the garrison from Fort Sumter, had not been fulfilled. Time was passing, and the necessity of some decided action became every day more apparent, if a conflict was to be avoided. On the 30th of March, the Governor of the State telegraphed the facts of Lamon's visit to the Commissioners at Washington, who at once communicated with Justice Campbell. Seeking an interview with the Secretary of State he left the telegram with him, with the understanding that a reply would be made on the 1st of April. On that day the Secretary informed Justice Campbell that "the President was concerned at the contents of the telegram." The question involved a point of honor, and that Lamon had no commission or authority from him; nor "any power to pledge him by any promise or assurance;" and so desirous was the President that Governor Pickens should be satisfied of this, that Justice Campbell was requested to question Lamon, who had been sent to an adjoining room by the President. This he declined, at the, same time inquiring what he should communicate upon the subject of Fort Sumter. To this the Secretary made no verbal reply, but taking material, wrote to the effect "that the President may desire to supply Fort Sumter, but will not undertake to do so without first giving notices to Governor Pickens," and handed the written statement to Justice Campbell. The effect was marked and immediate. The result of their previous interviews had been to convince him that the evacuation of the fort had been wholly: determined upon, and he had so informed the Commissioners, who, thus convinced; were only awaiting the action of the Government. When, therefore, he now received the written statement of the Secretary that the question of the supply of Fort Sumter was still an open one, it filled him with anxiety, and he at once inquired whether the President intended to make such an attempt. "I think not," replied the Secretary. The ease of access to the President was then stated, as well as the constant suggestions of plans for the relief of the fort. "I do not think he will attempt it," said the Secretary; "there is no intention to reinforce it." At once Justice Campbell urged that the evacuation of the fort had been regarded as settled, and that the expression of a desire would be regarded as an abandonment of the conclusion to do so," and might bring on an attack; that it was difficult to restrain South Carolina as it was, and that he would not recommend an answer that did not express the purpose of the Government. To this the Secretary replied; "I must see the President." Shortly afterward he returned, and modified the expression of the previous paper as follows: "I am satisfied the Government will not undertake to supply Fort Sumter without giving notice to Governor Pickens."*

It was understood, at the same time, that "the import of the conversation previously had" was unaffected by what had just taken place, and the result of the interview, with the verbal explanation of the Secretary, was to satisfy the Justice entirely with the good faith of the Government, "in everything except the time as to when Fort Sumter was to have been evacuated." The subject and the result of the interview were at once communicated to Montgomery by the Commissioners, who informed their Government that the truth in regard to the evacuation of Sumter "is, the promise was made *after* the Cabinet and President had agreed to the order for evacuation," and there was no reason to expect that "any influence whatever" would postpone it by the persons thus pledging its fulfillment; that the mission of Colonel Lamon was solely for the purpose of making the necessity for the evacuation more manifest, in order to justify the President and his administration "from the indignation consequent upon the act;" that Colonel Lamon had not returned to Sumter, as he had promised, "because the President had been forced to await the result of the elections in Connecticut and Rhode Island."

As there was no intention to revoke the order, the Commissioner thought it better to indulge the President in his "vacillating course" rather than to attack the fort. He also reported that the "Wall Street influence" had compelled the Secretary of the Treasury to declare that the administration would pursue a peaceful policy; that the whole want of the Confederacy was comprised in the word peace, and that the "question of force" became the important one to be first settled, and he asks that, the fort evacuated and the status preserved, would it not be better to make no demand which could be peremptorily refused?

---

* "I asked Mr. Seward, What does this mean? does the President design to attempt to supply Sumter ?" He answered, "No; I think not. It is a very irksome thing to him to surrender it. His ears are open to every one, and they fill his head with schemes for its supply. I do not think that he will adopt any of them. There is no design to reinforce it." (Campbell's MSS. p. 7.)

While they had not been able to obtain a recognition of their official position or the preservation of the military status, they had obtained from the General Government "an explicit promise" that no hostile movement should be made; and they had secured this with the advantage that the Confederate States "were not bound in any way whatever to observe the same course" toward the Government of the United States, and that they might go on and organize their army and concentrate their forces at their discretion.*

The policy to be pursued was thus defined by the Commission and approved of by the authorities at Montgomery. But events began to follow each other with a rapidity that finally disclosed the purpose of the Government. Upon the same date, and in anticipation of their letter, a telegram was sent by the Commissioners to Montgomery, to the effect that the President had not the courage to execute the order which the Commission knew to have been agreed upon in the Cabinet for the evacuation of the fort; that he intended "to shift the responsibility upon Major Anderson by suffering him to be starved out;" and they recommend the cutting off of all supplies, as an assault upon the fort would cause an unnecessary shedding of blood and concentrate public opinion in favor of the Government. On the 2d of April they again telegraphed that the "war wing" pressed upon the President, and that he leaned to that side and had consulted with certain naval engineers; and again on the 3d, that much activity prevailed in the War and Navy departments, and the movements of war vessels was reported, but that it was believed that a demonstration against Spain was intended. In the uncertainty that prevailed, Justice Campbell had stated that the Government dared not deceive him, as they knew that the Commission did not rely upon them, but upon him. Events were now rapidly developing. On the 6th the Commissioners telegraphed that the rumors of the warlike armaments, already referred to as destined for Forts Pickens and Sumter, were daily growing stronger.

The evidences of some movement upon the part of the Government were now so manifest as to induce the general belief that a vigorous policy had been determined upon, which pointed with all but official accuracy to Forts Sumter and

---

* Commissioner Crawford to Confederate Secretary of State, April 1, 1861;

Pickens. The concourse of nine Governors of Northern States in Washington, and their pledges of support to the Government, gave strength to the report which the unexplained movement of vessels of "war and transport seemed to confirm." "The tone of one party became more menacing, and of the other more anxious and despondent."

"The movement of troops, and preparation on board of vessels of war, of which you have already been apprised, are continued with the greatest activity. An important move requiring a formidable military and naval force is certainly on foot," wrote the Commissioner to his Government on the 5th of April, and he deemed it to be his duty to call at once upon the Justice for the fulfillment of the pledge made in regard to Fort Sumter "or for explanation." At once, upon the morning of the 7th Justice Campbell in a communication to the Secretary of State called his attention to the alarm that had been created by the preparation of the Government by the unusual movements of troops; and of the reports of conversations of the President that had "some appearance of authority." He recites the assurances he had given to the Commissioner, and he asks to be informed if they "were well or ill founded;" and he expresses his apprehension of a collision; and volunteers to go himself to Montgomery to aid in any arrangement of the difficulties. On the 8th, in response to his communication, an envelope to his address was received by Justice Campbell, containing a paper without date or signature; and upon which was written, "Faith as to Sumter fully kept; wait and see; other suggestions received, and will be respectfully considered."* The response was not satisfactory to the Commissioner. There was "no change in the activity of the warlike armaments, nor in the rumors assigning their operation to the South."†

The Commissioners concluded that the reinforcement of Fort Pickens was the object of the expedition, as it was not referred to in the reply of the Secretary, and that an attempt to supply, but not to reinforce, Sumter would be made. Under this conviction, they determined to call for an answer to their official note of the 12th of March, demanding an audience, at the same time notify-

---

* Original paper, Justice Campbell's MSS.

† Such Government by blindman's buff, stumbling along too far, will end by the general overturn. Fort Sumter, I fear, is a case past arrangement." (From draft of original letter, April 7, 1861. Justice Campbell's MSS.)

ing the Government that their Secretary would call for a reply upon the following day. This action was at once reported to their Government by telegram on the 7th of April, with the statement that a hostile movement was on foot and that part of it had sailed against the Confederate States. It might be Sumter, but it was "almost certain that it was Pickens and the Texas frontier." Should the reply of the Secretary of State be unsatisfactory, they should consider the gauntlet of war thrown down, and would close their mission.

The State authorities at Charleston were meantime wholly aroused to the situation, hourly becoming more complicated. On the 7th of April Governor Pickens had telegraphed to the Commissioners at Washington, inquiring if it had. been determined to reinforce Fort Sumter; so many extraordinary telegrams had been received, that he would like to be informed of the truth of the statement.

The Commissioners replied to the telegram of the Governor on the 8th of April, that the military and naval movements were conducted with extraordinary secrecy, but that they were assured that he would not be disturbed without notice, and that they thought that Fort Sumter would be evacuated and Fort Pickens provisioned. On the same day the Confederate general in command at Charleston, deeming the accounts so uncertain, called out several thousand volunteers; while a telegram from one of the Commissioners, Mr. Crawford, was received by the same officer to the effect that the reports were uncertain, on account of the constant vacillation of the Government; that they had been assured upon the previous day that the status at Sumter would not be hanged without previous notice to Governor Pickens, but that they had no faith in the assurance given.

A copy of the memorandum of the Secretary of State, on file in the State Department, was handed by the Assistant Secretary to the messenger of the Commissioners, who called for it on the 8th of April. It was dated March 15, and had long been awaiting the call of the Commissioners. The circumstances attending the presentation of the communication of the Commissioners were stated, and the reasons and grounds upon which their request for an interview with the President was based, were recapitulated; and the Secretary frankly confessed that he entertained a very different view of the recent events and the actually existing political condition from that of the Commissioners. He saw in them, not a rightful and accomplished revolution and an independent nation with an established Government, but, rather, a perversion of a temporary and partisan excitement to the purpose of an unjustifiable and unconstitutional aggression upon the rights and authority of the Government; and he looked not to irregular negotiations nor to agencies unknown to the Constitution, but to the regular and considerate action of the people of those States through Congress and through extraordinary conventions for the cure of the evils which had resulted from such unnecessary, unwise and unnatural proceedings. He denied that the Confederate States constituted a foreign power, to be dealt with diplomatically. His official duties were to conduct the foreign relations of the country, and did not embrace domestic questions; and as Secretary of State he had no authority to recognize them or hold any correspondence with them as diplomatic agents, and in this, he was supported by the President himself, whom he had consulted out of the respect for the people of the Union in whose name the Commissioners had presented themselves. The memorandum was received with deep feeling.

In view of the communication received by them through Justice Campbell, the Commissioners concluded that they had been "abused and overreached," and in this they were sustained by their Government at Montgomery; and they prepared an immediate rejoinder, violent in its expressions and denunciatory in its tone, and reflecting upon the intercourse held by Justice Campbell with the Secretary of State, and which they proposed to publish or to send to Montgomery. An earnest protest to this was at once made by Justice Campbell, who again urged that he had "assumed all of the responsibility of the intercourse, and had not appeared as the agent of the Secretary or to speak at his request," and that he had expressly informed the Commissioner with whom he dealt, that there was no inference to be drawn that the Justice derived information from the Secretary of State or from any special source. To this the Commissioners acquiesced, and expunged the objectionable features of their reply, and on the 9th of April transmitted to the Secretary their final communication. In it they alleged that the Government of the United States had not chosen to meet the Commissioners in the "conciliatory and peaceful spirit" in which they were commissioned, that in characterizing the "deliberate sovereign act" of the people of the Confederate States as a "perversion of a temporary and partisan excitement" was to deal "with delusions;" that the refusal to entertain overtures for a peaceful solution of the difficulties, the formal notice to the authorities in Charleston Harbor of the intention to provision Fort Sumter, by force if necessary, could only be received as a declaration of war, which the Commissioners, in behalf of their Government and people, accepted, and would appeal to God and to the judgment of mankind. Upon the receipt of this communication, the Secretary of State directed that the following "memorandum" should be filed in his department; and, if requested, a copy should be delivered to the Commissioners:

"MEMORANDUM.

"Messrs. Forsyth, Crawford and Roman, having been apprised by a memorandum, which has been delivered to them, that the Secretary of State is not at liberty to hold official intercourse with them, will, it is presumed, expect no notice from him of the new communication which they have addressed to him, under the date of the 9th inst., beyond the simple acknowledgment of the receipt thereof, which he hereby very cheerfully gives.

"DEPARTMENT OF STATE,
"WASHINGTON, April 10, 1861."

Upon the same day a telegram was sent to the authorities at Montgomery by the Commissioners, to the effect that "this Government politely declines, in a written paper, to recognize our official character or the power we represent."

Such parts of the despatches of the Commissioners as narrate their own proceedings are doubtless exact and entirely reliable. If those portions which refer to the opinions, acts and conversation of others are less so, it is to be remembered that these were necessarily based only upon such information as could be obtained in a period of high excitement.

Detained by freshets, they again telegraphed, on the 10th, both to Montgomery and to Charleston, that the public press had announced that the main object of the expedition was the relief of Sumter. On the 11th the Commissioners left Washington, having confided to their Secretary the transaction of such matters in their interest as might arise after their departure; and he was to furnish to such representatives of foreign Governments as were known to be friendly to their cause, copies of their correspondence with the General Government.

But before their departure, a telegram had come from the commanding general at Charleston on the 8th inst., announcing the arrival of the special messenger with the notice of the President of the United States that Fort Sumter was "to be provisioned either peaceably or otherwise forcibly."

Dissatisfied with the result, Justice Campbell, on the 18th inst., addressed a communication to the Secretary of State. Fort Sumter had been fired upon, and the intelligence had reached Washington, and it was with a view to same explanation of this occurrence that the communication was made. All of the steps taken, as well as the promises made, were recited, and the opinion given "that the equivocating conduct of the administration, as measured and interpreted inconnection with these promises, is the proximate cause of the great calamity;" and he concludes by stating that it was his "profound conviction" that the action of the authorities at 'Montgomery could be referred to nothing else than their belief that a systematic duplicity had been practiced upon them through him.

To this communication, no response was made by the Secretary. On the 20th, one week later, Justice Campbell enclosed a copy of his previous communication, disclaiming any conclusions unfavorable to the Secretary, nor any opinion not susceptible of modification by explanation. An explanation was, however, insisted upon, as the Justice thought that the assurances of the Secretary had been continued after the decision in regard to Sumter had been abandoned. In case of refusal he would not hold himself debarred from placing "these letters" before such persons as were entitled to an explanation from him. His full title as Associate Justice of the Supreme Court of the United States was signed to this communication.* Thus ended the "voluntary interposition" of an official high in position, and, whose sole object was to prevent a collision which would inaugurate war between the States. Like many of his countrymen, he believed that, in the preservation of peace, a settlement: would be ultimately reached that would satisfy the best and most patriotic minds, and to this end he devoted his best energies. He opposed the secession of his

---

* Justice Campbell to Secretary Seward, April 20, 1861; original paper.

State, and condemned all that resembled a conspiracy against the Union of the States. So anxious was he to interpose between the conflicting elements, that he had in January, and before the inauguration of the President-elect, initiated a correspondence with him through the medium of Mr. Montgomery Blair. In this he urged that the President-elect should define the principles which were to govern his administration and quiet the apprehension that was prevailing. A reply directed to John A. Gilmer was received from the President, declining to anticipate his inaugural.

But the firing upon Fort Sumter speedily and with great distinctness defined the positions of all who yet doubted as to their especial course. Justice Campbell, upon his return to the South, found that he had been misrepresented by one of the Commissioners, in his relations to the negotiation. He was styled an "emissary of Lincoln," and an attempt was made to discredit him with his people. As time rolled on and the war progressed, he gave in his' adhesion, and finally was promoted to high office under the Confederacy.

CHAPTER XXVII

Anderson's estimate of force necessary to relieve him–Referred to General Scott–His opinion–Plan of relief of Captain Fox–President calls for written opinions of his Cabinet in regard to Sumter–Views of the Secretary of State–Opinions of the Secretary of War, Postmaster-General, Secretary of the Treasury–Opinion of Brigadier-General Totten, Chief Engineer–General Scott changes his views–Abandonment of Fort Sumter a "sure necessity"–His Memorandum for the Secretary of War Francis P. Blair–His interview with the President–Letter of the Postmaster-General–Speculations upon the opinions of the Cabinet–Secretary Chase corrects statement of his position–His letters–Final position of the Secretary of War.

WHILE active preparations both within and without the work were in progress, a report, to the effect that the garrison was to be withdrawn and the fort evacuated, had been circulated, and in large measure credited. The question of its relief had been forced upon the attention of the President and his Cabinet, from the moment of the organization of the new administration. The estimate of Major Anderson in regard to the force necessary to relieve him, together with that of his officers, had been referred by the orders of the President, to Lieutenant-General Scott, who at once "concurred" with Major Anderson in opinion. He desired time, however, to reflect upon it, and at the end of four days, after consultation "with other officers both of the Army and Navy," came, "reluctantly but decidedly, to the same conclusion as before." This opinion of General Scott, sustained as it was by that of Brigadier-General Totten, the Chief Engineer, produced an effect upon the new Cabinet wholly unfavorable to any attempt to relieve Fort Sumter.

The question was the absorbing one to the administration, and the President, before coming to a decision, determined to again refer to General Scott. On. the 12th of March, he addressed to him an inquiry as to "what amount of means, and what description, in addition to those already at command, it would require to supply and reinforce the fort." In his reply the Lieutenant-General stated that "as a practical military question, the time for

346

succoring Fort Sumter had passed away nearly a month ago." Its surrender from assault or starvation was merely a question of time, and that he should require 5,000 regular troops and 20,000 volunteers to take the batteries. The co-operation of the Navy would be necessary, and this, in its scattered condition, could not be collected in less than four months, nor the army he required in less than six or eight.

While the plan of Commander Ward had now been abandoned even by himself, that of Captain Fox was first discussed at this meeting of the Cabinet. The Postmaster-General was his relative. He had warmly sympathized with Captain Fox in his views, and had urged their adoption upon the administration. He believed that the announcement by the President, that he would "hold, occupy and possess" the strong places and properties of the Government, committed him and his administration to the retention of Fort Sumter under all circumstances, and to this position he adhered with consistency and energy until the last. Both before and after his appointment to a Cabinet, position, he had been earnest in the expression of his views that relief should be sent, and in response to a telegram from him of the 12th of March, Captain Fox again arrived in Washington, and on the morning of the 13th accompanied him to the President. The plan in detail was explained. In reply to the objection now urged by General Scott, that the batteries established would render the plan impossible, it was urged by Captain Fox that a steam naval force could pass any number of guns there, and for the reason that the course was at right angles to the line of fire, and the distance, 1,300 yards, too great for accurate firing at night.

It was at this time (13th) that the idea of visiting Fort Sumter in person suggested itself to Captain Fox. In this the President acquiesced, provided that the consent of the Secretary of War and of General Scott could be obtained.

Cabinet meetings were now frequent, and at each of them the subject of the relief of Fort Sumter was the principal topic of discussion. In this consideration of the subject, the President determined to' obtain the written opinions of his Cabinet, and accordingly, on the 15th of March, he addressed to each the following inquiry.

"EXECUTIVE MANSION, March 15, 1861.

"*My Dear Sir:* Assuming it to be possible to now provision

Fort Sumter, under the circumstances is it wise to attempt it? Please give me your opinion in writing on this question.

"Your obedient servant,

"A. LINCOLN."

The responses of his Cabinet were soon laid before the President. The views of the Secretary of State were well known. He was in favor of a peaceful solution of the difficulties. He had not disguised his conviction that the garrison of Fort Sumter should be withdrawn, relying as he did upon the sober second thought of the South in view of the peaceful intentions of the North. His reply, therefore, to the inquiry of the President was in accordance with the views long held by him, and urged before his entry into the Cabinet of Mr. Lincoln. These convictions found clear and unmistakable assertion in his official despatch of April 10, to our minister at London.* He believed that our Federal system "had within itself adequate and recuperative forces," whereby the exercise of firmness in maintaining and preserving the public property, and in executing the laws where it could be done without "waging war," would be sufficient to secure the public safety until returning reflection should bring the "recusant members" back again to their "natural home." The Constitution provided for that return by a national convention, by which all real obstacles could be removed. If, however, civil war should break out during the present administration, it must come through the agency of those who had chosen to be its enemies, and that the President, for whom he spoke, did not doubt, in that case, that the American people would rise up with a unanimity which should vindicate their wisdom and their virtue, and save the imperilled Union.

When, therefore, the inquiry of the President was submitted to him, as to his associates in the Cabinet, he did not hesitate to express those convictions which influenced him in his official course, until Fort Sumter was fired upon by the Confederate authorities.

In his reply he said:

"DEPARTMENT OF STATE,

"WASHINGTON, March 15, 1861.

"The President submits to me the following question: 'Assuming it to be possible to now provision Fort Sumter, under all the circumstances is it wise to attempt it?'

---

* Seward to Adams, April 10, 1861. Diplomatic correspondence, 1861.

"If it were possible to peacefully provision Fort Sumter, of course I should answer that it would be both unwise and inhuman not to attempt it.   But the facts of the case are known to be that the attempt must be made with the employment of a military and marine force, which would provoke combat and probably initiate a civil war, which the Government of the United States would be committed to maintain through all changes to some definitive conclusion.

"History must record that a sectional party, practically constituting a majority of the people of the fifteen slaves States, excited to a high state of jealous apprehension for the safety of life and property by impassioned though groundless appeals, went into the late election with a predetermined purpose, if unsuccessful at the polls, to raise the standard of secession immediately afterwards, and to separate the slave States, or so many of them as could be detached from the Union, and to organize them in a new, distinct and independent Confederacy. That party was unsuccessful at the polls.

"In the frenzy which followed the announcement of their defeat, they put the machinery of the State Legislatures and Conventions into motion, and within the period of three months, they have succeeded in obtaining Ordinances of Secession by which seven of the slave States have seceded and organized a new Confederacy under the name of the 'Confederated States of America.' These States, finding a large number of the mints, custom houses, forts and arsenals of the United States situated within their limits, unoccupied, undefended and virtually abandoned by the late administration, have seized and appropriated them to their own use, and, under the same circumstances, have seized and appropriated to their own use large amounts of money and other public property of, the United States found within their limits. The people of the other slave States, divided and balancing between sympathy with the seceding slave States and loyalty to the Union, have been intensely excited, but at the present moment indicate a disposition to adhere to the Union if nothing extraordinary shall occur to renew excitement and produce popular exasperation. This is the stage in this premeditated revolution at which we now stand.

"The opening of this painful controversy at once raised the question, whether it would be for the interest of the country to admit the projected dismemberment, with its consequent evils, or whether patriotism and humanity require that it shall be prevented.

"As a citizen, my own decision on this subject was promptly made, namely, that the Union is inestimable, and even indispensable, to the welfare and happiness of the whole country, and to the best interests of mankind. As a statesman in the public service, I have not hesitated to assume that the Federal Govern-

ment is committed to maintain, preserve and defend the Union—
peacefully if it can, forcibly if it must—to every extremity.
Next to disunion itself, I regard civil war as the most disastrous
and deplorable of national calamities, and as the most uncertain
and fearful of all remedies for political disorders.   I have therefore made it the study and labor of the hour, how to save the
Union from dismemberment by peaceful policy and without civil
war.

"Influenced by these sentiments, I have felt that it is exceedingly fortunate that to a great extent the Federal Government
occupies thus far not an aggressive attitude, but practically a
defensive one, while the necessity for action, if civil war is to be
initiated, falls on those who seek to dismember and to subvert
the Union.

"It has seemed to me equally fortunate that the disunionists
are absolutely without any justification for their rash and
desperate designs. The administration of the Government had
been for a long time virtually in their own hands, and controlled
and directed by themselves, when they began the work of revolution. They had, therefore, no other excuse than apprehensions of
oppression from the new and adverse administration which was
about to come into power.

"It seems to me, further, to be a matter of good fortune that
the new and adverse administration must come in with both
Houses of Congress containing majorities opposed to its policy,
so that, even if it would, it could commit no wrong or injustice
against the States which were being madly goaded into revolution.
Under these circumstances, disunion could have no better basis
to stand upon than a blind, unreasoning, popular excitement,
arising out of a simple and harmless disappointment in a Presidential election—that excitement, if it should find no new ailment,
must soon subside and leave disunion without any real support.
On the other hand, I have believed firmly that everywhere, even
in South Carolina, devotion to the Union is a profound and
permanent national sentiment, which, although it may be sup-
pressed and silenced by terror for a time, could if encouraged, be
ultimately relied upon to rally the people of the seceding. States
to reverse, upon due deliberation, all the popular acts of Legislatures and conventions by which they were hastily and violently
committed to disunion.

"The policy of the time, therefore, has seemed to me to consist in conciliation, which should deny to Disunionists any new
provocation or apparent offense, while it would enable the Union-
ists in the slave States to maintain, with truth and with effect, that
the alarms and apprehensions put forth by the Disunionists are
groundless and false.

"I have not been ignorant of the objections that the administration was elected through the activity of the Republican party;

that it must continue to deserve and retain the confidence of that party; while conciliation towards the slave States tends to demoralize the Republican party itself, on which party the main responsibility of maintaining the Union must rest.

"But it has seemed to me a sufficient answer, first, that the administration could not demoralize the Republican party without making some sacrifice of its essential principles, while no such sacrifice is necessary or is anywhere authoritatively proposed; and secondly, if it be indeed true that pacification is necessary to prevent dismemberment of the Union, and civil war, or either of them, no patriot and lover of humanity could hesitate to surrender party for the higher interests of country and humanity.

"Partly by design, partly by chance, this policy has been hitherto pursued by the late administration of the Federal Government and by the Republican party in its corporate action. It is by this policy, thus pursued, I think, that the progress of dismemberment has been arrested after the seven Gulf States had seceded and the border States yet remain, although they do so uneasily, in the Union.

"It is to a perseverance in this policy for a short time longer, that I look as the only peaceful means of assuring the continuance of Virginia, Maryland, North Carolina, Kentucky, Tennessee, Missouri and Arkansas, or most of those States, in the Union. It is through their good and patriotic offices, that I look to see the Union sentiment revived, and brought once more into activity in the seceding States, and through this agency, those States themselves returning into the Union.

"I am not unaware that I am conceding more than can reasonably be demanded by the people of the border States They could, speaking justly, demand nothing; they are bound by the Federal obligation to adhere to the Union without concession or conciliation, just as much as the people of the free States are. But in administration we must deal with men, facts and circumstances, not as they ought to be, but as they are.

"The fact then is, that while the people of the border States desire to be loyal, they are at the same time sadly, though temporarily, demoralized by a sympathy for the slave States, which makes them forget their loyalty whenever there are any grounds for apprehending that the Federal Government will resort to military coercion against the seceding States, even though such coercion should be necessary to maintain the authority, or even the integrity, of the Union. This sympathy is unreasonable, unwise and dangerous, and therefore cannot, if left undisturbed, be permanent. It can be banished, however, only in one way, and that is by giving time for it to wear out, and for reason to resume its sway.   Time will do this, if it be not hindered by new alarms and provocations.

"South Carolina opened the revolution. Apprehending chastisement by the military arm of the United States, she seized all the forts of the United States in the harbor of Charleston, except Fort Sumter, which, garrisoned by less than one hundred men, stands practically in a state of siege, but at the same time defying South Carolina, and, as the seceding States imagine, menacing her with conquest.

"Every one knows, first, that even if Sumter were adequately reinforced, it would still be practically useless to the Government, because the administration in no case could attempt to subjugate Charleston or the State of South Carolina.

"It is held now because it is the property of the United States, and is a monument of their authority and sovereignty. I would so continue to hold it so long as it can be done without involving some danger or evil greater than the advantage of continued possession. The highest military authority tells us that, without supplies, the garrison must yield in a few days to starvation—that its numbers are so small that it must yield in a few days to attack by the assailants now lying around it, and that the case in this respect would remain the same even if it were supplied, but not reinforced. All the military and naval authorities tell us that any attempt at supplies would be unavailing without the employment of armed military and naval force. If we employ armed force for the purpose of supplying the fort, we give all the provocation that could be offered by combining reinforcement with supply. The question submitted to us, then, practically is, Supposing it to be possible to reinforce and supply Fort Sumter, is it wise now to attempt it, instead of withdrawing the garrison?

"The most that could be done by any means now in our hands, would be to throw two hundred and fifty to four hundred men into the garrison, with provisions for supplying it five or six months. In this active and enlightened country, in this season of excitement, with a daily press, daily mails, and an incessantly operating telegraph, the design to reinforce and supply the garrison must become known to the opposite party at Charleston as soon at least as preparation for it should begin. The garrison would then almost certainly fall by assault before the expedition could reach the harbor of Charleston. But supposing the secret kept, the expedition must engage in conflict on entering the harbor of Charleston; suppose it to be overpowered and destroyed, is that new outrage to be avenged, or are we then to return to our attitude of immobility? Should we be allowed to do so? Moreover, in that event, what becomes of the garrison?

"Suppose the expedition successful. We have then a garrison in Fort Sumter that can defy assault for six months. What is it to do then? Is it to make war by opening its batteries and attempting to demolish the defenses of the Carolinians? Can it demolish them if it tries? If it cannot, what is the advantage we shall have gained? If it can, how will it serve to check or prevent disunion?

In either case, it seems to me that we will have inaugurated a civil war by our own act, without an adequate object, after which reunion will be hopeless, at least under this administration, or in any other way than by a popular disavowal, both of the war and of the administration which unnecessarily commenced it. Fraternity is the element of union—war is the very element of disunion. Fraternity, if practiced by this administration, will rescue the Union from all its dangers. If this administration, on the other hand, take up the sword, then an opposite party will offer the olive branch, and will, as it ought, profit by the restoration of peace and union.

"I may be asked whether I would in no case and at no time advise force—whether I purpose to give up everything. I reply, no. I would not initiate a war to regain a useless and unnecessary position on the soil of the seceding States. I would not provoke war in any way *now*. I would resort to force to protect the collection of the revenue, because that is a necessary as well as legitimate public object. Even then, it should be only a naval force that I would employ for that necessary purpose, while I would defer military action on land until a case should arise where we would hold the defensive.

"In that case, we should have the spirit of the country and the approval of mankind on our side. In the other, we should peril peace and union, because we had not the courage to practice prudence and moderation at the cost of temporary misapprehension. If this counsel seem to be impassive and even unpatriotic, I console myself by the reflection that it is such as Chatham gave to his country under circumstances not widely different."

The opinion as expressed by the Secretary of War was important. He had given the subject careful consideration, and he was "reluctantly forced to the conclusion that it would, be unwise now to make such an attempt;" that it was perhaps impossible to succor the fort without capturing the batteries around it by means of a large expedition; and that the officers within the fort, together with Generals Scott and Totten, expressed the same opinion; and it seemed to the Secretary that the President could not "disregard such high authority without overruling considerations of public policy." The opinion of Major Anderson, that he would not risk his reputation at an attempt at reinforcement, and to retain possession of the fort, with less than 20,000 men, was quoted by the Secretary; as well as that of General Scott, in his reply to the inquiry of the President of the 12th inst. There were others, the Secretary stated, who believed that there might be limited relief of the fort without the employment of so large a force.

The plan of Commander Ward was referred to, and the probability of its success at the time, as assured by Lieutenant-General Scott, but the execution of which had been prevented by the late President. This plan had now been pronounced impracticable by competent officers, and in this Commander Ward himself "reluctantly concurs" before the present administration had assumed the government.

The proposition of Captain Fox, as approved by Commodores Stringham and Stewart of the Navy, to attempt the supply of the fort by vessels of light draught and boats protected by armed vessels, was commended by the Secretary, and would be entitled to his favorable consideration if he did not feel that it would inaugurate a bloody and protracted conflict.

The Secretary thought that what might have been done a month before, could not now be accomplished without great sacrifice, and as the fort must be abandoned sooner or later, it appeared to him "that the sooner it be done, the better;" that if Fort Sumter was relieved by this plan we could not hold it. No practical benefit would result from an acceptance of the proposal, and that "the cause of humanity" and the highest obligation to the public interests required an acquiescence in the counsels submitted. This important letter of the Secretary of War is given in full.

"EXECUTIVE MANSION, March 15, 1861.
"THE HONORABLE SECRETARY OF WAR:
"*My Dear Sir:* Assuming it to be possible to now provision Fort Sumter, under all the circumstances is it wise to attempt it? Please give me your opinion in writing on this question.
"Your obedient servant,
"A. LINCOLN."

Answer.

"In reply to the letter of inquiry addressed to me by the President, whether, 'Assuming it to be possible now to provision Fort Sumter, under all the circumstances is it wise to attempt it'? I beg leave to say that it has received the careful consideration, in the limited time I could bestow upon it, which, its very grave importance demands, and that my mind has been most reluctantly forced to the conclusion that it would be unwise now to make such an attempt.

"In coming to this conclusion, I am free to say I am greatly influenced by the opinions of the Army officers who have expressed themselves on the subject, and who seem to concur that it is, perhaps, now impossible to succor that fort substantially, if at all, without capturing, by means of a large expedition of ships of war and troops, all the opposing batteries of South Carolina. All the officers within Fort Sumter, together with Generals Scott and Totten, express this opinion, and it would seem to me that the President would not be justified to disregard such high authority without overruling considerations of public policy.

"Major Anderson, in his report of the 28th ultimo, says:

" 'I confess that I would not be willing to risk my reputation on an attempt to throw reinforcements into this harbor within the time for our relief rendered necessary by the limited supply of our provisions, and with a view of holding possession of the same with a force of less than twenty thousand good and well-disciplined men.'

"In this opinion Major Anderson is substantially sustained by the reports of all the other officers within the fort, one of whom, Captain Seymour, speaks thus emphatically on the subject:

" ' It is not more than possible to supply this fort by ruse with a few men or a small amount of provisions, such is the unceasing vigilance employed to prevent it. To do so openly by vessels alone, unless they are shot proof, is virtually impossible, so numerous and powerful are the opposing batteries. No vessel can lay near the fort without being exposed to continual fire, and the harbor could, and probably would, whenever necessary, be effectually closed, as one channel has already been. A projected attack in large force would draw to this harbor all the available resources in men and material of the contiguous States. Batteries of guns of heavy calibre would be multiplied rapidly and indefinitely. At least 20,000 men, good marksmen, and trained for months past with a view to this very contingency, would be concentrated here before the attacking force could leave Northern ports. The harbor would be closed. A landing must be effected at some distance from our guns, which could give no aid. Charleston Harbor would be a Sebastopol in such a conflict, and unlimited means would probably be required to ensure success, before which time the garrison of Fort Sumter would be starved out,'

"General Scott, in his reply to the question addressed to him by the President, on the 12th instant, 'What amount of means and of what description, in addition to those already at command, would it require to supply and re-enforce the fort'? says:

"I should need a fleet of war vessels and transports, which, in the scattered disposition of the Navy (as understood), could not be collected in less than four months; 5,000 additional regular troops and 20,000 volunteers; that is, a force sufficient to take all the batteries, both in the harbor (including Fort Moultrie) as well as in the approach or outer bay. To raise, organize, and discipline such an army (not to speak of necessary legislation by Congress, not now in session) would require from six to eight months. As a practical military question, the time for succoring Fort Sumter with any means at hand has passed away nearly a month ago. Since then a surrender under assault or from starvation has been merely a question of time.'

"It is true there are those, whose opinions are entitled to respectful consideration, who entertain the belief that Fort Sumter could yet be succored to a limited extent without the employment of the large army and naval forces believed to be necessary by the Army officers whose opinions I have already quoted.

"Commander Ward, of the Navy, an officer of acknowledged

merit, a month ago believed it to be practicable to supply the fort with men and provisions to a limited extent without the employment of any very large military or naval force. He then proposed to employ four or more small steamers belonging to the Coast Survey to accomplish the purpose, and we have the opinion of General Scott that he has no doubt that Captain Ward at that time would have succeeded with his proposed expedition, but was not allowed by the late President to attempt the execution of his plan. Now it is pronounced, from the change of circumstances, impracticable by Major Anderson and all the other officers of the fort, as well as by Generals Scott and Totten, and in this opinion Commander Ward, after full consultation with the latter-named officers and the Superintendent of the Coast Survey, I understand now reluctantly concurs.

"Mr. Fox, another gentleman of experience as a seaman, who, having formerly been engaged on the Coast Survey, is familiar with the waters of the Charleston Harbor, has proposed to make the attempt to supply the fort with cutters of light draught and large dimensions, and his proposal has in a measure been approved by Commodore Stringham, but he does not suppose or propose or profess to believe that provisions for more than one or two months could be furnished at a time.

"There is no doubt whatever in my mind that when Major Anderson first took possession of Fort Sumter he could have been easily supplied with men and provisions, and that when Commander Ward, with the concurrence of General Scott, a month ago proposed his expedition he would have succeeded had he been allowed to attempt it, as I think he should have been. A different state of things now, however, exists. Fort Moultrie is now rearmed and strengthened in every way; many new land batteries have been constructed; the principal channel has been obstructed; in short, the difficulty of re-enforcing the fort has been increased ten if not twenty fold.

"Whatever might have been done as late as a month ago, it is too sadly evident that it cannot now be done without the sacrifice of life and treasure not at all commensurate with the object to be attained; and as the abandonment of the fort in a few weeks, sooner or later, appears to be an inevitable necessity, it seems to me that the sooner it be done the better.

"The proposition presented by Mr. Fox, so sincerely entertained and ably advocated, would be entitled to my favorable consideration if, with all the light before me, and in the face of so many distinguished military authorities on the other side, I did not believe that the attempt to carry it into effect would initiate a bloody and protracted conflict. Should he succeed in relieving Fort Sumter, which is doubted by many of our most experienced soldiers and seamen, would that enable us to maintain our authority against the troops and fortifications of South Carolina?

Sumter could not now contend against these formidable adversaries, if filled with provisions and men. That fortress was intended, as her position on the map will show, rather to repel an invading foe. It is equally clear, from repeated investigations and trials, that the range of her guns is too limited to reach the city of Charleston, if that were desirable.

"No practical benefit will result to the country or the Government by accepting the proposal alluded to, and I am therefore of opinion that the cause of humanity and the highest obligation to the public interest would be best promoted by adopting the counsels of those brave and experienced men whose suggestions I have laid before you.

[Indorsement.]

"There was a signed copy of the within placed in the hands of President Lincoln.

"SIMON CAMERON.

"MARCH 17, 1861."

A like opinion was expressed by the remaining members of the Cabinet, with the exception of the Secretary of the Treasury, Mr. Chase, and the Postmaster-General, Mr. Blair.

The opinion of Mr. Blair was well known. He had urged the relief of Fort Sumter even before his entry into the Cabinet. He had induced his relative, Captain Fox, to come to Washington, in order that the President might consider the scheme for relief proposed by him; and now that he was a member of the newly formed administration, he neglected no opportunity to earnestly urge upon the President, both within and without the Cabinet, the propriety and the necessity of immediate action in accordance with the convictions he held. When, therefore, he received the inquiry of the President, he was at once prepared to respond to it, which he did upon the same day.

The Postmaster-General belonged to that school of Democrats of which President Jackson was the great exponent, when he declared, in defiance of the Nullification doctrines of South Carolina, that "the Union must and shall be preserved." His father, Francis P. Blair, was the intimate friend and counsellor of President Jackson, and of Martin Van Buren, his successor in office, and, as the controller of an official journal, was the accredited mouth-piece of their administration in the dissemination of their peculiar views, which became a school in contradistinction to the teachings of Jefferson, and whose disciples, as war Democrats, fought for the Union of the States.

In the reply to the President he at once announced himself as in favor of provisioning Fort Sumter, and in a resume of the considerations involved, he urged that the "rebellion" had been is enabled to attain its present proportions" only through "the connivance of the late administration;" that nothing had been done to check its growth or progress, or to prevent its recognition, "either at home or abroad, as a successful revolution;" that it had been treated practically as a lawful proceeding, and that even the Union-loving people must come to regard it as a rightful Government. He thought that it was proper to exercise the powers of the Government, only so far as to maintain its authority over the revenue, and hold possession of the public property, and that this should be done with as little bloodshed as possible; that the power and firmness of the Government must be exercised, as was done in 1833; that not alone upon Mr. Buchanan's weakness the rebels relied for success, but upon the belief they entertained that "Northern men were deficient in the courage necessary to maintain the Government." "The evacuation of Fort Sumter, when it is known that it can be provisioned and manned, will convince the rebels that the administration lacks firmness," will embolden them, and would not only fail to prevent collision, but would ensure it, unless all of the other forts are given up. Buchanan's policy had "rendered collision almost inevitable," and a continuance of it would go far to produce a permanent division of the Union. "Fort Sumter may be provisioned and relieved by Captain Fox with little risk." The rebellion would be demoralized, and a reactionary movement throughout the South would follow which would speedily "overwhelm the traitors," and whether the enterprise should succeed or not, those who directed it would receive honor from the President, as well as "from the lovers of free government in all lands." His response was as follows:

"POST   OFFICE DEPARTMENT,
"WASHINGTON, March 15, 1861.
"TO THE PRESIDENT.
"*Sir:* In reply to your interrogatory whether in my opinion it is wise to provision Fort Sumter under present circumstances, I submit the following considerations in favor of provisioning that fort.

"The ambitious leaders of the late Democratic party have availed themselves of the disappointment attendant upon defeat in the late presidential election to found a military government in the seceding States.

"To the connivance of the late administration, it is due alone that this rebellion has been enabled to attain its present proportions.

"It has grown by this complicity into the form of an organized government in seven States, and up to this moment nothing has been done to check its progress or prevent its being regarded either at home or abroad as a successful revolution.

"Every hour of acquiescence in this condition of things, and especially every new conquest made by the rebels, strengthens their hands at home and their claim to recognition as an independent people abroad.

"It has from the beginning, and still is treated practically as a lawful proceeding, and the honest and Union-loving people in those States must by a continuance of this policy become reconciled to the new Government, and, though founded in wrong, come to regard it as rightful government.

"I, in common with all my associates in your council, agree that we must look to the people of these States for the overthrow of this rebellion, and that it is proper to exercise the powers of the Federal Government only so far as to maintain its authority to collect the revenue and maintain possession of the public property in the States; and that this should be done with as little bloodshed as possible. How is this to be carried into effect? That it is by measures which will inspire respect for the power of the Government, and the firmness of those who administer it, does not admit of debate.

"It is obvious that rebellion was checked in 1833 by the promptitude of the President in taking measures which made it manifest that it could not be attempted with impunity, and that it has grown to its present formidable proportions only because similar measures were not taken.

"The action of the President in 1833 inspired respect, whilst in 1860 the rebels were encouraged by the contempt they felt for the incumbent of the Presidency.

"But it was not alone upon Mr. Buchanan's weakness the rebels relied for success.

"They for the most part believe *that the Northern men are deficient in the courage necessary to maintain the Government.*

"It is this prevalent error in the South which induces so large a portion of the people there to suspect the good faith of the people of the North, and enables the demagogues so successfully to inculcate the notion that the object of the Northern people is to abolish slavery, and make the negroes the equals of the whites.

"Doubting the manhood of Northern men, they discredit their disclaimers of this purpose to humiliate and injure them. Nothing would so surely gain credit for such disclaimers as the manifestation of resolution on the part of the President to maintain the lawful authority of the nation. No men or people have so many difficulties as those whose firmness is doubted.

"The evacuation of Fort Sumter, when it is known that it can be provisioned and manned, will convince the rebels that the administration lacks firmness, and will therefore tend, more than any event that has happened, to embolden them; and so far from tending to prevent collision, will ensure it unless all the other forts are evacuated and all attempts are given up to maintain the authority of the United States.

"Mr. Buchanan's policy has, I think, rendered collision almost inevitable, and a continuance of that policy will not only bring it about, but will go far to produce a permanent division of the Union.

"This is manifestly the public judgment, which is much more to be relied on than that of any individual. I believe that Fort Sumter may be provisioned and relieved by Captain Fox with little risk; and General Scott's opinion that, with its war complement, there is no force in South Carolina which can take it, renders it almost certain that it will not then be attempted.

"This would completely demoralize the rebellion. The impotent rage of the rebels and the outburst of patriotic feeling which would follow this achievement, would initiate a reactionary movement throughout the South which would speedily overwhelm the traitors. No expense or care should therefore be spared to achieve this success. The appreciation of our stocks will pay for the most lavish outlay to make it one. Nor will the result be materially different to the nation if the attempt fails and its gallant leader and followers are lost. It will in any event vindicate the hardy courage of the North, and the determination of the people and their President to maintain the authority of the Government, and this is all that is wanting, in my judgment, to restore it.

"You should give no thought for the commander and his comrades in this enterprise. They willingly take the hazard for the sake of the country, and the honor which, successful or not, they will receive from you and the lovers of free Government in all lands.

"I am, sir, very respectfully.
"Your obedient servant,
"M. BLAIR."

Mr. Chase was equally in favor of some attempt being made to relieve Fort Sumter, although he was not now, nor had he previously been, decided in his expressions to that effect. His opinion was as follows:

TREASURY DEPARTMENT, March 16, 1861.

"*Sir:* The following question was submitted to my consideration, by your note of yesterday.

" 'Assuming it to be possible to now provision Fort Sumter, under all the circumstances is it wise to attempt it'?

"I have given to this question all the reflection which the engrossing duties of this department have allowed.

"A correct solution must depend, in my judgment, on the degree of possibility; on the combination of reinforcement with provisioning; and on the probable effects of the measure upon the relations of the disaffected States to the National Government.

"I shall assume what the statements of the distinguished officers consulted seem to warrant—that the possibility of success amounts to a reasonable degree of probability; and, also, that the attempt to provision is to include an attempt to reinforcement, for it seems to be generally agreed that provisioning without reinforcement will accomplish no substantially beneficial purpose.

"The probable political effects of the measure allow room for much fair difference of opinion, and I have not reached my own conclusion without serious difficulty.

"If the proposed enterprise will so influence civil war as to involve an immediate necessity for the enlistment of armies and the expenditure of millions, I cannot, in the existing circumstances of the country, and in the present condition of the national finances, advise it. But it seems to me highly improbable that the attempt, especially if accompanied or immediately followed by a proclamation setting forth a liberal and generous, though firm, policy toward the disaffected States, in accordance with the principles of the inaugural address, will produce such consequences; while it cannot be doubted that, in maintaining a fort belonging to the United States, and in supporting the officers and men engaged, in the regular course of service, in its defense, the Federal Government exercises a clear right and, under all ordinary circumstances, discharges a plain duty.

"I return, therefore, an affirmative answer to the question submitted to me. And have the honor to be,

"With the highest respect, your obedient servant.

"S. P. CHASE.

"To the PRESIDENT."

At this meeting of the 15th the plan of Captain Fox was again discussed by General Totten, the Chief Engineer, in the presence of the President and his Cabinet, Captain Fox and Commodore Stringham, of the Navy, and General Scott. In the paper presented, General Totten discussed the several plans proposed for the relief of the fort—the entrance into the harbor by a squadron of war vessels in daylight—was condemned, both on account of the concentrated fire of the batteries and the total want of shelter, while small vessels would inevitably be destroyed, from the proficiency attained by practice with the batteries, as well as the vigilance displayed in guarding the harbor. The employment of a few fast tugs to enter the Swash Channel by night was also considered by General Totten, who thought that although these tugs-might pass the batteries without great risk, and that perhaps all of them might reach Fort Sumter, they must have light to take their bearings, and that in consequence they would be seen and would be intercepted by the steamers "lying in the channel-way full of men." He thought, too, that it would be "unreasonable to suppose" that this plan had not been anticipated and provided for,* and that it like any other, would inevitably involve a collision.

In reply, however, to this opinion of General Totten, it was claimed by Captain Fox that all he had urged was admitted by General Totten, and that the question of entrance into the harbor was a naval question solely. The opinion furnished by General Scott to the Secretary of War as a "Memorandum" was enclosed by the Secretary in his reply to the President. At this period, the views of General Scott naturally carried great weight, and upon such a subject his opinion was deemed by many as decisive. It was believed that he had been thwarted by the previous administration in his patriotic intentions, and his opinions ignored, and it was the whole desire of the present administration to accord to his counsels that respect and acquiescence which his high character and prominent position warranted. His relations to the Secretary of State, who had sustained him in his aspirations for the presidency, were close and cordial, as they had ever been, and his political views were largely influenced by those of the Secretary. When, therefore, the moment came for an expression of opinion upon the part of General Scott as to the final action of the administration in the case of Fort Sumter, the General was not only in accord with the views of the Secretary, but even far beyond them. In his "Memorandum" to the Secretary of War, the impossibility of succoring the fort without carrying the batteries around it, an opinion in which he and General Totten. concurred, was stated. Even if the expedition in small tugs prepared by Captain Fox should succeed once, the necessity of

---

* This opinion was confirmed by General Beauregard in a conversation with the author in New York, March, 1882. This plan of relief had been antici-pated by the military authorities at Charleston, and such provision made to meet it that its success was pronounced by him impossible.

its repetition would recur; and he concludes that an abandonment of the fort in a few weeks, sooner or later, would appear therefore to be a sure necessity, and if so, the sooner the more graceful on the part of the Government. The paper submitted to the Secretary of War by General Scott is here given:

"GENERAL SCOTT'S MEMORANDUM FOR THE SECRETARY OF WAR.

"It seems, from the opinions of the Army officers who have expressed themselves on the subject—all within Fort Sumter, together with Generals Scott and Totten—that it is perhaps now impossible to succor that fort substantially, if at all, without capturing, by means of a large expedition of ships of war and troops, all the opposing batteries of South Carolina. In the meantime-six or ten months—Major Anderson would almost certainly have been obliged to surrender under assault or the approach of starvation; for even if an expedition like that proposed by G. V. Fox should succeed *once* in throwing in the succor of a few men and a few weeks' provision, the necessity of repeating the latter supply would return again and again, including the yellow-fever season. An abandonment of the fort in a few weeks sooner or later would appear, therefore, to be a sure necessity, and if so, the sooner the more graceful on the part of the Government.

"It is doubtful, however, according to recent information from the South, whether the voluntary evacuation of Fort Sumter alone would have a decisive effect upon the States now wavering between adherence to the Union and secession. It is known, indeed, that it would be charged to necessity, and the holding of Fort Pickens would be adduced in support of that view. Our Southern friends, however, are clear that the evacuation of both the forts would instantly soothe and give confidence to the eight remaining slave-holding States, and render their cordial adherence to this Union perpetual.

"The holding of Forts Jefferson and Taylor, on the ocean keys, depends on entirely different principles, and should never be abandoned; and, indeed, the giving up of Forts Sumter and Pickens may be best justified by the hope that we should thereby recover the State to which they geographically belong by the liberality of the act, besides retaining the eight doubtful States."

This Memorandum of General Scott was written upon the day fixed for the final action on the question as to whether supplies, should be sent. The General was under the impression that the evacuation of Fort Sumter had been *determined upon* by the President, and he had also recommended the evacuation of Fort Pickens. Contrary to the expectation of the President, the question was not decided at the Cabinet meeting of the 15th, when some only of the opinions were presented and a discussion took place.

All of the members of the Cabinet agreed substantially in the views expressed by the Secretary of State and the Secretary of War, except the Postmaster-General and the Secretary of the Treasury, as has just been seen. Their opinions were in writing, and were handed to the President. No formal decision by vote was made, as such proceeding was unusual in Cabinet consultations, the decision being always left to the President alone. Although the majority of his Cabinet were decided in their opinion as to the policy to be pursued, which was against the attempt to relieve Fort Sumter, its effect upon the President was advisory only, and his ultimate decision, influenced as it was by subsequent circumstances, was adverse to it. After the Cabinet had separated, the Postmaster-General, Mr Blair sought an interview with his father, the venerable Francis P. Blair, to whom he related the circumstances of the meeting, and what he inferred was the decision arrived at. Mr. Blair at once sought the President, with whom he was upon terms of intimacy. He found him yet in his place in the Cabinet room, and engaged in securing the written opinions of the members of his Cabinet just handed to him. He was at once asked by Mr. Blair if it had been determined to withdraw Anderson from Sumter. The President replied that it had not yet been fully determined upon, but that the Cabinet were almost a unit in favor of it, "all except your son," said he, and that he thought that such would be the result. Mr. Blair then expressed his belief that such a course would not be endorsed by the people, that it would destroy the formation of the Republican party, and that impeachment would probably follow.* Upon subsequent occasions Mr. Blair repeated the statement, and always affirmed that his son the Postmaster-General was the only member of Mr. Lincoln's Cabinet who opposed the withdrawal of the garrison from Fort Sumter. The Postmaster-General himself was under the same impression, and frequently asserted it as the statement of Mr. Lincoln to him, and it was so believed in the country.

The subject of relief to Fort Sumter was now a constant source of discussion both within and without the Cabinet, while the impression became general that, with the exception of the

---

* Mr. Blair to author.

Postmaster-General, the entire Cabinet, yielding to the views of the Secretary of State, Mr. Seward, and influenced by the military counsel of Lieutenant-General Scott, was averse to any attempt to succor the fort under the then existing circumstances, and this gave rise to great feeling in the country. Mr. Blair himself was open in his expression and decided in his course; and in a letter to the writer, of the 6th of May, 1882, he has given so clear and detailed an account of what took place, and of his personal relation to it, that it is here given in his own language.

"You will see," said he, "by Mr. Seward's letter to Mr. Adams of April 10, 1861,* that he considered the Union dissolved at that time, and contemplated, at some future time, the call of a convention to bring about reunion. For this reason he opposed the use of force to retain possession of the fort. He thought this would engender bad blood, and prove an obstacle to his plan of a peaceful return of the States, which he regarded as the only practicable mode of securing reunion.

"General Scott, in the belief that the surrender of Fort Sumter had been determined upon, wrote to the President that it was necessary to surrender Fort Pickens also.

"This letter was written on the day fixed for the final action on the question, whether Sumter should be surrendered. But contrary to the President's previous intention, he did not decide the question at the Cabinet meeting that day. After dinner the President called the members out of the room where he had dined with them, and in an agitated manner read Scott's letter, which he seemed just to have received. An oppressive silence followed. At last I said, "Mr. President you can now see that General Scott, in advising the surrender of Fort Sumter, is playing the part of a politician, not of a general, for as no one pretends that there is any military necessity for the surrender of Fort Pickens, which he now says it is equally necessary to surrender, it is believed that he is governed by political reasons in both recommendations.

"No answer could be made to this point, and the President saw that he was misled, and immediately ordered the reinforcement of Fort Sumter. It is impossible to exaggerate the importance and merit of this act. It was an irrevocable decision that the

---

* "Diplomatic Correspondence of 1861," p. 58.

Union should be maintained by force of arms. It was assuming the greatest responsibility ever assumed by any man, and it was assumed by Lincoln with only the support of a single member of the Cabinet, and he represented no State, and was the youngest and least distinguished. member; and he was opposed by ail the others, who were the leaders of the Republican party, and the representative men of the great Republican States. Lincoln himself was inexperienced, and those who opposed the stand he took had not only great experience in public affairs, but they were regarded by Lincoln himself as his superiors. That he should resolve to stand by his convictions of duty against all these influences ought, and I believe will, crown him with immortal honor."

The replies given by the different members of the Cabinet to the President's inquiry-in regard to Fort Sumter gave rise to much discussion and speculation. The Secretary of the Treasury, Mr. Chase, in order "to correct misapprehensions," as early as the 28th of April, 1861, after Fort Sumter had been fired upon and taken, addressed a letter to the Hon. Alphonso Taft.

In this he not only defined his position in regard to the relief of Sumter at that time, but so clearly and forcibly set forth the views that animated him that the communication is given entire.

WASHINGTON, April 28, 1861.

"MY DEAR SIR: To correct misapprehensions, except by acts, is an almost vain endeavor. You may say, however, to all whom it may concern, that there is no ground for the ascription to me by Major Brown of the sentiment to which you allude.

"True it is that before the assault on Fort Sumter, in anticipation of an attempt to provision famishing soldiers of the Union, I was decidedly in favor of a positive policy and against the notion of *drifting*—the Micawber policy of 'waiting for something to turn up.'

"As a positive policy, two alternatives were plainly before us. (1) That of enforcing the laws of the Union by its whole power and through its whole extent; or (2) that of recognizing the organization of actual government by the seven seceded States as an *accomplished revolution*—accomplished through the complicity of the late administration. and letting the Confederacy try its experiment of separation; but maintaining the authority of the Union and treating secession as treason everywhere else.

"Knowing that the former of these alternatives involved destructive war, and vast expenditure, and oppressive debt, and thinking it possible that through the latter these great evils might be avoided, the union of the other States preserved unbroken, the return even of the seceded States, after an unsatisfactory experiment of separation, secured, and the great cause of freedom and constitutional government peacefully vindicated—thinking, I say, these things possible, I preferred the latter alternative.

"The attack on Fort Sumter, however, and the precipitation of Virginia into hostility to the National Government, made this latter alternative impracticable, and I had then no hesitation about recurring to the former. Of course, I insist on the most vigorous measures, not merely for the preservation of the Union and the defense of the Government, but for the constitutional re-establishment of the full authority of both throughout the land.

"In laboring for these objects I know hardly the least cessation, and begin to feel the wear as well as the strain of them. When my criticizers equal me in labor and zeal, I shall most cheerfully listen to their criticisms.

"All is safe here now. Baltimore is repenting, and by repentance may be saved, if she adds works meet for repentance. Soon something else will be heard of.

"Yours truly,
"S. P. CHASE.

"HON. ALPHONSO TAFT."

Years passed without correcting the impression which prevailed, when his attention was called to it in a letter to him from Judge J. S. Black, to whom he replied on the 4th of July, 1870, as follows:

"On one other point I wish to correct your information, lest not mentioning it I may seem to have admitted its exactitude.

"You state that 'the Cabinet (Mr. Lincoln's) voted six to one in *favor of surrendering Fort Sumter,* Mr. Blair being the only dissentient.' I never voted for the surrender of Fort Sumter. My grounds of opposition were not perhaps the same, nor so absolute as Mr. Blair's, but I was against it, and so voted. I make this statement, not for the public, but for yourself, because I was in a position to be well informed, and am sure you would not willingly remain in error. Before all things, justice.

"With great respect and regard,
"Yours very truly,
(Signed)   "S. P. CHASE."

The strong endorsement of General Scott had also produced its effect upon the Secretary of War, Mr. Cameron, who, up to the moment when the "Views" of Lieutenant-General Scott were read to the Cabinet by the President, had been against any attempt to relieve the fort as "too late." He now changed his mind, and became an advocate of the relief of the work, and so argued upon the final disposition of the subject by the Cabinet of Mr. Lincoln.

Among those present on the evening when the question in regard to Fort Sumter was determined, was Mr. George Harrington, then Assistant Secretary of the Treasury, who, in his recorded reminiscences, says, "I was at the White House one evening, and found there with the President Mr. Welles, Mr. Fox and Mr. Montgomery Blair, and ere they separated it was determined to relieve and provision Fort Sumter. I went to Mr. Seward and informed him of the fact, which, though, as he said, 'difficult to believe,' he subsequently found to be true."*

It would seem, however, from the subsequent statement of the President, in his message to Congress at the extra session of July, 1861, that he was brought to this conclusion and action mainly by the intelligence, just received, that "under the quasi armistice of the late administration" the company on board the *Sabine* had not been landed at Fort Pickens, as he had anticipated and directed, as will be fully narrated in a subsequent chapter.

---

*　"Harrington's Reminiscences."

CHAPTER XXVIII.

AFTER the important meeting of the Cabinet on the 15th of March, and before taking any positive steps, the President determined to obtain further information from Major Anderson himself. Accordingly, a communication was addressed to Lieutenant-General Scott on the 19th of March by the Secretary of War, requesting him to direct some suitable and competent person to proceed to Fort Sumter and to obtain "accurate information in regard to the command of Major Anderson." Upon being sent to Lieutenant-General Scott, he endorsed upon it, "The within may do good, and can do no harm. It commits no one." Captain G. V. Fox was the envoy selected by General Scott, and his selection was approved by the President. On the same day he left Washington for Charleston, arriving on the morning of the 21st of March.

On the morning of this day Dr. Robinson, of Charleston, had come to the fort on a mission to Major Anderson. He reported that a telegram authorizing the removal of the garrison had already come to Charleston, and he brought a message from the Governor that, while he was unwilling to trust the Cabinet at Washington, he had confidence in Major Anderson, who had never deceived him, and that he might leave as he saw fit; that Major Anderson had done right in all his course. Upon arriving at Charleston, Captain Fox sought an interview with Captain Hartstene, an old comrade—a native of South Carolina, formerly of the

United States Navy—who had now entered the service of his State. To him he expressed his desire to visit Fort Sumter, in order to learn the actual condition of its command and to inquire into the state of the provisions. After a consultation with Governor Pickens, which lasted half an hour, Captain Hartstene, accompanied by Captain Fox, waited upon the Governor, who received him, and at once asked for the orders under which he acted.   Captain Fox replied that he had no written orders, but Showed to him the letter of General Scott, and informed the Governor of his purpose to ascertain the state of Major Anderson's provisions and the actual condition of his command.   The conversation closed by an inference, upon the part of Governor Pickens, that the object of the visit was a peaceful one, in which Captain Fox acquiesced.* After some delay, Captain Hartstene was directed to accompany Captain Fox to Fort Sumter. They left at once and arrived at the fort after dark, where they were met by Major Anderson and some of his officers. Captain Fox was the bearer of three letters to Major Anderson, who showed them to the writer in confidence. One of these was a letter from General Scott to the Secretary of War, Mr. Holt, mentioning the services of Major Anderson, and stating that he was only the interpreter of the wishes of thousands when he expressed the desire that he should be suitably rewarded; and he recommends that a brevet of lieutenant-colonel be conferred upon him for moving his command from Fort Moultrie to Sumter; and for maintaining his position there, "aside of privation," in the face of a numerous and powerful force, he recommends him for a brevet of colonel.

The second letter was from the Secretary of War, Mr. Cameron, to Lieutenant-General Scott, stating the desire of the President for accurate information in regard to Anderson and his command, and directing that a special messenger should be sent at once. The remaining letter was from Governor Pickens to Major Anderson, stating that he had permitted Captain Fox and Captain Hartstene to go down to the fort, and he regretted that General Scott could not have been more formal with him, but that he trusted to Major Anderson as a man of honor. The visit of Captain Fox was short. After a general conversation in

---

* Captain Fox to author.

the room of the officer of the guard, at the sally-port of the work, Major Anderson moved off in company with Captain Fox, leaving Captain Hartstene in conversation with his officers. It was now dark; when they reached the parapet Major Anderson turned the conversation upon his position, and knowing that the author of the proposed scheme for his relief was before him, he at once earnestly condemned any proposal to send him reinforcements. He asserted that it was too late; he agreed with General Scott that an entrance by sea was impossible; and he impressed upon Captain Fox his belief that any reinforcements coming would at once precipitate a collision and inaugurate civil war, and to this he manifested the most earnest opposition, and dwelt at length upon the political results that would follow.

It was while engaged in this conversation, begun and maintained chiefly by Major Anderson himself, that the sound of oars was heard close to the work while no boat was visible The entire feasibility of the plan of relief by boats, seemed to be confirmed by this incident, and the attention of Major Anderson was drawn to it by Captain Fox, who showed to him that screened by the darkness, it would be impossible to fire upon the boats with any accuracy. A point at the pancoupe on the left flank of the work, where a landing might take place, was pointed out by Captain Fox.

But it was urged by Major Anderson that the naval preparations at the mouth of the harbor would prevent the tugs and boats from reaching him, when Captain Fox replied that his barbette guns would be sufficient to keep the channel open. So impressed was Captain Fox by the manner and arguments of Major Anderson, that he did not lay before him what he might otherwise have done, and he was conscious of no obligation on his part which would prevent his giving him all the information in his possession that affected his position. No proposal was made or discussed, or arrangement made for relieving the work, nor did Captain Fox refer Major Anderson again to his plan, now known to him; and while the object of his visit was to obtain more accurate knowledge for the President, there was in addition a strong personal reason, and which largely influenced him in making it. He had not before been in those waters, and the constant reference to that fact by those members of the Cabinet who opposed the sending of relief, strongly influenced him to visit the work and by personal observation do away with such objection. The President had not yet made up his mind to relieve the fort, the whole matter was in abeyance; nor was Captain Fox authorized to give Major Anderson to understand that reinforcements would probably be sent to him. Still less was it his purpose to arrange a plan with Major Anderson for his relief. The scheme long before proposed by him had been discussed openly in the public press, as well as by Major Anderson and his officers in the fort, to whom Lieutenant Hall upon his return from Washington had brought the report of the discussion of this plan in the presence of General Scott on the 6th of February. It was the plan of relief most feared by the South Carolina authorities. "The danger to be feared," said Major-General Bonham, afterwards Governor of South Carolina, "is that light-draught vessels, barges or boats in the night may be sent in through the two middle channels;" and General Beauregard had, on April 10, officially informed the commanding officer on Sullivan's Island, that Captain Hartstene and the naval officers were of opinion that boats could pass the batteries on a dark night.

The visit of Captain Fox was short; a statement of the provisions on hand was furnished to him, and it was understood between himself and Major Anderson that unless provisions were furnished to him, he could not hold his position beyond the 15th of April at noon, even if he should at once place his command on short rations, and for this he should await the orders of his Government.

Before leaving, Major Anderson desired that Captain Fox should converse with one of the engineer officers. He declined to bring him to Captain Foster, as his relations with that officer were not cordial, and he suggested Lieutenant Snyder. While in conversation with that officer, Captain Foster came up and made a rapid statement of his work, Saying that he was doing all in his power to strengthen the fort without instructions from Major Anderson, who, although he acquiesced, did not encourage him.*†

---

* Upon his return to Charleston, Captain Fox held a short conversation with General Beauregard, who was not present at his interview with the Governor, or indeed in Charleston, before he went to the fort. The interview was unimportant, as Captain Fox had accomplished his visit. In a conversation with Captain Hartstene, General Beauregard asked "Were you with Captain Fox all the time of his visit?" "All but a short period, when he was with Major Anderson," replied Captain Hartstene. "I fear that we shall have occasion to regret that short period," said General Beauregard. (Beauregard to author, N. Y., March, 1882.)

† Fox to author.

The visit of Captain Fox was made the subject of a communication to his Government by Major Anderson, who in reporting his visit informed the Department that he had examined the point alluded to by him, as a proper landing-place for supplies, and had found that a vessel lying there would be under the fire of thirteen guns from Fort Moultrie; and he gives the opinion of his engineer officer also, that at that point she would require at high tide a staging of forty feet, and he submitted that the Department could thus decide what chances there were of a safe debarkation and unloading at that point. The impression produced upon Major Anderson was that this idea, "merely hinted at" to him by Captain Fox, would not be carried out. Upon the conclusion of his visit, which lasted but little over an hour, Captain Fox returned to Washington that night.

Every hour now tended to strengthen the belief that the garrison was to be withdrawn, and the preliminary steps to be taken were considered upon both sides. The public press as well as private advices from Washington all seemed to place the fact of the withdrawal beyond doubt. The engineer officer had made his arrangements, and had reported to his chief his intentions, and had received from that official his instructions as to the disposition to be made of the property. He was to bring away his books and drawings, and, if it were possible, to secure the heavy articles of property. The hospital supplies were also packed up except such as were needed for immediate use. But official action on the subject was wanting, and the month of March closed leaving the matter still undecided, although the positive conviction, both within and without Fort Sumter, was that it would be evacuated. So confidently was the change anticipated, that on the 29th of March Major Anderson stated that the Government preferred that the transportation necessary should be procured in Charleston. Time passed without any change, when on the morning of the 25th a steamer bearing a white flag was seen approaching the work. She bore Colonel Ward H. Lamon, of Washington, who, accompanied by Colonel Duryea, of the Governor's staff, had been permitted by Governor Pickens to visit Major Anderson. Colonel Lamon had been for some time in Charleston, where he had registered himself from Virginia, and the public journals had announced his presence as connected with postal matters. He finally sought an interview with the Governor, as a "confidential agent of the

President," and informed him that he had come for the purpose of arranging for the removal of the garrison.* He had been courteously received by the Governor, who, under the escort of one of his aides, had sent him to Major Anderson, with whom he remained alone for an hour and a half. Upon the character of the interview Major Anderson was silent, although he informed the writer that he "would be amused at the confidential communications of the messenger." The impression produced upon Major Anderson, as well as upon the officers and men of the garrison, was that the command was to be withdrawn.

Upon his return to Charleston, Colonel Lamon inquired of the Governor if a war vessel could not be allowed to remove the garrison. He was answered that "no war vessel could be allowed to enter the harbor on any terms." He then informed the Governor that Major Anderson preferred an ordinary steamer, to which the Governor agreed. He also told him that the President professed a desire to evacuate the work. Upon his return to Washington he wrote to Governor Pickens that he hoped to return in a very few days to withdraw the command.

The month of March was now drawing to its close, and to the occupants of Fort Sumter there seemed to be a suspension of the work hitherto pushed with such activity around them. The guns and material landed on the beach near Cummings Point remained for some days undisturbed, and there seemed to be a cessation of the work on the mortar battery at Fort Johnson. Within the work, the engineer operations were confined "to the collection and counting of materials, the clearing of the parade of the stone slabs and temporary structures that encumbered it, and in perfecting the arrangements of the batteries of the first and third tier." On the 31st of March, the provisions of the engineer force being exhausted, it was proposed to discharge all of the laborers except enough to man one of the boats. The armament and condition of the fort, the supply of provisions, the number and extent of the batteries and works around him, as far as could be ascertained by him, as well as a careful estimate of the force necessary, in the judgment of himself and his officers, to relieve the work, had been communicated to Washington by Major Anderson, who, confirmed in his anticipations by the visit and statements of Lamon;

* Governor's Message, November, 1861.

as well as by the reports and statements of the public prints and the telegrams of the Commissioner, looked forward to his promised return and to the immediate withdrawal of his command. But the days passed without any official action in regard to such determination, and his position became daily more embarrassing. There were constantly recurring causes of irritability if not of danger.

It was now the 1st of April, and he had reported everything quiet around him. He had not made frequent mention of the question of rations, as he had kept the Department fully informed of the state of his supplies, and on the 27th of January a detailed statement had been sent on, "from which any one in the Commissary Department could have told the exact amount on hand at any given time." Meantime, positive orders had come from Montgomery that no one should be permitted to leave Fort Sumter, unless all went. This rendered it necessary to turn over to the Engineer Department provisions for the use of their men, which greatly reduced the amount on hand. Had the laborers been permitted to leave the fort, the amount of rations on hand would have been sufficient to last one week from April 1. On the 3d notice was sent to him by the authorities at Charleston that certain minor articles he required could not be permitted to go to him, and he feared that the intention was to stop his supplies altogether; and he earnestly asks for instructions as to his course when his provisions were exhausted, as his bread would last but four or five days longer. On the same day the garrison was startled by the sound of firing from the batteries bearing upon the entrance into the harbor. A small schooner, mistaking the harbor for that of Savannah, had attempted to enter, having failed to secure a pilot. She had crossed the bar and was coming up the harbor, and was passing Morris Island, when a shot was fired across her bow. She at once ran the United States flag to her peak, when two more shots were fired across her bow, and standing on her course, the batteries in range opened on her. The firing was wild and unskillful, and continued while she was in range. One shot only went through her mainsail above the boom, when she turned, lowered her flag, and went out to the bar. Within the fort the greatest excitement prevailed. The long roll was beaten, and the men manned the guns; the battery in the northeast angle of the work was made ready, and Lieutenant

Davis had reported himself in readiness to open fire. Again Major Anderson assembled his officers, and consulted with them as to what should be done. Five of them (Doubleday, Foster, Crawford, Davis, and Hall) were in favor of an immediate reply to the batteries. Three (Seymour, Snyder and Meade) advised that we should delay firing, and should send to the island and ask the authorities in regard to their action, and also, that we should send to the schooner and learn her purpose. She had now anchored just beyond the range of the batteries. The latter course was adopted by Major Anderson, who at once despatched two of his officers to the commanding officer on Morris Island, while the men remained at the guns. The officers were met upon landing by a sentinel, and the commanding officer soon made his appearance. He had, he said, simply carried out his orders, which were to fire upon any vessel carrying the United States flag that attempted to enter the harbor after being warned by a shot fired across her bow, which this vessel had done when she was fired into. The officers then visited the schooner, and they found from the statement of the captain that she was the *Rhoda B. Shannon,* of Boston, with a cargo of ice for Savannah. The weather was bad, and he had made a mistake in his reckoning; and he supposed that he was entering that harbor, and that when the first shot was fired across him, he hoisted his flag, as he supposed the shot was fired for that purpose. He had endeavored to secure a pilot by displaying his flag, but had failed. The captain had an imperfect idea of the condition of things, and appeared incompetent to any action. The Governor of the State and the general in command witnessed the whole proceeding from Sullivan's Island.

Despatches were at once prepared by Major Anderson, who again assembled his officers, on the 4th of April, and announced his intention to send an officer to Washington. Lieutenant Talbot had meantime been promoted to the Adjutant-General's Department, and it was necessary for him to join his post. Major Anderson had determined, therefore, to send him with his despatches to Washington. In his consultation with the officers he made known to them, for the first time, the instructions he had previously received from Washington of January 10 and February 23, in which he was earnestly directed to act strictly upon the defensive, and to avoid any collision by all means consistent with his safety.

This he regarded as the qualifying clause which would justify him in not opening his batteries. Captain Talbot, accompanied by Lieutenant Snyder, who was sent under a white flag to the Governor to give them a detail of the statement of the captain of the schooner, proceeded to Charleston. General Beauregard was present at the interview. The Governor replied, in response to Lieutenant Snyder's statement, that the commandant of the vessel whose duty was to warn vessels off the harbor, had left his post on account of rough weather, and would be dismissed, and that peremptory orders had been sent to stop the random firing. The Governor adhered to the promise given, and the captain in charge of the guard-boat *Petrel* was dismissed.

It was at this interview that the Governor informed Lieutenant Snyder of the despatch of Commissioner M. J. Crawford, on the 1st of April, from Washington; that no attempt would be made to reinforce Fort Sumter with men or provisions, and that the President intended to shift the responsibility upon Major Anderson by suffering him to be starved out.

Objection was made to the mission of Captain Talbot, but upon examining the orders of his War Department, the Confederate general concluded that they referred more especially to the engineer laborers and enlisted men, and Captain Talbot was permitted to depart. The authorities at Montgomery did not so construe the orders given, which were intended to cover the entire command at Fort Sumter, and an explanation was asked. It was answered by the commanding general, that Lieutenant Talbot was allowed to go in order to diminish the number of officers in Sumter, and with the hope that he would report the true condition of things, which Governor Pickens and himself had reason to believe was not satisfactory to them.

The despatch of Major Anderson to his Government was important, as it enabled him to define distinctly his position at the time. In his letter of April 4 he encloses the report made on the 3d instant, by Captain Seymour and Lieutenant Snyder, in regard to the firing upon the schooner, and then informs the Department that he had been under the belief that he would shortly receive orders to abandon the fort, and that this was confirmed by what Colonel Lamon had said to him, as well as from other sources. That he had concealed some of his guns by planking, and that when he was prepared to use them, the firing was over. And that in accordance with his orders of February 23, he determined not to open fire until he had "investigated the circumstances." With scanty ammunition, with provisions for a few days only, a collision with the superior force around him would have probably terminated in his destruction before relief could reach him; and in hourly expectation of receiving definite instructions, and bound, too, as he considered himself to be, by his explicit and peremptory orders, he deeply regretted that he did not feel himself at liberty to resent the insult to his flag. The conviction that the command was to be withdrawn was so assured in their minds at this time, that although it did not operate to suspend the preparations for the defense of the work, the mode of its accomplishment largely engaged the attention and thought of the garrison and its commander.

He blamed the State authorities for not communicating instructions to vessels desiring to enter the harbor, and he sends Captain Talbot to give the Department an opportunity to modify their orders to him, if it were deemed proper to do so; and he would "delay obedience thereto" until Captain Talbot should report and he should receive a telegram from the War Department, to which he thus wrote:

"FORT SUMTER, S. C., April 4, 1861.
        "(Received A. G. O., April 6.)
'Col. L. THOMAS, *Adjutant-General U. S. Army:*
    "*Colonel:* I have the honor to send herewith a report of the circumstances attending a firing yesterday afternoon by the batteries on Morris Island at a schooner bearing our flag, bound from Boston to Savannah, which, erroneously mistaking the lighthouse off this harbor for that of Tybee, and having failed to get a pilot, was entering the harbor.
    "The remarks made to me by Colonel Lamon, taken in connection with the tenor of newspaper articles, have induced me, as stated in previous communications, to believe that orders would soon be issued for my abandoning this work. When the firing commenced some of my heaviest guns were concealed from their view by planking, and by the time the battery was ready the firing had ceased. I then, acting in strict accordance with the spirit and wording of the orders of the War Department, as communicated to me in the letter from the Secretary of War dated February 23, 1861, determined not to commence firing until I had sent to the vessel and investigated the circumstances.
    "The accompanying report presents them. Invested by a force so superior that a collision would, in all probability, termi-

nate in the destruction of our force before relief could reach us, with only a few days' provisions on hand, and with a scanty supply of ammunition, as will be seen by a reference to my letter of February 27, in hourly expectation of receiving definite instructions from the War Department, and with orders so explicit and peremptory as those I am acting under, I deeply regret that I did not feel myself at liberty to resent the insult thus offer to the flag of my beloved country.

"I think that proper notification should be given to our merchant vessels of the rigid instructions under which the commanders of these batteries are acting; that they should be notified that they must, as soon as a shot is fired ahead of them, at once round to and communicate with the batteries.

"The authorities here are certainly blamable for not having constantly vessels off to communicate instructions to those seeking entrance into this harbor.

"Captain Talbot is relieved, of course, by order No. 7, from duty at this post. I avail myself of this opportunity of stating that he has been zealous, intelligent, and active in the discharge of all his duties here, so far as his health permitted him to attempt their performance. I send him on with these despatches, to give the Department an opportunity, if deemed proper, to modify, in consequence of this unfortunate affair, any order they may have sent to me. I will delay obedience thereto until I have time to receive a telegram after Captain Talbot's having reported to the War Department.

"I am Colonel, very respectfully, your obedient servant,

"ROBERT ANDERSON,
"Major, First Artillery, Commanding."

[Inclosure.]

"FORT SUMTER, April 3, 1861.
"Maj. ROBERT ANDERSON, *First Artillery, U. S. Army,*
"Commanding Fort Sumter, Charleston Harbor:

"MAJOR: In obedience to your directions, we visited Cummings Point, and the schooner bearing the United States flag, which was fired into by the batteries on Morris Island, and respectfully present the following statement concerning the affair:

"The commanding officer on Morris Island, Lieutenant-Colonel W. G. De Saussure, stated that a schooner with the United States flag at her peak endeavored to enter the harbor this afternoon about 3 o'clock; that in accordance with his orders to prevent any vessel under that flag from entering the harbor, he had fired three shots across her bows, and this not causing her to heave to, he had fired at her, and had driven her out of the harbor; that he thought one or two shots had taken effect, and that if he had a boat that could live to get out to her he would send and see if she were disabled, and inform Major

Anderson at once, but that he had no proper boat, as the schooner was at anchor in a very rough place; that the revenue cutter had gone out to examine her condition. We ascertained the schooner to be the *Rhoda B. Shannon.* Joseph Marts, master, of Dorchester, N.J., bound from Boston to Savannah with a cargo of ice, having left the former place on March 26. On account of unfavorable weather, the master had obtained but one observation and that was an imperfect one on yesterday. On his arrival off Charleston Bar, supposing himself to be off Tybee, and seeing a pilot-boat, he directed one of his men to hold the United States flag in the fore rigging as a signal for a pilot. As none came, the flag was taken down in a few minutes, and the master undertook to bring his vessel into the harbor without a pilot. He did not discover that he was not in Savannah Harbor until he had crossed the bar and had advanced some distance in the harbor. As he was passing Morris Island, displaying no flag, a shot was fired from a battery on shore across the bows of the schooner. The master states that he thought they wished him to show his colors, and that he displayed the United States flag at his peak. One or two shots were then fired across the schooner's bows, but he did not know what to do or what the people on shore wished him to do; that he kept the vessel on her course until they fired at her, and one shot had gone through the mainsail, about two feet above the boom, when he put her about and stood out to sea, anchoring his vessel in the Swash Channel, just inside of the bar; that the batteries kept on firing at his vessel for some time after he had turned to go out to sea.

"The master of the schooner stated that before leaving Boston, he had learned how affairs stood in Charleston Harbor, and that Fort Sumter was to be given up in a few days; that they had established a new confederacy down South.

"After satisfying ourselves that the vessel was uninjured, and as she was lying in a very rough place, we advised the master to move his vessel—either to stand out to sea and go on to Savannah, or to come into the harbor and anchor.

"On our return we stopped at Cummings Point, and stated the facts to Lieutenant-Colonel De Saussure. He said that the vessel would not be molested if she came into the harbor.

"The schooner weighed anchor a short time after we left, and stood in towards Morris Island for some distance, but finally turned about and went to sea.

"Respectfully submitted.

"T. SEYMOUR, *Captain, First Artillery.*
"G. W. SNYDER, *Lieutenant of Engineers."*

But the causes of irritation continued to increase. A revenue cutter came to anchor within two hundred yards of the work and the daily boat from the fort to Fort Johnson for the mails and provisions was stopped by the officer in command of the cutter and obliged to display a white flag, stating that such were his orders. This had been brought to the notice of the Governor by Lieutenant Snyder in his interview, by direction of Major Anderson, who at the same time addressed a communication to the Confederate general, expressing his disbelief that any such orders had been given by him. The letter was friendly and personal. He was unwilling, he said, that his officers should leave the fort, as they hoped to do in a few days, under such an impression; that he had never regarded himself as being in a hostile attitude towards the inhabitants of South Carolina, and had been very particular in his intercourse with them, treating all with civility and courtesy. But this was not the only cause of complaint. A mortar battery at Mt. Pleasant, in practicing for range had exploded shells so near to the work as to endanger its occupants. This too was made the subject of a remonstrance by Major Anderson. In reporting the location of this battery, not before known to him, the engineer officer reported to his chief that this battery, in connection with the other mortar batteries reported on the islands, would reach by their shells every part of the fort.

Both the Governor and the general in command disclaimed any knowledge of the authority exercised by the cutter, as far as the mail boat was concerned. Soon after, the cutter was removed to a greater distance and the firing from the mortar battery was not renewed. The firing of the battery was made the subject of a communication to his Government by Major Anderson, who urged that "the truth is that the sooner we are out of this harbor the better. Our flag runs an hourly risk of being insulted, and my hands are tied by my orders, and if that was not the case I have not the power to protect it."* There was marked depression among the officers, with constant reference to, and condemnation of, the failure to fire upon the batteries that had opened upon the schooner. An increased nervous sensibility was observable, which manifested itself in various ways. Increased vigilance upon the part of the guard-boats protecting the channel was now manifested and a large force put to work upon the batteries at Cummings Point, and the garrisons of the works around reinforced.

---

*Anderson to War Department, April 6, 1861. "War of the Rebellion."

On the 7th, the supply of provisions to the fort was stopped by orders from Montgomery. The mails, however, were still permitted to come, and on the afternoon of this day, an important communication from the Secretary of War was received by Major Anderson, informing him for the first time of the purpose of the Government in regard to him and his command. He was to be provisioned peaceably if possible, if not, an effort to provision and reinforce him was to be made, and he was to hold out, if possible, to a specified time and await the expedition for his relief. Confidence that he would act as a patriot and a soldier was expressed by the Secretary, who at the same time authorized a capitulation should it become a necessity. Upon the subject-matter of the despatch, Major Anderson was silent. He was deeply affected by it. The letter was as follows:

"WAR DEPARTMENT,
"WASHINGTON, D. C., April 4, 1861.
"Major ROBERT ANDERSON, *U. S. Army:*
"*Sir:* Your letter of the 1st instant occasions some anxiety to the President.

"On the information of Captain Fox he had supposed you could hold out till the 15th instant without any great inconvenience; and had prepared an expedition to relieve you before that period.

"Hoping still that you will be able to sustain yourself till the 11th or 12th instant, the expedition will go forward; and, finding your flag flying, will attempt to provision you, and, in case the effort is resisted, will endeavor also to re-enforce you.

"You will therefore hold out, if possible, till the arrival of the expedition.

"It is not, however, the intention of the President to subject your command to any danger or hardship beyond what, in your judgment, would be usual in military life; and he has entire confidence that you will act as becomes a patriot and soldier, under all circumstances.

"Whenever, if at all, in your judgment, to save yourself and command, a capitulation becomes a necessary, you are authorized to make it.

"Respectfully,
"SIMON CAMERON,
"Secretary of War."

On the morning of the 8th, by the destruction of a house which had hitherto wholly concealed it, a battery of four heavy guns, well constructed, with sod revetments, was unmasked at the upper end of Sullivan's Island. From its position, it could "enfilade the terrepleins of both flanks of the work," and would command by its fire the only anchorage near the fort that was practicable, that upon the left flank of the work. The discovery of this battery produced a marked and depressing effect upon Major Anderson. He seemed nervous and anxious. He thought that its fire, taking in reverse and enfilading his most efficient battery, the one that he depended upon to silence the breaching battery at Cummings Point, would, independent of the "shower of shells" upon him, render it impossible for his men to serve the guns. Some of the officers also seemed to share in this feeling, and there was a general depression in regard to it.

It was necessary to make provision at once, as far as the now almost exhausted means at the disposal of the garrison would allow, to meet this new condition of things. The engineers were promptly at work, and a traverse composed of a double curb of boards and scantling and filled in with earth in the absence of sand-bags, hoisted from the parade, was built upon the parapet to protect the guns and the important battery on the right flank. "Ladders and runways" to facilitate the reception of supplies were prepared, and one of the embrasures enlarged so as to admit a barrel. Openings were made in the walls of the officers' quarters so as to allow the freest communication from flank to flank. To protect the main gates more efficiently from the fire from Cummings Point, a heavy traverse was commenced, and some modification made by cutting the embrasures so as to allow the heavy guns on the right flank of the gorge to be used against the batteries at Cummings Point.

Upon the 8th, what had been before contemplated was now put into execution. The authorities at Charleston seized and opened the mails from Fort Sumter. Late on the previous day (8 P. M.) a notice was sent by the Confederate general to Major Anderson informing him that until further instructions from the Confederate Government, "no mails would be allowed to go to or come from Fort Sumter." The fort was to be "completely isolated." Anderson at once took alarm, and wrote requesting that the mails sent previously to the notification he had received should be returned to him, and he confidently hoped that his request might be complied with.

But this was not done, and he was informed by the Confederate general that while the private letters were sent to their destination, those that were "official" were sent to the Confederate Government, in return for "the treachery of Captain Fox," who was reported as having violated his word to Governor Pickens.

The same accusation was made by Governor Pickens in a communication to the President of the Confederate States, and who also informed the Confederate Secretary of War that he had seized the mails because he considered that a state of war had been "inaugurated by the authorities at Washington," and that "all information of a public nature" was necessary to them. "You will see," said he, "by these letters how it is intended to supply the fort."

On the 8th, the stoppage of the mails for Fort Sumter had been determined upon, and Anderson was so informed. Judge Magrath had been sent to Postmaster Huger to tell him that the Governor had determined to seize the mail.*

Among the letters thus seized were two from Major Anderson, and one from the engineer officer to the Government. Their contents were of the highest importance, as they made known to the Confederate authorities not only what was being then done as to the defenses of the work, but revealed to them the personal sentiments of Major Anderson. His despatch was in response to the communication of the Secretary of War of the 4th inst, and was as follows:

No. 96.]   "FORT SUMTER, S. C., April 8, 1861.
    "Col. L. THOMAS, *Adutant-General U. S. Army:*
    "COLONEL: I have the honor to report that the resumption of

---

* A staff-officer of the Governor was sent to the postmaster on the 9th of April demanding their delivery to him. The bag containing Major Anderson's mail was handed to him and taken to the headquarters of the Government. The bag was thrown upon the table around which sat the Governor's advisers, including the Governor himself and also General Beauregard. It was opened, and passed over to Judge Magrath to examine. This he declined, saying, "No, I have too recently been a United States' Judge, and have been in the habit of sentencing people to the penitentiary for this sort of thing, so, Governor, let General Beauregard open them." General Beauregard replied, "Certainly not: Governor, you are the proper person to open these letters." Governor Pickens then took up one of the letters in an official envelope, turned it over nervously, saying, "Well, if you are all so fastidious about it, give them to me."

He held the letter for some time, when Judge Magrath said, "Go ahead, Governor, open it." The Governor then tore open the letter so nervously as almost to destroy it. Nothing but the official mail was opened. Private letters were not disturbed, but sent to their destination. A private letter directed to Mrs. Anderson was opened, for the reason that it had an official backing; when its character was recognized, it was at once closed.

work yesterday (Sunday) at various points on Morris Island, and the vigorous prosecution of it this morning, apparently strengthening nearly all the batteries which are under the fire of our guns, shows that they either have received some news from Washington which has put them on the *qui vive,* or that they have received orders from Montgomery to commence operations here. I am preparing by the side of my barbette guns protection for our men from. the shells, which will be almost continuously bursting over or in our work.

"I had the honor to receive by yesterday's mail the letter of the honorable Secretary of War, dated April 4, and confess that what he there states surprises me very greatly, following as it does and contradicting so positively the assurance Mr. Crawford telegraphed he was authorized to make. I trust that this matter will be at once put in a correct light, as a movement made now, when the South has been erroneously informed that none such will be attempted, would produce most disastrous results throughout our country.

"It is, of course, now too late for me to give any advice in reference to the proposed scheme of Captain Fox. I fear that its result cannot fail to be disastrous to all concerned. Even with his boat at our walls the loss of life (as I think I mentioned to Mr. Fox) in unloading her will more than pay for the good to be accomplished by the expedition, which keeps us, if I can maintain possession of this work, out of position, surrounded by strong works, which must be carried to make this fort of the least value to the United States Government.

We have not oil enough to keep a light in the lantern for one night. The boats will have, therefore, to rely at night entirely upon other marks. I ought to have been informed that this expedition was to come. Colonel Lamon's remark convinced me that the idea, merely hinted at to me by Captain Fox, would not be carried out. We shall strive to do our duty, though I frankly say that my heart is not in the war which I see is to be thus commenced. That God will still avert it, and cause us to resort to pacific measures to maintain our rights, is my ardent prayer.

"I am, Colonel, very respectfully, your obedient servant,
"ROBERT ANDERSON,
"Major First Artillery, Commanding.."

[Inclosure No. 1.]

"FORT SUMTER, S. C., April 8, 1861.
"General JOSEPH G. TOTTEN,
"Chief Engineer U. S. Army, Washington, D. C.:
"GENERAL: The increased activity and vigilance of the investing force, as reported yesterday, still continues. Three large traverses are nearly completed on the front, from battery Nos. 3 to 5, on Morris Island, and traverses are also being erected in the

interior of battery No. 5. Additions of sand-bags are being made to the covering of the magazine, between Nos. 2 and 3, and to the left flank of No. 1, where I think they are constructing a service magazine.

"I am busily at work constructing splinter-proof shelters on the terreplein. I obtain timber by taking the gun-carriages to pieces, and form the covering of the 2-inch iron pieces for embrasures, as seen below. The plates are spiked on, so as to be securely retained in their places, even if struck by a shell, which I am confident it will turn.

"Our supplies are entirely cut off from the city, and those on hand are very limited.

"The besieging forces worked all day yesterday, whenever the intervals between the showers of rain would allow.

"Very respectfully, your obedient servant,

"J. G. Foster, *Captain   Engineers.*

"P. S.—I received yesterday a letter from the Secretary of War to Major Anderson, which, by mistake, had been enveloped to me. I handed it to Major Anderson without reading.

"Respectfully, &c.,

"J. G. Foster, *Captain   Engineers."*

———

[Inclosure No. 2.]

"Col. L. Thomas, *Adjutant-General:*

"Dear Colonel: In another envelope I shall send a No. 96, which you will be pleased to destroy.

"That God will preserve our beloved country, is the heartfelt prayer of your friend,   "R. A."

It was upon the expressions of this letter that the allegations against Captain Fox were based, and upon them their action in regard to the mails was taken.

Captain Fox was ignorant of any guarantee or pledge made by Captain Hartstene on his account. He had told Captain Hartstene, as before stated, of his desire to visit Sumter to learn its condition and to inquire into the state of the provisions; and whatever guarantee that officer may have given, or promise made, was unknown to him. His plan for the relief of the work had long been known, and its execution was only suspended. No necessity for making any arrangement with Anderson existed, nor was any plan suggested to him. The basis of the accusation made against Captain Fox rests solely upon the statements in Major Anderson's letter of the 8th of April, which was seized and opened by the State authorities on the 9th. This letter, as has been stated, was a reply to the communication of the Secretary of War of the 4th of April, that the President, upon the information of Captain Fox, had supposed that Major Anderson could hold out until the 15th instant, and had prepared an expedition to relieve him. Captain Fox's plan, long in abeyance, had finally been determined upon, and it was the carrying out of this "proposed scheme" whose results he feared. It was the proposal of Captain Fox, not originated or agreed upon at the time of his visit to Fort Sumter, but long before submitted to the Government, and now adopted by them.

In his message to the Legislature of South Carolina at the extra session of November, 1861, the Governor of the State, in reference to his visit, stated that Captain Fox said that he desired to visit Fort Sumter, and that his objects were "entirely pacific."

"Upon the guarantee of the officer introducing him, Captain Hartstene, he was permitted to visit Major Anderson in company with him, expressly upon the pledge of pacific purpose. Notwithstanding this, he actually reported a plan for the reinforcement of the garrison by force, which was adopted. Major Anderson protested against it."

The tone of his communication, and his admission that his heart was not in the war which was thus brought on, gave rise to severe criticism and reflection upon Major Anderson, who, conscious probably of the effect it would produce, had made the unusual request that his letter might be destroyed.

CHAPTER XXIX.

WHILE the events related were transpiring, the Convention of South Carolina was holding its session in the city of Charleston. Resolutions and various amendments, all looking to the immediate possession of the public property in the harbor, as well as recommending an aggressive military policy, and even specifying Executive action in regard to the forts, were offered from time to time, and renewed as events occurred which seemed to precipitate action. Propositions were made instructing the Commissioners in Washington, and expressing the sense of the Convention in reference to the occupation of Fort Sumter. Two days after the passage of the Ordinance of Secession, the Committee, at the head of which was Ex-United States Judge Magrath, and to which had been referred so much of the message of the President of the United States as referred to the property of the United States in South Carolina, made their report. They held that the possession of places within the territorial limits of the State by a power now in all its relations foreign, would be inconsistent with the safety and honor of the State, and that the possession of the forts should be restored to her, and asserted that any armament of them would be regarded as an act of hostility. Resolutions of inquiry into the condition of the forts were offered, as well as instructions to

388

the Commissioners at Washington, to demand the delivery of the forts. Upon the movement of Major Anderson to Fort Sumter a resolution was offered, to the effect that it was the sense of the Convention that the occupation of Fort Sumter ought to be regarded "as an authorized occupation and vigorous military defenses provided immediately." But this, in common with all similar resolutions, was ordered to lie upon the table by a large majority of the Convention.

While propositions expressing the sense of the Convention in favor of vigorous military preparations and defense were at once adopted, all resolutions or amendments whose purpose was to direct or guide the Executive or the Commissioners in Washington, or in any way to assume Executive action, were promptly laid upon the table. But the disposition to interfere was constantly manifested. The Convention had adjourned on January 5, to meet at the call of the President, who reconvened it on the 26th of March, to consider the new Constitution of the Confederate States; and similar resolutions were again introduced, and again laid upon the table.

Towards the close of the session on the 6th of April, 1861, it was determined to inquire and report what resolutions and orders passed in secret session, and what portion of the secret journal, could now be made public. The resolution was referred to the engrossing Committee, who reported in favor of removing the injunction of secrecy and of the publication of the proceedings. But it was objected, that there was a class of resolutions the publication of which might give rise to a misconception of the real views of the Convention and a misconstruction of its action, and to these the attention of the Convention was called. The resolution offered upon the day after Major Anderson's movement from Fort Moultrie to Fort Sumter was one of this class. It provided that it was the sense of the Convention that the occupation of Fort Sumter ought to be regarded as "an authorized occupation" and vigorous military defenses provided immediately. It was ordered to lie on the table. Many similar resolutions were presented, and either in like manner disposed of or rejected altogether. And it had been suggested that to publish them now to the world would seem to imply that the Convention had failed to assert the principles involved in these resolutions or even denied them, and had thus antagonized the action.

of the Commissioners at Washington. The Committee, however, took a different view; they held that it was not the intention of the Convention to express any opinion as to the authority and character of Major Anderson's occupation, as neither had been affirmed or denied by the then administration, and the whole question had been confided to the hands of the Commissioners. This did not appear upon the record, but this the Committee suggested, like the proceedings of all legislative bodies, must depend for "explanation and vindication upon contemporaneous history." The injunction of secrecy was removed and the proceedings published. On the 8th of April, a resolution was offered in secret session, as the opinion of the Convention, that the military posts at Morris and Sullivan's islands should be strengthened by large reinforcements, that the Government should be requested to call 3,000 volunteers, or more if necessary, for the protection of the harbor. Amendments were offered to the effect that military operations in the harbor should be placed under the charge and control of Brigadier-General Beauregard, and that the volunteers should be placed at his disposal. But these resolutions and amendments were also ordered to lie upon the table, as well as others of a like effect.

Upon the same day, as already noticed, the Ordinance was passed transferring to the Government of the Confederate States the use and occupance of the forts, arsenals and public property, until by a convention of the people of the State the Ordinance should be repealed.   Resolutions of thanks to the volunteers, and various officers, as well as to General Beauregard and his assistants, and also a complimentary resolution to Major-General Twiggs, for his patriotic devotion and loyalty in resigning his commission and turning over the public property in his control to the State of Texas, and tendering to him the thanks of South Carolina therefor, were passed.   On the 10th of April the Convention called by the people of South Carolina, having wholly performed the duty required, and having prepared the State as far as it was possible to meet the issue, adjourned *sine die.*

Communication between the Commissioners and friends at Washington, and the authorities at Charleston and Montgomery, was now frequent. On the 1st of April Commissioner Crawford transmitted to Governor Pickens the following important telegram, which was forwarded at once to the Confederate Secretary of War.

"CHARLESTON, S. C. April 1, 1861.
"The HON. L. P. WALKER, Montgomery, Ala.
    "The following telegram, just received from Commissioner Crawford: 'I am authorized to say that this Government will not undertake to supply Sumter without notice to you. My opinion is that the President has not the courage to execute the order agreed upon in Cabinet for the evacuation of the fort, but that he intends to shift the responsibility upon Major Anderson by suffering him to be starved out. Would it not be well to aid in this by cutting off all supplies?'
                                        "CRAWFORD."

    "Batteries here ready to open Wednesday or Thursday. What instructions?
                                    "G. P. BEAUREGARD."

    The report of this telegram sent by Commissioner Crawford greatly impressed Major Anderson, if it did not alarm him, and upon the 5th of April it was made the subject of an earnest communication to the Government. He thought that the Commissioner had misunderstood what he had heard in Washington, as he could not think "that the Government would abandon, without instructions and without advice," his command, that had sought to do its duty. He thought that if the Government determined to be passive in regard to "a recognition of the fact of a dissolution of the Union," it would not compel him to an act which would leave his "motives and actions liable to misconception." After his long service, he did not wish it to be said that he had treasonably abandoned his post, and that he was entitled to this act of justice. What to do with the public property, and where to take his command, were questions to which he earnestly sought a response; and he closes his communication with the statement that unless he was supplied, he would be compelled to stay without food or to "abandon his post" very early next week. He wrote:

No. 94.]   "FORT SUMTER, S. C., April 5, 1861.
                            "(Received A. G. O., April 8.)
                    "Colonel L. THOMAS, *Adjutant-General U. S. Army:*
    "*Colonel:* I have the honor to report everything still and quiet, and to send herewith the report of Lieutenant Snyder, whom I sent yesterday with a short note and a verbal message to the Governor of South Carolina. No reply has been received to my note.
    "I cannot but think that Mr. Crawford has misunderstood what he has heard in Washington, as I cannot think that the Gov-

ernment would abandon, without instructions and without advice, a command which has tried to do all its duty to our country.

"I cannot but think that if the Government decides to do nothing which can be construed into a recognition of the fact of the dissolution of the Union, that it will, at all events, say to me that I must do the best I can, and not compel me to do an act which will leave my motives and actions liable to misconception.

"I am sure that I shall not be left without instructions, even though they may be confidential. After thirty odd years of service I do not wish it to be said that I have treasonably abandoned a post and turned over to unauthorized persons public property intrusted to my charge. I am entitled to this act of justice at the hands of my Government, and I feel confident that I shall not be disappointed. What to do with the public property, and where to take my command, are questions to which answers will, I hope, be at once returned. Unless we receive supplies, I shall be compelled to stay here without food or to abandon this post very early next week.

"Confidently hoping that I shall receive ample instructions in time,

"I am, Colonel, very respectfully, your obedient servant,

"ROBERT ANDERSON,

"Major First Artillery, Commanding."

[Inclosure.]

It was this telegram that produced the effect upon Major Anderson, already noticed. At Montgomery, the Government was kept equally apprised of every indication of movement. On the 2d the Commissioner telegraphed that the "war wing" pressed upon the President, and that he had been in conference with military and naval officers, which was supposed to be in reference to Fort Sumter, and that Mr. Chase, the Secretary of the Treasury, had been found by Senator Dixon to be much moderated and strongly inclined to the peace policy. On the same day, the Confederate Secretary of War addressed a communication to General Beauregard, in which he expressed to him the distrust entertained by the Confederate Government in regard to the evacuation of Sumter, or of the indisposition of the United States Government to concede or yield any point unless driven to it by absolute necessity, and he was in no degree to remit his efforts to prevent the reinforcement of Fort Sumter; he was to be prepared to repel any invading force, and to act as f he was in the presence of an enemy intending to surprise him. The status which he must enforce was "that of hostile forces in the presence of each other, who may at any moment be in actual conflict." All communication between the city and fort was to be "inhibited," and this was to be rigidly enforced, and specific instructions would be sent him upon the withdrawal of the Commissioners from Washington. Telegrams announcing the movements or rumored movements of ships or of troops were sent daily to the authorities at Montgomery or at Charleston, either by the Commissioners or by Southern emissaries or friends. The putting in commission of the *Powhatan,* the sailing of the Minnesota, the orders to the *Pawnee,* the sending of three companies of artillery to New York, were all subjects of telegraphic information and caution. That some military expedition was in contemplation and in preparation, was plain. And in spite of the rumor that it was intended for San Domingo or for Spain, it became daily more evident that it was intended for Fort Sumter or for Fort Pickens, and the authorities were advised to show equal activity to receive them if they came. The advices gradually became more positive. On the 6th of April a telegram was sent to the Hon. A. G. Magrath at Charleston to the following effect: "Positively determined not to withdraw Anderson. Supplies go immediately, supported by naval force under Stringham, if their landing be resisted." It was signed a "Friend," and was thus endorsed: "To Charleston office: the above is by a reliable man.   Caldwell."

But the telegraph office was not satisfied unless the despatch was confirmed by some responsible name, when the following endorsement was made upon it:

"MONDAY, April 8.
Sent by James E. Harvey by telegraph, last Saturday morning."

The telegram was duly received by Judge Magrath, who upon the same day communicated it to the Confederate Secretary of War at Montgomery, saying also that he had asked as to the identity of the "Friend" who had signed it, and was satisfied that he was high in the confidence of the Government at Washington, but upon the same day a totally different despatch was communicated to Judge Magrath and others in Charleston and signed James E. Harvey. It was as follows:

"Orders issued for withdrawal of Anderson's command. Scott declares it military necessity.   This is private."

It was followed by another, to the effect that great efforts were making to reconsider the withdrawal, but would fail, and again by a third, that there was no decision yet reached; the final order was reserved, and that the Cabinet was six for withdrawal and one against it.   A rumor, too, had been circulated that the people of South Carolina were opposed to the voluntary withdrawal of Anderson's command, and demanded a capitulation, and eager inquiries had been made from the emissaries in Washington as to the truth of their being opposed to Anderson's voluntary withdrawal. The request of Captain Foster, to be allowed to send away his mechanics and laborers from Fort Sumter, was on the 2d of April, as has been already seen, peremptorily refused by the Confederate Secretary, who replied that no portion of the garrison must be permitted to go unless all go.   This decision added to the embarrassment of Major Anderson, whose stock of provisions was now being rapidly exhausted.   Meantime, Major Anderson was allowed to receive his mails only, and for the reason that they might carry to him authority to withdraw. A strict surveillance was to be kept up, and any courtesies required were to be determined by the necessities of his position. No one was to be allowed to leave the fort, or any messenger favorable to the Washington Government to visit it, except he bore an order for the evacuation of the fort.

On the 8th an ordinance was passed by the Convention, transferring the forts, navy yards and arsenals, together with Fort Sumter, to the Confederate Government, to be controlled at its discretion until the ordinance should be repealed by a convention of the people.   Meantime, Captain Talbot had arrived in Washington and had presented the despatch of Major Anderson to the Government, which had now wholly determined upon its course. Formal notice of its intention was to be given to the authorities in Charleston.

On the 6th instant an order was issued by the Secretary of War directing Captain Talbot to proceed directly to Charleston, S. C., to procure an interview with Governor Pickens, if Fort Sumter was still held, and to read to him a notice that an attempt would be made to provision the fort.   If the fort had been evacuated or surrendered, he was not to seek the interview, but was to return forthwith.* The promise given to the Commissioner, that

---

* Secretary of War, April 6, 1861.

due notice should be given of such an attempt, was thus to be fulfilled, and Mr. R. L. Chew, of the Department of State, was selected
as the messenger to proceed to Charleston in company with Captain Talbot and deliver his message to the Governor of the State.

On the 6th they left Washington, and arrived in Charleston
on the 8th instant, when an immediate interview with the Governor was sought by Captain Talbot, who informed him of the
nature of his mission and of his written instructions, and asked
that his Excellency would accord an interview to Mr. Chew at his
earliest convenience. This was at once accorded at the headquarters of the Governor, when Mr. Chew read to him a message
from the President of the United States, leaving a copy with him.
On page 396 appears a facsimile of the paper read to the Governor.

As the State had ratified the Constitution of the Confederate
States, the Governor desired that General Beauregard, who was
in command under that authority, should be present when the
Governor read and handed to him a copy of the message. A
request upon the part of Captain Talbot, that he might proceed
to Fort Sumter for duty, was peremptorily refused by both Governor Pickens and General Beauregard, as well as permission to
communicate with Major Anderson, even with the understanding
that Captain Talbot should return at once to Charleston; and
very significant hints were given that the immediate departure of
these gentlemen would be prudent. At the hotel there were signs
of excitement and disapprobation at the presence of Mr. Chew,
the object of whose mission had become rumored about the city.
They were conveyed quietly from the hotel in a carriage, and
under the escort of an aide of the Governor and one from General Beauregard to the station near midnight. By direction of
General Beauregard their journey was impeded and broken. At
Florence they were detained for some hours, and all telegrams
sent by them were, by the same authority, communicated to him
at Charleston. They reached Washington on the fourth day.

On the 8th, the day upon which the communication of the
President was delivered, a telegram from one of the Commissioners had come, affirming the uncertainty of "accounts," and
that a reassurance, in which, however, they had no faith, had
been made that the status of Sumter would not be changed
without notice, and that the war policy prevailed in the Cabinet.
Upon the same day the Confederate War Department was

I am directed by the President of the United States to notify you to expect an attempt will be made to supply Fort Sumter with provisions only, and that, if such attempt be not resisted, no effort to throw in men, arms or ammunition, will be made, without further notice, or in case of an attack upon the Fort.

The above was communicated to us on the evening of 8th of April by [Mr] Robert S. Chew Esqr of the State Department in Washington & Capt: Talbot who stated it was from the President of the U. States as did Mr. Chew & was delivered to him on the 6th inst. at Washington & they are read in this presence and admitted.

8 April 1861–

F.W. Pickens

G.T. Beauregard

informed by the general in command at Charleston of the message of the President to the Governor, when he was answered that under no circumstances was he to allow provisions to be sent. Owing to the premature publication of the proceedings of the South Carolina Convention, in which was a detailed report of the State Secretary of War, giving "the exact condition, strength and number of batteries and troops in the harbor," the general in command at once called out the balance (5,000 men) of the contingent forces, a measure he deemed necessary on account of the warlike preparations made by the United States. Upon the same date the Confederate Secretary of War recommended to the Governor the calling out of 3,000 volunteers, to be held in readiness for any service, and a similar request was made to the Governors of Louisiana, Texas, Alabama and Mississippi.

Events of great import now rapidly succeeded each other. The forces on Morris Island were increased to 2,100 men, as the Governor now informed his Government, and ten companies of 800 men and two more regiments were to arrive the following day (10th); that he had 3,700 men at the different posts and batteries, and that by the 10th he would have 3,000 more which he had "called down." He anticipated a landing in boats on the lower end of Morris Island, but he had a fine rifle regiment and two Dahlgren guns, with four 24-pounders in battery, as well as forty enfilade rifles to give them a cordial welcome. A valuable addition to their armament, a Blakely gun, arrived on the 9th from England. It was the latest improvement in ordnance, and was a gift from Charles K. Prioleau, a citizen of South Carolina then residing in London, of the firm of Frazer & Co. It was inscribed, "Presented to the State of South Carolina by a citizen resident abroad, in commemoration of the 20th December, 1860."

Composed of steel coils, with an elevation of seven and one-half degrees to the mile, the Governor had informed the authorities at Montgomery that it would throw a shell or twelve-pound shot with the accuracy of a duelling pistol, and with only half a pound of powder. This gun was placed in position on Cummings Point, and fully justified the anticipations in reference to it; its fire was accurate and searching, and did more towards effecting a breach in the work than any other ordnance.

The garrison of Fort Sumter numbered at this period ten

officers and sixty-five enlisted men. Meantime vigorous prosecution of the work around the fort was noted and reported, although the mails had been stopped and no communication allowed. The heightening and strengthening of the works, their reinforcement, as well as the increased activity of the guard-boats in the channels and the signal vessels now far out "beyond the bar," were all observed, as well as the addition of a heavy Dahlgren gun to the new battery on Sullivan's Island, the unmasking of which had so greatly impressed Major Anderson.

The rations were fast diminishing; there was but little bread and rice, but by putting the command on half rations, he thought that he could make his bread ration last until the 13th. The strictest economy was enjoined, and the officers compelled to take with them the fragments of bread or crackers that remained after any meal; one cracker to a man morning and evening, none at dinner, was now ordered. The greatest enthusiasm prevailed among the men. While their long confinement was telling upon them, they were yet in good spirits, although unfit for any fatiguing labor, and they worked by day and night at the preparations made to protect the anticipated landing. The construction of the splinter-proof traverses on the parapet was now approaching completion, and the sound gun-carriages taken to pieces to obtain necessary timber. For their greater protection the whole command was now moved into the gun-casemates by Major Anderson's orders. All of the surplus blankets and extra company clothing, as well as the bed-clothing of the hospital, were used to make cartridge bags, while shot and shell were now distributed to the guns. The men worked cheerfully and in the greatest elation of spirits, and it was after witnessing this that the writer descended from the parapet to the lower battery on the morning of the 10th, when he saw Major Anderson alone, walking slowly backward and forward among his guns. He was greatly depressed; he seemed to realize that upon himself rested mainly the great responsibility. He had endeavored to avert the crisis upon him by every means in his power; he had failed, and the struggle was unavoidable and imminent. His sense of duty now overcame every other consideration, and he prepared to meet the worst. The morning of the 11th of April dawned brightly over the harbor of Charleston; nothing could exceed the activity everywhere manifested. From the early hours of the morning the waters were covered with the white sails of the shipping putting hastily to sea. The guard-boats were busily plying between the harbor and the bar, incessantly signalling. Constant communication was kept up between the batteries and forts, and the town. Steamers conveying men and material left to the last moment, passed at times under the guns of the fort, while small boats with officers bearing special and final instructions crossed and recrossed the waters of the harbor at all hours. At early dawn the floating battery, which had been towed down in the night, was discovered firmly stranded on the upper end of Sullivan's Island, behind and protected by the stone breakwater. The fire of its guns would cover the whole of the left flank of Fort Sumter and command the anchorage for boats, and, as Anderson reported to his Government, "was admirably placed for pouring a murderous fire" upon any vessels attempting to lay alongside of the left flank of the fort. The activity around him, and the especial direction given to it in the "judicious arrangements" made to prevent the landing of supplies, induced Anderson to believe and to report that, had the authorities about him been in possession of the intentions of the Government, they could not have made better arrangements. He suggests another plan, as the least dangerous course, and this was for the supply vessels to run directly into the wharf of the fort after passing Cummings Point, where they would be less exposed to fire from the new batteries on the west end of Sullivan's Island. In reporting the good health and spirits of his men, he says that they were under greater anxiety for those whom he expected to come to their relief than for themselves. The bread ration was now exhausted; damaged rice* was used with broken pieces of crackers which had remained, and this with salt pork was the only food left. The greatest eagerness was manifested among the men, as they anticipated an immediate solution of the existing difficulty. All of the command were now in the casemates, the hospital arrangements completed, the traverses to protect the battery upon the parapet and also the main gates were finished, and the officers assigned to the various batteries. The men could be seen at all hours upon

---

* Some rice that had been wet was spread upon the floor of the upper story of the officers' quarters to dry. In firing the national salute upon the 22d of February the glass in the window was shattered, and mixed with the rice so as to render it unserviceable. This was now sifted and used.

the parapet, watching the preparations going on around them and looking anxiously seaward, when at four o'clock in the afternoon, in the midst of the uncertainty and suspense, a boat bearing a white flag was seen approaching the work.

CHAPTER XXX.

In order to a clear understanding of the circumstances which
from the moment of its advent to power surrounded the new
administration with difficulties that were unprecedented, it is
necessary to recur again to the condition of affairs affecting Fort
Pickens under the former administration.

On the 6th of February the United States steamer *Brooklyn*
with a company of artillery under Captain Vodges, of the First
United States Artillery, from Fortress Monroe, had arrived at
Pensacola, off Fort Pickens, with the intention of reinforcing that
fort. But upon his arrival, Captain Vodges was met by orders
from the War Department, to the effect that his company was not
to be landed unless Fort Pickens should be attacked or preparations made for such attack. He was, however, to land the provisions necessary. The communication of the War Department
contained the following enclosure:

"WASHINGTON, January 21, 1861.
'To James Glynn, commanding the *Macedonia;* Captain F.
Walker, commanding the *Brooklyn,* and other officers in com-
mand; and Lieutenant Adam J. Slemmer, First Regiment of
Artillery, United States Army, commanding Fort Pickens,
Pensacola, Florida:
"In consequence of the assurances received from Mr. Mallory,

in a telegram of yesterday to Messrs. Slidell, Hunter and Bigler, with a request it should be laid before the President, that Fort Pickens would not be assaulted, and an offer of such an assurance to the same effect from Colonel Chase, for the purpose of avoiding a hostile collision, upon receiving satisfactory assurances from Mr. Mallory and Colonel Chase that Fort Pickens will not be attacked, you are instructed not to land the company on board the *Brooklyn* unless said fort shall be attacked or preparations shall be made for its attack. The provisions necessary for the supply of the fort you will land, &c., &c.

"J. HOLT, *Secretary of War.*
"ISAAC TOUCEY, *Secretary of the Navy.*"

On this quasi truce, the "status quo" in the harbor of Pensacola was maintained.

The pressure brought to bear upon the President in regard to Fort Sumter, after the meeting and action of his Cabinet on the 15th of March, was unremitting, as either side urged upon him their peculiar views. A conviction seemed now to prevail in the Cabinet that an attempt to succor Anderson would inaugurate civil war, and this belief was sustained and supported by the highest military authority.

From his official relation to the military questions involved, and upon which he conceived that great political events were about to turn, the Chief Engineer* deemed it to be his duty, in addition to what he had heretofore said, to state his "strongest convictions" in regard to the question of defending or abandoning Forts Sumter and Pickens. Accordingly, on the 3d of April he addressed a communication to the War Department. He thought that even were Fort Sumter now filled with men and munitions, it could hold out but a short time, that it would be bravely defended with much loss of life, and that the issue could only be averted by sending a large "army and navy" to capture the batteries and forts; that there was now no time to do this, and that if Fort Sumter was not evacuated it would be taken by force. He did not advise as to the policy of the Government, but he presented facts of a military nature which he thought might bear upon the political question. He thought, too, that no measures "within our reach" would prevent the loss of Fort Pickens. Cabinet meetings were now of almost daily occurrence, when the subject was earnestly discussed. The President had not yet wholly made up his mind. The views

---

* General Totten.

of Lieutenant-General Scott and other military authorities had greatly impressed him, and these, taken in connection with the letter of Major Anderson of the 28th of February, with the estimate of himself and his officers as to the force required to relieve him, supported as it was by the highest military authority, and especially by that of General Scott, appeared to the President, "in a purely military point of view," to reduce the duty of the administration "to the mere matter of getting the garrison out of the fort." But the counsels of those who had so consistently urged that the fort should be relieved had now prevailed. In spite of the great weight of authority, both military and civil, against such action, the President resolved that the property of the Government should not be abandoned nor its garrison withdrawn under the plea of any necessity, without some effort upon his part to relieve it; he thought that to abandon Fort Sumter "under the circumstances would be utterly ruinous;" that the necessity pleaded for it would be misunderstood, and "would be construed as a part of a voluntary policy," and that "it would be our national destruction consummated." If, however, before the provisions. at Sumter were exhausted Fort Pickens could be reinforced, it would indicate a policy which would "better enable the country to accept the evacuation of Fort Sumter as a military necessity." The month of March was drawing to a close before the President had finally determined as to the policy he would adopt, and his responsibility and action under it. But he had already begun to take the necessary steps to carry into execution the plan that should be selected. Accordingly, towards the end of March an order was sent directing that the company of artillery on board the Brooklyn should be at once landed and reinforce that work.

In order to replenish her stores, the *Brooklyn* on the 22d of March had transferred the troops on board to the frigate *Sabine,* and had left for Key West. The messenger proceeded by sea. When the order arrived,* the commanding officer of the *Sabine,* "acting upon the quasi armistice of the late administration—and of the existence of which the present administration, up to the time the order was despatched, had only too vague and uncertain rumors to fix attention—had refused to land the troops."†

---

* On the 31st of March.

† The words of the President himself. (See President's Message, Extra session of Congress, July, 1861.

The messenger, with the news of this refusal, and the consequent failure to reinforce the work, reached Washington "just one week before the fall of Fort Sumter." No time now remained to renew the attempt to reinforce Fort Pickens before the crisis would have arrived at Fort Sumter, through the absolute want of provisions. Some days before, a provisional expedition had been ordered by the President in person. On the 29th of March he addressed to the Secretary of War a communication desiring that an expedition to move by sea should be in readiness to sail upon the 6th of April, in co-operation with the navy, and "preliminary orders" were enclosed to the Navy and War departments.*

Upon the following day Captain Fox proceeded to New York, under the verbal instructions of the President to make ready, but "not to incur any binding engagements." Here he consulted with prominent citizens who had had experience in naval affairs, with a view of coming to an understanding authorized by the President's instructions. One of them, Mr. Charles H. Marshall, declined to give him any assistance, and for the reason that the attempt to relieve Fort Sumter would kill the proposed loan and bring on civil war, and because the people had made up their minds to abandon Sumter and make the stand upon Fort Pickens.† On the afternoon of the 4th of April Captain Fox was sent for by the President, and informed by him for the first time of his final determination to send the expedition for the relief of Sumter. He told him, also, of his intention to send a messenger to inform the authorities at Charleston of his purpose to provision Fort Sumter peaceably. When, in response, Captain Fox had stated that there were but nine days in which to organize such expedition and also to reach Charleston, six hundred and thirty-two miles distant, the President replied, "You will best fulfill your duty to your country by making the attempt." The orders to Captain Fox directed him to take charge of the transports in

_____

*To the Navy: Specifying the steamers required to be placed under sailing orders, with supplies for one month, and three hundred men to be kept ready on the receiving ships at New York. *Pocahontas, Pawnee* and *Harriet Lane* specified. To the War Department: To hold two hundred men in readiness to leave Governor's Island, New York, Supplies for one hundred men for one year, to be put into portable shape, and one large steamer and two tugs conditionally engaged.

† Captain G. V. Fox, "Old Residents' Historical Association," Vol. II., No. 1. Lowell, Mass., p 46.

New York, with the troops and supplies on board, to the entrance of Charleston Harbor, and to endeavor to deliver the subsistence. If he was opposed in this, he was to report the fact. to the senior naval officer, who was instructed to force a passage. The necessary orders were issued by Lieutenant General Scott to his aide-de-camp in New York, who was directed to organize a detachment of two hundred recruits, with the proper complement of officers and arms and subsistence. All of the necessary orders were to be given in General Scott's name.

Captain Fox proceeded at once to New York, where he arrived on the 5th of April, and at once pushed forward his preparations with the utmost energy. He delivered his confidential orders to Colonel H. L. Scott, the aide-de-camp of the Lieutenant-General, but that officer "ridiculed the idea of the Government relieving Fort Sumter, and by his indifference and delay half a day of precious time was lost."* The recruits ordered were undrilled, raw and wholly unfit for the service required. The tugs necessary were hired with difficulty, the owners objecting to the secrecy required, but finally yielded after securing exorbitant rates.

At this period there were but two small vessels of war in the Atlantic waters, the *Pocahontas* and the *Pawnee.* The *Powhatan* had arrived at New York on the 13th of March, and by order of the Navy Department had gone out of commission at 5 o'clock P. M. on the 1st of April. The *Powhatan* had been selected by Captain Fox as a part of the provisional expedition now organizing, because it was deemed impracticable to crowd the transport *Baltic* with all of the troops and material required; and with her large boats she was deemed indispensable to success. But the service of the ship had been anticipated, for on the 31st of March, as will be subsequently seen, in his interview with the President both the ship and her commander had been named by Captain Meigs, and there was at that time no mention of her in connection with other service until she was ready for sea. It was the intention that she should sail on the ad of April, but her condition was such as to render that impossible.

At 7 P. M. on that day (April 1) an order from the Secretary, of the Navy, revoking the previous order, directing the detachment of the officers and the transfer and discharge of the crew of

---

* Statement of Captain G. V. Fox.

the *Powhatan* was received by the commandant of the Brooklyn Navy Yard, who was directed to hold the ship in readiness for sea service. This was followed by a telegraphic order from the same source, and of the same date, to "fit out the ship to go to sea at the earliest possible moment." These orders were in the ordinary routine of the Navy Department. But upon the evening of the same day an order was received by telegram from the President himself, in similar language, with the addition that the ship was to sail under "sealed orders," and that orders would go forward by a confidential messenger upon the following day. On the 2d the recall of the officers of the *Powhatan* was directed by the Secretary of the Navy, who again, upon the following day, urged all despatch upon the commandant in preparing the vessel for sea. That officer at once devoted himself to the carrying out of his instructions, pushing the work by night and day, and by the 5th of April he informed the Department that the ship was ready for sea, and that she would drop down off the Battery at daylight and await the orders of the Secretary. The orders to guide the officer under whose command the naval force was placed were duly transmitted to him on the 5th of April. The steamers *Powhatan, Pocahontas, Pawnee* and *Harriet Lane* were to proceed under his command to the vicinity of Charleston, S. C., to assist an expedition in charge of the War Department. The primary object of the expedition was to provision Fort Sumter. If this was not resisted, no further special service would be required by his force, which was, in that event, to return to the North. If, however, resistance should be made, he was then to open the way to afford security for the boats, and to remove all obstructions and reinforce the fort by force. He was to co-operate with Captain Fox, who had charge of the expedition under the War Department. He was to leave New York with the *Powhatan* in time to be off Charleston bar, ten miles east of the light-house, on the morning of the 11th of April, there to await the arrival of the transports. After the service was rendered, the several vessels were to return to their respective posts. Upon the same day confidential communications were sent to the commanders of the several vessels composing the expedition, to report off Charleston bar on the 11th inst., in accordance with the orders given to the commanding officer of the *Powhatan* for special service, and to await his arrival if necessary. This expedition was contingent upon the necessity for its use, and, in the language of the President, "as well adapted as might be to relieve Fort Sumter, and it was intended to be ultimately used or not, according to circumstances."

The news of the failure to reinforce Fort Pickens reached the President in March, when the information was officially received that, "under the quasi armistice of the late administration" the company of artillery on board the Sabine had not been landed at Fort Pickens, as he had anticipated and directed. Unobstructed communication with that fort was possible by sea only, and it was now too late to renew it before the provisions at Fort Sumter would be wholly exhausted and the fort abandoned. In regard to the expedition provisionally prepared, the President believed, that "the strongest anticipated case for using it was now presented, and it was resolved to send it forward;"* and on the 4th of April Major Anderson was duly and officially informed of the determination of the Government by the Secretary of War.

Meanwhile, preparations for another expedition were in progress, which, although originating by the direct and personal authority of the President himself, were unusual, and so contrary to official custom and departmental routine that it is deemed proper, in view of the serious controversy which followed, to recount in detail the steps taken.

On the morning of the 29th of March a messenger was despatched by the Secretary of State, Mr. Seward, with a request to Captain M. C. Meigs, a prominent officer of the United States Engineers, then on duty in the city of Washington, to confer with him. Captain Meigs was at that time in charge of the extension of the Capitol and other public works, and was personally and favorably known to the Secretary. Upon the evening of that day, the Secretary, accompanied by Captain Meigs, proceeded to the President's residence, where, in a long interview—in which the possibility of relief to Fort Sumter was canvassed, and the subject of the reinforcement of Fort Pickens and the means to effect it were discussed—it was suggested by Captain Meigs that the danger of losing the fort lay principally in the transportation of troops in boats across the bay to attack it before a relieving expedition could be fitted out in the North and arrive there. He believed that a ship of war under some energetic officer of the Navy should be made

---

* President's message. Extra session of Congress, 1861.

ready for sea, and, if possible, reach Fort Pickens in time to anticipate any attack. The return from sea of the United States steamer *Powhatan* had been noticed, and she was mentioned in this connection by Captain Meigs as being immediately available.

The President seemed to be impressed with what had been said to him, and wholly favored the scheme.

Meantime it had become necessary to inform General Scott of the purpose of the President. On the morning of the 30th the Secretary of State proceeded to the headquarters of General Scott, whom he found at his desk, when the following interview took place: "Lieutenant-General Scott," said the Secretary, "you have advised the President that in your opinion it is *impossible* to reinforce Fort Sumter or Fort Pickens. I now come to you from the President, to say that he orders that Fort Pickens shall be reinforced, and that you give the necessary instructions." General Scott rose, and drawing himself up to his full height, replied: "Well, Mr. Secretary of State, the great Frederick used to say that, 'when the King commands, nothing is impossible.' The President's orders shall be obeyed, sir."*

But General Scott was not yet satisfied that the difficulties attending the reinforcement of Fort Pickens were thoroughly known, and accordingly, on the morning of the 31st of March, he sent his military secretary, Lieutenant-Colonel E. W. Keyes, to the Secretary of State. Colonel Keyes bore with him a map of Pensacola Harbor, upon which the difficulties of reinforcing Fort Pickens were to be explained. The Secretary at once ignored the "difficulties," and desired Colonel Keyes to find Captain Meigs immediately, and to return with him. Shortly afterward, finding Captain Meigs, they returned to the Secretary's residence, when he at once desired them to make a plan for the reinforcement of Fort Pickens, submit it to General Scott, and bring it to the President's mansion before 3 o'clock that afternoon. A plan looking to the complete reinforcement and supply of Fort Pickens was prepared by each. But upon the completion of their work it was found to be too late to consult General Scott and arrive at the President's mansion at the hour designated. They went directly to the executive mansion, where they found the President and Secretary awaiting them. The plans in detail were read by

* F. W. Seward, Ex-Assistant Secretary of State.

each. The President became bewildered at the scientific and technical detail, while the attentive and silent Secretary protested that he did not understand them. But there were no suggestions made or any modifications proposed.

It was at this interview that the name of Lieutenant D. D. Porter, United States Navy, was first suggested to the President by Captain Meigs as a suitable officer to command the man-of-war to be employed in the expedition. His daring achievement in his entrance with his ship into the harbor of Havana in 1854, in spite of the prohibition of the Governor-General of the island, was told to the President. He had inherited a name illustrious in naval annals, and he seemed from his personal characteristics to be eminently fitted for the service required. The whole subject was thoroughly discussed and determined upon at this interview, and immediately afterward assumed the shape of definite orders for its execution. The President simply directed that the plans should be taken to General Scott, who was to be told that he "wished this thing done," and that there must be no failure unless he refused something asked for as necessary. Prompt and immediate action was now taken. This same Sunday afternoon the officers mentioned submitted their plans to Lieutenant-General Scott, who after some discussion approved them, and undertook to give the necessary orders at once. At the latter part of this interview Secretary Seward was present.

On the 1st of April Lieutenant Porter was sent for by the Secretary of State. He reported to him upon the same day, when the Secretary informed him that it had been determined to save Fort Pickens, and asked if it were yet possible. Lieutenant Porter replied that it was possible, but that it was essential to adopt a very unusual course.

The plan submitted by Captain Meigs was again gone over by Lieutenant Porter, who urged its adoption upon the Secretary, at the same time explaining the naval details involved.

The Secretary was assured that, however practicable the scheme might be, it would be found to be impossible if the war vessel should be fitted out in the usual way. In that event the orders must pass through the ordinary channels of the Navy Department. As many of the clerks were suspected of secession sympathies, the news would be communicated and the fort would be taken. So he proposed to the Secretary that the *Powhatan,*

then lying at the Navy Yard at New York,' should at once be fitted out "by a secret order of the President." So much impressed was the Secretary by the proposition of Lieutenant Porter,
that he proposed to him to see the President, and in company with
Captain Meigs they proceeded to the Executive mansion. The
President entered heartily into the scheme—with which he was now
familiar, after his conversation with Captain Meigs—and readily
endorsed all the plans proposed. Recognizing the fact that the
procedure involved an ignoring of the Secretary of the Navy, he
thought that he could overcome that objection. No allusion was
made to any other expedition whatever, involving the use of the
Powhatan, as none such had yet been authorized, while the ship
had been named and her use recommended by Captain Meigs in
his interview with the President. The proposal of Lieutenant
Porter was naturally warmly supported by Captain Meigs, who had
originally proposed it. To him was committed the duty of accompanying the expedition as engineer officer, his rank not being sufficient to command, while to Lieutenant-Colonel Keyes was confided the preparation in New York of the direct military details
of the expedition. The orders to Lieutenant Porter directed him
to proceed with all despatch to the harbor of Pensacola in the
steamship *Powhatan,* to run into the harbor with his ship, to prevent any expedition from crossing to attack Fort Pickens, to
cover the landing of reinforcements, and to remain and protect the
fort with his guns.

But Captain Mercer was still in command of the *Powhatan.*
It now became necessary to detach him, when the following letter
was written by Lieutenant Porter and signed by the President.

"SIR: You will, on receipt of this order turn over the command of your vessel to Lieutenant David D. Porter, who is to
proceed in her on an important service.

"In depriving you of your command of your vessel I do not
desire in the least to reflect upon your zeal or patriotism; on the
contrary, I have the fullest confidence in your ability to perform
the duty in question. There are reasons, however, which make
it necessary for the officer who goes in command of the ship to
be well informed personally of my views and wishes, and time
will not admit of the delay necessary to communicate with you
personally.

"Having to give up your command, I can assure you that
you may ask of me the command of any other vessel, which will
be freely given to you. (Signed) "ABRAHAM LINCOLN,"

But it became equally necessary that the commandant of the New York Navy Yard should be informed of the new command, of the *Powhatan,* and of the urgent despatch and secrecy required, when the following despatch was written by Lieutenant Porter, and also signed by the President:

"SIR: Lieutenant David D. Porter is directed by me to assume command of the United States frigate *Powhaton,* and goes on important duty, which it is desirable he should accomplish without delay, and you will, therefore, give him every aid in fitting out the vessel. The duty is to be performed with the greatest secrecy.

(Signed) " ABRAHAM LINCOLN. "

This was an extraordinary course to pursue, and only to be justified by the exigency and the high source that directed it, and from which there was no appeal. These communications were both committed to Lieutenant Porter, to be delivered in person to the officer addressed, and it was thus, under two distinct sources of authority, unknown to each other, and both entitled to obedience and respect, that the *Powhatan* was made ready for sea service.

But before proceeding to fit out the expedition, it became necessary to arrange for the funds requisite to carry it forward, and a difficulty presented itself which threatened to postpone, if not to prevent entirely, the success of the expedition. Congress had adjourned without making provision for any military or naval secret-service fund for those departments. The expedition proposed was an extraordinary one, and its incidental expenses must be met by funds for such service. There were funds for ordinary expenses, with open accounts, but to use them publicly would be to make known and render futile the proposed expedition.

There was but one officer of the Government who had at his command any secret-service fund, and this was the Secretary of State. He was in possession of a fund which he was entitled to expend for secret purposes. Of such expenditure no record was to be made. According to law, the moneys were to be paid, and the approval of the President settled the account. An entry of the President's sanction and order was the only record made of the transaction. When, therefore, upon the statement of Captain Meigs, that $10,000 would be required, the Secretary of State proceeded to his Department, procured the amount in coin, and for greater privacy went to his own residence and there transferred the sum to Captain Meigs, who gave his receipt for it and for the incidental expenses of the expedition, turning over to Colonel Keyes and Lieutenant Porter the sums necessary for their immediate use. The expedition itself was fitted out by the Quartermaster's Department, Colonel Keyes conducting the negotiations for the hire of the steamer, while the charter-party was executed by the Department quartermaster. The *Atlantic* was to go at once, other vessels were to follow, and the safety of the forts in the Gulf was to be assured. On the conclusion of the expedition, Captain Meigs returned to the Government the unexpended balance of the fund entrusted to him, amounting to nearly $6,000.

On the 1st of April Lieutenant Porter left for New York, under the general public impression that he was *en route* for California. Captain Meigs followed the next day. Upon the morning of the 2d Lieutenant Porter reported in person to the acting commandant of the Navy Yard (Foote), and presented to him the orders of the President. That officer was naturally "very much astonished" at a proceeding so unusual and so contrary to all naval and official precedent; and even the name and signature of the President failed to reconcile him, nor did he inform Lieutenant Porter of the order he had received and acknowledged, at 7 P. M. the previous day from the Secretary of the Navy, to refit the *Powhatan* with "the quickest despatch," which had been repeated by telegram twice upon that day.

The commandant hesitated to obey the order of the President, and insisted upon telegraphing to the Secretary for instructions.* But the secrecy of the orders, and their high source, was insisted upon; the particulars of the enterprise were all made known to him before he would consent; and after a deliberation of two hours, the commandant at last concluded to act. The ship was at that moment all dismantled. She had been surveyed, and pronounced unseaworthy; her boilers were worn out, her hull was rotten, her machinery was all apart, her stores had been removed, her crew transferred to the receiving ship, and her officers allowed to go home. The captain was the only officer who remained, and he was anticipating his detachment. The commandant pronounced the ship unfit to go, but it was impossible to delay, and

---

* "Porter, these are ticklish times. How do I know that you are not going to run off with the ship? I must telegraph immediately to the Secretary," –Admiral Porter to author.

Lieutenant Porter resolved to take her as she was. It now became necessary to inform the captain of the ship of the intentions of the President, and to admit him into the confidence of the transaction. The letter of the President gratified him, and he had no regrets that the course of events had excluded him from an active participation in the expedition. He thought the ship unfit for service, and that she would be knocked to pieces in going into Pensacola; but he at once took charge of the refitting of the ship, recalled his officers and laid in the necessary stores, as if personally concerned. The *Powhatan* was fitted for sea with a rapidity that was wholly unprecedented. The work was pushed by night and by day, and it is probable that no such task was ever accomplished in less time; when on the evening of the 5th of April the commandant of the yard was enabled to report to the Secretary that she was ready, and would leave her berth on the following morning and await his orders.

Meantime, Lieutenant Porter had not shown himself at the Navy Yard or at the ship, and his connection with her remained generally unknown. When the ship was ready, his luggage was sent on board marked "American Minister, Vera Cruz," which seemed to decide the destination of the ship. The commandant had apprised the Secretary of the visit of Captain Meigs to him, and the authority of the Government he bore, to make certain preparations and to ship certain articles. The orders did not come directly to him, but he had gone on with the preparations desired, in order to save time, and would report his action, and that he was executing orders received from the Government through both Navy and Army officers.

It would appear, from the communication made to the Navy Department by the commandant, that something unusual was in progress at the Brooklyn Navy Yard, but it does not seem that any suspicion was awakened in the mind of the Secretary that the destination of the *Powhatan* was other than that intended and ordered by him, until she was reported as "ready to sail" and awaiting his orders. He now determined to retain the ship, and on the morning of the 5th he transmitted a telegram personally to the commandant in New York, directing him to delay the *Powhatan* for further instructions. The receipt of this telegram produced so decided an impression upon the mind of the commandant that he determined that it was his duty to obey the last order, but the President's order and signature was again shown to him, and insisted upon by Lieutenant Porter as taking precedence, notwithstanding the priority of date. The captain of the ship had come to a similar decision, and felt obliged to give up the command. Captain Meigs was of a similar opinion, and it was determined that the ship should sail on that day, the 6th, at 1 o'clock. Upon the receipt of the Secretary's telegram, both Lieutenant Porter and Captain Meigs put themselves in communication with the Secretary of State. Lieutenant Porter informed him that the Secretary of the Navy had altered the destination of the *Powhatan,* and asked whether this or the President's order was to be obeyed. If the former, Colonel Brown would be "entirely crippled." The following telegram was sent to the Secretary of State by Captain Meigs:

"NEW YORK, April 5, 1861.

"HON. W. H. SEWARD:

"*Powhatan* was ready to sail at 6 P. M.; telegram received by Captain Foote, commandant of Navy Yard, to detain. First, disobedience of orders, came through Stringham; second, Secretary of the Navy. President's orders were to sail as soon as ready. This is fatal; what is to be done ? Answer 110 Astor House.

M . C . MEIGS."

But without awaiting a reply, it was determined that the ship should sail that evening, notwithstanding the receipt of a telegram from the Navy Department that an officer would deliver a despatch, and accordingly, at 1 o'clock P. M. on the 6th, she left her moorings with Captain Mercer in command—and with Lieutenant Porter unseen and unknown, seated in the stateroom of the captain—and steamed down the harbor. When opposite Staten Island the engines stopped, and sending for the ship's First Lieutenant, Captain Mercer introduced him to Lieutenant Porter as the future commander of the ship, and putting on citizen's dress, went at once ashore. Directing the executive officer not to mention his presence until the pilot had left the ship, Lieutenant Porter remained in his stateroom. The *Powhatan* had hardly left to go down the harbor when a telegram from the Secretary of State arrived for Lieutenant Porter. The commandant of the Navy Yard at once despatched an officer to employ a fast vessel in New York and go in pursuit, and the ship was only just under way again after the departure of Captain Mercer, when a small but swift steamer was seen approaching, and making signals that she desired to communicate with her. Again the engines stopped, when an officer went on board and delivered to Lieutenant Porter the following telegraphic despatch:

> "Deliver up the *Powhatan* to Captain Mercer.
> (Signed) "W. H. SEWARD."

Porter at once replied:

"I have received orders from the President which I cannot disobey;" and at the same time he transmitted a verbal message to Commander Foote, that he regretted that the despatch came too late to change his plans, as the *Atlantic,* which he was to convoy, had already gone to sea.

The telegram and message were committed to the officer, who left the ship, which proceeded immediately and rapidly to sea.

Meanwhile a change in the relative condition of things at Pensacola had taken place, which from its very nature could not be known to Lieutenant Porter, now coming in the *Powhatan.* Lieutenant Slemmer, the commandant of Fort Pickens, believing that an attack upon him was threatened, had officially applied for assistance on the 12th of April. He was yet in correspondence with Captain H. A. Adams, of the *Sabine,* as to the necessity, when Lieutenant Worden, of the Navy, arrived from Washington with the renewed order to land the company of artillery, which was at once accomplished, and had thus partially reinforced the fort six days after the sailing of the *Atlantic.*

That ship, with the troops and material under Colonel Harvey Brown, with Captain Meigs on board as the engineer to the expedition, had arrived on the 16th, and her stores were being rapidly landed, when on the morning of the 17th the *Powhatan* hove in sight off the harbor.

The situation had wholly changed, and Colonel Brown, the officer now in command, naturally considered that the entrance at this time of a ship of war into the channel would bring on a collision which might threaten the success of his operations.

He therefore directed Captain Meigs to hail and board the *Powhatan,* and inform its commander of the exact status of things. Meantime Porter was coming in rapidly with his ship, which he had disguised as a British man-of-war, her thick smoke from soft coal aiding in misleading as to her nationality. He had hoisted the British colors, intending to run in with them under the enemy's guns, and then to display the national flag, and he was making directly for the channel upon which bore the guns of Forts MCRae and Barrancas. His port battery was ready for action, his extra ports being filled with guns, when Meigs in the *Wyandotte* appeared, making constant signals. Disregarding these, Porter changed his course to avoid them, when the *Wyandotte* was thrown across the ship's path, and Porter reluctantly stopped. Meigs boarded at once, when the new situation was explained. Lieutenant Porter yielded, and soon after brought his ship to anchor near the *Atlantic* to cover the landing of her stores.

With the men and stores from the *Atlantic,* Fort Pickens had now been reinforced and supplied, and the valuable harbor of Pensacola thus saved to the nation.

The fleet intended for the relief of Sumter had now put to sea. Before it sailed, it had been suggested by Captain Fox "to the Secretary of the Navy, to place Commodore Stringham in command of the naval force,' but that officer thought it now too late to succeed, and that it would jeopardize the reputation of the officer who should undertake it, and the fleet sailed without any instructions and without a head. Captain Mercer, when relieved from his ship by the President's order, wisely transmitted a copy of the secret orders to him from the Navy Department of the 5th instant, through Captain Faunce, of the *Harriet Lane,* directing him at the same time to report to the senior naval officer he might find off Charleston.   The *Harriet Lane* sailed on the 8th, and was the first to arrive off Charleston bar; the tugs *Uncle Ben* and Yankee, together with the transport *Baltic,* with the troops and material on board, dropped down to Sandy Hook on the same day, and went to sea on the 9th at 8 A. M. The *Pawnee* sailed promptly on the 9th, the *Pocahontas* only on the 10th. She was the last to sail and the last to arrive. Captain Fox, in charge of the expedition, embarked on board of the transport *Baltic* with First Lieutenant Edw. McK. Hudson, Fourth Artillery, in command of the troops, with First Lieutenants R. O. Tyler, Third Artillery and C. W. Thomas, of the First Infantry regiment, as subordinates. Hardly had the fleet got off the coast when it encountered a heavy northeast gale, which continued during the passage. Before daylight on the 12th, the rendezvous agreed upon was reached off the Charleston bar. The *Harriet Lane* had already arrived, but at 6 A. M. the *Pawnee* was seen, and shortly after was boarded by Captain Fox, who then informed Commander Rowan of his orders from the Secretary of War, and requested him "to stand in for the bar" with him. This that officer declined to do. He replied that his orders required. him to remain "ten miles east of the light and await the *Powkatan,* and that he was not going in there to begin civil war."* The *Baltic* then went in, followed by the *Harriet Lane.* As they approached the land, the firing of the guns at Sumter was

PARAPET OF GORGE TOWARDS CUMMINGS POINT, PAGE 433.

heard, and the smoke and shells of the batteries "were distinctly visible." Commander Rowan having received his orders by the *Harriet Lane,* was now coming in with his ship. Comprehending at once the situation, he asked for a pilot, and announced his intention of running in and sharing the fate of the garrison. Captain Fox went at once on board, and explained to him "that the Government did not expect such gallant sacrifice"

---

* Contributions of the old Residents' Historical Association, Lowell, Mass. Vol. II, No. 1, p. 48.

in the instructions given either to Captain Mercer or to himself. The 12th passed without the arrival of any other vessels of the fleet; some merchant vessels lingered about the rendezvous, giving indication of a large naval fleet off the bar. Anticipating the arrival of the *Powhatan* during the night, and yet ignorant of her change of destination, Captain Fox returned in the *Baltic* to the rendezvous and signalled for her all night. Neither the *Pawnee* nor the Harriet Lane was furnished with the proper boats to carry in supplies or troops to the fort, when Lieutenant Tyler, a zealous and efficient officer attached to the troops, organized a boat's crew, and notwithstanding the heavy sea prepared them for service, that there might be "at least one boat by which to reach Sumter." The ground swell was so heavy that the *Baltic,* in steaming towards the harbor, ran aground on Rattlesnake Shoals, and was subsequently obliged to anchor in deep water, several miles away from the ships of war.

The bombardment was now at its height; the quarters were in flames, and the flash of Anderson's guns could be distinctly seen from the fleet as he strove to reply to the enemy's fire, his guns sounding like signals of distress. There was no movement for his relief, "as it was the opinion of the officers that loaded boats could not reach Sumter in such a heavy sea." None of the tug-boats had arrived, when a schooner loaded with ice was seized and preparations made to use her in lieu of them on "the following night." At 2 o'clock, the *Pocahontas* at last arrived. The flag-staff of the fort had been shot away at 1:30 P. M. and the firing shortly afterward ceased. It was on the morning of this day that, for the first time, Captain Fox was apprised that the captain of the *Powhatan* had informed Commander Rowan, on the 6th, of the special service of the ship elsewhere, under superior authority. Although the *Baltic* did not leave New York until two days afterward, no information of this fact was communicated to Captain Fox. Upon his arrival the commanding officer of the *Pocahontas* manifested every disposition to go to the relief of the fort and to attempt to pass the batteries, "as the impulse was strong to render assistance;" but there were no pilots for the channel on board. The buoys and marks had all been removed, and he feared that his ship would run aground. Preparations were made, however, under a proposition of Captain Fox and Lieutenant Hudson, to run provisions and some men into Sumter that night in the schooner, accompanied by boats containing some of the ship's crew, but the cessation of the firing, and the arrangements for the evacuation soon after, rendered the attempt unnecessary.

The northeast gale that had detained the war ships had been equally severe upon the tugs. The owners of the tug *Freeborn* prevented her leaving New York at all. "The *Uncle Ben* was driven into Wilmington, N. C., and seized by the rebels."* The gale drove the tug *Yankee* to the entrance of Savannah, and she repassed Charleston only after the transport Baltic had returned to the North. Thus almost every element that was essential to the success of the expedition was wanting. As it failed, it is impossible to estimate what might otherwise have been the result. The secrecy of the instructions which required the different use of the *Powhatan* had been so carefully observed that Captain Fox had depended upon her as the flag-ship of the little fleet, and her detachment, in his estimation, largely increased the risk of failure. But it was all too late—too late in conception, too late in execution; mainly due to the political exigency that existed. Much was left to hazard, and the information sent to the authorities in Charleston of the intention of the Government at once precipitated the collision. Had the *Powhatan* remained with the fleet, her usefulness, even had she arrived in time, is questionable. She could not pass the bar, drawing as she did twenty-one feet, and her boats, so much relied upon, were worthless for service, and swamped when put into the water. Had she lost a man overboard, it would have been impossible to save him by her boats. The storm dispersed the tugs when the conditions for their use were most urgent, and the *Pocahontas* arrived only in time to witness the surrender.

In thus taking the *Powhatan,* it is certain that the President and the Secretary of State were not aware of any intention or action of the Secretary of the Navy in regard to her. There was no desire to slight either the War or Navy departments. They were yet in an unorganized condition and the Secretary of State did not even trust his own Department, and nothing at that time was more natural than to conceal, as far as possible, an important transaction whose success depended upon its secrecy; but why the Secretary of the Navy, the chosen and trusted coun-

* Captain Fox's statement.

sellor of the President should have been included in this determination, is not so clear, unless the reasons previously given should
fully account for it. The Secretary of State had not favored
the expedition. He had believed that it would bring on a collision
and inaugurate war. He had, however, no idea of thwarting the
Secretary of the Navy, for upon the demand of that official he
made every effort to transfer the ship to him.

The President himself was surprised at the confusion resulting
from the conflicting orders emanating from the Navy Department
and himself, but while regretting the failure to relieve Fort Sumter,
he was gratified at the reinforcement of Fort Pickens, and
rewarded the officers connected with the expedition. At the same
time, he was not without misgivings lest he should have done
injustice to a gallant officer, and with characteristic generosity
he assumed the responsibility, and transmitted to Captain Fox the
following communication:

"WASHINGTON, D. C., May 1, 1861.
"CAPTAIN G. V. FOX.

"My Dear Sir: I sincerely regret that the failure of the
late attempt to provision Fort Sumter should be the source of
any annoyance to you.   The practicability of your plan was not,
in fact, brought to a test.

"By reason of a gale, well known in advance to be possible,
and not improbable, the tugs, an essential part of the plan, never
reached the ground, while by an accident, for which you were in
nowise responsible, and possibly I to some extent was, you were
deprived of a war vessel, with her men, which you deemed of
great importance to the enterprise. I most cheerfully and truly
declare that the failure of the undertaking has not lowered you a
particle, while the qualities you developed in the effort have
greatly heightened you, in my estimation. For a daring and
dangerous enterprise of a similar character you would to-day be
the man of all my acquaintances whom I would select. You and
I both anticipated that the cause of the country would be
advanced by making the attempt to provision Fort Sumter, even
if it should fail; and it is no small consolation now to feel that
our anticipation. is justified by the result.

"Very truly, your friend,
"A. LINCOLN."

CHAPTER XXXI.

Effect of notice of President upon authorities in Charleston–Their action–
Reply of Montgomery Government–Demand for the immediate surrender
of the fort–Anderson's reply–Verbal statement to the messenger–Reported to Montgomery–Reply of Confederate Secretary of War–Anderson
declines its terms–Bombardment opened on morning of the 12th of April–
Description of the fire of the batteries–Maintained all day–Mortar fire all
night–Sumter opens fire at 7 o'clock–Service of its batteries–Effect
of the enemy's fire upon the fort–Fleet arrives–Men withdrawn from the
batteries at night.

THE intention of the President to attempt relief to Fort Sumter, as made known to the authorities at Charleston, produced an
effect and action immediate and decided. A telegram was at
once despatched to the Confederate Secretary of War by the
general commanding at Charleston, informing him of the arrival
of the messenger from the President of the United States, and of
his purpose to provision Fort Sumter "peaceably if they can,
forcibly if they must." The receipt of the telegram gave rise to
an extended discussion in the Confederate Cabinet. While it
was under discussion Mr. Toombs, the Secretary of State, came
in, when-the telegram was handed to him. Upon reading it, he
said, "The firing upon that fort will inaugurate a civil war greater
than any the world has yet seen; and I do not feel, competent to
advise you."* Any reply to the telegram was delayed until the
morning of the 10th, when the following despatch was sent to the
general commanding at Charleston:

"If you have no doubt of the authorized character of the
agent who communicated to you the intention of the Washington
Government to supply Fort Sumter by force, you will at once
demand its evacuation and, if this is refused, proceed in such
manner as you may determine to reduce it.   Answer.
                                      "L.P. WALKER."

To this the commanding general immediately replied that the
demand would be made at 12 o'clock upon the following day

---

* L. P. Walker to writer.

(11th April). But the authorities at Montgomery considered that unless there were "special reasons" connected with his own condition, the demand should be made earlier. The reasons were "special," although not communicated. The supply of powder on hand was insufficient for more than a few hours' bombardment, and the commanding general was unwilling to open his batteries unless with a supply on hand to last him for forty-eight hours. Such supply had been contracted for in Augusta, Ga., and only arrived that evening.

The action of the Montgomery Cabinet was unavoidable, and, in a manner, forced upon it. The current of events had set manifestly towards the near commencement of hostilities, but it was hoped by those in favor of a peaceful settlement that something might yet be gained by delay. A large number of influential men had not yet defined their position. In the harbor of Charleston the preparations for an attack were not complete, and the Confederate Commissioners were yet in Washington. But the communication of the President precipitated the issue, and forced it to an unavoidable conclusion. The temper of South Carolina was well known. Her people had long chafed under the restraint that prevented her from taking possession of a fort that controlled her principal harbor, and, through her Governor, her Legislature and her Convention, had again and again asserted her anxious desire and her deliberate purpose. Hesitation now upon the part of the Governor, to which she had entrusted this vital interest, would have been fatal. The anticipation too that the State would herself act—and thus inaugurate separate State action, which, if followed by the other seceded States would have thrown the new Confederacy into confusion at its very birth—greatly influenced the action of the Government at Montgomery. The end had been reached, and the demand for the immediate surrender of the fort was now to be made with all the formality and authority of the Confederate Government. Shortly after noon on the 11th of April a boat flying a white flag pushed off from a wharf in Charleston, and made its way down the harbor towards Fort Sumter. In her stern sat three men. They were: Colonel James Chesnut, recently United States Senator from South Carolina; Captain Stephen D. Lee, a graduate of West Point, who had resigned his commission in the United States Army, and who, with his companion, was an A. D. C.

of the commanding general. The third was Lieutenant-Colonel Chisholm, an aide-de-camp and representative of the Governor of the State. At half-past three the boat arrived at Fort Sumter, where it was met by Lieutenant J. C. Davis, the officer of the day, and its occupants at once conducted to the guard-room, where they were met by Major Anderson in person. The object of the visit was soon declared. They bore a communication from the Confederate general to Major Anderson demanding the evacuation of the work. Believing, he said, that an amicable settlement would be reached, and to avert war, the Confederate Government had made no demand for its surrender, but they could now no longer refrain, and in obedience to the orders of his Government he demanded the evacuation of the work. His aides were authorized to make such a demand. "All proper facilities will be afforded for the removal of yourself and command, together with company arms and property, and all private property, to any post in the United States you may select. The flag which you have upheld so long, and with so much fortitude, under the most trying circumstances, may be saluted by you on taking it down." Anderson at once summoned his officers, who gathered in silence around him, when he announced to them that he had a communication to make, that not only involved their position but possibly their lives, and he submitted the demand of the Confederate general.

The session lasted for an hour, when the whole subject of the position was gone over, and when for the first time the confidential communication of December, 1860, by Major John Withers was made known to the officers. The decision was soon reached, and it was determined without dissent to refuse the demand, when the following response was made by Major Anderson and handed to the messengers:

"FORT SUMTER, S. C., April 11, 1861.
"GENERAL: I have the honor to acknowledge the receipt of your communication demanding the evacuation of this fort, and to say, in reply thereto, that it is a demand with which I regret that my sense of honor, and of my obligations to my Government, prevent my compliance. Thanking you for the fair, manly and courteous terms proposed, and for the high compliment paid me,
"I am, General, very respectfully, &c."

The messengers at once, and without further conversation,

took their leave. Anderson accompanied them as far as the main gate, where he remained; and as the messengers were about to enter their boat a few yards distant, he asked, "Will General Beauregard open his batteries without further notice to me?" This interrogatory caused a momentary hesitation and embarrassment, when Colonel Chesnut replied, "I think not," and finally said, "No, I can say to you that he will not, without giving you further notice." Anderson then remarked that he would await the first shot, but that he would be starved out anyway in a few days, if General Beauregard did not batter him to pieces with his guns.

This remark was but partially heard by the messengers, who had now entered their boat. The writer was present, when Colonel Chesnut asked him in regard to the remark of Anderson, when, upon a request to that effect, Major Anderson repeated it. Colonel Chesnut then asked if he might report it to General Beauregard. Anderson declined to give it the character of a report, but stated that it was the fact of the case. The boat then left the work. Within the fort, the men had already become aware of the nature of the visit, and manifested the greatest enthusiasm. The little that remained to be done upon the parapet was now rapidly completed. The day closed without further action, and the garrison had gone to rest, when at 1 o'clock. on the morning of the 12th a boat again approached the work and was hailed by the sentinel. It contained Colonel Chesnut and Captain Lee, two of the aides of the Confederate general, who had returned with the final proposition of the Confederate authorities.

The refusal of Anderson, as well as his verbal statement as to his condition, had been promptly telegraphed to Montgomery by the commanding general. The reply was immediate, and as follows;

MONTGOMERY, April 11, 1861.

"GENERAL BEAUREGARD: Do not desire needlessly to bombard Fort Sumter. If Major Anderson will state the time at which, as indicated by him, he will evacuate, and agree that in the meantime he will not use his guns against us unless ours should be employed against Fort Sumter, you are authorized thus to avoid the effusion of blood. If this, or its equivalent, be refused, reduce the fort as your judgment decides to be most practicable.

"L. P. WALKER."

It was this proposition that was now presented to Major Anderson, when he again summoned his officers, and a long and protracted conference took place, in which all the officers took part. The principal question considered was, how long the garrison could hold out effectually with the insufficient supply of food, now beginning to be felt by the men. It was greatly desired that the fort should hold out at least until the date specified as desirable by the Government, the 15th instant. The professional opinion of the writer, which was called for by Major Anderson, was given to the effect that the men could hold out for five days, when they would be three days entirely without food. There was no thought of according to the proposal made to reserve or restrain the fire of the fort, and no consideration given except to reject it, and Major Anderson replied in a written communication to the messengers, as follows:

4.] "FORT SUMTER, S. C., April 12, 1861.
   "GENERAL: I have the honor to acknowledge the receipt by Colonel Chesnut of your second communication of the 11th instant, and to state in reply that, cordially uniting with you in the desire to avoid the useless effusion of blood, I will, if provided with the proper and necessary means of transportation, evacuate Fort Sumter by noon on the 15th instant, and that I will not in the meantime open my fires upon your forces unless compelled to do so by some hostile act against this fort or the flag of my Government, by the forces under your command, or by some portion of them, or by the perpetration of some act showing a hostile intention on your part against this fort or the flag it bears, should I not receive prior to that time controlling instructions from my Government or additional supplies.

   "I am, General, very respectfully, your obedient servant,
                              "ROBERT ANDERSON,
                    "Major, First Artillery, Commanding.
"Brig.-Gen. BEAUREGARD, *Commanding."*

Three hours had been consumed in the discussion of the subject, which was commented upon by the messengers in their report of their mission, who thought that a longer time was taken than was necessary to decide upon their communication, but that they could not prevent it.

The terms of this reply were considered by the messengers as "manifestly futile;" and, as far as they were concerned, as placing them at a great disadvantage, and not within the scope of the verbal instructions given to them. They promptly refused them, and handed to Major Anderson the following notice:

"FORT SUMTER, April 12, 1861.
"3:30 A.M.

"SIR: By authority of Brigadier-General Beauregard, commanding the provisional forces of the Confederate States, we have the honor to notify you that he will open the fire of his batteries on Fort Sumter in one hour from this time.

"We have the honor, &c.,

"CHESNUT,
"LEE."

PARAPET OF FORT SUMTER AFTER BOMBARDMENT, PAGE 443.

The messengers now hastily took their leave. The batteries around were lighted, their fires burning brightly, as the busy hum of preparation was borne across the water to the beleaguered fort. Anderson, accompanied by his officers, then went through the casemates where the men were quartered and sleeping; he aroused them, informing them of the impending attack, and directed them not to move until they had received orders from him; that he would not open fire until daylight, and that they were then to fire slowly and carefully.

The sea was calm, and the night still under the bright starlight,

when at 4:30 A. M. the sound of a mortar from a battery at Fort
Johnson broke upon the stillness. It was the signal to the batteries around to open fire. The shell, fired by Captain George
S. James, who commanded the battery, rose high in air, and
curving in its course, burst almost directly over the fort. A silence
followed for a few moments, when a gun opened from the Iron-
clad battery on Cummings Point. It was fired by Edward Ruffin of Virginia, who had volunteered for the service. Hardly had
the echo of this opening gun died upon the air, when the mortars
nearest to the fort opened their fire, which was at once followed
by others in the neighborhood, and in succession by the batteries
around, until the fort was "surrounded by a circle of fire." At
a distance between 1,200 and 1,300 yards from the fort, and nearest to it upon Cummings Point, an array of heavy armament had
been established, whose construction had been anxiously watched
by the garrison, and whose value was now to be tested. There
were three distinct batteries, the result of protracted labor and
of engineering skill. Upon the right was the "Trapier" battery,
consisting of three 10-inch mortars, well placed and protected.
On the left stood the "Point" battery, consisting of three 10-inch
mortars, two 42-pound guns, and one 12-pound rifled Blakeley.
In the centre rose the Iron-clad battery, mounting three 8-inch
Columbiads. The mortars in the "Trapier" battery, under the
command of Captain J. Gadsden King, with the Marion Artillery,
of Charleston, opened their fire immediately after the signal gun.
They were followed by the mortars in the Point battery, which, in
connection with the Iron-clad battery, were assigned to the supervision of Major P. F. Stevens, of the Citadel Academy, in Charleston. They were manned by the Palmetto Guard under Captain
G. B. Cuthbert.

Fort Moultrie was ready with its fire, and opened with its
guns and neighboring mortars soon after the opening gun was
fired from Cummings Point. Of the thirty guns constituting its
armament, nine bore directly upon Sumter, and were designated
as the "Sumter/battery," and were under. the immediate command of Lieutenants Alfred Rhett and Mitchell, They were the
heaviest of the ordnance of Fort Moultrie, and included the guns
that had been spiked and whose carriages had been destroyed
by Major Anderson upon his movement from Fort Moultrie to
Fort Sumter, The batteries upon Sullivan's island were com-

manded by Lieutenant-Colonel R. S. Ripley, an able and experienced officer of artillery, long an officer of the old army, and
whose name and service became identified with the defense of
Charleston Harbor until the last. "Of these batteries, three
8-inch Columbiads, two 32-pounders and six 24-pounders in Fort
Moultrie; two 24-pounders and two 32-pounders in the enfilade
battery; one 9-inch Dahlgren gun, two 32-pounders, two 42-
pounders at the 'Point,' and on board the floating battery, and
the six 10-inch mortars—bore upon Fort Sumter."* The fire,

MAIN GATE, SALLY-PORT OF GORGE, AFTER BOMBARDMENT OF 1863.

from Moultrie was at first wanting in precision, the shots passing
over the work; but with the advancing daylight this was soon
corrected, until almost every shot took effect, either striking the
scarp wall, or, passing closely over the crest, plunged into the
quarters on the gorge wall opposite. These were soon destroyed.
Projecting above the crest of the walls, the roofs and gables
afforded the easiest marks, and were soon riddled by the shots.

* Ripley's report, p. 39, "War of the Rebellion." Vol. I., Series I.

The fire was steadily kept up through the day-and only lessened upon the approach of night.

The enfilading and adjoining batteries at the north end of Sullivan's Island, under the command of Capt. J. H. Hallonquist, opened fire early on the morning of the 12th and maintained it steadily through the day. Their fire was especially directed upon the parapet of Fort Sumter. The enfilading battery mounted two 32-pound and two 42-pound guns. It was this battery which was suddenly unmasked on the morning of the 9th of April, and which so impressed Major Anderson. Taking the most important battery upon the parapet in reverse, its guns were so actively worked, and at such short intervals of fire, that six hundred and eleven shots were fired from it alone. "The object of our firing," said the officer who immediately commanded it,* in his official report, "was to sweep the crest of the parapet, the roofs of the quarters within Fort Sumter, to dismount the bar-bette guns, if practicable, and to drive the enemy from the parapet. The latter object was accomplished."†

The floating battery of Captain Hamilton, at the extreme northern end of the island, also opened promptly, and maintained its fire from its two 32 and two 42 pound guns, under the direct command of Lieutenant Yates, but with less effect than had been anticipated by the garrison. The mortar batteries upon Johnson and at Mount Pleasant were also served steadily, and added to the effective fire. To the fire of the two 10-inch mortars at Mount Pleasant no response was made by the garrison of Fort Sumter.

It was not until 7 o'clock that Fort Sumter opened its fire. Its entire armament now consisted of forty-eight available guns in casemate and barbette, with five 8-inch and 10-inch Columbiads on the parade, and so mounted as to bear upon the city, Fort Moultrie and the batteries at Cummings Point. The details to serve the guns had been made from Captain Double-day's company. There were three. The first, commanded by Captain Doubleday in person, took position at the battery of the two 32-pounders, in the right gorge angle on the lower tier, and which bore upon the batteries at Cummings Point. It

---

  * Lieutenant Jacob Valentine.

  † The troops were withdrawn from the parapet by Major Anderson's order, as will be subsequently seen.

was the first to open fire, and one of its shots "passed a few feet above the upper bolts of the shed."* A constant and heavy fire was maintained all day, producing but little effect, the balls glancing harmlessly off the iron roof of the battery, that answered with its three 8-inch Columbiads effectively. This, with the 12-pound rifled Blakeley, well served, together with the three 10-inch mortars of the Point battery and the two 42-pounders, poured their fire at regular intervals through the whole day upon the fort in answer to its guns.

The second detail was under the command of First Lieutenant J. C. Davis. It manned the guns on the left of Doubleday.†

The third detail was under the command of Assistant Surgeon Crawford. It manned the three 32-pounders on the western face of the work, and opened fire upon the floating battery at the upper end of Sullivan's Island, as well as upon the enfilading battery and heavy Dahlgren gun that had opened early and whose fire was sweeping the parapet.

The effect of the fire upon the floating battery was slight. Nearly all of the shot failed to penetrate the roof, and were deflected; one only, striking the angle between the front and roof, penetrated through the iron covering and woodwork beneath. The sea wall behind which it had taken position protected its water line from our ricochet shots. This battery with its 32-pounders, from which so much was expected on both sides, failed to realize the hopes or fears so long formed of it. Failing to produce any sensible effects from his fire, the writer sought Major Anderson, and requested authority to move his command along the casemates on the right to a battery of one 42 and two 32 pounders that bore directly upon Moultrie, whose fire had been steadily kept up upon the fort since the early opening of its guns and without reply from the fort.

Major Anderson was in the magazine, whose exposed condition already caused him anxiety. He gave the requisite authority, and moving the men, fire was opened at once in reply to Moultrie, and maintained for four hours, when the writer was relieved by Lieutenant R. K. Meade, who continued the fire until night

---

* Captain Cuthbert, South Carolina Infantry. Official report, p. 54, "War of the Rebellion;" Vol. I, Series I.

† There is no record of this service.

Meantime, Captain Seymour relieved Doubleday at the batteries and maintained their fire for several hours.

A few shots were fired at the mortar batteries at Fort Johnson by Captain Seymour, but with no appreciable effect. It was now noon. The constant fire of the fort had largely reduced the number of cartridges. There were but seven hundred when the fire began, and the six needles were kept busy in their manufacture, but the supply was now so reduced that the fire of the fort slackened, and was at last confined to six guns: two bearing upon Cummings Point, two upon Moultrie and two upon the batteries upon the western end of Sullivan's Island. The effect of the vertical fire of the mortars, and of the enfilading batteries upon the parapet, was so soon manifested that Anderson determined not to serve the guns *en barbette* at all. He took, he said, the whole responsibility, and would not expose his men to a fire in reverse that would be fatal. The men were at once withdrawn from the parapet by Anderson's order. And thus the long toil and engineering care expended upon the erection of the most formidable battery in the fort, and whose construction was wholly in reference to the array of heavy armament at Cummings Point, was lost. The guns thus left to the sport of the enemy's fire were the heaviest in calibre, and must if properly served have produced a serious effect.

The men displayed great enthusiasm, and even the workmen caught the spirit of the hour and helped to serve the guns. After the abandonment of the casemate by Doubleday's command, by Anderson's order, a party of the workmen who had been watching the firing, voluntarily took possession of the battery and renewed the fire on Cummings Point, when they were "organized into a firing party."

Knowing that the guns on the parapet were loaded and trailed, one of the men made his way to them, and without orders fired them." In the discharge of one 10-inch Columbiad, the proper arrangements for controlling the recoil of the piece were neglected, and running back off its chassis it entirely overturned, dismounting an 8-inch seacoast howitzer next to it and adding greatly to the appearance of destruction produced by the fire. The rapid fire from Moultrie dismounted one 8-inch

---

* Private Carmody, Co. E.

Columbiad and cracked another on the right flank of the work in the barbette tier. The fire from the enemy's mortars upon the parapet, and especially that from the enfilading battery and from the "Sumter battery" of Moultrie, besides silencing the guns *en barbette,* completely riddled the officers' quarters above the lowest story. Three times the quarters were set on fire by shells from Cummings Point and by hot shot from Moultrie, but this was promptly extinguished, and mainly by the active co-operation of Sergeant Peter Hart, an old soldier who had seen service with Anderson as first sergeant, and had come to him voluntarily and was now employed as a workman by the engineer.

The enemy's shots had cut the iron cisterns over the hallways, and the rush of water aided in controlling the fire. It was now first made known to us that the fleet so earnestly looked for had arrived, and their flags could be seen as they lay off the bar.

Upon the approach of night the enemy slackened his fire, and finally reduced it to his mortars, which fired at intervals of fifteen minutes, and with great precision, through the night, which passed in storm and with high wind and tide. The men were withdrawn from the batteries, as the scarcity of the cartridges forbade any service of the guns through the night.

At midnight the making of cartridges was stopped by Major Anderson, as nearly all of the extra clothing and material from the hospital had been used.

At the request of Lieutenant Snyder, the writer, just before midnight, accompanied him upon an inspection of the outside of the work. Everywhere, but especially upon the wall of the gorge, and on the faces opposite to Fort Moultrie, were deep indentations made by the solid shot. That from the 8-inch Columbiad had penetrated about twelve inches, crumbling the bricks and leaving a wide crater. The twelve-pound projectile from the rifled gun had penetrated but little deeper, but its fire was more accurate, and the attempt to breach around the lower embrasure of the right gorge angle had progressed to a depth of twenty inches and must in the end have succeeded. Some of the hastily constructed devices of the engineers had yielded to the enemy's fire; a shot having passed through the filling of one of the embrasures of the second tier and one through the main gate. But the resistance of the fort was unaffected: its walls were intact, its casemates uninjured, and its lower tier of guns untouched.

The parapet had suffered most; it had been undefended, and, in the destruction of the projecting roofs and chimneys, the crumbling of its walls and the injury to its guns, presented a picture of havoc and ruin.

CHAPTER XXXII.

Mortar firing through the night–Anticipating the fleet–Heavy firing opened in the morning–Fort Sumter replies "early and spitefully–Scarcity of cartridges–Fire restricted in consequence–Quarters set on fire by shells and hot shot–Increased fire of the batteries–Fort threatened with explosion –Magazines closed–Flames spread–Woodwork consumed–Flagstaff shot away–Flag restored at once–Colonel Wigfall crosses in small boat from Cummings Point–His visit unauthorized–Enters the fort–Interview with Major Anderson–Terms of evacuation proposed–Major Anderson consents–Wigfall departs–White flag raised–Three aides of Confederate general come to fort under white flag–Interview with Anderson–Aides return to Charleston–Wigfall's visit without knowledge or Confederate general–"Formal and final terms" presented–Anderson accepts–condition of the fort–Effect of the fire upon it–Casualties slight–Four men wounded–Salute to the flag permitted–Serious explosion, and result– State troops take possession–-Captain Ferguson, aide-de-camp to commanding general, raises Confederate flag over the work–Garrison transferred to the steamer *Baltic,* which leaves for the North.

THE night closed in rain and darkness; the wind from the sea blew in storm. The men rested undisturbed, while an anxious and expectant watch was kept in anticipation of the relief promised, but which failed to appear. The enemy were equally upon the alert, and through the night his batteries guarding the channels were manned, and a ceaseless watch kept upon the approaches to the harbor, while his enfilading batteries were kept in readiness to sweep the landings and faces of Fort Sumter should any force attempt to succor the garrison. The light wood upon the hulks that had been anchored at the entrance to the inner harbor, under the guns of Fort Moultrie, was now ignited in anticipation of the approach of the fleet, while the fire of the mortar batteries was kept up at intervals of fifteen minutes through the night, which passed without further incident.

Early in the morning of the 13th the firing was renewed.

In anticipation of a movement of the fleet, and to save ammunition, the firing from Sullivan's Island was at first confined to the mortars and enfilading battery. The direct fire of Fort Moultrie was restricted to two of the guns; of the Sumter battery, until the fire broke out at Sumter, when the entire battery was manned and served. At Cummings Point the mortar batteries opened early, and maintained their fire steadily at regular intervals, while the fire of the heavy Columbiads in the Iron-clad battery was concentrated to breach the work as well as to destroy the granite defenses of the main gate.

"Fort Sumter opened early and spitefully," said the commander of Fort Moultrie, in his official report, "and paid especial attention to Fort Moultrie, almost every shot grazing the crest of the parapet and crushing through the quarters." After their limited breakfast of pork and the last of the damaged rice, the details went again to their guns. Those bearing upon "Cummings Point" were not served, the guns in the casemates bearing upon the inner channel and upon Fort Moultrie being the only ones used. A rapid and accurate fire was maintained for hours, when the supply of cartridges became so much diminished as to restrict the fire to one gun every ten minutes. Before 8 o'clock the officers' quarters had been twice set on fire by the mortar shells; the flames had been promptly extinguished, when between 9 and 10 the fire was renewed from the same cause, and was being again controlled, when Moultrie opened with hot shot, which was poured into the fort, spreading the conflagration and greatly adding to the destruction. Every battery around the fort now increased its fire, and Major Anderson forbade any further attempt to control the flames, which were now spreading in every direction through the wooden floors and partitions of the quarters. It spread to both barracks and quarters, and by noon all of the woodwork was in flames. The officers, seizing the axes that were available, exerted themselves in cutting away whatever woodwork was accessible. It soon became evident that the magazine with its 300 barrels of powder was in danger of the flames, and every man that could be spared was placed upon the duty of removing the powder, toward which the fire was gradually progressing, now separated from the magazine by only one set of quarters. Not a third of the barrels could be removed; so thick was the cloud of smoke and burning cinders, that penetrated everywhere, that a cause of serious danger arose from the exposed condition of the powder taken from the magazine, and Major Anderson now ordered that all but five barrels be thrown into the sea.

The men, almost suffocated as the south wind carried the cloud

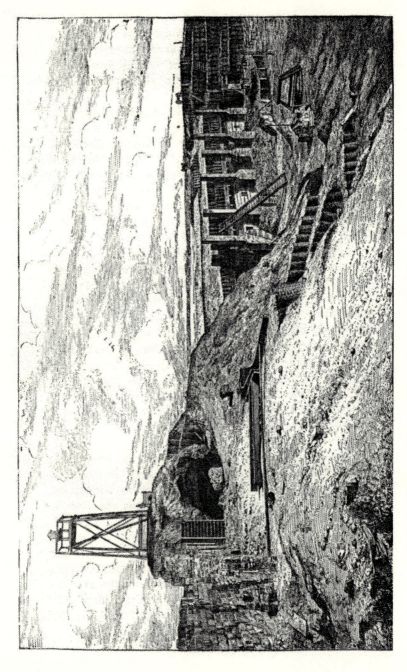

INTERIOR OF FORT SUMTER, SHOWING ITS CONDITION WHEN REOCCUPIED BY THE GOVERNMENT.

of hot smoke and cinders into the casemates, threw themselves upon the ground and covered their faces with wet cloths, or rushed to the embrasures, where the occasional draught made it possible to breathe. The enemy maintained his increased fire. The nine-inch shells which had been filled, and located in different parts of the work, to be used as grenades in repelling an assault, now exploded from time to time as the fire spread, adding greatly to the danger and destruction.

A large number had been placed in the towers on the spiral staircase of granite. They exploded, completely destroying these structures at the west gorge angle, as well as the interior of the other. It was at this moment that the writer, in obedience to Anderson's orders, had ascended to the parapet to report any movement of the fleet. It was with the greatest difficulty that he could make his way amid the destruction and reach the parapet at all. The fleet had made no movement.

The magazines were now closed, when a shot from the enemy's batteries "passed through the intervening shield, struck the door, and bent the lock in such a way that it could not be opened again."

For some time our batteries had ceased even their restricted fire, when some single shots were fired by Doubleday, and were answered by cheers from the enemy.

The scene was wellnigh indescribable. It was now noon. The enemy's fire from his mortars and gun batteries had been so increased that there was scarcely an appreciable moment that shot and shell were not searching the work. The flames of the burning quarters were still spreading, shooting upward amid the dense smoke as heavy masses of brick and masonry crumbled, and fell with loud noise. All of the woodwork had now been consumed. The heavy gates at the entrance of the work, as well as the planking of the windows on the gorge, were gone, leaving, access to the fort easy and almost unobstructed.

In the midst of the fire, the flag-staff, which had borne the flag since the demand for the surrender, having been repeatedly struck, was shot away at 1:30 P. M. and fell heavily to the ground, it being down but a few moments, and, in the words of Major Anderson, "merely long enough to enable us to replace it on another staff."*

---

* Anderson, April 13, 1861,

The flag halliards had been cut, and the flag itself had been sustained by one only, that had become twisted around the staff. Upon the disappearance of the flag the enemy slackened his fire. It was at once secured by Lieutenant Hall, and attached to a short spar brought promptly by Sergeant Hart and carried to the parapet, where under the superintendence of Captain Seymour, assisted by Lieutenant Snyder and Sergeant Hart, it was again

INSIDE OF ONE OF THE MAGAZINES, FORT SUMTER.

raised and the temporary staff secured to a gun-carriage on the parapet amid the renewed and concentrated fire of the enemy's guns.

Meantime a group of officers had been watching the progress of the bombardment and its effect upon the fort from the Iron-clad battery at Cummings Point, when one of them, Lieutenant-Colonel De Saussure, the officer commanding the artillery on

Morris Island, suggested that, from the silence of the fort, the spread of the flames, as well as the evident effect of their fire, they should send and inquire into the status of the garrison as a matter of humanity. Brigadier-General James Simons, commanding upon the island, was present, but objected to such a course, as beyond the scope of his authority, as well as from the fact that he had no one whom he could send. Upon this, an aide-de-camp of General Beauregard (Colonel Louis Wigfall), who had been with the batteries for two days, at once volunteered for the service. Upon consultation with Colonel Manning and Colonel Chesnut, two aides of the commanding general, who, with Colonel Chisholm, of Governor Pickens's staff, had come to the island to learn the condition of the batteries and to establish communication with the city," the general commanding upon the island reluctantly gave the authority. Colonel Wigfall anticipated the action of the aides, who, seeing the flag of the fort down, had determined to renew the demand for the surrender. Their boat was being prepared, when Colonel Wigfall, securing a skiff in a creek near by, and joined by private Gourdin Young, of the company of the Palmetto Guard on duty on the Iron-clad battery, with two negroes as oarsmen, pushed off at once amid the firing for Fort Sumter. Colonel Ripley, in Fort Moultrie, seeing the boat push off, fired a shot across her bow, which she disregarded, when, continuing her course, she finally reached the wharf of the fort. Seeing no one, and finding the entrance to the fort obstructed by the burning ashes, Colonel Wigfall went alone around the enrockment to the left face of the work. Meantime, Anderson being informed of the arrival of the boat with a white flag by a private soldier that had seen it land, passed out of the fort through the blazing gateway, accompanied by Lieutenant Snyder, who followed Colonel Wigfall around the work. Arriving near an embrasure on the left flank, where a sentinel was standing, Colonel Wigfall displayed his white flag upon his sword, and said he wished to see Major Anderson, when after some discussion he was permitted to enter. The writer saw him enter the work, Lieutenant Snyder entering after him. He at once asked for Major Anderson, saying that General Beauregard desired to stop "this firing." In passing down the casemates some of the

Simons, p. 33, "War of the Rebellion," Vol. I, Series I,

officers were met, and to them Colonel Wigfall at once appealed. "Your flag is down," said he, "you are on fire, and you are not firing your guns. General Beauregard desires to stop this," and he proposed that a white flag be displayed towards Moultrie, as the batteries on Cummings Point, from which he had come, had ceased' firing. "No, sir," said Lieutenant Davis, "our flag is not down; if you will step this way you will see it floating." He then said, "Let us stop this firing. Will you hoist this?" holding out his sword, to which he had attached his handkerchief. "No;" said Davis, "it is for you to stop it." "Will no one hold it?" said Wigfall. Receiving no response, he sprang into an embrasure looking toward Moultrie, that was keeping up a steady fire, and waved his flag backward and forward without attracting attention, so great was the distance. Upon seeing this Lieutenant Davis said, "As you have put the flag out yourself, I will let one of the soldiers continue to hold it;" and directed a corporal, who stood near, to continue to wave it. He had hardly been in the embrasure a moment, when a shot struck just over him, when springing back inside he announced with an oath, that the flag was not respected. "I have been fired upon with that flag two or three times," replied Wigfall; "I think you might stand it once."*

It was at this moment that Anderson came up, when Colonel Wigfall immediately addressed him. "Major Anderson, I am Colonel Wigfall; General Beauregard wishes to stop this, and to ask upon what terms you will evacuate this work; you can have almost any terms which General Beauregard will arrange with you." Major Anderson replied: "I have already stated to General Beauregard the terms upon which I will evacuate this fort.   Instead of noon on the 15th, I will go now." "Then, Major Anderson, I understand that you will evacuate the fort upon the same terms proposed to you by General Beauregard." "Yes, sir," replied Anderson," and upon those terms alone." "Then," said Colonel Wigfall, inquiringly," the fort is to be ours?" "Yes," replied Major Anderson, upon those terms." "Very well; then I will return to General Beauregard."

The conditions for the evacuation were gone over. Anderson was to evacuate the fort with his command, taking arms and all pri-

---

* Personal observation and record.

vate and company property, saluting his flag upon taking it down, and transportation secured to any port in the North. After some appreciative remarks in regard to the defense, Colonel Wigfall left the fort, when the flag was taken down and a white flag raised by Anderson's order, when the firing entirely ceased. Colonel Wigfall returned at once in his boat to Cummings Point, where the command received him with enthusiasm, and to whom he announced, although mistakenly, the unconditional surrender of the fort. The aides of the general commanding had awaited his coming, when he accompanied them at once in their boat on their return to Charleston.

The visit of Colonel Wigfall was wholly unauthorized. It was a voluntary act, not to be justified even by the exigency. But he gave Anderson to understand that he came from and upon the part of the general commanding the opposing forces, and upon that representation alone was he received. He had scarcely left the fort, when a boat containing three aides-de-camp* of the commanding general came, under a white flag.

The commanding general had noticed the absence of the flag and the burning of the quarters, and had sent to offer assistance. On their way to the fort they recognized that the flag had again been raised on Sumter, and were about to return, when the white flag was again seen, and they pushed on. Anderson declined any assistance, and then inquired if they had come directly from General Beauregard. Upon being answered in the affirmative, he then gave the incident of the visit of Colonel Wigfall, "as an aide to and by authority of General Beauregard," and as authorized to propose terms for the evacuation. He was then informed that Colonel Wigfall had been absent from headquarters, and had not seen General Beauregard for' two days. Vexed at the misunderstanding and the awkward position in which he found himself, Anderson determined to restore his flag, that he regretted had ever been taken down, and to re-open his batteries, that his flag was lowered only because he had understood Wigfall to come directly from Beauregard. But he was persuaded to postpone any such action until General Beauregard could be advised of the terms to which he would consent. Meantime he reduced to writing the terms proposed by Colonel Wigfall and those upon which he

---

* Captain S. D. Lee, Colonels Roger A. Pryor and W. Percher Miles,

would evacuate the fort, and sent it to General Beauregard by Captain S. D., Lee, one of the aides.*

The visit of Colonel Wigfall, and its purpose, had been communicated to General Beauregard, who at once sent two officers † of his staff "to receive any propositions he might wish to make." The note sent by Anderson to General Beauregard by Captain Lee was read, when the officers informed Anderson that they "were authorized to offer him those terms, excepting only the clause relating to the salute to the flag," and this they were not authorized to grant. When asked what his answer would be if not permitted to salute his flag, he replied that he would not urge it, but would refer the matter again to General Beauregard. At this interview a message was sent by Anderson to Governor Pickens and to General Beauregard, which under the circumstances may be deemed extraordinary. It was that, "as an evidence of his desire to save the public property as much as possible, he had three times on Friday and twice on Saturday sent up his men to extinguish the flames under the heavy fire of our batteries, and when the magazines were in imminent danger of being blown up.‡

The formal and final terms agreed to by the general commanding, were presented to Anderson by some messengers from General Beauregard at 7 o'clock P. M., in regard to which

---

* An incident now occurred which might have had a serious ending. The aides of the Confederate general had been introduced into the only gun casemate which was habitable, and which was occupied as quarters by Captain Foster and the surgeon of the fort. Colonel Roger A. Pryor, one of the aides, had taken his seat near a table at the head of the camp-bed occupied by the surgeon. The latter had been seriously ill, and was under the course of a strong medicine that stood in a large bottle upon the table. Without reflection Colonel Pryor poured out a large portion of the medicine and drank it. Discovering his mistake, he appealed at once to Major Anderson, who, in an angle of the casemate was writing down the terms upon which he would agree to evacuate the work. The surgeon was at once sent for, when Colonel Pryor rapidly recounted the circumstances, when the surgeon said to him, "If you have taken the amount of that solution that you think you have, you have likely poisoned yourself." "Do something for me, doctor, right off," said he, "for I would not have anything happen to me in this fort for any consideration." The surgeon took him to his improvised dispensary down the line of casemates, where he was shortly afterward relieved, and returned to the city.

† D. R. Jones, Assistant Adjutant-General; Charles Allston, Jr., Colonel and aide-de-camp.

‡ Official report, Jones and Allston, April 15, 1861.

Anderson expressed his gratification; and it was arranged that he should leave in the morning, after communicating with the fleet, but that he must be responsible for the fort in the meantime, as otherwise four companies of artillery would be ordered there. After the cessation of the firing the fort was left in comparative quiet, and an opportunity offered to examine its, condition. It was a scene of ruin and destruction. For thirty-four hours it had sustained a bombardment from seventeen 10-inch mortars and heavy guns, well placed and well served. The quarters and barracks were in ruins. The main gates and the planking of the windows on the gorge were gone; the magazines closed and surrounded by smoldering flames and burning ashes; the provisions exhausted; much of the engineering work destroyed; the cartridges gone; and with four barrels of powder only available— the command had yielded to the inevitable. The effect of the direct shot had been to indent the walls, where the marks could be counted by hundreds," while the shells well directed had crushed in the quarters, and, in connection with the hot shot, setting them on fire, had destroyed the barracks, and quarters down to the gun casemates, while the enfilading fire had prevented the service of the barbette guns, some of them comprising the most important battery in the work. The breaching fire from the Columbiads and rifled gun at Cummings Point upon the right gorge angle had progressed sensibly, and must eventually have succeeded if kept up, but as yet no guns had been disabled or injured at that point. The effect of the fire upon the parapet was most pronounced. The gorge, the right face and flank, as well as the left face, were all taken in reverse and a destructive fire maintained until the end, while the gun-carriages on the barbette of the gorge were destroyed in the fire of the blazing quarters.

Fort Sumter had been built with all the careful appliance of the most improved engineer science. Its beautiful arches were models of strength and grace; and it was with natural pride that the engineer officer in his official report remarked upon the fact that so good was the masonry of one of the fifteen-inch arches of the second tier, that a 10-inch shell from Cummings Point failed to go through it, although it was not covered by concrete or flagging.

---

* 600. Foster.

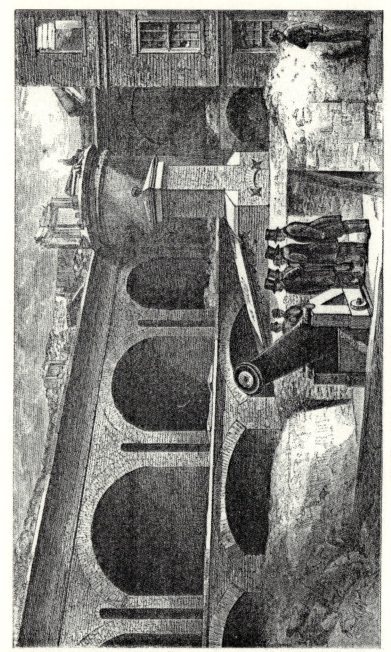

GOVENOR PICKENS, AT FORT SUMTER AFTER THE BOMBARDMENT.

But the fort had been constructed without reference to an attack by those who should have been its defenders, and in con-, sequence its weakest part, the gorge, undefended by a flanking fire, became its most vulnerable point, and its destruction the object of the able engineer who conducted the attack upon the work. Its walls, standing upon a stone foundation twelve feet thick at the base, and lessening to eight and a half feet at the parapet, were built to resist smooth-bore projectiles, which at that time was the adopted system; but strong as they were, they showed how little fitted such construction was to resist rifled ordnance when the twelve-pounder Blakely gun from Cummings Point put one of its shot through the masked wall of the magazine. But the offensive strength of the fort was not felt.   The powerful battery upon the barbette bearing upon the batteries on Cummings Point was not used, although to its erection and completion the best efforts of officers and men had been given. The heavy Columbiads mounted upon the parade and bearing upon the city, Fort Moultrie and Cummings Point were not once loaded, and the hot shot furnaces remained untouched. The guns of the lower tier were the only ones used, and the strength of the casemates protected the men serving them, while they remained uninjured to the last. Had the garrison been sufficient in numbers, and supplied with men and provisions, and proper munitions, the resistance could have been greatly protracted. The substantial part of the fort was uninjured, and its subsequent history showed to what an extent a resistance supported by men and material, and sustained by intelligence and determination, might be sucessfully carried, when the crumbling of its walls under a fierce bombardment only served to strengthen its defensive power. From the result of the bombardment, it is clear that the projecting roofs and gables about the parapet should have been removed. The heavy moldings about the windows and doors of the officers' quarters, unnecessary and in bad taste, only afforded fuel to the fire. The almost destitute condition of its little garrison, rendered the evacuation of the fort unavoidable. Within a few days, if not hours, the fort must have surrendered if no gun had been fired, and it must be left to history to account for the fact that while such an assurance was positive, any necessity for such an attack should have existed beyond the gratification of a sentiment. Notwithstanding the persistence and accuracy of the fire to which the fort had been subjected, the casualties were light. Four men were slightly wounded by fragments of concrete and mortar, one of these a mechanic in the employ of the engineer. Anderson had promptly withdrawn his men from all exposure, and the protection afforded by the casemates was almost complete.

The men, released now from all responsibility, seemed to change in feeling. They became reserved and silent. The enthusiasm that had so long inspired them seemed to have gone, and they made ready to leave with unconcealed expressions of disappointment.

But little now remained to be done. It had been arranged that the fort should be evacuated on Sunday morning, the 14th. The preparations began at an early hour. Permission to salute his flag had been accorded to him, and Anderson made arrangements to fire one hundred guns. Every resource to obtain material for cartridges was exhausted, and when the command was in readiness the firing began under the officers designated, the flag still flying from the rampart. The guns yet serviceable on the parapet were used, and the firing was in progress, when, by the premature discharge of one of the large guns on the right flank, the right arm of one of the gunners was blown off. The wind was blowing stiffly from the sea, and directly into the muzzles of the guns. The cartridges to be used had been placed by the side of each gun, amid the debris of broken brick and mason work and fragments of slate and lead in a confused mass. Upon one of the discharges an ignited fragment of one of the cartridge bags was blown back by the wind, and lighting upon the pile of cartridges in rear of the piece, immediately ignited them with fatal explosion. The loose fragments of masonry were driven in every direction. Of the gunners on duty at the piece, Private Daniel Hough, Co. E, was instantly killed; Private Edward Galloway, Co. E, was mortally wounded, and died on the 19th, at the Gibbes Hospital in Charleston, to which he had been kindly removed and treated. Private James Fielding, Co. E, severely wounded and burned, was removed to the "Chisholm" Hospital, cured, and finally sent North without exchange. Three others were injured, but were enabled to accompany the command. The occurrence of this accident delayed the departure of the command, and induced Anderson to satisfy himself with a salute of fifty instead of one hundred guns. "Because of an unavoidable delay," said General Beauregard, in his official report, "the formal transfer of the fort to our possession did not take place until 4 o'clock on the afternoon of the 14th, when the United States troops evacuated the place."

The State troops detailed to occupy the work now took possession. They consisted of the Palmetto Guard, under Captain Cuthbert, and a company (B) of regular troops, under Captain Hallonquist, all under the command of Lieutenant-Colonel Ripley. The Confederate flag was raised upon the rampart by Captain Samuel Ferguson, aide-de-camp, who had received the keys of the work. The flag of the State was also. raised at the same time.

In making his preliminary report to his Government, the Confederate general used the following language:

"Whilst the barracks in Fort Sumter were in a blaze, and the interior of the work appeared untenable from the heat and from the fire of our batteries (at about which period I sent three of my aides to offer assistance in the name of the Confederate States), whenever the guns of Fort Sumter would fire upon Fort Moultrie the men occupying Cummings Point batteries (Palmetto Guard, Captain Cuthbert) at each shot would cheer Anderson for his gallantry, although themselves still firing upon him; and when on the 15th instant he left the harbor on the steamer *Isabel* the soldiers of the batteries on Cummings Point lined the beach, silent, and with heads uncovered, while Anderson and his command passed before them, and expressions of scorn at the apparent cowardice of the fleet in not even attempting to rescue so gallant an officer and his command were upon the lips of all. With such material for an army, if properly disciplined, I would consider myself almost invincible against any forces not too greatly superior.

"The fire of those barracks was only put out on the 15th instant, P. M., after great exertions by the gallant fire companies of this city, who were at their pumps night and day, although aware that close by them was a magazine filled with thirty thousand pounds of powder, with a shot-hole through the wall of its anteroom."

By Anderson's orders the men were formed upon the parade, and marched out under Doubleday with their flags, the drums beating the national air. A large crowd had collected on vessels and steamers and in boats, and had surrounded the fort to witness its evacuation. Great enthusiasm prevailed as the command embarked upon the boat that was to convey them to the steamer. Owing to the accident, their departure had been delayed-the surgeon of the fort remaining until the last, in attendance upon the mortally wounded man, who expired-until near sundown, when it was too late to cross the bar. Early on the morning of the 15th the steamer proceeded to the bar, where the entire command was transferred to the *Baltic,* where every attention was shown to them by the officers of the fleet. The *Baltic* was soon underway northward, and as she put to sea the men lingered upon her deck until the receding fort had sunk upon the horizon.

CHAPTER XXXIII.

Return of the garrison of Fort Sumter to New York–Their separation for service–Their individual careers in the war–Present condition of the fort–Wholly changed in appearance and in its armament–Main defense of the harbor.

A QUARTER of a century has now passed away, since the events related in the preceding pages took place, and it may be of interest to trace the record of the officers whose accidental position brought them so prominently into view at the very beginning of the difficulties. Upon the evacuation of the fort, the transport *Baltic,* with the officers and men of the garrison of Fort Sumter, made its way to the North. As she entered the harbor of New York, the flag they had defended was placed at the fore as the vessel passed along amid the loud welcome of the people. It was now that Anderson made the only report he ever made of the attack upon the fort. His physical as well as his mental condition was such that he requested Captain G. V. Fox to write the despatch for him, which was accordingly done and telegraphed to Washington upon the arrival of the ship. It was as follows:

"STEAMSHIP *Baltic,* OFF SANDY HOOK,
"April 18, 1861, 10:30 A. M., via New York.
"Having defended Fort Sumter for thirty-four hours, until the quarters were entirely burned, the main gates destroyed by fire, the gorge walls seriously impaired, the magazine surrounded by flames, and its door closed from the effects of the heat, four barrels and three cartridges of powder only being available, and no provisions remaining but pork, I accepted terms of evacuation offered by General Beauregard (being the same offered by him on the 11th instant, prior to the commencement of hostilities), and marched out of the fort on Sunday afternoon, the 14th instant, with colors flying and drums beating, bringing away company and private property, and saluting my flag with fifty guns.
"ROBERT ANDERSON, *Major First Artillery.*
"Hon. SIMON CAMERON, Secretary of War.
"WASHINGTON, D. C."

Upon their arrival they were received with an enthusiasm and
449

demonstration seldom exceeded and wholly exceptional, and the interest then manifested by the generous heart of New York continued to follow them through their subsequent service. In the issues of the fiercely contested war that followed the firing upon their fort, they were temporarily lost to view, as each one followed the career incidental to his position, and they parted not to meet again until its close. Widely separated, they served mainly in different armies, and in every section of the country; and, with the exception of Major Anderson himself, in every condition of active service. On the 20th of April, by the direction of the President, the following communication was made by the War Department to the officers and men:

"WAR DEPARTMENT,
"WASHINGTON, April 20, 1801,
"Major ROBERT ANDERSON,
        "*Late Commanding at Fort Sumter.*
    "*My Dear Sir:* I am directed by the President of the United States to communicate to you, and through you to the officers and the men under your command, at Forts Moultrie and Sumter, the approbation of the Government of your and their judicious and gallant conduct there, and to tender to you and them the thanks of the Government for the same.
    "I am, sir, very respectfully,
"SIMON CAMERON,
        "*Secretary of War.*"

Of the officers of Fort Sumter one alone failed in his allegiance: Second Lieutenant R. K. Meade, Corps of Engineers, who had distinguished himself in his service at Fort Sumter, and who had commanded a battery during the bombardment, resigned his position upon the secession of Virginia, to follow the fortunes of his State. He was on duty in the fortifications of Richmond, and falling ill, he died in July, 1861. Of the ten officers of the garrison of Fort Sumter, six rose to the position of general officers, and exercised active command, from the brigade to the corps. But three survive.

Major Anderson was made a brigadier-general in the regular army, and "was soon after sent to his native State, Kentucky, to assist in organizing and directing the Union element there." He was subsequently placed in command of the Department of the Cumberland. His health failing, he was relieved from duty shortly afterward, and in October, 1863, he was, at his own

INTERIOR OF FORT SUMTER AFTER BOMBARDMENT OF 1861.

request, placed upon the retired list of the army. He traveled abroad, his health continuing to fail him, when on the 27th of October, 1871; he died at Nice, Italy. He was brevetted "a major-general for gallant and meritorious service in Charleston Harbor."

Captain J. G. Foster, the senior engineer officer, a native of New Hampshire, was tendered the position of major of the Eleventh United States Infantry shortly after the return of the command from Fort Sumter, which he declined. He was shortly afterward appointed a brigadier-general of volunteers, and was engaged in the Roanoke Island expedition and the capture of Newbern. He rose to the rank of major-general of Volunteers, and was assigned to the command of the Department of Virginia and North Carolina; subsequently, for a short period, to the command of the Army and the Department of the Ohio, and finally to that of the South and of Florida, serving through the war. He was brevetted major in the regular army for the distinguished part taken by him in the transfer of the garrison of Fort Moultrie to Fort Sumter, and lieutenant-colonel and colonel for gallant and meritorious service at Roanoke Island and at Newbern. For the capture of Savannah he was brevetted a brigadier-general in the army, and major-general "for gallant and meritorious services in the field during the Rebellion." At the close of the war he returned to duty in his corps as lieutenant-colonel of engineers, and was upon temporary duty in Washington. He died on the 2d of September, 1874.

First Lieutenant George W. Snyder, Corps of Engineers, who was in immediate charge of the work at Fort Sumter before the movement from Moultrie, remained on duty with his corps after the return of the command to the North. He was on duty in the fortifications of Washington, and as engineer of the third division of the Army of Northeastern Virginia, and participated in the first battle of Bull Run, or Manassas. For gallant and meritorious services at Fort Sumter he was brevetted captain in the regular army and major for similar service "in the Manassas campaign." While on duty near Washington he fell ill, and died on the 17th of November, 1861.

Assistant Surgeon S. W. Crawford was appointed from Pennsylvania. After the return of the command from Fort Sumter to New York he was tendered the position of major in the Thirteenth United States Infantry, which he finally accepted, and was ordered to duty under Major-General Rosecrans, then actively engaged in West Virginia. He served upon his staff as Inspector-General of the Department until the retreat of Floyd and the successful close of the campaign. He was one of the two officers named by General Rosecrans in response to a request from Washington for promotion to brigadier-general, and was assigned to duty in the Army of the Shenandoah. He was present at the second battle of Winchester, and commanded the advance to Culpepper and to Cedar Mountain, where in the attack upon the right he lost one-half of his brigade. His corps being incorporated with the Army of the Potomac, he was present at South Mountain, and commanded a division at the battle of Antietam after the death of General Mansfield—his corps commander-and where he was severely wounded. He rejoined the army on the march to Gettysburg, having been placed in command of the Third Division of the Fifth Corps (Pennsylvania Reserves), participating in the battle upon the left of the line at the Round Tops. Upon the expiration of the term of service in this organization he was placed in command of the regiments of the old First Corps, then incorporated with the Fifth as the Third Division of that corps. This division he commanded through the Rapidan campaign, from Bethesda Church through the siege of Petersburg, the battle of Five Forks and the surrender of Lee's army at Appomattox. For "gallant and meritorious services at the battle of Gettysburg" he was brevetted colonel in the regular army; brigadier-general "for gallant and meritorious service at the battle of Five Forks;" major-general of volunteers "for conspicuous gallantry in the battles of the Wilderness, Spotsylvania Court House, Jericho Mills; Bethesda Church, Petersburg and Globe Tavern (Weldon Railroad), and for faithful service in the campaign;" major-general in the regular army "for gallant and meritorious service in the field during the war." He became colonel of the Sixteenth United States Infantry in 1869, and upon the reduction of the army, which immediately followed, he was transferred to the Second Regiment of Infantry, and was assigned to duty at Huntsville, Ala., under the reconstruction act, for three years. His disability increasing, he made application for retirement, when he was retired by special enactment with the rank of brigadier-general (19th of February, 1873).

Of the officers of the line, Captain Abner Doubleday, a native of New York, had been second in command at Fort Sumter. After its fall he was appointed major in the Seventeenth United States Infantry, and served in the Shenandoah Valley, and subsequently 'in the artillery defenses of Washington. Early in 1862 he was made a brigadier-general of Volunteers. In May he joined the army under General McDowell. He commanded a brigade, and subsequently a division, in the Army of the Potomac, at the second battle of Bull Run. His brigade soon after formed part of the Army of the Potomac, and with it he served at the battles of South Mountain and Antietam. In the latter action he commanded a division after the wounding of General Hatch. In November, 1862, he was made a major-general of Volunteers, and commanded a division of the First Corps at Fredericksburg under Burnside, and subsequently under Hatch at Chancellorsville. At Gettysburg he commanded the first corps of the army in the fight of the first day, when it sustained the fierce attack of the Confederate forces until overpowered. At the close of the war he assumed his position as lieutenant-colonel of his regiment. He became colonel of the Thirty-fifth United States Infantry, and was on duty in California and Texas, when from impaired health he retired from the active service of the army in December, 1873, on the lineal rank of colonel. After thirty years service he was brevetted lieutenant-colonel in the regular army "for gallant and meritorious service in the battle of Antietam;" colonel by brevet for gallant and meritorious service in the battle of Gettysburg; brigadier and major general by brevet for gallant and meritorious service during the war.

Brevet Captain Truman Seymour was a native of Vermont. He served in the defenses of Washington and as chief of artillery of McCall's division, in which he subsequently commanded a brigade. He was appointed a brigadier-general of Volunteers in April, 1862, and participated in the Peninsular campaign, the second battle of Bull Run, and in the campaign in Maryland at South Mountain and Antietam. Subsequently he served in the Department of the South as chief of staff and of artillery to the commanding general, and later in command of a division in the operations in Charleston Harbor. He commanded at the assault upon Fort Wagner, in July, 1863, where he was severely wounded.

In 1864 he was in command of the District of Florida and fought the battle of Olustee. Subsequently he commanded a brigade in the Army of the Potomac on the Rapidan, where he was captured. He rejoined the army upon being exchanged, and commanded a division at the siege of Petersburg and the capitulation of Lee's army at Appomattox C. H. For gallant and meritorious service during the defense of Sumter he was brevetted major in the regular army; lieutenant-colonel and colonel for gallant and meritorious service at South Mountain and Antietam; brigadier-general for gallant and meritorious service in the capture of Petersburg; major-general of volunteers "for ability and energy in handling his division, and for gallantry and valuable service in action," and major-general in the regular army for "gallant and meritorious service during the war." In November, 1876, he was retired from the active service of the army with the lineal rank of major.

First Lieutenant Jefferson C. Davis, born in Indiana, was appointed colonel of the Twenty-second Indiana Volunteers, 1861, and participated in the campaigns in Missouri and Arkansas. In May, 1862, he was appointed a brigadier-general, and in the battle of Stone River and the campaign against Chattanooga, and the actions of Chickamauga, Missionary Ridge and the operations around Atlanta, he rendered valuable service. He marched in command of the Fourteenth Army Corps "with Sherman to the sea," and was present at the capture of Savannah and the surrender of Johnson. He was subsequently in command of the Department of Kentucky, and finally of Alaska in 1867-70. All of the brevets conferred upon him were for gallantry in action. For gallant and meritorious conduct at the battle of Pea Ridge he was made major by brevet in the regular army. For similar conduct at the battles of Resaca and of Rome, in Georgia, he was made lieutenant-colonel and colonel by brevet, and both brigadier-general and brevet major-general in the regular army for gallant and meritorious conduct at the battles of Kenesaw Mountain and of Jonesboro, Ga. He became colonel of the Twenty-third infantry by regular promotion, and was on duty in Alaska, and continued in active service until the 30th of November, 1879, when he died.

First Lieutenant Theodore Talbot was appointed from Kentucky in 1847. He served in Fort Sumter as first lieutenant

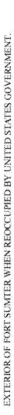

EXTERIOR OF FORT SUMTER WHEN REOCCUPIED BY UNITED STATES GOVERNMENT.

of Captain Seymour's company; an intelligent and able officer, he was employed by Major Anderson as the bearer of confidential despatches to Washington, but was refused permission by the South Carolina authorities to return to the fort. He was appointed Assistant Adjutant-General in the army on the 15th of March, 1861, while, in Fort Sumter.. He was chief of staff to General Mansfield, commanding the defenses of Washington. He became major in his corps, and while serving as chief of staff to General Wadsworth, Military Governor of the District of Columbia, he died, April 22, 1862. He was brevetted captain and Assistant Adjutant-General, 16th of March, 1861, and brevetted major in the same Department in July of same year.

Second Lieutenant Norman J. Hall, who was Major Anderson's adjutant at Fort Sumter, was a native of New York, and appointed from Michigan. After the fall of the work he was on duty with his regiment, when he was made Chief of Artillery of Hooker's Division, and served with the army of the Potomac in the Peninsular campaign, and in 1862 upon the staff of the commanding general. He was appointed colonel of the Seventh Michigan Volunteers, which he commanded at Antietam, where he was brevetted captain in the regular army for gallant and meritorious services in that battle. He was made major by brevet for similar services at Fredericksburg. At the battle of Gettysburg he rendered distinguished services while in command of a brigade, and was made lieutenant-colonel by brevet. Falling ill, he was discharged from the volunteer service on "surgeon's certificate of disability" in 1864, and was finally retired from the active service of the army on the 22d of February, 1865, for disability resulting from long and faithful service, and disease contracted in the line of duty. In May, 1867, he died.

Of the fort itself, but a semblance of its original structure remains, the requirements of modern warfare having wholly changed its character. Its lofty walls of fifty feet, enclosing its three tiers of guns, have been reduced to a low battery of half the size, with its 100-pounder guns in casemate, and a battery of 11-inch rifles upon its barbette. The walls in front of the gun casemates on the channel front still show the marks of Moultrie's fire. Its old armament has been replaced by a powerful battery, which may yet be strengthened; its old barracks and quarters are gone and not replaced, while upon its restricted parade stand its bomb-proof magazines and its covered ways communicating with its tiers of guns.

In its reconstruction, as in its original structure, the Government has been indifferent to any other purpose than that of securing the defense of the harbor.

More powerful than ever, it stands to-day, as it has ever stood, that main defense, as its brilliant history has abundantly shown. It commands by its guns the only approach by the new channel for ships of war, while above it and over the shores of the beautiful harbor of Charleston floats in peace the flag of the country.

APPENDIX I.

SOURCES OF INFORMATION.

IN my work I have had the valuable assistance of many distinguished people. Documents of greater or less value have been placed in my hands by citizens representing both sides of the question. From the South I have exhaustively drawn, whenever information could be obtained, either from official or private sources. No application was ever made by me for authentic documents bearing upon the transactions, to anyone in possession of them, without being met by a cordial and prompt acquiescence. No suggestion tending to bias my judgment was ever made to me; and, in placing the documents in my possession, the simple wish was expressed that the truth might be told. The course of the war, and its vicissitudes in South Carolina, the partial destruction of its principal city, and subsequently of its capital, the pillage of the public records in Columbia at a later date, together with the mutilation of what was left, rendered the compilation of any history from the public papers a very difficult task. What is now left of the minutes of the Executive Council of the State is but a fragment of what would otherwise have been a most valuable contribution to the history of the time. It is now impossible to compile from any public documents anything like a complete history of South Carolina. The proceedings of the Convention which passed the Ordinance of Secession, as also the official reports of its public men, were published at the period of their occurrence. Copies of these were secured shortly after the close of the war, and are now in my possession. Much, however, was in manuscripts and in private hands, either of the actors in the scene or their families. To these I have had access. Among the most valuable are those of the late Governor Francis W. Pickens. He was the chief figure of the early days of the revolution, and I desire here to acknowledge gratefully the action of her who generously placed in my hands the papers of her husband. without reserve or imposition of a single obligation.

While in command at Huntsville, Ala., in 1869-70 I was brought into association with General L. P. Walker, the first Secretary of War of the Confederacy, from whom I obtained much information of value. He placed in my hands the Official Letter-Book of the Confederate War Department from the beginning of the war, containing over 600 letters.*

In the archives at Washington, with the exception of the War Department, there is no connected record of the events of this period, and scarcely a mention of the political complications in the matter of Fort Sumter in any of the Departments.

The latter portion of Mr. Buchanan's administration has been portrayed in an important and valuable narrative written immediately after the war, by the Hon. W. H. Trescot, Assistant Secretary of State during Mr. Buchanan's administration. Conspicuously prominent in the events, his able narrative is valuable as that of an eyewitness to the transactions, and much of it is given in his own graphic language.

During two winters spent at York, Penn., I was admitted to the friendship of Judge J. S. Black, the Attorney-General, and subsequently the Secretary of State in Mr. Buchanan's Cabinet. To him, and to his son, Lieutenant-Governor C. F. Black, and to his clear and able views, I feel an indebtedness for assistance in my work that merits more than this mere acknowledgment. In many and exhaustive conversations, oft repeated, his wonderful memory still vigorous, Judge Black recalled the events of those days with a freshness equal almost to the written record. From the survivors in Charleston and in the State I have received all the assistance they could render. It seems invidious to discriminate, yet I may be permitted to mention especially my great indebtedness to Ex-Governor A. G. Magrath, Ex-Judge of the United States District Court, who was perhaps the most potential factor of the period, and who influenced its course at the moment of

---

* Upon the breaking up of the Confederate Government at Richmond, in 1865, one of the clerks of the War Department possessed himself of this "Letter-Book." Some years afterward he approached "Parson" Brownlow, of Tennessee, with an offer to transfer the book to him for $100. Parson Brownlow replied that he would not give 100 cents for all of the correspondence of the Confederacy; when the person in possession of the book offered it to General L. P. Walker, who secured it and placed it in my hands. —*General L. P. Walker to author,* 1871.

separation more than any other single person, as well as to R. B. Rhett, Jr., to the Hon. Isaac Hayne, to Colonel R S. Simonton, to Edward McCready, Jr., to Mayor Courtenay, all of whom exerted themselves to the utmost to place me in possession of all the facts in their knowledge. From General J. Holt, who was the Postmaster-General, and subsequently the Secretary of War of Mr. Buchanan's Cabinet, I have obtained interesting and valuable details. Of that period of Mr. Lincoln's administration from the inauguration until Fort Sumter was fired upon, I have obtained the fullest information from the Hon. F. W. Seward, who was the Assistant Secretary of State at that time. Access to the papers of his father, the Secretary of State, has been accorded me, and also to his private correspondence during that period. To him and to the Ex-Associate Justice Jno. A. Campbell, I am indebted for important papers relating to the period just prior to the surrender of Fort Sumter. To the Postmaster-General, Mr. Montgomery Blair, I owe a great obligation for the frank and outspoken statements furnished to me, both oral and written; and to the Secretary of War, Mr. Cameron, whose singularly clear memory of the events still remains, and was cheerfully given. The principal sources from which I have drawn the material of my narrative are as follows:

1. Reports, resolutions and journals of the General Assembly of South Carolina, 1861.
2. Conventions of South Carolina, 1832, 1853 and 1857.
3. Messages of Governors Gist and F. W. Pickens, of South Carolina, 1860, 1861 and 1862.
4. Private and public papers, letters of Governor F. W. Pickens, 1860, 1861 and 1862.
5. Journal of the Convention of South Carolina, 1860, 1861.
6. Reports of Heads of Departments, South Carolina, 1860, 1861, after the secession of the State.
7. Confederate documents relative to Fort Sumter: These were obtained from Montgomery Blair, Ex-Postmaster-General.
8. Official correspondence of L. P. Walker, Secretary of War, 1861, Confederate War Department.
9. Ordinances and Constitution of the State of Alabama, with the Constitution of the Provisional Government, 1861.
10. Reports and private letters of General P. T. Beauregard, C.S.A.

11. Acts and resolutions of the Provisional Congress of the Confederate States, 1861.

12. Correspondence of the Confederate Commissioners Crawford, Roman and Forsyth with the Confederate Government at Montgomery, from February 7, 1861, to April 11, 1861. (These are from the original papers purchased by the Government through John A. Pickett, of Washington.)

13. Executive Document No. 5. Correspondence between the Hon. J. W. Hayne and the President relative to Fort Sumter, 1861.

14. "The record of Fort Sumter from its occupation by Major Anderson to its reduction by Confederate Sates troops, 1862." Columbia, S. C., 1862, W. A. Harris.

15. From "Buchanan's Administration" I have drawn largely, and often in the words of the writer, as more forcible than any I could use, and it may be that credit has not always been given in the text. Especial acknowledgment is due, therefore, to this important work for the part his expressions will play in this narrative.

16. Contributions of the Old Residents' Historical Association. Lowell, Mass., Vol. II., No. 1, 1880.

17. Statement, letters and reports of Captain G. V. Fox, United States Navy. *Powhatan* and relief of Sumter expedition.

18. Papers of Ex-Associate Justice John A. Campbell, United States Supreme Court. Historical sketch. Correspondence with Southern Commissioners. MSS. "Facts of History."

19. The "War of the Rebellion;" A Compilation of the Official Records of the Union and Confederate Armies. Washington: Government Printing Office, 1880. Vol. I, Series I.

20. Messages and accompanying documents of Presidents Buchanan and Lincoln, 1860-1861.

21. Congressional Record, 1860-1861.

22. Official opinions, public and private papers, of the Hen. W. H. Seward, Secretary of State.

23. Notes and journal of letters, official and private, of Major-General M. C. Meigs, U. S. A., Powatan and Fort Pickens.

24. Doubleday's "Moultrie and Sumter."

25. Statement of Admiral D. D. Porter, relating to the *Powhatan.*

26. Executive Documents, South Carolina. No. 1 to No. 6.
27. Personal journal of daily events, from the meeting of the South Carolina Convention until the evacuation of Fort Sumter.
28. "Life of James Buchanan," by George Ticknor Curtis.

In the course of the preparation of my work I have twice visited the scene of the events related in my narrative, and have gone over the record with the prominent survivors. There are yet many facts of detail and of interest unrecorded, which must now remain to be incorporated, should the reception of the work warrant further illustration. It might be alleged that subjects not immediately connected with the "Genesis of the Civil War" have been introduced into the narrative; but these belong wholly to the "Story of Sumter," and, as in the case of the *Powhatan* and the reinforcement of Fort Pickens, could not be told intelligently except in detail.

Other high and important sources of information have been freely drawn upon, and probably there are none of greater historic value than the responses made to specific inquiries addressed by me to the prominent survivors of the struggle, and which are nowhere else a matter of record. The authorities above mentioned will show the character of the references I have relied upon to form my story, and to strengthen my own recorded observations and recollections of the events as they occurred.

THE AUTHOR.

APPENDIX II.

HEADQUARTER, PROV. FORCES,
CHARLESTON, S. C., U. S. A., April 6, 1861.

GENERAL ORDER }
No. 9.   }

THE following general instructions are issued for the government of commanders of batteries, and will be furnished by them to captains of batteries under their command.

I. Should Fort Sumter at any time fire upon the works on Morris, James, or Sullivan's islands, or on any vessel or steamer in the service of or friendly to the Confederate States, this act of aggression will be the signal for the commencement of hostilities; the mortar, enfilade and other batteries of the harbor bearing on Fort Sumter will immediately open their fire upon it, with a view, first, to dismount as many of the guns as possible, and then to effect a breach, if practicable. Great care should be taken not to fire rapidly, but accurately.

The order to fire slowly but surely should be strictly enforced. There must be no waste of powder, shot or shells, the object being to worry out the garrison, if practicable.

II. The mortar batteries will continue their firing day and night at the rate, collectively, in the daytime, of one shell every two minutes, and at night of one every ten minutes. There being sixteen mortars in position (four at Fort Johnson, two near the Moultrie House, two near Sullivan's Island point, two at Mount Pleasant, and six at Cummings Point), each mortar will be fired every thirty-two minutes in the first case, and once every two hours and forty minutes in the second.

III. The batteries opposite to each other will endeavor to fire in succession in relative proportion to their armaments, and so as to cause their shells to explode sometimes immediately over and within Fort Sumter, and at other times on its parade or interior ground. The firing, having been commenced by the Moultrie House mortar battery (Captain Butler), will be continued in the following order: first by the Fort Johnson (Captain James), in

464

the proportion of two shells from the latter to one from the former; then by Cummings Point mortar batteries (Major Stevens and Captain King), followed by Sullivan's Island point mortar battery (Captain Hallonquist), and then last by the Mount Pleasant mortar battery (Captain Martin), in the proportion of three shells from the Cummings Point mortar battery to one from each of the two batteries.

IV. Commanders of batteries to make application for additional ammunition.

V. Lights carefully placed, and batteries to open on Sumter at the signal.

APPENDIX III.

EXTRACT from the message of President Lincoln transmitted to the 37th Congress, called in general session in July, 1861.

At the beginning of the present presidential term, four months ago, the functions of the Federal Government were found to be generally suspended within the several States of South Carolina, Georgia, Alabama, Mississippi, Louisiana and Florida, excepting only those of the Post Office Department.

Within these States all the forts, arsenals, dock-yards, custom houses and the like, including the movable and stationary property in and about them, had been seized, and were held in open hostility to the Government, excepting only Forts Pickens, Taylor and Jefferson, on and near the Florida coast, and Fort Sumter, in Charleston Harbor, South Carolina.

The forts thus seized had been put in improved condition, new ones had been built, and armed forces had been organized, all avowedly with the same hostile purpose. The forts remaining in the possession of the Federal Government, in and near those States, were either-besieged or menaced by warlike preparations, and especially Fort Sumter was nearly surrounded by well-protected hostile batteries, with guns equal in quality to the best of its own, and outnumbering the latter as perhaps ten to one. A disproportionate share of the Federal muskets and rifles had somehow found their way into those States, and had been seized to be used against the Government.

Accumulations of the public revenue lying within them had been seized for the same object. The Navy was scattered in distant seas, leaving but a very small part of it within the immediate reach of the Government. Officers of the Federal Army and Navy had resigned in great numbers, and of those resigned a large proportion had taken up arms against the Government. Simultaneously, and in connection with all this, the purpose to sever the Federal Union was openly avowed.

An ordinance was adopted in each of these States so declaring, . . . a formula for instituting a combined government promulgated, and this illegal combination in the character of Confederate States was already invoking recognition, aid and intervention from foreign powers. Finding this condition of things, and believing it to be an imperative duty upon the incoming Executive to prevent, if possible, the consummation of such an attempt to destroy the Federal Union, a choice of means to that end became indispensable. This choice was made and declared in the inaugural. . . exhaust all peaceful measures, hold all of the public places and property not already wrested from the Government, and to collect the revenue, relying for the rest on time, discussion, and the ballot. It promised a continuation of the mails at Government expense, to the very people who were resisting the Government, and repeated its pledges to maintain the rights of the people. Of all that which a President might constitutionally and justifiably do in such a case, everything was forborne without which it was believed possible to keep the Government on foot.

Major Anderson's letter on the 5th of March (the present incumbent's first full day in office) was placed in his hands. It was laid before General Scott, who concurred in Major Anderson's opinion, having conferred with other officers of the army and navy, and at the end of four days came to the same conclusion. No such force available. In a purely military point of view this reduced the duty of the administration in the case to the mere matter of getting the garrison out of the fort.

It was believed, however, that to abandon that position under the circumstances would be utterly ruinous; that the necessity under which it was to be done would not be fully understood; that by many it would be construed as a part of a *voluntary* policy; that at home it would discourage the friends of the Union, embolden its adversaries, and go far to ensure to the latter a recognition abroad. That, in fact, it would be our national destruction consummated. This could not be allowed. Starvation was not yet upon the garrison, and ere it would be reached Fort Pickens might be reinforced. This fact would be a clear indication of policy, and would better enable the country to accept the evacuation of Fort Sumter as a military necessity.

An order was at once directed to be sent for the landing of

the troops from the steamship *Brooklyn* into Fort Pickens. This order could not go by land, but must take the longer and slower route by sea. The first return news from the order was received just one week before the fall of Sumter. The news itself was that the officer commanding the *Sabine,* to which vessel the troops had been transferred from the *Brooklyn,* acting upon some quasi armistice of the late administration (and of the existence of which the present administration; up to the time the order was despatched, had only too vague and uncertain rumors to give attention), had refused to land the troops. To now reinforce Fort Pickens before a crisis would be reached at Fort Sumter was impossible, rendered so by the near exhaustion of provisions in the latter-named fort. In precaution against such a conjunction, the Government had a few days before commenced preparing an expedition, as well adapted as might be, to relieve Fort Sumter, which expedition was intended to be ultimately used or not, according to circumstances. The strongest anticipated case for using it was now presented, and it was resolved to send it forward.

As had been intended in this contingency, it was also resolved to notify the Governor of South Carolina that he might expect that an attempt would be made to provision the fort, and that if not resisted no attempt to reinforce would be made, or arms or ammunition sent without previous notice or in case of attack.

The notice was given; the fort was bombarded without awaiting the arrival of the expedition. It is thus seen that the assault upon and the reduction of Fort Sumter was in no sense a matter of self-defense on the part of the assailants. They well knew that the garrison in the fort could by no possibility commit aggression upon them. They knew, they were expressly notified, that the giving of bread to the few brave and hungry men of the garrison was all which upon that occasion would be attempted, unless themselves, by resisting so much, should provoke more. They knew that the Government desired to keep the garrison in the fort, not to assail them, but merely to, maintain visible possession, and thus to preserve the Union from actual and immediate dissolution, trusting, as hereinbefore stated, to time and discussion and the ballot-box, for final adjustment, and they assailed and reduced the fort for precisely the reverse object, to drive out the visible authority of the Federal Union, and thus force it into immediate dissolution.

That this was their object, the Executive well understood and having said to them in the inaugural address, "You can have no conflict," &c., &c., he took pains not only to keep this declaration good, but also to keep the case so freed from ingenious sophistry that the world should not be able to misunderstand it. By the affair at Fort Sumter, with its surrounding circumstances, that point was reached. Then and thereby the assailants of the Government began the conflict of arms, without a gun in sight or in expectancy to return their fire, save only the few in the fort, sent to that harbor years before for their own protection in whatever was lawful.

In this act, discarding all else, they have forced upon the country the distinct issue, "immediate dissolution or blood," and this issue embraces more than the fate of these United States. It presents to the whole family of man the question whether a constitutional republic or democracy, a government of the people by the same people, can or cannot maintain its territorial integrity against its own domestic foes. Must a government of necessity be too *strong* for the liberties of its own people or too weak to maintain its own existence?"

APPENDIX IV.

Steamship *Baltic,*
"Thursday, April 18, 1861.

"GENERAL:

"I have the honor to submit to you the following report of killed and wounded during and after the engagement at Fort Sumter, South Carolina, on the 12th, 13th and 14th of April, 1861.

"WOUNDED IN THE ACTION

"April 12   Sergt. Thomas Kernan, Co. E., 1st Art'y. Severely.
"   Private James Hays, Co. E, 1st Art'y. Slightly.
"   Private Edward Gallway, Co. E, 1st Art'y. Slightly.
"   John Swearer, mechanic, Eng'r Dep't. Severely.

"KILLED AND WOUNDED AFTER THE ACTION:

"April 14, Killed: Daniel Hough, Private, Co. E, 1st Artillery, while firing salute.

"WOUNDED:

"April 14, Edward Gallway, Co. E, mortally wounded; died on April 19.

April 14, John Irwin, Co. E, severely burned on thigh and leg.
"   James Fielding, Co. E, severely wounded.

"   John Pritchard, Co. E, slightly wounded—face with fire.
"   James Harp, Co. E. slightly wounded,

"Respectfully,
S. W. CRAWFORD,
"Assistant Surgeon, U. S. A."

APPENDIX V.

"New York, December, 1862.

"HON. E. M. STANTON, *Secretary of War.*

"SIR: Although by the strict advice of my medical advisers I am prevented from undertaking any correspondence, the subject upon which I now have the honor to address you is one involving so much that I am induced to incur a risk, in order to bring it to your notice. I have observed in published Orders No. 181 that the brevet of major for the distinguished part taken by him in the transfer of the garrison of Fort Moultrie to Sumter, South Carolina, has been conferred upon Captain John G. Foster, Engineer Corps, to date from December 26, 1860. It is proper that I should here refer to the part taken by the different officers in that move; the only part Captain Foster took in the removal was his, compliance with my request in directing Lieutenants Snyder and Meade to report to me with their boats' crews to and in the move. To Lieutenants Snyder and Meade we were greatly indebted for their active and laborious exertions in making the transfer. I regret more deeply that neither of those officers can, receive the favorable notice of our Government; the former is dead, and the latter has left our service. Assistant Surgeon Crawford returned to Fort Moultrie on the 27th, and was very active in sending over some ammunition, which was of material and essential service to us during our fight; and articles which Lieutenant Hall, to whom I was greatly indebted for his activity and energy in sending off the greater part of the stores which I had been unable to take over. From this it will be seen that if the Department desires to reward any officers for this service, that Brevets should be conferred upon those just named.

"In my letters to the Adjutant-General, whilst at Fort Sumter, numbered 43, 44, 45, 58, 62, 74, 54, 66, 83, 93 and. 94, I make a special mention of the services of Captain Seymour, Dr. Crawford, Lieutenants Snyder and Meade; these officers, in addition to their appropriate duties, contributed in no small degree to

471

the maintenance of our position at Fort Sumter, and whose service deserves a special mention from me. If the Government deems any brevets due, it is to these officers.

"It will be seen by reference to my letters I have mentioned, I have in letter No. 83 given credit to Captain Doubleday for an important suggestion; I now take advantage of this occasion to renew the commendation thus made, and to respectfully recommend that as a measure of justice to the officers named, a brevet, to date from April 14, 1861, should be bestowed either upon those of whom a special mention is made, or, as an act of justice to all, each one of the officers under my command should alike receive a brevet; and I again implore the Department that the distinction now contemplated for one only of the officers shall not be bestowed alone, it being in my estimation neither deserved upon his part nor just to his brother officers. As this matter has become the subject of official notice, it renders it more important that I should, as soon as possible, undertake an official report of the closing scenes of the occupancy of that work, which I have been thus far prevented from complying with from the strict orders of my physician. As soon as I can write, with the assistance of my friends I will make the report.

"Very   respectfully,

(Signed)   "ROBERT ANDERSON,
"Brigadier-General.

"Letter No. 54, thanks to Dr. Crawford, and to Lieutenant Snyder, and Lieutenant Meade."

I N D E X

Abolitionists, stringent measures against, by Gov. Gist, 17.

Adams, J. H., at Secession Convention, 46; appointed commissioner to Washington. 142.

Anderson, Maj. R., appointed to command at Moultrie, 59, 60; recommends occupation of Sumter and Pinckney, 60, 62, 64; sketch of, 61; report of, on work at Moultrie, 62; urges reinforcement of forts, 63; force of, at Moultrie, 64; report of, on work, 66; refuses rolls of men to State, 67; reports Moultrie in danger, 68, 69; letter of, to R. N. Gourdin, 69, to his rector, 70; desires to remove sand-hills, 70, 71; views of, regarding Sumter, 73; authorized to defend forts, 73; occupies Pinckney, 75, 76; suggests change in construction at Moultrie, 92; desires entire control and to occupy Sumter, 93, 94; interpretation by, of Buell's orders, 100; determines to transfer to Sumter, 101, plan carried out, 40, 41, 43, 102-112, report on, 106; receives messengers from Pickens, 110; refuses to leave, 111; requests protection for non-combatants, asks for private effects, 117; sends messenger to Moultrie, 118; surrounded by difficulties, 126; reasons of, for removal to Sumter, 127-130; visited by his wife, 133; interview of, with his brother, 136; despatch of, to Floyd, reply, 143; condemned by Cabinet, 146; tribute of Judge Black to, 154, 155; informed of relief expedition, 175; instructed to protect relief ship, 175, 176; praised by Secretary of War, 177; action of, as to *Star of the West*, 185, does not fire, 186; threatens to close harbor. 187, letter thereon to Governor, 188; sends messenger to Washington, 190, 191; will not surrender, 192; reply of, to Magrath, 193, to Pickens, 194; reply of, to offer of supplies, 201, returns them, 202; reports of, on supplies, 202, 203; course of, approved by Government, 204, 205; sends women and children North, 206, 207; reports of, on works in harbor, 279-281, 291; estimate of, of force for relief, 283, 355; Government's erroneous impression of position of, 284, 288, notwithstanding reports of Anderson, 289, 290; reasons of, for not asking reinforcements, 290; instructions to, on floating battery, 292, 293; despondent, improvements in fort, 295-297; letter of, to Beauregard on removal, 303; letter to, from Beauregard on surrender, 308, reply, 309; protests against reinforcement, 371, against Fox's expedition, 385, because impracticable, 373; can hold out till 15th April, 372; misled by Lamon's statements, 374, 377, 378; report of, on *Shannon* affair, 376-380; complains of cutter and shell-firing, despatch on, 381; notice to, of relief by Government, 382; mails of, seized, 383, 384-386; alarmed at report of no relief, 391; allowed to receive mails, 394; suggestion of, as to supply vessels, 399; informed of relief expedition, 407; called on to surrender, refuses, 423; receives final proposition of Confederate Government, 424, his answer, 425; notified of immediate attack, 426; withdraws men from parapet, 431; stops making of cartridges, 432; agrees to surrender at once, 440; raises white flag, submits terms to Beauregard, 441; letter of, to Pickens and Beauregard, 442; Beauregard's tribute to, 447; reports surrender to Cameron, 449; subsequent career of, 450.

Army, U. S., social relations of officers of, in Charleston, 7, 64; loyalty of, to Union, 8; force of, in February, 1861, 167.

Arsenal, U. S., at Charleston, watched by State troops, 57; seized, 119-122; value of stores at, 123.

473

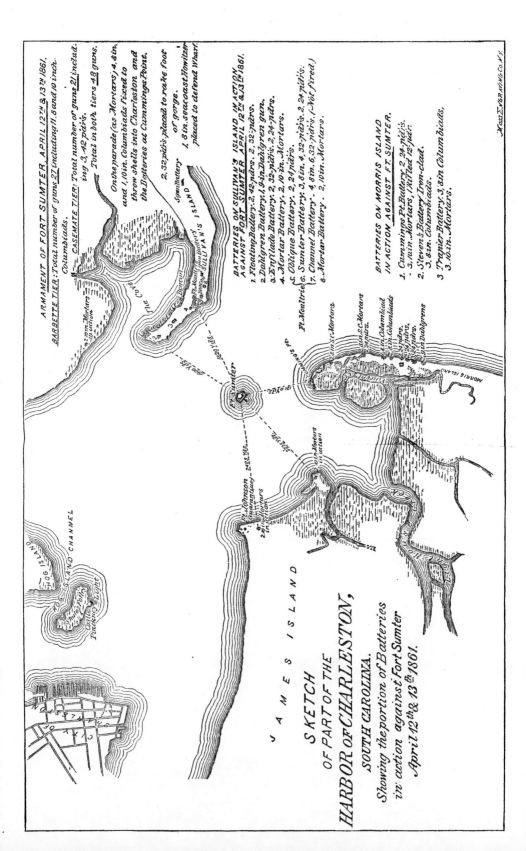

Bringing the Past into the Future

More Great Books Brought Back by DSI

Series 1: Lincoln

Special Series 1 includes a total of nine volumes: *The Life of Abraham Lincoln* by Ida Tarbell, a four-volume set; *Debates of Lincoln and Douglas; Six Months at the White House with Lincoln* by F. B. Carpenter; and *Herndon's Lincoln: The True Story of a Great Life*, three volumes unabridged, written by Lincoln's law partner of more than twenty years.
CD-ROM ISBN 1-58218-084-9

The Life of Abraham Lincoln

By Ida M. Tarbell. Illustrations and maps. 4 vols. Originally published by the Lincoln Historical Society in 1900.
Discover the incredible facts of the life of Abraham Lincoln, a man who changed the fabric of America forever. Read in his own words his views on equality and ending slavery. This work details Lincoln's entire life including the origins of the Lincoln family, his entry into the military during the Black Hawk War, his important law cases, his entire political career, the Civil War, his personal life with Mary Todd, the devastating loss of one of their children, and his constant battles with depression.
CD-ROM ISBN 1-58218-017-2
Softcover ISBN 1-58218-002-4

Debates of Lincoln and Douglas

Carefully prepared by the reporters of each party at the times of their delivery. Originally published by Follett & Foster in 1860.
Perhaps the most consequential artifact of American election campaigning and its political arguments. Political debates between Hon. Abraham Lincoln and Hon. Stephen A. Douglas, in the celebrated campaign of 1858 in Illinois. Included are the preceding speeches of each at Chicago, Springfield, etc., as well as the two great speeches of Lincoln in Ohio in 1859, published at the times of their delivery.
CD-ROM ISBN 1-58218-009-1
Softcover ISBN 1-58218-000-8

Series 2: Custer

Special Series 2 includes both *A Life of Major Gen'l George A. Custer* by Frederick Whittaker and *Tenting on the Plains* by Custer's wife, Elizabeth. Also included are the National Archives' transcripts concerning the Court Martial of Custer (1867) and the Court of Inquiry of Reno (1879) for his actions at Little Big Horn.
CD-ROM ISBN 1-58218-081-4

A Life of Major Gen'l George A. Custer

By Frederick Whittaker. Originally published in 1876.
With no marked advantages of education or wealth to command his situation, Custer yet passed through a career so brilliant that his deeds are household words, his "Last Stand" against Sioux and Cheyenne warriors at Little Big Horn an enduring legend in American history. Truth and sincerity, honor and bravery, tenderness and sympathy, unassuming piety and temperance were the mainspring of Major Gen'l Custer, the man.
CD-ROM ISBN 1-58218-042-3
Softcover ISBN 1-58218-040-7

Tenting on the Plains

By Elizabeth Custer. Includes illustrations by Frederic Remington. Originally published in 1889.
Elizabeth Custer was just a young girl when she fell in love with one of the most controversial Indian fighters of the late 1800s, and barely a woman when she defied her father to marry him. She went on to earn literary fame as well as financial independence with her entertaining tales of frontier life as the wife of General George Custer. Her stories of life on the Plains are as colorful today as when they first appeared over a century ago.
CD-ROM ISBN 1-58218-052-0
Softcover ISBN 1-58218-050-4

Series 3: Generals

Special Series 3 includes *Personal Memoirs of U. S. Grant, Memoirs of General W. T. Sherman, Personal Memoirs of P. H. Sheridan*, and *McClellan's Own Story*.
CD-ROM ISBN 1-58218-082-2

Personal Memoirs of U. S. Grant

Illustrations, Maps, and Facsimiles of Handwriting. 2 vols. Originally published in 1885.
Published by Mark Twain under the Charles L. Webster Company imprint, this memoir is widely admired as one of the finest military autobiographies ever written. Grant recounts the failings and triumphs of his leadership in strong, clear prose including his boyhood in Ohio, his graduation from West Point, his marriage to Julia Dent, his brilliant military campaigns, and his presidency.
CD-ROM ISBN 1-58218-029-6
Softcover ISBN 1-58218-005-9

Memoirs of General W. T. Sherman

With a map showing the marches of U.S. forces under his command. 2 vols. Originally published in 1890.
General William Tecumseh Sherman, a great man both in his gifts and his achievements, was altogether a solider in the habits of mind. A natural student of the topography of the countryside, this characteristic of true military genius served Sherman well in planning his devastating march from Atlanta, across Georgia to the sea, the most striking achievement of the Civil War. The memoirs of this courageous, patient, and self-sacrificing "Old Warrior" are certain of a permanent place in literature.
CD-ROM ISBN 1-58218-025-3
Softcover ISBN 1-58218-004-0

Personal Memoirs of P. H. Sheridan

Illustrated. Twenty-six maps, prepared specially for this book by the War Department. 2 vols. Originally published in 1888.
General Phil Sheridan revolutionized the handling of mounted men in this country and abroad as commander of America's army. A hell-for-leather cavalryman, Sheridan was as deliberate and careful as he was brave. His memoirs vividly depict the brilliant campaigns he masterminded, including his victory at Appomattox where his men blocked Lee's retreat to force his surrender, ending the Civil War.
CD-ROM ISBN 1-58218-033-4
Softcover ISBN 1-58218-006-7

Digital Scanning, Inc. • 344 Gannett Road, Scituate, MA 02066 • www.digitalscanning.com • toll-free 1-888-349-4443

McClellan's Own Story
Illustrations from sketches drawn on the field of battle by A. R. Waud, the great war artist. Originally published in 1886.
After Bull Run, Lincoln appointed 34-year-old Gen. George B. McClellan as commander of the newly created Army of the Potomac. An able administrator and drillmaster, McClellan proceeded to reorganize the army for what he expected to be an overwhelming demonstration of Northern military superiority. "Our George," as his soldiers lovingly called him, was one of the ablest commanders which the United States has ever produced.
CD-ROM ISBN 1-58218-037-7
Softcover ISBN 1-58218-007-5

History of Massachusetts in the Civil War
By William Schouler, Late Adjutant-General of the Commonwealth. Originally published in 1868.
Massachusetts played a prominent part in the Civil War, from the beginning to the end; not only in furnishing soldiers for the army, sailors for the navy, and financial aid to the government, but in advancing ideas, which though scoffed at in the early months of the war, were afterwards accepted by the nation, before the war could be brought to a successful end.
CD-ROM ISBN 1-58218-013-X
Softcover ISBN 1-58218-001-6

Series 4: Indians
Special Series 4 includes George Catlin's *North American Indians* and *Indian Tribes of North America.* Also included are Indian Treaties from the National Archives.
CD-ROM ISBN 1-58218-083-0

North American Indians
By George Catlin. Illustrations and maps. 2 vols. Originally published in 1903.
Explore the territories of the North American Indian with the historical text, illustrations, and maps of George Catlin. Catlin gave up the practice of law to pursue his self-taught art, travelling throughout the American West from 1832 to 1840, painting portraits and writing on his encounters with various Indian tribes. Scholars and researchers alike will delight in the descriptions and portraits that portray this moment in history with such vivid detail.
CD-ROM ISBN 1-58218-021-0

Civil War Prison Stories

Daring and Suffering: A History of the Great Railroad Adventure
By Lieut. William Pittenger, One of Andrews' Raiders. Originally published in 1863.
This courageous raid into Georgia ranks high among the striking and novel incidents of the Civil War. Pittenger and his comrades embarked on a secret raid deep into Confederate territory to cut the rail link between Marietta and Chattanooga, only to run out of fuel after a long and dangerous chase. Those that survived the mission were the first soldiers at rank of private to be awarded the Congressional Medal of Honor.
CD-ROM ISBN 1-58218-077-6
Softcover ISBN 1-58218-075-X

Beyond the Lines: A Yankee Loose in Dixie
By Capt. J. J. Geer. Originally published in 1864.
Geer narrates the suffering endured as a prisoner in the Southern Confederacy. After being captured at the battle of Shiloh, Geer was tried on the most frivolous charges and subsequently chained with slaves' chains and cast into military prisons and common jails. He managed to escape, overcoming malarious marshes and bloodhounds only to be recaptured!
CD-ROM ISBN 1-58218-085-7
Softcover ISBN 1-58218-088-1

Prison Life in Dixie
By Sergeant Oats. Originally published in 1880.
The author describes his harrowing capture and imprisonment by the Rebels at Sumter Prison a.k.a. "Andersonville Prison Pen". Renowned as one of the worst prisons of the Civil War, the Andersonville pen spread over only 11 acres, with a 12-foot wall surrounding over 33,000 Union soldiers. The writer endeavors to furnish such descriptions and incidents that give the reader a true picture of Rebel prisons and the means and methods of either surviving or dying in them.
CD-ROM ISBN 1-58218-101-2
Softcover ISBN 1-58218-100-4

Forthcoming Titles

Herndon's Lincoln: The True Story of a Great Life
By William H. Herndon, Lincoln's friend and law partner

Six Months at the White House with Lincoln
By F. B. Carpenter

Reminiscences of Winfield Scott Hancock
By his wife, A. R. Hancock

The Battle of Gettysburg
By Comte de Paris

Sheridan's Troopers on the Border
By De B. Randolph Keim

Genesis of the Civil War
By Samuel Wylie Crawford

Following the Guidon
By Elizabeth Custer

The Indian Tribes of North America
By McKenney and Hall

The History of Philip's War
By Thomas Church

Book of the Indians of North America
By Samuel G. Drake

Digital Scanning, Inc. • 344 Gannett Road, Scituate, MA 02066 • www.digitalscanning.com • toll-free 1-888-349-4443

Printed in the United States
1193600002B/57